A Grammar of Patwin

Studies in the Native Languages of the Americas

EDITORS
Douglas R. Parks
Raymond J. DeMallie

Recipient of the Mary R. Haas Award
Presented by
The Society for the Study of the
Indigenous Languages of the Americas

A Grammar of Patwin

LEWIS C. LAWYER

UNIVERSITY OF NEBRASKA PRESS, LINCOLN
In cooperation with the American Indian Studies
Research Institute, Indiana University, Bloomington

Portions of chapters 2 and 3 first appeared as "Patwin Phonemics, Phonetics, and Phonotactics," *International Journal of American Linguistics* 81, no. 2 (April 2015): 221–60.

RECOVERING
LANGUAGES & LITERACIES
OF THE AMERICAS

This book is published as part of the Recovering Languages and Literacies of the Americas initiative. Recovering Languages and Literacies is generously supported by the Andrew W. Mellon Foundation.

Library of Congress Cataloging-in-Publication Data
Names: Lawyer, Lewis C., author.
Title: A grammar of Patwin / Lewis C. Lawyer.
Description: Lincoln: University of Nebraska Press; Bloomington: In cooperation with the American Indian Studies Research Institute, Indiana University, [2021] | Series: Studies in the native languages of the Americas | Includes bibliographical references.
Identifiers: LCCN 2020023740
ISBN 9781496221193 (hardback)
ISBN 9781496230423 (paperback)
ISBN 9781496222770 (pdf)
Subjects: LCSH: Patwin language—Grammar.
Classification: LCC PM2136 .L39 2021 | DDC 497/.41—dc23
LC record available at https://lccn.loc.gov/2020023740

Set in Merope by Tseng Information Systems, Inc.

For Laurie

CONTENTS

ILLUSTRATIONS

MAPS

ILLUSTRATIONS

TABLES

ACKNOWLEDGMENTS

First and foremost I would like to thank the language consultants upon whose words this book is ultimately based. I list them here in alphabetical order: William Benjamin, Jesse Berryessa, George Bill, Minnie Bill, William Bush, George and Mary Byers, Samuel Capita, James Cooper, Fred Gonzales, Hazel Gonzales, Sarah Gonzales, George Howell, John Hudson and his mother, Lewis James, "Juana," Carlos Lewis (Luis), Daisy Lorenzo, Harry Lorenzo, Anderson Lowell, Anderson Lowell's mother, Nelson Lowell, Nora Lowell, Stephen Luluk, Oscar McDaniel, Old Man McGill, Bill Mitchell, Joe Mitchell, Tony Bill Mitchell, Ida Benjamin Mitchum, William Mitchum, Amelia Nunes, Jim O'Brian, Thomas Odock, Jim Perdue, "Philip," Henry Pulsifer, Jennie Regalado, Julia Richards, Jim Tomaso Smith, Antōn Taylor, Platon Vallejo, Bill Wiley, Helen Wiley Baker, Ruth Wiley, Bob Wilson, Peter Wilson, Charlie Wright, and all of the language consultants whose names were not recorded. These men and women, whom I never met, took the time to share their knowledge of their language with the field linguists who were my predecessors. I am profoundly grateful to all of them. Because of their work, it is possible now to study and describe the Patwin language.

I am also deeply grateful to the researchers who preceded me in studying the Patwin language. I list them here, in approximate chronological order according to when each was active studying the language: Felipe Arroyo de la Cuesta, George Gibbs, Platon Vallejo, John Bartlett, Jeremiah Curtin, H. B. Wilson, C. E. Kelsey, C. Hart Merriam, John Alden Mason, Alfred Kroeber, T. T. Waterman, Samuel Barrett, William E. Myers, Jaime de Angulo, Paul Radin, A. M. Halpern, Mary Haas, Richard H. Reeve, Elizabeth Bright, Morris Swadesh, Sally McLendon, Dorothy Hill, Donald Ultan, Warren Snyder, Robert Rathburn, and Kenneth Whistler. The creation of a grammatical description of Patwin has been a slow process—the work of decades rather than years, and the work of many people rather than one. It has been two hundred years since Arroyo de la Cuesta recorded the first word list of Patwin from Suisun speaker Samuel Capita, 118 years since C. Hart Merriam began his work making sense of Patwin dialect geography, and ninety-two years since Jaime de Angulo sketched the first grammatical description of a Patwin dialect (Cortina Hill Patwin, with data from consultant Fred Gonzales). The analysis in this book is a synthesis of the data and analyses that these researchers collectively created over a period of two centuries. I am standing on all of their shoulders, and that is exactly as difficult as it sounds.

I would especially like to thank Ken Whistler, for taking the time to personally walk me through his own valuable and insightful work, and for sharing his thoughts and manuscripts concerning the Patwin language. Ken is my link to the chain of Patwin researchers who came before me, and I am grateful for his friendship and assistance. I am also happy to have learned a bit about Unicode and the Unicode Consortium from Ken. I hope that we can talk again soon about Patwin, character encoding, databases, or really anything at all. We seem to be the same kind of nerd.

I would also like to express my gratitude to the Survey of California and Other Indian Languages at UC Berkeley, the Berkeley Language Center, the Bancroft Library at UC Berkeley, the Hearst Museum of Anthropology at UC Berkeley, the American Philosophical Society in Philadelphia, the National Anthropological Archives at the Smithsonian Institution, the Archives of Traditional Music at Indiana University, the Braun Research Library at the Autry Museum of the American West, the Meriam Library at CSU Chico, and the Department of Special Collections at the UC Davis Library. These institutions and their wonderful staffs are responsible for the important job of keeping the collective archive of Patwin language materials safe and accessible, now and into the future. Special thanks to Ken Whistler, Martha Vallejo McGettigan, Dorothea Theodoratus, Robert Rathburn, Alex Walker, Todd Gettleman, and the Yocha Dehe Wintun Nation for helping me obtain difficult-to-find or non-archived materials, and for helping to ensure that these materials become properly archived for future research.

Next I would like to acknowledge a particularly inspiring group of people: those who are working to sustain and revitalize the Patwin language in the community. While I have worked over archival materials in creating an academic reference for the language, many people have been working to ensure that the Patwin language maintains a presence in contemporary Patwin communities, and it has been my honor to occasionally play a supporting role in their work. Language revitalization and conservation programs in the Yocha Dehe Wintun Nation, the Cachil Dehe Band of Wintun Indians, and the Kletsel Dehe Band of Wintun Indians are a continuing source of inspiration.

Turning now to my personal path in completing this book, I thank my academic advisers and mentors. If I were to be a completist, I would here list the names of practically all of the linguistics faculty members at USC, at the Research Centre for English and Applied Linguistics at Cambridge and at UC Davis. However, the indulgent reader has already read enough lists of names, so I will mention only two here in particular. Years ago I enrolled in an introductory linguistics elective course at USC, which happened to be taught by the great Jack Hawkins, and I was hooked. Jack subsequently got me my first research jobs as a linguist and inspired me to pursue degrees at Cambridge and at UC Davis. I am grateful for Jack's mentorship in my navigation of the tangled worlds of linguistics and academia, and I will always try to remember to "see the forest through the trees." I am also particularly grateful to Martha Macri, for plopping this particular project in my lap a few years ago. For the life of me I cannot remember what inspired me to take a U-turn in the middle of my graduate studies, seek out Dr. Macri, and begin an entirely new project unrelated to my work at the time in linguistic typology. I still don't know why it happened but I know that it was meant to be. Thanks are due to Martha for getting this project started and for establishing its character. Martha impressed upon me the vital importance not only of publishing in the academic world, but also of making information and knowledge available to the community outside of academia, and working with the community to ensure that my work is both useful and culturally appropriate.

Thanks to Patrick Farrell, Raúl Aranovich, Justin Spence, Martha Macri, and Pam Gonzales for interesting and elucidating discussions about the Patwin language and about linguistics in general that informed various parts of this book. Thanks also to Martha McGettigan, Julie Ngo, Rachael Duke, Annie Welch, and others who shall remain anonymous, for assisting me in the digitization of the large and unruly Patwin language archive. Special mention goes to Julie, who is responsible for a whopping 21,060 entries in my database. This transcription has been instrumental in navigating the archive in the production of this book, and will continue to be useful in the future as lexicographical and further grammatical work proceed.

Work on the dissertation that became this book was completed with the financial and material support of the Department of Linguistics at UC Davis, the Yocha Dehe Wintun Nation, and a Doctoral Dissertation Research Improvement grant from the Documenting Endangered Languages program at the National Science Foundation (BCS-1264305). I also deepened my understanding of Patwin grammar—River Patwin in particular—in the course of my contract work for the Cachil Dehe Band of Wintun Indians.

Thanks to the wonderful team at the University of Nebraska Press, who helped bring my complicated manuscript to a high polish for publication. Any remaining out-of-place punctuation marks or wonky capitalizations are my own. Thanks also to the anonymous reviewer and the eponymous Dave Costa, for giving the text a good read-over and helping to bring more clarity to some of the content. Special mention goes to to Dr. Costa for being the first person to notice that I had misspelled *both* words in "Carquinez Strait."

Many thanks also to my family and friends, who have helped to keep me happy and sane in the course of writing this book. How could I have survived grad school without lunches at the Delta of Venus with Ben, Lily, Scotty, and Laurie? Pioneers all in the art of five-hand cribbage. Muggins. Special and unending thanks to my parents, without whose support none of this would have been possible at all. Thank you for cultivating the kind of careful analyticity that it takes to do this kind of work, and thank you for your tolerance when I ended up in the humanities rather than the sciences. Thank you for instilling in me the value of always doing the Right Thing. You are wonderful parents, and wonderful grandparents, and it was truly a pleasure to live so near you during the time I was writing this book. Mom, you didn't live to see the publication of this book, but I know it would have made you proud. Like everything else I am, this is part of your legacy.

Last, and the opposite of least, I wish to express my deepest gratitude to my wife, Laurie. Without your steadfast love and support this book never would have been completed. Thanks for the humor. Thanks for the intellectual conversation, and the frivolous. Thanks for geeking out with me about English etymology with a Compact OED, a magnifying glass, and a cup of tea—and thanks for the cups of tea. Thanks for letting me know when I have "crazy eye" and should probably get up from my desk. Thanks for fixing my computer(s) when I lose patience to do so myself. Laurie—we did it. We both finished our dissertations near simultaneously (you won by two and a half months) and collectively amassed more years of graduate education than I care to count, all while raising a happy girl and keeping two goofy animals out of trouble. Let's not try that again. I love you.

ABBREVIATIONS

1, 2, 3	first person, second person, third person
ABL	ablative case
ABS	absolutive suffix (on kinship terms)
ADV	adverbial participial
ALL	allative case
AN	animate
APPL	applicative voice
APS	American Philosophical Society
AUX	active auxiliary (RP)
be.AN	stative auxiliary (animate subject)
be.IN	stative auxiliary (inanimate subject)
CARD	cardinal suffix (on numerals)
CAUS	causative voice
CERT	certainty
COM	comitative case
CONC	concessive
COND	conditional suffix (RP)
CONN	connector enclitic
COP	copula
DECL	declarative
DIM	diminutive
DIST	distal
DU	dual number
EXCL	exclusive
FIN	finite suffix
FUT	future tense
GEN	genitive
HAB	habitual aspect
HORT	hortative mood
HP	Hill Patwin
HP_C	Cortina Hill Patwin

HP_L	Lodoga Hill Patwin
HP_R	Rumsey Hill Patwin
HP_T	Tebti Hill Patwin
IN	inanimate
INCEP	inceptive aspect
INCL	inclusive
INS	instrumental case
INS_{AN}	animate instrumental
INS_{IN}	inanimate instrumental
INTR	intransitive
IRR	irrealis
LOC	locative case
LOC_{AN}	animate locative
LOC_{IN}	inanimate locative
MOVT	movement suffix (on directionals)
NAA	National Anthropological Archives
NEG	negation
NMLZ	nominalizer
$NMLZ_{AG}$	agentive nominalizer
NMNL	nominalized verb
nSG	non-singular number
OBJ	objective case
PART	participle
PASS	passive voice
PAST	past tense
PL	plural number
POSS	possessive case
$POSS_{AN}$	possessor of animate noun
$POSS_{IN}$	possessor of inanimate noun
$POSS_{K}$	possessive pronominal (on kinship terms)
$POSS_{K\text{-}F}$	free possessor of kinship term
$POSS_{V}$	possessor of nominalized verb
PROL	prolative case
PROX	proximal
Q	interrogative

RECIP	reciprocal voice
REDUP	reduplicant
REFL	reflexive voice
REL	relativizer
REL_{OBL}	oblique relativizer
REM	remote suffix (on directionals and cardinals)
REM2	remote suffix (on directionals and cardinals)
REPRT	reportative
RL	kinship-relational suffix
RP	River Patwin
RPAST	remote past tense
SBJ	subjective case
SBJV	subjunctive mood
SCOIL	Survey of California and Other Indian Languages
SG	singular number
SP	South Patwin
SP_M	Merriam's South Patwin
SP_V	Vallejo's South Patwin
STAT	stative suffix (on directionals and cardinals)
TRANS	transitive
VBL	verbalized nominal
VBLZ	verbalizer
$VBLZ_A$	active verbalizer
$VBLZ_S$	stative verbalizer
VOC	vocative

ALPHABETICAL LIST OF MORPHEMES

Here each functional morpheme discussed in the text is listed alphabetically. For each morpheme, a description and a gloss is given, if applicable, and the primary section(s) in which the morpheme is discussed.

-ʔa	stative verbalizer 'VBLZ$_S$': 4.10.2
ʔan	coordinating particle 'and': 6.6.2
ʔa·na	quantifier 'much': 6.4.3
-ba	plural 'PL': 4.5
-be	interrogative 'Q': 8.2.1.3
be·, beh	stative auxiliary 'be.IN': 9.1.2
-bes	finite suffix 'FIN': 8.2.1.1
-beti	certainty 'CERT': 8.2.2.8
-bi	second-person to first-person hortative '2>1HORT': 8.2.2.1
-bo	interrogative 'Q': 8.2.1.3
bo·, boh	stative auxiliary 'be.AN': 9.1.2
-bosa	habitual 'HAB': 8.2.1.9
-bota	habitual interrogative 'HAB.Q': 8.2.1.10
-boti	certainty 'CERT': 8.2.2.8
-bu(da)	first-person plural inclusive hortative '1PL.INCL.HORT': 8.2.2.1
-bus	finite suffix 'FIN': 8.2.1.1
-busa	habitual 'HAB': 8.2.1.9
čaket	collective quantifier 'all': 6.4.1
čeh	active auxiliary 'AUX': 9.1.3
-či,-ču	resultative: 8.2.1.11
-čin	modal 'lest': 8.2.2.4
-ču	kinship-relational suffix 'RL': 5.3.1.3.4
ču·-	first-person singular root '1SG': 5.2.1
ču*(y)-	first-person plural root '1PL': 5.2.4
-č'u·	plural 'PL': 5.3.2.3
-da	comitative case 'COM': 4.6.2.2, 5.3.1.4, 6.6.1
-da*k	ablative case 'ABL': 4.6.2.6
-di	third-person hortative '3HORT': 8.2.2.1

-do	possessive case 'POSS': 5.3.1.3
-e·	vocative case 'VOC': 4.8
ʔe·-	proximal root 'PROX': 5.2.7.1
-e·l	remote suffix 'REM': 7.1, 7.2
ʔele·	negative auxiliary 'NEG': 9.1.4
ʔew-	proximal root 'PROX': 5.2.7.1
halihali	distributive quantifier 'all.kinds': 6.4.2
he·-	indefinite locational root 'where': 5.2.8
heče-	indefinite root 'which': 5.2.8
hečew-	indefinite root: 5.2.8
heka-	indefinite root 'where': 5.2.8
heke-	indefinite root 'which': 5.2.8
-her(e)	passive voice 'PASS': 8.2.4.1
-hil	comitative voice 'COM': 8.2.4.4
-ho(·)	active verbalizer 'VBLZ_{A}': 4.10.1
-hu	active verbalizer 'VBLZ_{A}': 4.10.1
-hVm	relativizer 'REL': 6.5
ʔi(h)	copula 'COP': 9.1.1
-i·n	demonym suffix 'people': 7.2
-in	instrumental case 'INS': 4.6.2.3
-in	directional suffix: 7.1
ʔiro	coordinating particle 'and': 6.6.2
-ka	concessive 'CONC': 8.2.6
ka	irrealis particle 'IRR': 9.2.3
-kam	concessive 'CONC': 8.2.6
kam	irrealis particle 'IRR': 9.2.3
-kin	instrumental case 'INS': 4.6.2.3
-ko	iterative, delimitative: 8.3.4.2
-k^{h}e·	vocative case 'VOC': 4.8
-k^{h}o	iterative: 8.3.4.1
-k°a	SP pronoun suffix: 5.3.4
-le(da)	first-person exclusive hortative '1EXCL.HORT': 8.2.2.1
-le	ability 'can': 8.2.2.3
-le·	plural 'PL': 4.5, 5.3.2.3
-len	ability 'can': 8.2.2.3
-lena	first-person exclusive hortative '1EXCL.HORT': 8.2.2.1

-les	ability 'can': 8.2.2.3
-ła	locative case 'LOC': 4.6.2.4, 5.3.1.4, 9.3.2
-m	objective case 'OBJ': 4.6.1.2, 5.3.1.2
-m	subjunctive 'SBJV': 8.2.2.2
-ma	objective case 'OBJ': 4.6.1.2, 5.3.1.2
-ma	causative voice 'CAUS': 8.2.4.2
-ma	confident inference 'must': 8.2.2.7
-ma	nonsingular 'NSG': 4.5
-mʔa	confident inference 'must': 8.2.2.7
ma·-	second-person root '2': 5.2.5
-me	comitative voice 'COM': 8.2.4.4
-mele·	negative 'NEG': 9.4
=men	diminutive 'DIM': 8.4.5
-mi	second-person to first-person hortative '2>1HORT': 8.2.2.1
mi·-	second-person root '2': 5.2.5
-min	possessive case 'POSS': 4.6.1.3, 5.3.1.3
-m(i)t°a	past interrogative 'Q.PAST': 8.2.1.6
-m(i)t°at	8.2.1.6
-mt°i	8.2.1.6
-mu	subjunctive 'SBJV': 8.2.2.2
-muʔa	confident inference 'must': 8.2.2.7
-mur	negative 'NEG': 9.4
-m(u)te·	past tentative inference 'might.PAST': 8.2.2.6
-m(u)t^{h}ere	tentative inference 'might': 8.2.2.5
-m(u)ʔu	negative 'NEG': 9.4
-·n	kinship absolutive suffix 'ABS': 4.7
-n	adverbial participle 'ADV': 8.2.3.2
-n	possessive case 'POSS': 5.3.1.3
-n	remote past tense 'RPAST': 8.2.1.5
-na	prolative case 'PROL': 4.6.2.7, 5.3.1.4
-na	remote suffix 'REM2': 7.2
na·-	first-person singular root '1SG': 5.2.1
-na·k	ablative case 'ABL': 4.6.2.6, 5.3.1.4
-nan(a)	reflexive voice 'REFL': 8.2.4.6
ne-	exclusive root '1.EXCL': 5.2.3
-net	remote past tense 'RPAST': 8.2.1.6

-ni	adverbial participle 'ADV': 8.2.3.2
-ni	past tense 'PAST': 8.2.1.6
-ni	remote past tense 'RPAST': 8.2.1.5
-nini	conditional 'COND': 8.2.7
-no	possessive case 'POSS': 4.6.1.3, 5.3.1.3
-nomin	possessive case 'POSS': 4.6.1.3, 5.3.1.3
-nu	possessive case 'POSS': 5.3.1.3
-o	active verbalizer '$VBLZ_A$': 4.10.1
-oho	contiguous: 8.3.4.1
-pa	applicative voice 'APPL': 8.2.4.3
-pa	movement suffix 'MOVT': 7.1
pa	interrogative particle 'Q': 9.2.2
-pe·	dual 'DU': 5.3.2.2
pe·-	indefinite impersonal root 'what': 5.2.8
-pel(e·)	dual 'DU': 4.5, 5.3.2.2
pi	declarative particle 'DECL': 9.2.1
pi·-	third-person root '3': 5.2.6
pi·-	distal root 'DIST': 5.2.7.2
po·-	indefinite personal root 'who': 5.2.8
p'e-	inclusive root '1.INCL': 5.2.2
-p'ir(i)	reciprocal voice 'RECIP': 8.2.4.5
-ro	participle 'PART': 8.2.3.1
-s	finite suffix 'FIN': 8.2.1.1, 8.4.2
-s	objective case 'OBJ': 4.6.1.2, 5.3.1.2
-sa	past declarative 'PAST': 8.2.1.2
-say	interrogative 'Q': 8.2.1.3
-se	first-person dual inclusive hortative '1DU.INCL.HORT': 8.2.2.1
-se·	vocative case 'VOC': 4.8
-sem	relativizer 'REL': 6.5
-sey	interrogative 'Q': 8.2.1.3
-sin	instrumental case 'INS': 4.6.2.3, 5.3.1.4
-so	active verbalizer '$VBLZ_A$': 4.10.1
-sok	oblique relativizer 'REL_{OBL}': 6.5
-t	objective case 'OBJ': 4.6.1.2, 5.3.1.2
-t	possessive case 'POSS': 4.6.1.3, 5.3.1.3

-t	remote past tense ‘RPAST’: 8.2.1.6
-ta	participle ‘PART’: 8.2.3.1
-ta	human nominal suffix: 4.2.2
-ta	cardinal suffix ‘CARD’: 6.3.1
-ta·	past interrogative ‘Q.PAST’: 8.2.1.4
-taro	participle ‘PART’: 8.2.3.1
-te·	past interrogative ‘Q.PAST’: 8.2.1.4
-ti	ablative case ‘ABL’: 4.6.2.6, 5.3.1.4
-ti	stative suffix ‘STAT’: 7.1, 7.2
-tin	instrumental case ‘INS’: 4.6.2.3, 5.3.1.4
-tin	locative case ‘LOC’: 4.6.2.4, 5.3.1.4
-tk°a	8.2.9
-to	possessive case ‘POSS’: 4.6.1.3, 5.3.1.3
-to	delimitative: 8.3.4.1
-to	single event: 8.3.4.2
-tok	possessive case ‘POSS’: 5.3.1.3
-tom	possessive case ‘POSS’: 5.3.1.3
-tomin	possessive case ‘POSS’: 4.6.1.3, 5.3.1.3
-tu	agentive nominalizer ‘NMLZ$_{AG}$’: 8.4.3
-t(’)uka	allative case ‘ALL’: 4.6.2.5, 5.3.1.4
-t^hi	second-person non-singular hortative ‘2nSG.HORT’: 8.2.2.1
-t^hi,-t^hu	semelfactive: 8.3.4.3
-t’i	future tense ‘FUT’: 8.2.1.7
-t’o	inceptive ‘INCEP’: 8.2.1.8
-t°i	finite suffix ‘FIN’: 8.2.1.1, 8.4.2
-ʔu	verbalizer ‘VBLZ’: 5.4
=ʔu	clause connector ‘CONN’: 9.6
ʔu·-	third-person root ‘3’: 5.2.6
ʔupu(m)	reportative particle ‘REPRT’: 9.2.4
-wa	8.2.8
-win	instrumental case ‘INS’: 4.6.2.3
-y	plural ‘PL’: 5.3.2.3
-y	possessive case ‘POSS’: 4.6.1.3, 5.3.1.3
-yo	active verbalizer ‘VBLZ$_{A}$’: 4.10.1
ʔ	prosodic marker ‘‖’: 3.2.3

A Grammar of Patwin

ONE

Background

1.1. THE PATWIN LANGUAGE

Patwin is a Native American language, historically spoken in the southwestern drainage of the Sacramento River. Formerly spoken by hundreds of communities with a combined population estimated at between six thousand and thirty thousand people, it is now spoken as a first language by only one living person known to me (Kroeber 1932:420; Cook 1976; Whistler 1976:59; Golla 2011:145).[1]

1.1.1. Genetic Affiliation and Contact

Patwin (ISO code pwi) is a member of the Wintuan language family, along with Wintu (wnw) and Nomlaki (nol).[2] The historical relation of Patwin, Nomlaki, and Wintu is evident even from a casual examination of lexical similarities. In the published literature, Latham (1856) was the first to note the existence of the Wintuan family, which he called "Copeh."[3] The Wintuan family grouping has never been challenged. Wintu and Nomlaki are closely related to one another, and may even be mutually intelligible (Golla 2011:143; Cody Pata, pers. comm.). They can be grouped together in a subfamily of Wintuan: the Northern Wintuan languages. Patwin is by itself the southern branch of the Wintuan language family.

Pitkin (1984) finds that the Wintuan languages are related to one another at about the same time-depth as the Romance languages. Whistler (1976, 1977b) finds that the Proto-Wintuan homeland was probably in southern Oregon or far-northern California. Shepherd (2005) is a first stab at a reconstruction of Proto-Wintuan, and Whistler (1980) is a detailed reconstruction of Proto-Wintuan kinship terminology. The entire Wintuan language family is categorized as "moribund" in Whalen and Simons (2012), in the technical sense that no Wintuan language is currently being learned as a first language by children. Of the Wintuan languages, only Wintu has a previously published grammar (Pitkin 1984) or dictionary (Pitkin 1985; Schlichter 1981).

The Wintuan family was part of the earliest formulation of the Penutian hypothesis, and has consistently been a member of that proposed classification (Dixon and Kroeber 1913a, 1913b, 1919; Sapir 1929; Callaghan 1958; Silverstein 1979; DeLancey and Golla 1997). The Penutian hypothesis is a proposal uniting several Native American language families into a superfamily called Penutian. This proposal is not uncontroversial. For optimistic overviews of the Penutian hypothesis in its various formulations, see Silverstein (1979) and Foster (1996:87–90). For a substantial set of resemblant forms in Penutian languages, see Tarpent (1997). For more critical views, see Campbell (1997:309–24) and Callaghan (2014:1–7).

Patwin is situated in an area of extreme linguistic diversity, being bordered by languages in six language families (Maiduan, Utian, Pomo, Wintuan, Yukian, and Yokuts), in three distinct stocks (Penutian, Pomoan, and Yukian; see Golla 2011). Patwin speech communities would have been in frequent contact with all of these groups, and the Patwin language is known to play a central role in some areal religious practices (Golla 2011; Barrett 1908; Kroeber 1932). In more recent times Patwin speech communities have come into contact with Spanish and English. The introduction of Spanish and English terms for introduced referents is well documented (see section 3.7), but the structural and lexical influence of other Indigenous languages on Patwin is poorly understood.

1.1.2. Dialects

There are three major dialect groups of Patwin: Hill Patwin (HP), spoken by communities living in the valleys of the Coast Range west of the Sacramento Valley; River Patwin (RP), spoken along the banks of the Sacramento River north of the northern border of present-day Yolo County; and South Patwin (SP), spoken in the Sacramento Valley and in the hills north of the Sacramento River delta. Significant structural and lexical isoglosses clearly differentiate each of the dialect groups, and the grammatical features of each group will often be discussed separately in this work. Of the three groups, South Patwin is the most divergent.

Figure 1.1 shows each identifiable dialect and the grouping into dialect groups. It also shows the speakers recorded in the archive for each dialect and the researchers who worked with each speaker in parentheses. For those dialects that will be discussed in this work, abbreviations are also given. In the abbreviations the major dialect group is represented in capital letters (HP, RP, SP) and individual dialects are represented with subscript letters. My identifications of dialects are informed by Whistler (1980:ch.3), Merriam (1966, 1967), Kroeber (1932), and others as described in more detail in the following sections. The form of this tree in figure 1.1 should not be taken as a strong claim for genetic lineages of Patwin dialects. More lexicography is needed to solidify the relationships among the dialects, and further work on language contact in the region is needed to determine how much of the differentiation is from language contact, as opposed to language-internal change over time.

I endeavor to describe all of the observable interdialectal variation that can be found in the archival record, although some of the less well-attested dialects are difficult to describe in detail. Of the three dialect groups Hill Patwin has been the most studied and has the most accumulated archival material. South Patwin is the least studied, and little South Patwin material is known to exist. See discussions of dialects and available materials in the following sections.

1.1.2.1. Map of Patwin Dialects

Map 1 shows the dialects in their geographic context.[4] The boundary of Patwin-speaking territory shown in map 1 is based on the maps in Kroeber (1932), Merriam (1967), Heizer (1966), Bennyhoff (1968), Johnson (1978), Whistler (1980), and Golla (2011), as described below. The dialect boundaries shown in map 1 are based on the map in Merriam (1967:260). Dialect boundaries should be understood to be approximate, and are not the same as political boundaries. Historically there were many more than nine politically independent Patwin polities. Individual village sites are not depicted here, out of respect for the privacy of Patwin people and their cultural heritage.

Merriam (1967) tentatively shows the area around the Marysville Buttes as being in Patwin language territory. I follow Kroeber (1932), Johnson

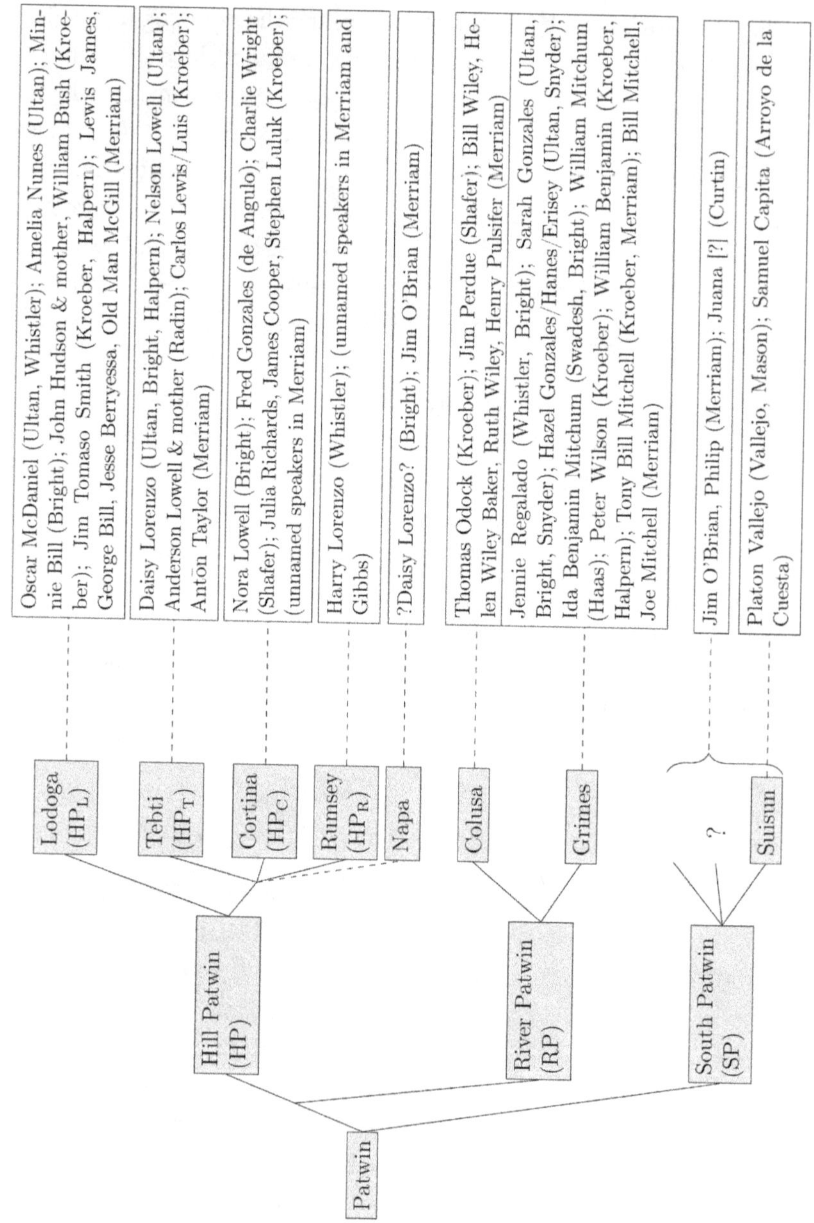

Fig. 1.1. Patwin dialects and speakers.

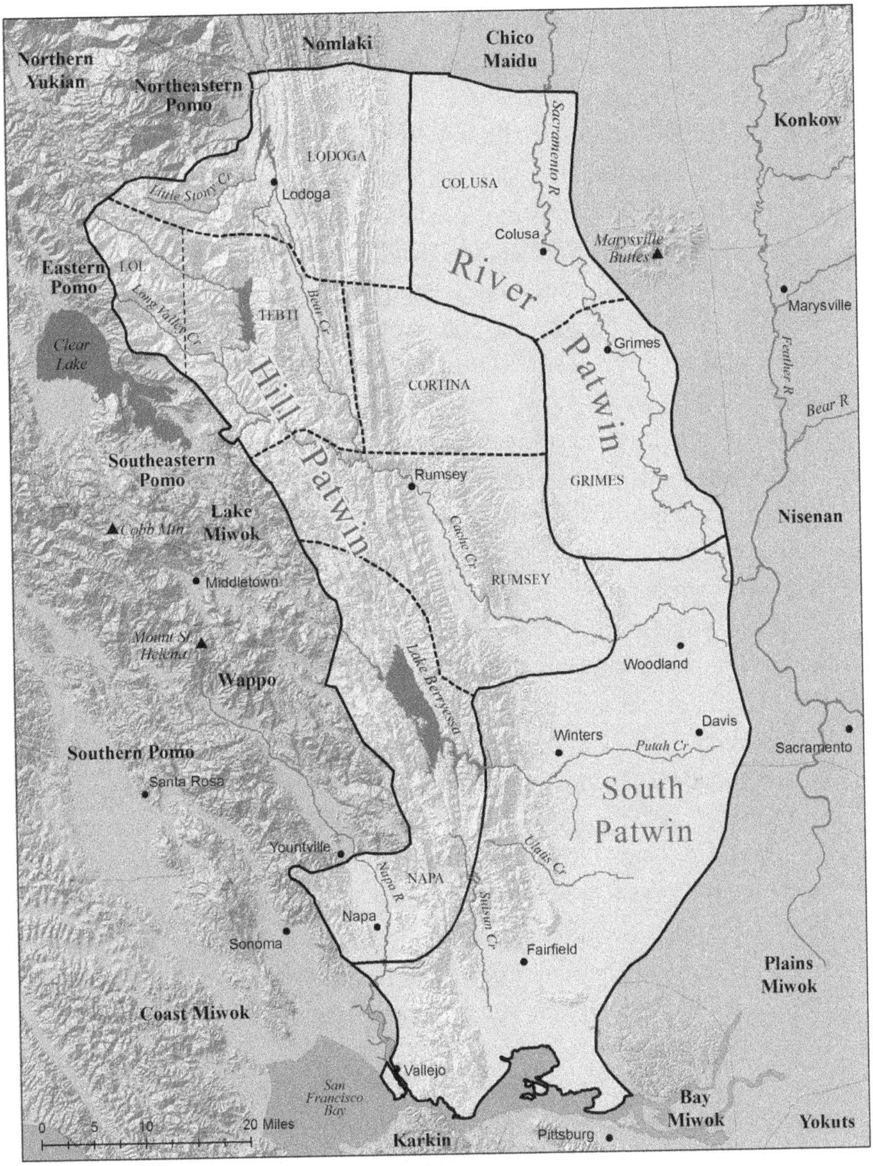

Map 1. Patwin dialects in their geographic context. Created by Jacquelyn Bjorkman. © The Regents of the University of California, Davis.

(1978), Whistler (1980), and Golla (2011) in depicting this territory as unclaimed, shared with the Maiduan peoples to the east (i.e., the westernmost Nisenan and the Konkow polities). A similar region is the Yolo Basin, the area immediately west of the Sacramento River, south of the confluence with the Feather River. This is a low-lying seasonal wetland, and may not have been permanently inhabited. It is likely to have been a shared resource among Patwin, Nisenan, and Plains Miwok tribes in the area (Bennyhoff 1968). I follow Kroeber (1932), Bennyhoff (1968), Johnson (1978), and Whistler (1980) in drawing the boundary through the middle of the Yolo Basin, a bit west of center. The map in Golla (2011), presumably following Merriam (1967), shows Patwin territory extending all the way to the Sacramento River in this area, thus encompassing the entire Yolo Basin. Wilson and Towne (1978) and Levy (1978) show the Nisenan and Plains Miwok territories stopping at the river here, though Kroeber (1932) shows these territories extending west of the river. Generally the Indigenous political and linguistic boundaries in this region are poorly understood.

The map in Golla (2011) shows the area around the city of Vallejo as Karkin Ohlone (Costanoan) territory, following Kroeber (1957:217 ff.) and the revised Kroeber map published in Heizer (1966:map 4). Kroeber cites a discussion in Beeler (1954:274) for this decision, which he admits is based on scant evidence. Almost all other maps (Kroeber 1932; Merriam 1967; Johnson 1978; Whistler 1980) show the Vallejo area as Patwin territory, and Bennyhoff (1968:141–42) provides good evidence that this is correct. Drawing from mission records and a careful analysis of documents from the Spanish period, Bennyhoff argues convincingly for Patwin occupation of the north shore of the Carquinez Strait (i.e., the strait south of Vallejo). I therefore follow Bennyhoff, and most other maps, in identifying this area as Patwin territory.

Map 1 differs from most previous maps in identifying the area immediately northwest of Vallejo as Coast Miwok territory. In this I follow Bennyhoff (1968), who identifies a named Coast Miwok village in this area.

The map in Golla (2011) shows the area around the city of Napa as being of uncertain linguistic affiliation, which I do not indicate in map 1. The area immediately north of the city of Napa may be Wappo territory—see

Sawyer (1965:xii). Generally it is to be understood that the language borders in the southern part of Patwin territory are not definitely known.

Of the lakes shown on the map, only Clear Lake is natural. The lakes in Lodoga, Tebti, and Napa territories are modern reservoirs.

1.1.2.2. *Language and Dialect*

In Patwin, as in many other languages, the boundary between *language* and *dialect* is not easily discerned. On the one hand anecdotal statements from Patwin speakers suggest that even the major dialect divisions did not present a boundary to mutual intelligibility, from which it follows that all the varieties of Patwin are dialects of the same language. On the other hand the Indigenous cultures of this region are characteristically multilingual (Golla 2011:6 ff.). It may be that speakers of the various Patwin varieties could understand each other not simply because of the similarity among the varieties, but because most people happened to know more than one of the Patwin languages. The lexical and grammatical differences between South Patwin on the one hand and River and Hill Patwin on the other certainly give one the impression of a division between two separate languages, rather than two dialects of the same language. Even the differences between Hill Patwin and River Patwin are in some cases notable enough that one is tempted to call them distinct languages.

Another level of complexity here is the Indigenous conceptualization of what a language is. Tatsch (2006:43 ff.) notes that a speaker of an Indigenous California language is likely to say, upon hearing a recording of a closely related dialect, "This is not my language." This indicates that each small speech community has its own strongly differentiated identity, despite close cultural contact with surrounding communities, formal linguistic similarities, and mutual intelligibility. To give the reader an idea of just how different these Patwin cultures are from one another: Elliott (2011) argues that Hill Patwin and River Patwin cultures belong to two entirely separate cultural regions of California—the North Coast Ranges cultural region and the Central Valley cultural region, respectively—citing differences in political affiliations and material culture. We can therefore be sure that the differences among the various dialects of Patwin carry important cultural significance and may be important for language revitalization projects, as well as for academic studies in anthropology and linguistics (e.g., historical linguistics or contact phenomena in the Patwin region). Therefore the term *language*, applied to Patwin, is somewhat misleading, insofar as this term carries connotations of social and/or political unity. The Patwin tribes are not and never were a homogeneous unit socially or politically (see, for example, Kroeber 1932).

We are therefore in somewhat of a conceptual and terminological quagmire when approaching the idea of *language* versus *dialect* in Patwin. I take an academically conservative route: I call Patwin one *language*, basing this tentative classification primarily on the anecdotal evidence of mutual intelligibility. Accordingly, I call the varieties of Patwin *dialects* of the language. More specifically, I divide the language into three major *dialect groups*—Hill Patwin, River Patwin, and South Patwin—each of which is further divisible into individual *dialects*. This is academically conservative in that (a) it follows the general convention in linguistics of using mutual intelligibility as the primary or only factor in determining the sameness of two linguistic varieties, and (b) the Patwin language is generally recognized to be one *language* in the existing academic literature (though with some disagreement about the place of South Patwin). In using these terms I do not however wish to alienate readers who draw sharp distinctions among the languages spoken in each of the ancestral Patwin regions. These are indeed different languages in the important sense that they are each traditions carried on by different tribes, and different peoples, which outsiders have grouped together as "Patwin" for analytical reasons. I also do not intend to obscure the structural differences among the various dialects of Patwin, which are in some cases quite significant.

Terminology aside I have taken care always to indicate which Patwin dialect is represented in each of the examples throughout the text, and to describe the variation I have observed within Patwin in as much detail as I am able, given the information in my sources. I hope this will be useful for researchers interested in specific Patwin varieties.

1.1.2.3. Hill Patwin

Hill Patwin territory is located in the coast range immediately west of the southern Sacramento Valley. Hill Patwin is the primary heritage language of two contemporary, federally recognized tribes: the Yocha Dehe Wintun Nation and the Kletsel Dehe Band of Wintun Indians. It is also one of the primary heritage languages of the Grindstone Indian Rancheria of Wintun-Wailaki Indians. Before contact with European peoples Hill Patwin was spoken by about nineteen politically independent tribes (Kroeber 1932:262–64). Permanent settlements were mostly located in the narrow valleys running through this mountainous terrain, although the southwestern extremity of Hill Patwin territory may have included the lower Napa Valley (see below). Cook estimates the combined pre-1830 population of Hill Patwin tribes at four thousand people (Cook 1976:14).

The Hill Patwin group can be divided into a number of dialects. Figure 1.1 shows those dialects of which we can be most certain. The Lodoga (HP_L), Tebti (HP_T), and Cortina (HP_C) dialects are moderately well documented, and the Rumsey dialect (HP_R) somewhat less so. The Napa dialect is barely attested (see below). Of the Hill Patwin dialects Lodoga is the most divergent, possibly because of close cultural connections to neighboring Yuki, Northeastern Pomo, and Nomlaki communities. Whistler (1980) describes Cortina and Rumsey as being particularly close to one another, placing them together in a subgroup of Hill Patwin that he calls Southern Hill Patwin, which excludes both Lodoga and Tebti. As far as I can see, Lodoga is clearly the most divergent but Tebti is not particularly more distinct from Rumsey and Cortina than these latter two are from one another. I have therefore grouped Tebti, Cortina, and Rumsey together in the main branch of Hill Patwin, excluding only Lodoga—like the classification in Whistler (1976). In any case this classification of Hill Patwin dialects is preliminary. Further lexicographical work is needed to make any strong claims about dialect similarities or genetic relationships.

Napa: The Napa dialect is very poorly attested. What little is known about the Napa subdialect is due to Merriam. He records a few Napa words in three lists that are otherwise primarily River Patwin lists (Merriam:V74,

NH71, NH72), from which we may tentatively conclude that Napa is similar to the Cortina dialect of Hill Patwin (Whistler 1980). Merriam's communication with his consultant Jim O'Brian about the Napa dialect seems to have been somewhat garbled, but in Merriam's judgment it was enough to draw conclusions about the boundaries of Napa territory and to affiliate Napa with Hill Patwin.[5] I associate Napa with Hill Patwin here as a best guess, in agreement with the standard source (Whistler 1980). No specific mention of linguistic features of the Napa subdialect will appear in this work, however, since there is no substantial source.

The introduction to Elizabeth Bright's unfinished Patwin grammar discusses the dialect affiliation(s) of each speaker she worked with. Here Bright suggests that Daisy Lorenzo's mother was born at Topaydihi (Monticello), which could make Lorenzo a source for Napa (Bright, b:6). In other sources we find contradictory information, however. In Ultan's notebooks we see that both of Lorenzo's parents speak the Tebti dialect (Ultan, d:6.27,6.74). Halpern's field notes also show that both of Lorenzo's parents are from the Lake County region, in agreement with Ultan (Halpern, c:7.10). I conclude that Lorenzo is not a source for Napa data, being instead a speaker of the Tebti dialect.

Putah: Whistler (1980) identifies an additional dialect of Hill Patwin: Putah, spoken in the Berryessa Valley. However, there is not sufficient evidence to demonstrate the existence of a Putah dialect distinct from Napa. Whistler's source for Putah data, Gibbs's "Cop-éh" word list, is in fact a Rumsey source.[6] Gibbs states that this vocabulary is from a speaker from the village of Cop-éh (i.e., Kope), on Putos Creek (i.e., Putah Creek, in the Berryessa Valley). However, Merriam (1929) points out that the village Kope is in fact on Cache Creek, in the Rumsey area. This leaves the purported Putah dialect without any available materials, and with no solid reason to consider it a separate dialect. I therefore follow Merriam in tentatively considering the Berryessa Valley to belong to the Napa dialect area (Merriam 1966, 1967).

Subdivisions of Tebti: The Tebti dialect may be further divided into two very close subdialects: Tebti proper and Lol, spoken farther upstream of Tebti.

These varieties are so close that I generally refer to them collectively as Tebti. Grouping these varieties together as one dialect is the prevailing opinion in the small literature on Patwin dialects (i.e., the work of Whistler and Merriam). There is at least one formal difference between the Lol and Tebti subdialects, however; see section 8.2.1.4.

1.1.2.4. River Patwin

River Patwin territory is located along the Sacramento River in present-day Colusa County. River Patwin is the primary heritage language of the Cachil Dehe Band of Wintun Indians, a contemporary, federally recognized tribe. Before contact with European peoples River Patwin was spoken by sixteen to eighteen politically independent tribes, with permanent settlements on both sides of the Sacramento River (Kroeber 1932:259–61). Cook (1976:12 ff.) estimates the combined pre-1830 population of River Patwin, Valley Nisenan, and Valley Maidu (Michopda) population at forty-seven thousand people, but does not provide a separate estimate for River Patwin territory. Using Cook's methodology, but restricting the search area to River Patwin settlements, we can estimate a pre-1830 population of about twenty thousand people.[7]

Older ethnological sources sometimes group River Patwin and South Patwin into one group, possibly for cultural reasons (e.g., Barrett 1919; McKern 1922). However, they are undoubtedly distinct dialect regions, with clear structural and lexical differences.

The River Patwin group may be divided into two closely related dialects: Colusa in the north and Grimes in the south. Because they are so similar grammatically, these two dialects are generally not differentiated in this work. Of the two dialects, Grimes is much better documented, and most of the River Patwin data in this work is from Grimes.

1.1.2.5. South Patwin

South Patwin was spoken by an unknown number of tribes located in the southwestern Sacramento Valley. Cook estimates the combined pre-mission population of South Patwin tribes at five thousand people (Cook 1976:6 ff.), though this does not include South Patwin tribes north of Putah Creek. Though the ethnogeography of the South Patwin region is sketchy, in Kroeber (1932) and Heizer and Hester (1970) we find mention of three distinct villages in South Patwin territory north of Putah Creek (in the Knight's Landing area). Therefore, following Cook's methodology as explained in footnote 7, a further 1,500 people can be conservatively added to Cook's estimate, bringing the total combined pre-mission population of South Patwin tribes to at least 6,500 people.

Linguistically South Patwin (SP) is the most divergent dialect group—so much so that some scholars consider South Patwin to be a distinct but closely related language (e.g., Whistler 1976, 1980, 1986; Shepherd 2005). Others consider South Patwin to be a Patwin dialect (e.g., Kroeber 1932; Johnson 1978; Goddard 1996). The historical paucity of South Patwin materials has prevented a definitive statement on this issue. Most general resources on the classification of Native American languages remain wisely agnostic (e.g., Mithun 1999; Golla 2011).

Some anecdotal evidence suggests that South Patwin was mutually intelligible with other dialects of Patwin. A South Patwin speaker named Jim O'Brian informed Merriam in 1906 that his people spoke the same language as the people at Cortina—that is, Hill Patwin (Merriam 1967:270 ff.). The writings of Platon Vallejo also suggest that South Patwin was the same language as that spoken further inland (e.g. P. Vallejo, c:10.1).[8] Because of this evidence of mutual intelligibility I consider South Patwin to be a dialect of Patwin for the purposes of this work.

The dialect divisions within South Patwin are difficult to discern, since the whole language is poorly documented. The best documented dialect is Suisun, which Platon Vallejo learned as a child from a Suisun man named Tomó. Vallejo later wrote down what he remembered of the language, including word lists, sentences, and some translations of Christian texts. Vallejo was also the speaker consulted by Mason for his Suisun vocabulary (see Mason). Suisun territory lies immediately north of Suisun Bay; the exact extent of the territory is unknown.

Other South Patwin sources represent different dialects from what is seen in Vallejo. Merriam documented a dialect of South Patwin from speakers he identifies as Jim O'Brian and Philip (Merriam 1967:270 ff.). This dialect, which Merriam calls "Poo´-e-win," is clearly different from the Suisun dialect, but its geographic provenance is not known. Arroyo de la Cuesta's word list of "Suisun" appears to be yet another dialect of South Patwin, morphologically distinct from both Vallejo's Suisun and Merriam's Poo´-e-win (see Arroyo de la Cuesta). Barrett's slip files have a few South Patwin words (labeled "puyuwin"), but not enough grammatical information to associate this data with a specific South Patwin dialect (Barrett, b). We therefore have evidence for at least three distinct dialects of South Patwin, although not enough information to assign specific geographic areas to each of them. For discussions of some of the most salient differences among the South Patwin dialects, see sections 8.2.1.6 (about verbal morphology unique to the Vallejo materials) and A.2.7 (about pronouns).

Whistler (1980:21) tentatively identifies three dialects of South Patwin with geographic regions: Knight's Landing, Dixon, and Suisun. Chairman Harry Lorenzo of Rumsey, one of Whistler's consultants, was able to give a few rough characterizations of each of these (Suisun "was drawled out," Knight's Landing was "all mumbly," etc.) and to provide two example sentences from the Dixon dialect (Whistler, d:G99–100). It is not known how these three geographically delimited dialects might line up with the linguistic varieties represented by Vallejo's Suisun, Arroyo's Suisun, and Merriam's Poo´-e-win.

1.1.3. Nomenclature and Synonymies

The word *patwin* means '(Indian) person' in the Patwin language. Some Patwin people prefer the word *Wintun* /wint^{h}un/ to refer to their language (Pamela [Pulsifer] Gonzales, pers. comm.), while others use the word *Patwin* (see, for example, Dubin 2010). I will use *Patwin*, because (a) this is the current practice among linguists, and (b) *Wintun* is sometimese used to refer to the Nomlaki language and to the Wintuan language family as a whole.

The Patwin language has also been called "Cop-éh" (Gibbs 1853), and is sometimes synonymous with "Southern Wintun" or "Southern Wintuan" (e.g., Mithun 1999; Golla 2011). The term *Patwin*, used in this work, is used also in Powers (1877), Kroeber (1932), Whistler (1980), Goddard (1996), Mithun (1999), and Golla (2011). Other names for the Wintuan language family include "Copeh" (Latham 1856), "Copehan" (Powell 1891; Hodge 1907), "Wintoon" (Merriam 1962, 1966, 1967), and "Wintun" (Whistler 1976,

1980; Boas 1911; Sapir 1929; Pitkin 1984; Shepherd 2005). The term *Wintuan*, used in this work, is used also in Goddard (1996), Campbell (1997), Mithun (1999), and Golla (2011).

The complicated array of synonymies for the various dialects of Patwin is well summarized in Whistler (1980:33–46); I will not duplicate that summary here. My terminology for Patwin dialects is the same as in Whistler (1980), except that his "Lake County" is my "Tebti." My abbreviations are different from Whistler's, however. These differences are summarized in figure 1.2, along with the differences in dialect group divisions.

1.2. MATERIALS

The linguistic forms discussed in this work are drawn entirely from the archival record. Using the archival record is necessary for the goals of this study, since the few known living speakers of Patwin do not represent the entire dialect spectrum of the language, and since these speakers are hesitant to work with linguists. In spite of the difficulties in working with a large collection of archival sources of varying quality, I argue here that having varied sources is a kind of strength: the researcher gains a kaleidoscopic perspective on the language, from many speakers, filtered through the observations of many researchers.

In terms of phonetic transcription, the highest quality written materials are those gathered most recently by linguists Donald Ultan and Kenneth Whistler in the 1960s and 1970s. By this time the phonemic contrasts of Patwin were more or less established, and these researchers were well trained in phonetic transcription. However, the speakers that linguists worked with at this time represented only a few dialects; the vibrant speech communities of first-language Patwin speakers were already long past. Older records such as C. Hart Merriam's vocabulary lists represent a wider variety of dialects, and speakers at this time were more likely to be speaking Patwin on a regular basis. However, the poor phonetic transcription in these sources and the often flawed glosses makes them more difficult to interpret than more modern sources.

While each individual source comes with its difficulties of interpretation, a large study encompassing many sources can overcome some of

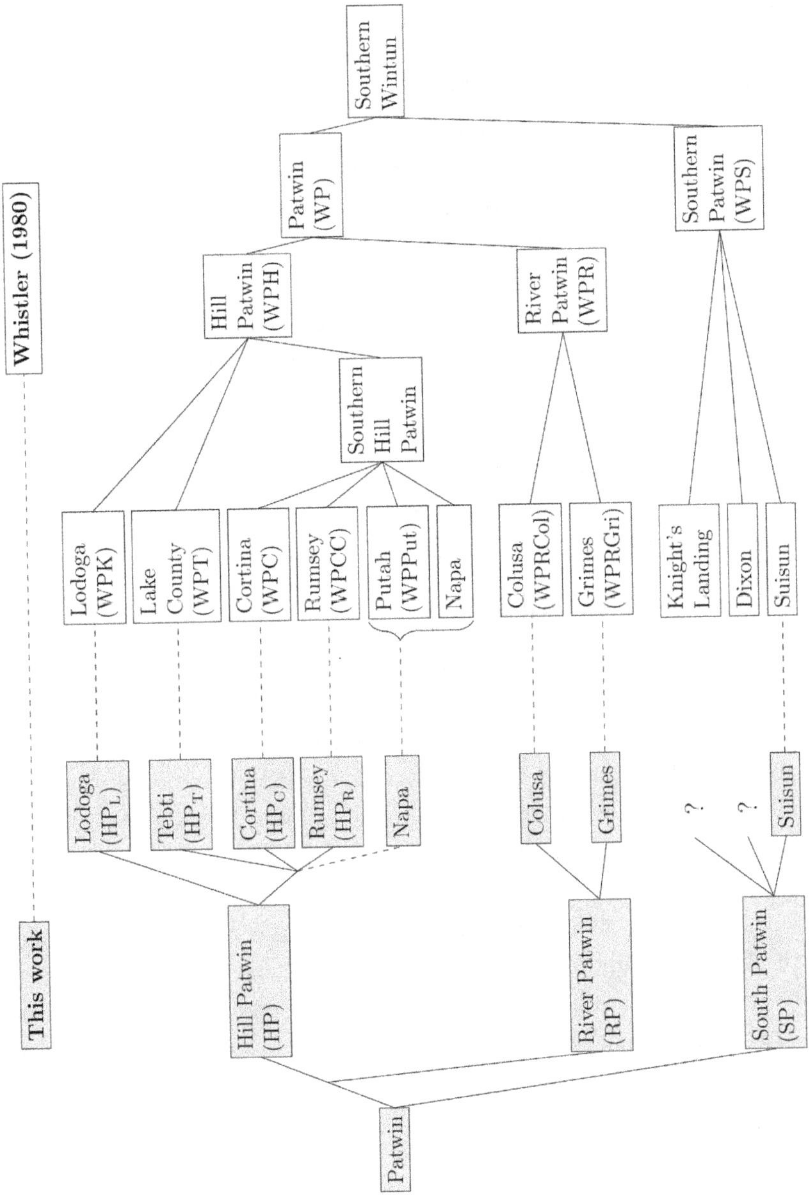

Fig. 1.2. Dialect synonymies between the present work and Whistler (1980).

these difficulties. Data from older, less reliable sources can be compared with data from newer sources to fill in phonetic detail and correct semantic misinterpretations. This older data can then fill in some of the gaps in knowledge inherent in the newer sources. Thus variation that may have the appearance of errors on the part of speakers or researchers can be checked across multiple sources: patterns of variation attested from multiple speakers or across multiple decades can be trusted more than those peculiar to a single speaker or a single researcher. Finally, archival audio recordings can be used to fill in the phonetic detail that does not appear in the written record. The author has no control over the data collection in this kind of study, and one can expect a certain amount of unwanted variation across sources whose authors may have had different methodologies or goals. (In this case the amount of unwanted variation across sources is very high.) On the other hand the multiplicity of sources itself is a strength. A pattern observed in multiple cases by multiple authors is a pattern indeed.

1.2.1. Materials Consulted

Following are brief descriptions of available Patwin materials, all of which have been consulted to some extent in the research for this work. Sources are organized below by resource type, and within each section resources are ordered roughly chronologically. I have listed the speakers consulted by each researcher where possible. In examples throughout this work speakers are referred to by their initials, which are given here as well. In the discussion below, the names of the following institutions are abbreviated: the National Anthropological Archives in Washington, DC (NAA); the American Philosophical Society in Philadelphia (APS); the Survey of California and Other Indian Languages at UC Berkeley (SCOIL); and the Bancroft Library at UC Berkeley (the Bancroft). A complete list of archival sources can also be found in the first part of the references.

1.2.1.1. Major Sources

Major collections of archival and published materials are listed here, presented roughly in chronological order and grouped by researcher.

Vallejo: Platon Vallejo (son of General Mariano Vallejo) learned Suisun South Patwin as a child from his caretaker, a Suisun speaker named Tomó. As an older man, Vallejo wrote down what he remembered of the language. These materials are now archived primarily at the Autry Museum in Los Angeles (P. Vallejo, c). The collection consists of nine notebooks of words and phrases glossed in English, and about a dozen word lists and translations of Christian prayers.[9,10] Additional South Patwin documents by Vallejo are archived at SCOIL (P. Vallejo, a) and in the private collection of Martha Vallejo McGettigan (P. Vallejo, e, f, g, h). J. Alden Mason also obtained a South Patwin word list using Vallejo as his informant, providing a valuable phonetic transcription of some sounds that Vallejo did not transcribe in his own writings. Mason's list is part of the Pitkin Papers archived at the APS (see Mason). Additionally there are at least two documents written by Vallejo's brother Napoleon, using Platon as an informant: N. Vallejo (a, b). These documents are archived at the Vacaville Heritage Council.

Kroeber: A. L. Kroeber collected linguistic, ethnographic, and ethnogeographic Patwin data between 1909 and 1924, from Lodoga Hill Patwin speakers Jim (Tom/Tomaso) Smith [JS], William Bush, John Hudson, and Hudson's mother, Maggie; Tebti Hill Patwin speaker Carlos Lewis/Luis; Cortina Hill Patwin speakers Julia Richards, James Cooper, and Stephen Luluk; and River Patwin speakers Thomas Odock [TO], Bill Wylie, Peter Wilson, William Benjamin [WB], and Tony Bill Mitchell. The results of Kroeber's work are codified in his *Handbook of the Indians of California* (Kroeber 1925) and his Patwin ethnography (Kroeber 1932). Most of his field notebooks (Kroeber, b) and his Patwin slip file (Kroeber, c) are archived in the Pitkin Papers at the APS. A few of Kroeber's notes on River Patwin and its phonetics are archived at the Bancroft (Kroeber, a; Kroeber and Waterman).

Merriam: Naturalist and ethnographer C. Hart Merriam collected a large amount of data on the Native languages of California, including Patwin. Near-identical copies of Merriam's vocabulary lists are archived at the Bancroft Library in Berkeley and at the Library of Congress in Washington, DC.[11] Merriam collected Patwin vocabulary between 1903 and 1936, from South Patwin ("Poo´-e-win": V76, NH73), River Patwin ("Ko´-roo": V74, V75, NH71, NH72), and five dialects of Hill Patwin: Lodoga ("Choo-hel´-mem-shel": V70, NH67), Tebti ("Chen´-po-sel win": V71, NH68), Cortina ("Klet´-win": V72, V74, NH71, NH72), Rumsey ("Ko-peh´": V73, NH70, NH72), and a small amount from Napa ("Nap´-pa": V74, NH71, NH72). Taken together this collection represents the widest sample of Patwin in terms of dialects represented. The phonetic transcription however is not of high quality, and some forms are mistranslated.

Merriam consulted the following speakers in the creation of his vocabulary lists (as indicated on each list): Lewis James [LJ], George Bill [GB], Jesse Berryessa [JB], and Old Man McGill [McGill] (Choo-hel´-mem-shel); Antōn Taylor [AT] (Chen´-po-sel); Tony Bill Mitchell [TM], Bill Mitchell [BM], Joe Mitchell [JM], Bill Wiley [BW], Ruth Wiley [RW], and Helen Wiley Baker [HW] (Ko´-roo); and other unnamed speakers.

Merriam also published on the ethnography, ethnogeography, and linguistic affiliations of Patwin (Merriam 1929, 1962, 1966, 1967).

De Angulo: Jaime de Angulo wrote a grammar of Patwin based on one week of fieldwork conducted in 1929 with Cortina Hill Patwin speaker Fred Gonzales [FG] (who also spoke River Patwin). Some of the data in this grammar appears to be extrapolated rather than being based on directly observed linguistic data (see discussion in section A.2.4, for example). Although de Angulo's grammar is thought-provoking and valuable as an initial attempt at creating a grammatical description of Patwin, his field notebooks will have to be consulted in order to determine which structures he actually observed and which he only extrapolated from other data. Unfortunately his field notebooks have not yet been located.

In addition to the grammatical description, de Angulo's grammar also contains a word list with more than six hundred entries (the "Semasiology" section) and three translated texts in the valuable genres of conversation (Text I) and personal narrative (Texts II and III). The word list and texts are the most valuable sections of de Angulo's grammar, being valuable, near-primary resources of the under-documented Cortina dialect.

Radin: Anthropologist Paul Radin collected Tebti Hill Patwin data in 1931 from speaker Anderson Lowell [AL] and his mother. His field notebook (Radin, d), sixteen texts (Radin, c), dictionary (Radin, a), and grammar (Radin, b) are all archived in the Pitkin Papers at APS. The grammar, dictionary, and texts are handwritten rough drafts. The texts are the largest collection of connected Patwin narrative ever collected. These sources are informationally rich but difficult to interpret both phonetically and semantically.[12] So far eight of the texts have been analyzed in enough detail to use for the present study. Radin formatted his texts such that the Patwin and the corresponding English glosses are on separate pages, roughly 130 pages apart. Therefore examples from Radin's texts are cited with two page numbers, as in (1) below.

Halpern: A. M. Halpern collected Patwin linguistic and ethnographic data in 1936. His linguistic data, from speakers Jim Tomaso Smith [JS] (HP_L), Daisy Lorenzo [DL] (HP_T), and William Benjamin [WB] (RP), is archived in the Pitkin Papers at the APS (Halpern, c). Halpern's ethnographic notes at SCOIL (Halpern, a) and the Bancroft (Halpern, b) also contain some linguistic information.

Bright: Elizabeth Bright conducted extensive fieldwork in 1952 with speakers Minnie Bill [MB] (HP_L), Nora Lowell [NL] (HP_C), Daisy Lorenzo [DL] (HP_T), Sarah Gonzales [SG] (RP), and Ida Mitchum [IM] (RP). Her field notes (Bright, c) and draft grammar (Bright, b) are archived at SCOIL, and can be viewed online at the California Language Archive.[13]

Ultan: Donald Ultan conducted extensive fieldwork between 1961 and 1962, with speakers Oscar McDaniel [OM] (HP_L and other dialects), Amelia Nunes [AN] (HP_L), Nelson Lowell [NeL] (HP_T), Daisy Lorenzo [DL] (HP_T), Sarah Gonzales [SG] (RP), and Hazel Hanes (Gonzales) [HG] (RP). Ultan's original field notebooks are in the Pitkin Papers at APS, and microfilm copies are at SCOIL and viewable online through the California Language Archive (Ultan, d).[14] The quality of phonetic transcription is high. Ultan also began compiling an electronic dictionary, a printout of which is archived in the Pitkin Papers at APS (Ultan, c).

Snyder and his students: Warren Snyder conducted a small amount of fieldwork on River Patwin with speaker Sarah Gonzales [SG] in 1969 and 1970. His field notebooks have not been located, but his slip file containing lexical and grammatical data is archived at the Bancroft (Snyder, b). Snyder also wrote a draft paper on River Patwin phonemics, also archived at the Bancroft (Snyder, a).[15] Snyder also led students into the field to gather their own River Patwin data. Robert Rathburn's field notebook of data from Sarah Gonzales [SG] is archived at the Bancroft.

Snyder also worked with Bernadine Claire Morgan, who wrote a preliminary phonemic and morphemic analysis of River Patwin for her master's thesis (Morgan 1971). Morgan's phonemic analysis was based on Snyder's (of River Patwin), and her morphemic analysis is based on de Angulo's (of Cortina Hill Patwin). She also gathered her own data from Hazel Erisey (Gonzales) [HG] (RP) and Sarah Gonzales [SG] (RP), but the location of her field notebooks is not known. Her notebooks would be particularly useful, since the data presented in the morphemic sketch is undifferentiated between Hill Patwin (from de Angulo's work with Cortina Hill Patwin) and River Patwin (from Morgan's own River Patwin data).

Whistler: Between 1975 and 1979 Kenneth Whistler conducted fieldwork with Patwin speakers Oscar McDaniel [OM] (HP_L), Harry Lorenzo [HL] (HP_R), and Jennie Regalado [JR] (RP). This research led to a master's thesis on Patwin plant and animal taxonomy (1976), a doctoral dissertation on Wintuan kinship terminology (1980), published papers on Hill Patwin verb stems (1981) and evidentiality (1986), two published Hill Patwin texts (1977a, 1978), and presentations on Wintuan geographical prehistory (1977b) and Patwin numerals (1979). Whistler's seven field notebooks and some ethnobiological specimens are archived at SCOIL (Whistler, a, d).[16] The quality of phonetic transcription in these sources is very high. Other unpublished work remains in Whistler's possession, including an unfinished chapter on Hill Patwin phonology (Whistler, c).

1.2.1.2. *Smaller Written Sources*

Word lists are relatively minor sources for grammatical information, but can help to fill in gaps in lexical knowledge, which is of course necessary to fully parse any sample sentence. Additionally, some morphological and syntactic information can be gleaned from word list data.

The first word list of Patwin was taken down in 1821 by Fray Felipe Arroyo de la Cuesta, from South Patwin speaker Samuel Capita. This word list is now archived at the Bancroft (see Arroyo de la Cuesta). John Bartlett obtained a short River Patwin word list from an unknown speaker in San Diego in the mid-nineteenth century, now part of NAA MS 1627 (see Bartlett). George Gibbs gathered a short word list of Rumsey Hill Patwin that became the first published Patwin word list (Gibbs 1853). Powers gathered a word list from Tebti Hill Patwin speaker Antonio ("Chief of the Chenposel tribe"), published as "Pat-win´" in Powers's *Tribes of California* (Powers 1877:530). Jeremiah Curtin gathered South Patwin data from an unknown speaker in 1884 and 1889, now archived at the NAA (Curtin, a, b). H. B. Wilson gathered Grimes River Patwin data in July 1903 from George Howell, Bob Wilson, George Byers, and Mary Byers. Wilson's field notebook is in the Pitkin Papers at APS (Wilson, notebook). C. E. Kelsey gathered numerals from a large number of California languages in the first decade of the twentieth century, and his lists are now archived at the Bancroft (see Kelsey). S. A. Barrett's ethnographic work in the early twentieth century resulted in a comparative slip file with Patwin data from Frank Wright and Dick, both of Rumsey, and others. Barrett's slip file is housed at SCOIL (Barrett, b). Some Patwin language data also appears in Barrett's Pomo ethnogeography (Barrett 1908).[17] T. T. Waterman obtained some River Patwin vocabulary and two valuable texts from Thomas Odock, now archived in the Pitkin Papers at the APS (see Waterman). Some Patwin words can be found in W. C. McKern's ethnological papers on River Patwin (McKern 1922, 1923). William E. Myers obtained Patwin vocabulary for Edward Curtis's *North American Indian* project (Myers 1924). Mary Haas gathered a short River Patwin word list from Ida and William Mitchum, also housed at SCOIL (see Haas). Robert Shafer gathered word lists of Hill and River Patwin from Charlie Wright and Jim Perdue, published in Shafer (1961).

1.2.1.3. Audio Sources

In this section I list the spoken audio archival Patwin material known to me. There are recordings of both (a) elicitation sessions, where individual words and short phrases are elicited, and (b) connected speech. I exclude recordings of songs and religious speeches, since some people consider these kinds of recordings to be culturally sensitive. The language in these kinds of recordings is specialized in any case and would require its own separate discussion.

Elizabeth Bright recorded Cortina Hill Patwin speaker Nora Lowell in 1952, obtaining elicited words and some songs. The entire recording is available at the Berkeley Language Center (Bright, a).[18] Richard Reeve obtained an audio recording of Chairman Harry Lorenzo (HP_R) in 1952, which includes a few elicited words and phrases. Reeve's recording is archived at Sacramento State (see Reeve). Morris Swadesh and Robert Melton recorded a one-hour elicitation session with River Patwin speaker Ida Benjamin Mitchum, as part of Swadesh's Penutian vocabulary survey (see description in Swadesh 1954). This recording is archived at the Archives of Traditional Music at Indiana University (Swadesh and Melton). Sally McLendon made a series of Northeastern Pomo recordings in 1958, but one of her recordings contains Lodoga Hill Patwin speakers Oscar McDaniel and Minnie Bill having a conversation in Patwin—mostly a monologue with McDaniel speaking, and Bill responding minimally. This recording is archived at the Berkeley Language Center (see McLendon).[19] Donald Ultan recorded an elicitation session and some texts from Lodoga Hill Patwin speaker Oscar McDaniel in 1961 (Ultan, b), and one text from River Patwin speaker Sarah Gonzales in 1962 (Ultan, a). Both recordings are archived at SCOIL. Kenneth Whistler obtained more texts from Oscar McDaniel in 1975, and these are also archived at SCOIL (Whistler, b). Donald Jewell is said to have recorded River Patwin speaker Jennie Regalado telling a story, circa 1970, but this recording has not been found.

The Dorothy M. Hill collection in the Special Collections of the Meriam Library at Chico contains some audio recordings, including interviews with Lodoga Hill Patwin speaker Oscar McDaniel and River Patwin speaker Jennie Regalado (see Hill). The collection also contains transcriptions of some of the recordings. The Dorothy Hill material has not been consulted in the creation of the present work, but should be consulted for future work.

1.3. GRAMMATICOGRAPHY

This study demonstrates the richness of description that can be achieved by studying complex and varying linguistic forms through the kaleidoscopic lens of archival materials. The information is presented in such a way that it may be of use both to linguists engaged in language comparison, typology, and so on, and to scholars interested in the Patwin language specifically, or in one of its dialects. This has all been done without attempting to reduce the variation apparent in the Patwin archive into a single, simplified system. Instead the variation in the data is embraced and explained, including dialect variation, individual variation, meaningful formal variation, and free variation. This work is a description of Patwin grammar, but is also a work of comparative linguistics, comparing the various grammatical systems found in Patwin dialects and speakers to one another.[20] A noticeable downside of this is that the resulting information is complicated, and may be difficult to approach for a nonspecialist. Therefore in addition to the academic style of presentation, the author assumes the responsibility of creating more easily digested summaries and descriptions, and of distributing these to Patwin communities or individuals, should they be interested in the perspective gained by an academic study such as this one.

1.3.1. The Utility of Language Description

What is the purpose, then, of reassembling all of the existing archival materials into a grammatical description? This project is not generating any new primary records for Patwin. Therefore it falls outside of what Himmelmann (2006) defines as "language documentation proper." But this document has a different purpose. A descriptive grammar adds value to a collection of primary material by providing an analysis of the grammatical structures found in the data, reducing the noisy data in the archive into a manageable description. This description should be useful for language revitalizationists and academic researchers alike, saving them the trouble of sifting through the archive for answers to questions about Patwin grammar. Because of the utility of descriptive grammars to academic and community researchers in making sense of raw language data, this kind of document is in fact central to the purpose of language documentation: the creation of a record of a language useful for further inquiry into any arbitrary facet of the language (Rehg 2014).

Of course Patwin grammar is not closed to further inquiry with the publication of this document. On the contrary I hope that the availability of a grammatical description of Patwin will stimulate further research into the Patwin language, relationships among the languages of California, and any and all fields touching on these areas.

I also hope that this book will be a reference for the creation of more "user-friendly" Patwin materials for use in language revitalization. This document is not itself intended for pedagogical purposes—the intention here is to present and discuss the data with all of its complexity, and not to sweep any confusing variation under the rug. So although this book can inform the creation of pedagogical materials, the book is not itself recommended as a learning tool for the language student unless no other options are available.

1.3.2. Managing Uncertainty

Fundamentally a study of this nature is a process of distilling the chaotic data found in the archival record into a comprehensible summary of attested forms, their meanings and uses, and the patterns of their variation. Using multiple sources and comparing attested forms among them, it is generally possible to arrive at a good analysis. Nevertheless much uncertainty is inherent in such a process. Following Spence (2015) we can conceptualize a process of "managing uncertainty" with archival data sources.

The aim of cross-source comparison is to filter out variation by researcher, to the extent possible. For example, Elizabeth Bright consistently transcribes the first-person plural exclusive pronoun stem as if it were /ne·ču-/ in every dialect, but she is the only researcher to transcribe this stem with a long vowel. I therefore assume that the long vowel in this stem is an artifact of her analysis and not a phenomenon in the language, and I do not discuss this as a point of linguistic variation. Similarly some older sources do not differentiate aspirated from unaspirated stops, or glottalized from nonglottalized obstruents. Thus for example the glottalization on the first-person inclusive pronoun root /p'e-/ is often not transcribed in older sources; whereas the more phonetically reliable sources (Whistler, d; Ultan, d) always transcribe this root with a glottalized /p'/. I therefore assume that the form of this root is in fact /p'e/, and analyze every instance of it as such.

In some cases however the form, meaning, or dialect affiliations of a linguistic element remain obscure. In these cases I describe what I can about the element, but also make sure to clearly point out the limits of my knowledge. The following conventions are used to represent uncertainty in attested forms: a centered asterisk ⟨∗⟩ following a vowel indicates that the length of that vowel is not known, as in *na∗nu*. A superscript circle after a consonant indicates that its laryngeal series is not known. For example, the South Patwin finite suffix (see section 8.2.1.1) may be /-ti/, /tʰi/, or /t'i/, so that suffix is rendered ⟨t°i⟩ here. Other uncertainties in forms are also present, such as vowel quality uncertainty and uncertain word boundaries. These have no special symbols, but are discussed in the text in a way I hope is clear. For uncertainty of meaning I simply place a question mark after the gloss.

To make the analyses in this work maximally transparent, I adhere to the following conventions in presenting evidence: (1) All examples are found in the archive, not made up for the purposes of easy exposition. (2) Each example is presented both in its standard phonemic form and in the exact form found in the written source. (3) Each example is accompanied by a page citation (or time point for audio sources), researcher and speaker names, and dialect affiliation. (4) Glosses provided match the glosses in the source closely, with only minor corrections (capitalization, spelling out abbreviations, modern species names, etc.). If a gloss departs significantly from that found in the source, it is because the gloss found in the source is either incorrect or worded in a way that is misleading. In this case the original gloss is also provided.

1.3.3. Theoretical Alignment

I endeavor to make this description as straightforward as possible, such that it will be as accessible as one could reasonably expect to non-specialists and to practitioners working in various linguistic frameworks. The structure of the Patwin language is of interest not only to linguists but also to anthropologists, language learners, and teachers involved in language revitalization. What this means in terms of my employing one linguistic theory or another in this work is that I will select representations that I judge to be as non-technical as possible, while still allowing for a complete and accurate description.

For example it is generally felicitous to analyze Patwin morphology in terms of morphemes in the classical sense: the smallest linguistic forms that bear meaning, and that can be combined together to form complex words. For instance the pronoun *mipelet* can be analyzed as consisting of the root /mi·-/ 'second person', the suffix /-le·/ 'plural number', and the suffix /-t/ 'objective case'. Linguists working with other models may choose to conceptualize these elements differently (e.g., as exponents of realizational rules in Word and Paradigm models). It is not the purpose of the present study to argue in favor of one theoretical approach or the other. I will instead endeavor to describe the structure of and variation in Patwin morphology in a way that is theory-neutral (or "framework-free" *per* Haspelmath 2010), in the sense that the description will be accessible to readers working in any theoretical framework. However, I will be obliged to use certain concepts such as *phoneme, morpheme, construction,* and so on, which in some strict interpretations could be taken to imply a strong theoretical stance. I choose this terminology not to make any claims about the existence of the phoneme, the morpheme, or the construction as a "real" categories in the language (or in Language), but simply as convenient, basic structural terminology that a reader with some knowledge of linguistics should be able to interpret.

Another theoretical question concerns those grammatical functions that have no overt exponents. For example the subjective case and the singular number are not explicitly marked in Patwin nominals. One can conceptualize this state of affairs either as the presence of null markings (markers that are present but phonologically null), or as the absence of marking (e.g., the absence of case marking indicates subjective case). The data here does not particularly favor one interpretation over the other I therefore remain theoretically agnostic on this issue. For the present description I will represent the form of these categories with the null symbol ⟨Ø⟩ when it is necessary to refer to their form, but this is not to be taken as a strong claim that null morphemes are present. This symbol is simply a device for referring to the phonologically null realization of these categories, and for representing their forms alongside the other paradigmatically related forms in the description.

1.4. ORTHOGRAPHY AND FORMATTING

Orthography: The orthography in this work is most similar to that of recent academic scholars of Wintuan languages, notably Kenneth Whistler and Alice Shepherd (*née* Schlichter).

A superscript ⟨h⟩ indicates aspiration, a distinctive feature of certain plosives: *p*^{h}*uki* 'to sweat'; *t*^{h}*uli* 'to swim'. An apostrophe indicates glottalization, of oral stops or affricates: *č'esi* 'to sneeze'; *k'ir* 'dirt'. Voiceless plosives with neither of these diacritics are unaspirated and not glottalized. Where the laryngeal state of an obstruent is not known, a superscript circle follows the symbol: *k°owé* 'to deceive' (SP); /*-t°i*/ [finite suffix] (SP). ⟨ł°⟩ represents some lateral obstruent, either /ł/ or /ƛ'/.

The (voiceless) postalveolar affricate is rendered ⟨č⟩, as in *či·li* 'star thistle', *ʔuču·* 'to catch'. The glottalized alveolar lateral affricate is ⟨ƛ'⟩, as in *ƛ'et* 'ground squirrel'. This sound is always glottalized. The voiceless alveolar lateral fricative is ⟨ł⟩, as in *łori* 'to poke'. Standard Americanist practice is to use a barred l ⟨ɬ⟩ for this sound, but I prefer ⟨ł⟩ as it is more clearly visually differentiated from ⟨t⟩. The palatal glide is rendered ⟨y⟩: *yet* 'name', *ƛ'eye·* 'to smile'. Patwin /s, ł, ƛ'/ have a retracted articulation (i.e., IPA [s̠, ɬ̠, t͡ɬ̠']), but this is not indicated in the orthography.

The five distinctive vowel qualities are represented with the symbols for the five closest cardinal vowels: ⟨i, e, a, o, u⟩. Long vowels are indicated with a following raised dot: *k'i·r* 'cloud'. A centered asterisk ⟨*⟩ following a vowel indicates that the vowel length is not known, but that the vowel may be long: *he*ła* 'where' (SP).

I indicate stress on the nucleus of the syllable rather than at the onset of the syllable. Primary-stressed syllables are indicated by an acute accent

Table 1.1. IPA equivalents

Patwin	IPA
č	t͡ʃ
č’	t͡ʃ’
s	s̠
ł	ɬ̠
ƛ’	t͡ɬ̠’
y	j
V·	Vː
V́	ˈ[σ

over the nucleus ⟨V́⟩. Stress is usually not indicated at all—I show stress only where it is directly relevant to the discussion at hand.

I use the same symbols in phonemic transcription and ordinary Patwin writing, thus *ƛ’optʰi* ~ /ƛ’optʰi/ ‘to put in’.

Slash-brackets “/X/” indicate phonemic transcription, square brackets “[X]” indicate phonetic transcription of speech sounds, angle brackets “⟨X⟩” indicate an orthographic symbol, and *italicized text* indicates a non-English word/phrase or any word/phrase under analysis. In example sentences, the word or morpheme under discussion is underlined, and subordinate clauses appear in square brackets.

In some of the discussion of phonetics in chapter 2 I use IPA symbols for subphonemic variation: For example I use ⟨ɺ⟩ for a lateral flap (section 2.3.3) and ⟨r̥⟩ for a voiceless alveolar trill (section 2.3.4).

Table 1.1 summarizes the IPA equivalents of my orthographic symbols, where the two systems differ.

Formatting of examples: Throughout this work example words, phrases, and sentences are provided to illustrate descriptive points. All reported words, phrases, and sentences are drawn directly from the archival record, or from previously published material. No examples have been fabricated to illustrate a point.

All examples show (the surface form of) the Patwin, a morpheme-by-morpheme gloss, and a free translation. Meta-information associated with each example includes the source document, the page or time-point at which the example is located, the speaker (if known), and the dialect (aligned to the right margin for easy reference). For examples sourced from written material, the original orthographic form is also given.

For examples where the surface form differs from the underlying form of at least one morpheme (i.e., where a morphophonological process has applied), the surface form is shown first, followed by the morpheme-by-morpheme underlying form, followed by the morpheme-by-morpheme gloss. Where the surface form and underlying form are identical, only the morpheme-parsed underlying form is shown.

An example with all of these features is shown in (1). The first line shows the original orthography, the second line is the surface form (where the last /e/ has been inserted by a phonological process), followed by the morpheme-level parse in Patwin, the morpheme-level gloss in English, and finally the free translation. The source (Radin's texts), page number(s), and speaker's initials follow parenthetically, and the dialect (HP_T = Tebti Hill Patwin) is indicated at the right margin.

(1) ⟨nɛ´n·tcup'ɛlɛt⟩
ne·nčupelet
ne·n-ču-pel-t
mother-RL-DU-OBJ
my parents (OBJ)
(Radin, c:33/164, AL) [HP_T]

Summary lists: Where the variation of a morpheme is particularly complicated, I include a list summarizing its most common forms. In these lists I show the most widespread form first (where applicable), labeling it *regular* to indicate that it is the regular form associated with the function at hand.[21] Forms with more limited distributions follow. Any common suppletive forms are also listed. These lists are intended to be quick reference points, complementing the richer discussions in the text.

Allomorphs of OBJ

-t	regular
-s	RP *mis, ʔe·s*
-ma	*pima, pe·ma*
-m	SP_V

Suppletive form

ʔe·	'PROX.SG.OBJ.IN' (HP)

For an example, see the list at section 5.3.1.2 showing the allomorphs of the objective case suffix in pronouns (reproduced here). This list shows that /-t/ is the regular allomorph of the objective case suffix found on pronouns, and explains the more limited distributions of the other allomorphs /-s, -ma, -m/: /-s/ occurs only in two River Patwin pronouns, /-ma/ occurs only in two pronouns, and /-m/ is found only in Vallejo's South Patwin materials. The list also shows the suppletive form *ʔe·* 'this (PROX.SG.IN.OBJ)', found only in Hill Patwin, which has no overt objective case suffix at all.

TWO

Phonemics and Phonetics

This chapter describes Patwin speech sounds phonemically and phonetically.[1] The phonemic inventory is described in section 2.1, minimal pairs for similar sounds are given in section 2.2, and phonemes are described in phonetic detail in section 2.3.

2.1. PHONEME INVENTORY

Table 2.1 schematically represents the consonant phonemes of Patwin, arranged by place of articulation, manner of articulation, and laryngeal state (voicing, aspiration, glottalization) where applicable. Some of the phonemes in the alveolar series may more accurately be described as "retracted alveolars." Since there is no phonemic contrast between this retracted position and a true alveolar position, I have simply labeled this series *alveolar*. (See section 2.3.2 for discussion.)

The vowel inventory is shown in table 2.2. Patwin has five contrastive vowel qualities, which are represented in this work as /i, e, a, o, u/.[2] There is also a simple length contrast—long versus short.

The phoneme inventory is stable across all dialects. Whistler gives identical inventories for Hill Patwin and River Patwin (Whistler, c), and Shepherd (2005:5–7) gives identical inventories for all Patwin dialects, including South Patwin.

2.2. MINIMAL PAIRS

Table 2.3 shows minimal pairs for each of the five vowel qualities. Table 2.4 shows minimal pairs for vowel length. Table 2.5 gives minimal pairs at all places of articulation for the four laryngeal series.[3]

Table 2.1. Patwin consonant phonemes

		Bilabial	**Alveolar**		**Post-alveolar**	**Palatal**	**Velar**	**Glottal**
			Central	Lateral				
Plosive	Voiceless	p	t				k	ʔ
	Aspirated	pʰ	tʰ				kʰ	
	Glottalized	p’	t’				k’	
	Voiced	b	d					
Nasal	Voiced	m	n					
Fricative	Voiceless		s	ɬ				h
Affricate	Voiceless				č			
	Glottalized			ƛ’	č’			
Trill/flap			r					
Approximant	Liquid			l				
	Semivowel	w				y	w	

Table 2.2. Patwin vowel phonemes

	Front		**Back**
High	i, i·		u, u·
Mid	e, e·		o, o·
Low		a, a·	

Table 2.3. Minimal pairs of vowel quality

ba·	‘to eat’	*be·*	‘to be (IN)’
k’ar	‘to cut the ends off; to mow’	*k’ir*	‘dirt’
bak	‘wild cucumber’	*bok*	‘milkweed’
sayi	‘light to shine in the dark’	*suyi*	‘to suck’
t’e·t	‘big rope’	*t’i·t*	‘sore’
bo·le	‘dreaming person’	*bo·lo*	‘to soak’
pʰe·ɬ	‘wild hemp’	*pʰu·ɬ*	‘whistle!’
t’ik	‘fish scale’	*t’ok*	‘wood’
ʔih	copula (RP)	*ʔuh*	‘to say’ (RP)
bok	‘milkweed’	*buk*	‘pus’

Table 2.4. Minimal pairs of vowel length

Short		**Long**	
k'ay	'gopher'	*k'a·y*	'old woman'
tep	'groin'	*te·p*	'forked'
k'ir	'dirt'	*k'i·r*	'cloud'
pot	'guts'	*po·t*	'whom'
ʔut	'catch!'	*ʔu·t*	'him/her (3SG.OBJ)'

Table 2.5. Minimal pairs between the laryngeal series

Aspirated vs. plain				
Bilabial	*p*^{h}*o·*	'fire'	*po·*	'who'
Alveolar	*t*^{h}*ep*	'hit.2SG.HORT'	*tep*	'groin'
Velar	*k*^{h}*o·wa*	'cradle basket' (RP)	*ko·wa*	'back'
Aspirated vs. glottalized				
Bilabial	*p*^{h}*oka·*	'to clap'	*p'oka·*	'to pop, crackle'
Alveolar	*-t*^{h}*i*	2PL.HORT	*-t'i*	FUT
Velar	*k*^{h}*ay*	'goose'	*k'ay*	'gopher'
Aspirated vs. voiced				
Bilabial	*p*^{h}*o·*	'fire'	*bo·*	'to be'
Alveolar	*-t*^{h}*i*	2PL.HORT	*-di*	3.HORT
Plain vs. glottalized				
Bilabial	*paki*	'fish trap'	*p'aki*	'to hammer'
Alveolar	*tipa*	'to try' (HP)	*t'ipa*	'bread'
Velar	*kewe*	'house'	*k'ewe*	'headdress'
Postalveolar	*či·li*	'star thistle'	*č'i·li*	'deer horns'
Plain vs. voiced				
Bilabial	*pa·*	'now'	*ba·*	'to eat'
Alveolar	*toyi*	'to stop (intr.)'	*doyi*	'to give'
Glottalized vs. voiced				
Bilabial				
Alveolar	*t'eče·*	'hair, fur'	*deče·*	'to climb'

2.3. DETAILED PHONETIC AND PHONEMIC DESCRIPTIONS

In this section Patwin phonetics and phonemics will be discussed in greater detail. In some cases this will involve analyses of written texts or reporting the findings of previous research. In other cases a quantitative or qualitative analysis of audio recordings is possible.

2.3.1. Laryngeal Series

Patwin, and the Wintuan languages generally, are notable in having four series of plosives differentiated by laryngeal state: voiceless unaspirated ("plain"), aspirated, glottalized, and voiced.[4] All four of these series are contrastive syllable-initially (see minimal pairs in table 2.5).

Clear examples of bilabials from each of the four plosive series are shown in the wave forms in figure 2.1. In each of these examples, the plosive is in word-initial position, from the stressed syllable of a word uttered in isolation by Lodoga Hill Patwin speaker Oscar McDaniel in an elicitation session (Ultan, b). In each word the plosive is followed by a short /a/. The oral stricture releases have been vertically aligned at the point marked "0.0" (seconds) and each wave form progresses on the same timescale, lasting until 100 milliseconds after the oral release.

The first wave form in figure 2.1 is a plain plosive, characterized by periodic vocal vibrations beginning very soon after the oral release. The second wave form (b) is an aspirated plosive, characterized by a longer period of time between the oral release and the onset of periodic vocal vibrations. The third wave form (c) is a glottalized plosive, characterized by a period of continued glottal stricture after the oral release. The oral release in (c) is the small noisy burst. It is followed by a completely silent period of continued glottal stricture. Periodic vocal vibrations begin only once the glottal stricture is released (in this example after about 75ms). The fourth wave form (d) is a voiced plosive. In this wave form the periodic vocal vibrations begin *before* the release of the oral stricture.

Syllable-finally there is no contrast of aspiration or glottalization, though the voicing contrast remains. Plosives in utterance-internal codas are unreleased—that is, plosives appearing as the first consonant in a consonant cluster, whether within a word or between words. At the end of

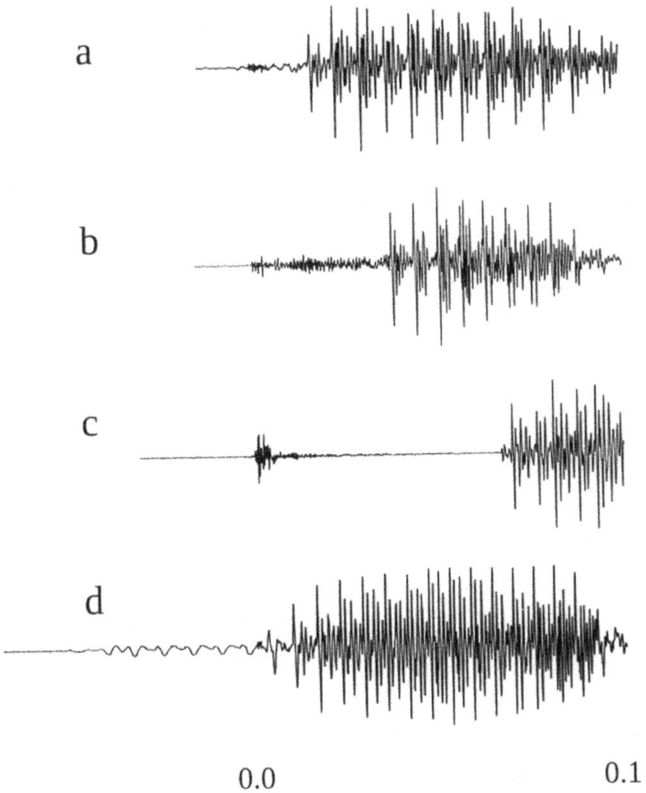

Fig. 2.1. Utterance-initial bilabials from the four manner series: (a) plain *pak* 'bone', (b) aspirated *pʰákpʰak* 'egg', (c) glottalized *p'ákibus* 'is nailing', and (d) voiced *bak* 'wild cucumber'; all uttered at approximately the same speaking rate, in isolation in an elicitation session by Lodoga Hill Patwin speaker Oscar McDaniel. Oral releases are vertically aligned (at 0.0 sec.), and each wave form is on the same time scale.

utterances plosives are usually released, and sometimes voiceless plosives in this position have a long aspiration.

There is no voiced velar plosive, although there are voiced plosives at the bilabial and alveolar places of articulation. This is not an unexpected pattern. In order for a speaker to produce a voiced plosive, a pressure differential must be maintained across the glottis. During the production of a voiced velar plosive the supralaryngeal cavity is small, so the pressure differential decreases rapidly as air passes through the glottis. On the other hand, during the production of an alveolar or bilabial plosive the supralaryngeal cavity is relatively large, and the transglottal pressure differential is easier to maintain.[5] Probably for this reason, a voiced plosive series that lacks /g/ (and other dorsal voiced plosives) is fairly common in the languages of the world.[6] Thus given Patwin's three places of articulation for plosives, the velar place of articulation is the most likely place to lack a voiced plosive.

Patwin affricates do not have all four laryngeal series. No distinction of aspiration or voicing is made for the affricates, but there is a contrast between glottalized (/č', ƛ'/) and plain voiceless (/č, ł/).

2.3.1.1. *Voice Onset Time*

Three of the Patwin laryngeal series (the aspirated, plain, and voiced series) are differentiated primarily by Voice Onset Time (VOT). For plosives, VOT is defined as the length of time between the beginning of the release of the oral stricture and the onset of voicing (periodic laryngeal vibration) that carries on into the following vowel. The VOT can be expected to be smallest for voiced plosives, larger for plain plosives, and largest for aspirated plosives.

To best describe the Patwin plosives, some quantitative data on the VOTs of the plosives is desirable. Since VOT is commonly measured in careful speech, elicited forms are desirable for analysis. There are three possible sources for this kind of data.; Here the two most robust sources will be used: Ultan (b) for Hill Patwin, with speaker Oscar McDaniel (HP_L), and Swadesh and Melton for River Patwin, with speaker Ida Mitchum. Following Cho and Ladefoged (1999), only utterance-initial plosives followed by non-high vowels are considered. The narrow oral aperture characteristic of high vowels could be expected to increase the impedance of the airflow, possibly affecting VOT. Also following Cho and Ladefoged, only words uttered in isolation are considered, not words uttered as part of sentences or multiword phrases. An additional constraint on the present samples is that only primary-stressed syllables are considered. Since unstressed syllables in many languages are characterized by general "hypo-articulation" (see Lindblom 1990), it is plausible that the presence or absence of stress may have a significant effect on the VOT of a syllable onset.

From Ultan's recording of Lodoga Hill Patwin speaker Oscar McDaniel (Ultan, b), a balanced sample of eighty-nine speech sounds was gathered.[7] The sample contains between seven and ten word-initial instances of each Patwin plosive. For each plosive, at least two distinct words are used, to diminish any VOT effects that may be specific to a particular lexical item. There are between two and five instances of each word in the sample.

A similar sample of seventy-five plosives was collected from Swadesh and Melton's recording of River Patwin speaker Ida Mitchum.[8] This sample is not as balanced or complete as the Hill Patwin sample, however, because some of the plosives are not adequately represented in the recording. Specifically there are no instances of word-initial /p'/ preceding a non-high vowel in a stressed syllable, and there are only two and three such instances of /d/ and /t/, respectively. The River Patwin sample is therefore less complete than the Hill Patwin sample. Other than /p'/ and /d/, each phoneme in this sample is represented by at least two distinct words, with between one and three instances of each word.

The results of these measurements are shown in figures 2.2 and 2.3, and table 2.6. In figures 2.2 and 2.3, the vertical axes represent VOT in milliseconds. For every plosive phoneme where more than five data points were collected, a boxplot shows the distribution of the VOTs measured.[9] Table 2.6 shows the mean VOT and standard deviation for each plosive phoneme in each sample.

The data confirms the general observation that voiced plosives have the smallest VOTs, plain plosives have larger VOTs, and aspirated plosives have the largest VOTs. The voiced plosives /b, d/ have consistently negative VOTs, ranging between about -20ms and -160ms. This indicates that voicing for these phonemes begins consistently before the oral stricture is released. No other plosive in any of the other laryngeal series was found to have a negative VOT (with the exception of one outlying instance of /p/ in the Hill Patwin sample). The VOTs for the plain series are small but positive. For /p/ and /t/ especially, the observed VOTs are very close to zero, meaning that the release of the oral stricture approximately coincides with the onset of voicing (but always precedes it). The aspirated plosives have relatively large VOTs, with mean values between 50ms and 100ms. Pairwise Welch's *t*-tests comparing VOTs of homorganic plain, aspirated, and voiced

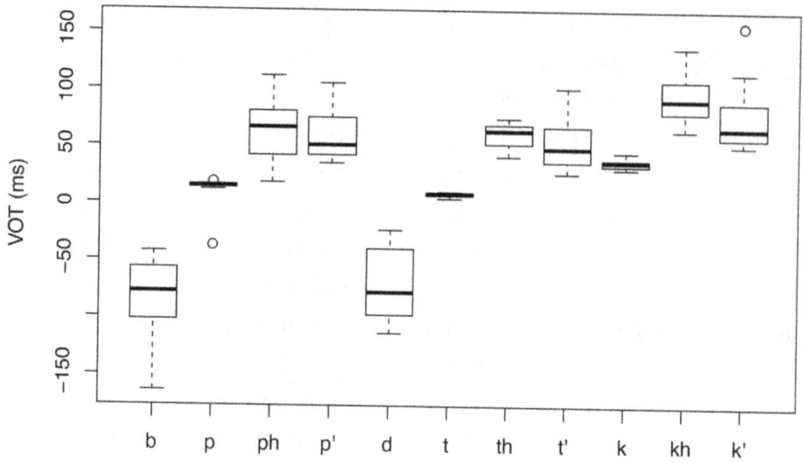

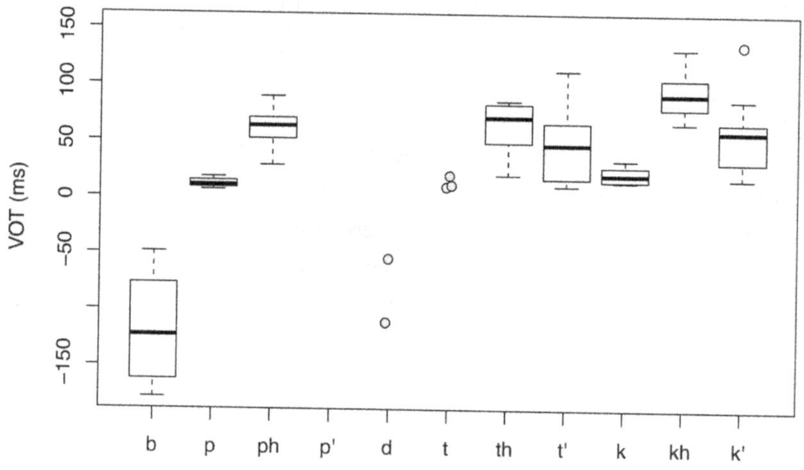

Figs. 2.2 and 2.3. Voice Onset Times from utterance-initial sounds. From stress-initial words uttered in isolation in elicitation sessions. Boxplots given only for categories with enough exemplars. 2.2 Oscar McDaniel (Lodoga Hill Patwin); 2.3 Ida Mitchum (River Patwin).

plosives all yield highly significant *P*-values ($P < 0.01$), confirming that the VOT differences among these series are not random artifacts of the study.

Cho and Ladefoged (1999:223) describe different degrees of aspiration for plosives in various languages. Drawing from samples of elicited forms in eighteen languages, they calculate the language-specific mean

Table 2.6. Voice Onset Time measurements

	μ	σ	n		μ	σ	n
b	-85.0	40.0	8	b	-118.8	47.8	8
p	14.8	1.4	7	p	11.1	3.6	13
pʰ	63.1	31.4	7	pʰ	60.7	20.0	7
p'	59.7	23.8	8	p'			0
d	-69.9	35.9	7	d	(-82.9)		2
t	8.3	2.1	8	t	(13.3)		3
tʰ	60.8	11.7	8	tʰ	63.4	24.3	9
t'	55.1	24.2	9	t'	47.7	33.3	9
k	37.0	5.0	7	k	21.7	7.6	6
kʰ	95.0	24.5	8	kʰ	93.6	21.3	11
k'	71.4	20.5	9	k'	50.5	21.5	11
(a) Oscar McDaniel (HP_L)				(b) Ida Mitchum (RP)			

VOT means () and standard deviations () from utterance-initial plosives followed by non-high vowels. From stress-initial words uttered in isolation in an elicitation session. Measurements shown in milliseconds. Standard deviation shown only for categories with enough exemplars. Outliers not included in calculations.

VOTs for the various plosives in these languages. They find that a distinction of aspiration is not a simple binary category crosslinguistically, but that there is a continuous range of attested VOTs for plosives. They suggest four categories of aspiration for voiceless plosives, based on the mean VOTs of dorsal plosives from the languages in their sample: unaspirated (mean VOT ≈ 30ms), slightly aspirated (mean VOT ≈ 50ms), aspirated (mean VOT ≈ 90ms), and highly aspirated (mean VOT ≈ 140ms). By these categories, Hill Patwin plain velar /k/ falls between the unaspirated and slightly aspirated types, with a mean VOT of 37ms; while River Patwin /k/ is squarely of the unaspirated type (μ = 22ms). Aspirated velar /kʰ/ falls squarely into the aspirated type in both Hill Patwin and River Patwin, with a mean VOT of ≈ 95ms.

In addition to the differences in VOT among the laryngeal series themselves, there is a noticeable effect of place-of-articulation. Specifically the plain and aspirated velar plosives have larger VOTs than their bilabial and alveolar counterparts. Welch's *t*-tests comparing VOTs of plain and aspirated velar plosives with individual nonvelar plosives of the same laryngeal series for each speaker all show significant results, with *P*-values ≤ 0.05.[10] This place effect is expected and in accordance with the crosslinguistic pattern discussed in Cho and Ladefoged (1999). Almost without exception plain and aspirated dorsal plosives have larger VOT values than their non-dorsal counterparts crosslinguistically. Interestingly the glottalized velar /k'/ does *not* have a larger VOT than its bilabial or alveolar counterparts in either Hill Patwin or River Patwin. In pairwise Welch's *t*-tests comparing observed VOTs for /p', t', k'/ for each speaker, no evidence was found that VOT varies according to place of articulation (*P*>0.1 for every test). This too is consistent with the data from Cho and Ladefoged: VOTs for ejective phonemes display no consistent place-of-articulation patterns crosslinguistically.

There is also a noticeable difference in the *variance* of VOTs for the different laryngeal series in both Hill Patwin and River Patwin.[11] The variance of VOTs for each of the plain plosives is very small, while the VOT variance for the voiced, aspirated, and glottalized plosives is relatively large. The plain series' small variance can be observed in the narrowness of the box-plots for /p, t, k/ in figures 2.2 and 2.3, and in the small standard deviations (σ) shown in table 2.6. This disparity in VOT variance is consistent with the crosslinguistic data in Lisker and Abramson (1964). Lisker and Abramson report VOT mean and VOT range for each plosive phoneme in eleven languages, including languages with two-way, three-way, and four-way laryngeal distinctions for plosives. In every language in Lisker and Abramson's study, the range of VOT values for plain voiceless plosives was smaller than the range of VOT values for plosives in other laryngeal series (voiced, aspirated, and breathy-voiced ['voiced aspirated']). Unfortunately Lisker and Abramson do not discuss this interesting result or even acknowledge it; nor has any other phonetician, to my knowledge.[12] A plausible explanation for the strikingly small variance in voiceless unaspirated plosives could be offered in gestural terms: the release of oral stricture and the onset of voicing are roughly simultaneous for a voiceless unaspirated plosive. Simultaneity of release is a concrete gestural goal, leaving little room for error. Plosives with nonsimultaneous voicing onset, on the other hand, may have no particular temporal goal for the voicing onset. This could result in increased variability in VOT for these categories. The phenomenon warrants further crosslinguistic investigation.

Although VOT is not the primary distinctive characteristic of plosives in the glottalized series, it is nevertheless worth noting that their VOTs have similar distributions to those of aspirated plosives.[13] Both aspirated and glottalized plosives would fall into Cho and Ladefoged's "aspirated" category for VOT. The mean VOT for each glottalized plosive in both the Hill Patwin and River Patwin data is lower than the mean VOT of the homorganic aspirated plosive, but only for the velars is this difference statistically significant (Hill Patwin $P \approx 0.05$; River Patwin $P < 0.01$).

2.3.1.2. Glottalization

The glottalized series is characterized by an airstream modification whereby the oral stricture is accompanied by a glottal stricture. Before either stricture is released the glottis moves upward, causing increased supraglottal pressure that is released when the oral stricture is released. This gesture means that the glottalized sounds in Patwin are initiated in a fundamentally different way from all other Patwin speech sounds. Glottalized sounds are initiated by glottalic pressure, whereas all other Patwin speech sounds are initiated by pulmonic pressure.[14] In some languages glottalized plosives may have audibly very prominent oral release bursts. Patwin glottalization, however, is often subtle, and glottalized plosives may be difficult to discern from plain or aspirated plosives in connected speech. On the other hand glottalized plosives in elicited speech are usually clear, and their VOTs are sometimes long enough for the oral release and the glottal release to be perceived as distinct events.

Lindau (1984:154) describes the shape of the onset of vowels following glottalized consonants in Hausa (Afro-Asiatic, Chadic) and Navajo (Athabaskan). She notes that the glottal release in Hausa is not distinct, but rather the voice onset occurs gradually, beginning with aperiodic vibrations. In Navajo glottalized consonants, however, the glottalic release occurs abruptly, and the following vowel begins abruptly with the glottalic release. In Patwin apparently both of these vowel-onset shapes occur in free variation. Of three occurrences of the word *t'e·t* 'rope' spoken by Oscar

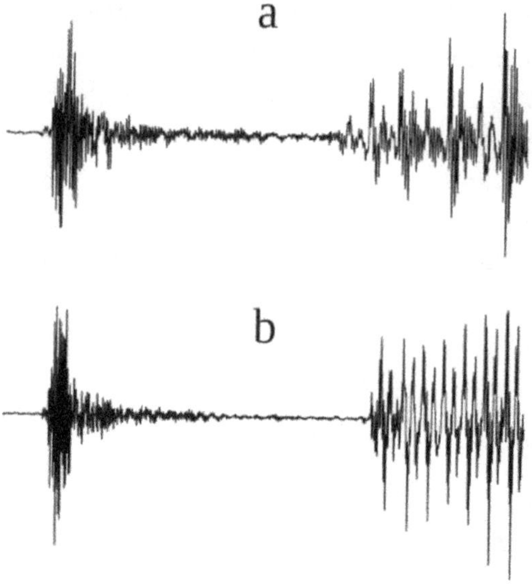

Fig. 2.4. Vowel-onset shapes after glottalized /t'/: (a) Hausa-like onset, and (b) Navajo-like onset; both in the word *t'e·t* 'rope', uttered in isolation in an elicitation session by Lodoga Hill Patwin speaker Oscar McDaniel.

McDaniel in an elicitation session, two have Hausa-like vowel onsets (gradual) and the other a Navajo-like vowel onset (abrupt). See figure 2.4.

It is also worth repeating here that Patwin glottalized obstruents are often perceptually confusable with nonglottalized obstruents. The glottalization may be emphasized by a clear articulation, as in a recording session where the researcher is attempting to elicit a clear form. But in connected speech glottalized obstruents are often subtle and not clearly differentiated from plain obstruents. This may account for why researchers of Wintuan languages use the term *glottalized* rather than *ejective,* since the latter tends to connote perceptually very salient oral releases. The glottalization of obstruents in Patwin may involve a laxly articulated glottal stricture, resulting not in the kind of sudden, intense supraglottal pressure of a canonical ejective, but rather a slight difference in the quality of the oral release.

Glottalized plosives contrast with plain plosives followed by /ʔ/. This contrast is not necessarily purely phonemic, since the sequence /Cʔ/ will always span a morphemic boundary. Thus one distinguishing characteris-

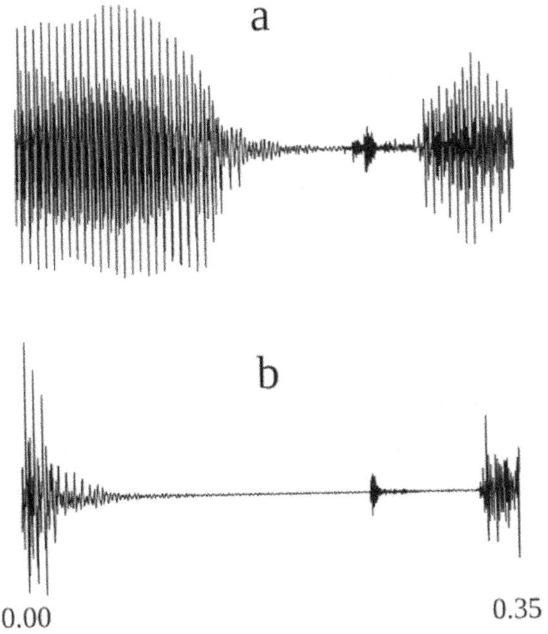

Fig. 2.5. /C'/ vs. /Cʔ/: (a) /k'/ from *se·k'oro* 'to float', and (b) /kʔ/ from *sekʔa* 'green'; both uttered in isolation at roughly the same speaking rate in an elicitation session.

tic of the /Cʔ/ sequence is that the C has a longer closure duration than the oral closure duration for /C'/, consistent with its morpheme-final position. Compare the wave forms in figure 2.5. The small burst about two-thirds down each wave form is the release of the velar closure. Note that both wave forms have the same overall duration (0.35 seconds), and the oral closure is significantly longer in the /Cʔ/ sequence (b). The period of time between the oral release and the following vowel onset is also noticeably longer in the /Cʔ/ sequence. This is consistent with the glottal stop being its own separate segment in this case.[15] In spite of this contrast Whistler notes an "occasional" tendency for /ʔ/ to merge with preceding plosives, forming glottalized plosives (Whistler, c:F2). More research is required to find out how often this happens and whether anything conditions it. Whistler's example is /honok-ʔa/ → [honok'a]. But this suffix /-ʔa/ is the same suffix that appears in my nonmerged /Cʔ/ example in figure 2.5 (/sek-ʔa/ → [sekʔa])!

2.3.2. Alveolars

The alveolar series as represented in table 2.1 may not be a homogeneous set, descriptively or phonologically. Whistler notes that the place of articulation for the voiceless laterals /ɬ, ƛ'/ may be retracted (Whistler, c:B4). On the other hand, Ultan describes Tebti Hill Patwin speaker Daisy Lorenzo's /t/ as dental throughout his notebooks, and next to an elicitation of the word *mato* 'your', he writes, "t is inter-dental" (Ultan, d:6.114).[16]

Unfortunately no palatograms were ever produced for Patwin, and analyzing formant transition information from audio recordings is very unlikely to shed any light on this subject. Whether some of the Patwin alveolars are better described as retracted alveolars is an open question. Possibly, later phonological analysis will reveal some phonological difference between an alveolar class and a retracted-alveolar class, though no such difference has yet been detected.

2.3.3. Laterals

/ɬ/ varies between a fricative and an affricate ([ɬ̠] ~ [t͡ɬ̠]). In an examination of the audio recordings of Hill Patwin speakers Oscar McDaniel and Nora Lowell, no clear pattern of allophony suggests itself. In Mr. McDaniel's speech the fricative allophone is preferred in general, the affricate occurring only word-initially (though the fricative occurs word-initially as well). In Ms. Lowell's speech the affricate allophone is preferred in general, but the fricative allophone occurs in some cases postvocalically. In River Patwin speaker Ida Mitchum's speech the affricate allophone is preferred in general and in all environments, especially utterance-initially and utterance-finally. However, the fricative allophone occurs in almost all environments as well. For all three speakers the affricate and the fricative may freely vary even in different instances of the same elicited word. The fricative and affricate allophones of /ɬ/ may thus safely be described as being in free variation, their distribution being possibly subject to individual speaker preferences. Note that since /ɬ/ may manifest as an affricate, the only reliable phonetic distinction between /ɬ/ and /ƛ'/ is glottalization.

Patwin /l/ may be a plain liquid like the English /l/, but in word-final position it is sometimes accompanied by a slight obstruction at its onset—

a lightly articulated lateral flap [ɺ] or even a chaotic series of light lateral flaps resembling a trill. This obstruction is not contrastive, and freely varies with plain /l/. It has been observed in both Hill Patwin with speaker Oscar McDaniel (Ultan, b) and River Patwin with speaker Ida Mitchum (Swadesh and Melton). /l/ is never fricated.

2.3.4. The Rhotic

The rhotic /r/ has two basic allophones: a voiced alveolar flap [ɾ] and a voiceless trill [r̥]. The voiceless trill occurs word-finally and in some cases syllable-finally within a word. The flap occurs intervocalically, and in some cases syllable-finally within a word. In slow speech the intervocalic /r/ may manifest as a voiced trill.

2.3.5. The Sibilant

Patwin has only one sibilant, which varies in its pronunciation between alveolar [s] and postalveolar [ʃ]. Its target place of articulation is somewhere between the two—in other words it is a clear instance of a retracted s, or "California s." See Bright (1984) for a good crosslinguistic discussion of the California s, which he transcribes ⟨ṣ⟩. Bright finds that the retracted [ṣ] is more common in the California linguistic area than the European-like alveolar [s]. It is not clear whether the California s is the only alveolar with a notably retracted articulation in the California linguistic area. It may be that California languages have retracted alveolar sounds in general (see discussion of Patwin alveolars in section 2.3.2). Perhaps English-speaking linguists are simply more likely to notice fine place distinctions for coronal sibilants than for other coronal sounds.

2.3.6. The Glottal Fricative

The glottal fricative is generally voiceless but may sometimes be a voiced fricative [ɦ]. This phonetic difference is not contrastive, and the two variants are in free variation. For example, in a single elicitation session Oscar McDaniel pronounces the word *hu·s* 'buzzard' alternately as [hu·s] and [ɦu·s]. The glottal fricative occurs rarely in syllable-final position in surface forms but it does occur, as in *behna* 'the next day'. Syllable-final /h/ is more common in River Patwin than in Hill Patwin.

2.3.7. The Glottal Stop

Other than a special prosodic use of the glottal stop (for which see section 3.2.3), the glottal stop occurs only morpheme-initially. Therefore it is tempting to discard the phoneme /ʔ/ altogether. Perhaps a glottal stop is simply inserted by a morphophonological process wherever a morpheme would otherwise begin with a vowel. However, the distribution is not as predictable as this explanation would suggest. There are a handful of morphemes that begin with a vowel and never with a glottal stop: /*-e·*/ (an allomorph of the vocative case), /*-e·l*/ (the remote suffix), /*-in*/ (animate plural), /*-in*/ (an allomorph of the animate locative case), /*-i·n*/ (demonym suffix), and /*-o*/ (an allomorph of the active verbalizer). Since the glottal stop is arbitrarily absent from some morpheme boundaries, it cannot be analyzed merely as the result of a morphophonological process. The glottal stop is therefore phonemic in Patwin, although it has an unusual distribution.

The glottal stop is sometimes not fully articulated, and may be reduced to an incomplete stricture or even simply a creaky phonation on an adjacent vowel.

2.3.8. The Postalveolar Affricate

There is no phonemic distinction of aspiration for the postalveolar affricate /č/. Shepherd (2005) finds that all dialects of Patwin use only an unaspirated /č/ except for Lodoga Hill Patwin, which, she claims, has an aspiration distinction for postalveolar affricates. Shepherd believes that in the other dialects /č/ and /$č^h$/ were historically distinct but have recently merged into one phoneme. Shepherd's claim that /č/ and /$č^h$/ were distinct in the recent history of Patwin seems unlikely. She describes Patwin /$č^h$/ and /č/ as deriving historically from Proto-Wintuan /k^h/ and /k/, respectively. However, modern reflexes of this putative distinction in the proto-language have disappeared in the Northern Wintuan languages as well! This leaves a single dialect of Patwin as evidence of an otherwise unattested distinction.

Though in earlier work Whistler sometimes transcribes phonemic /$č^h$/ (i.e., in his analysis of Rumsey Hill Patwin in Whistler 1977a), in his later work this distinction is explicitly rejected. Whistler finds that in Rumsey

Hill Patwin /č/ is often aspirated, "but non-distinctively"; while the Grimes dialect of River Patwin tends toward a non-aspirated /č/, again with no phonemic distinction of aspiration (Whistler, c).

2.3.9. The Semivowels

/y/ is a palatal glide, having roughly the same tongue position as the high front vowels /i, i·/ but being phonologically a consonant. The palatal glide tends to be pronounced with a higher tongue position than the vowels /i, i·/ (see figure 2.6). In syllable-initial position /y/ is sometimes pronounced with such extreme height that there is audible palatal frication. This fricated /y/ is present in the audio recordings of Lodoga Hill Patwin speaker Oscar McDaniel (Ultan, b) and River Patwin speaker Ida Mitchum (Swadesh and Melton). Shafer (1961) transcribes it as ⟨ÿ⟩ in both Hill and River Patwin, calling it "a y with friction."

/w/ is a labiovelar glide, having roughly the same articulation as the high back vowels /u, u·/ but even more high and back (see figure 2.6). Phonologically /w/ is a consonant. Ultan notes some amount of occasional labial friction or closure in the articulation of /w/ for Hill Patwin speakers Daisy Lorenzo and Oscar McDaniel (Ultan, d: 1.46, 6.114).[17]

2.3.10. Vowels

2.3.10.1. Vowel Quality

Table 2.2 represents the five Patwin vowel qualities schematically, but a more detailed description is desirable. To obtain such a detailed description it is desirable to examine clear vowels produced in careful speech. Only Ultan's elicitation session with Lodoga Hill Patwin speaker Oscar McDaniel is clear enough to use for this purpose (Ultan, b). The other Hill Patwin elicitation session (Bright, a) and the only River Patwin elicitation session (Swadesh and Melton) are both too noisy to use. Persistent and inconsistent low-frequency noise in both of these recordings obscures the relevant acoustic information. The quantitative data on the Patwin vowel space is thus even more limited than other Patwin linguistic data, as it is limited to a single speaker of a single dialect. Nevertheless it is important to glean what we can from the little data available.

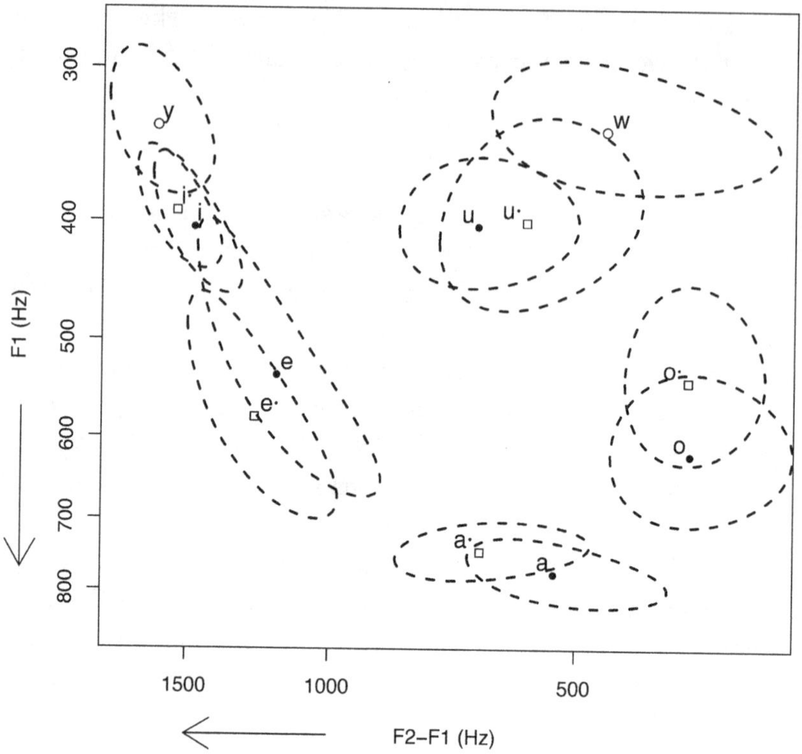

Fig. 2.6. Hill Patwin vowel space: mean values of F_1 and F_2–F_1 for each vowel and semivowel phoneme. From stressed syllables of words uttered in isolation in an elicitation session by Lodoga Hill Patwin speaker Oscar McDaniel. Long vowels are indicated by unfilled squares, short vowels by filled circles, semivowels by unfilled circles.

A sample of 148 vowels was examined from the speech of Oscar McDaniel.[18] The sample contains between ten and twenty-eight instances of each of the ten Patwin vowel phonemes. Each of these is from a stressed syllable in a word uttered in isolation by Mr. McDaniel in an elicitation session (Ultan, b). The semivowels /y, w/ are also included in the sample, since they are also felicitously described in terms of their formant frequencies. Eight instances of /w/ and six instances of /y/ are in the sample. For each vowel and semivowel phoneme between two and six distinct words are used, to diminish lexeme-specific effects. To get the quantitative measure-

Table 2.7. Vocoid formant measurements from stressed syllables

Phoneme	F_1		F_2		$F_2–F_1$		F_3		*n*	
a	775	32	1307	82	532	92	2399	107	12	(8)
a·	744	26	1399	118	655	110	2540	325	12	(9)
e	534	88	1698	125	1163	192	2558	133	28	(15)
e·	578	77	1817	117	1238	166	2563	210	17	(10)
i	405	33	1877	93	1472	115	2581	129	11	(8)
i·	393	29	1941	102	1548	118	2769	442	18	(12)
o	620	54	982	78	362	56	1846	55	9	(7)
o·	540	57	904	73	364	45	1770	47	13	(7)
u	404	31	1067	110	663	104	1972	121	15	(7)
u·	401	45	978	119	578	101	1713	207	12	(8)
w	337	26	799	104	462	109	2169	250	8	(7)
y	335	27	1971	132	1637	141	3020	213	6	(5)

Means () and standard deviations () for F_1, F_2, $F_2–F_1$, and F_3 for each vowel and semivowel phoneme, in hertz. From stressed syllables of words uttered in isolation in an elicitation session by Lodoga Hill Patwin speaker Oscar McDaniel. Final column indicates the number of data points for F_1 and F_2 measurements, then the number of data points for F_3 measurements in parentheses.

ment of vowel quality, spectrograms of each vowel were generated using Praat (Boersma and Weenink 2011), and the frequencies of the first and second formants were observed.[19]

The results are shown in figure 2.6 and table 2.7. In figure 2.6 the vertical axis shows the first formant F_1 in hertz (Hz), whose value is roughly inversely related to vowel height (Ladefoged 2001:176). The horizontal axis shows the difference between the second and first formants ($F_2–F_1$) in hertz, an interval commonly used as an approximate indicator of vowel backness (see Ladefoged and Maddieson 1996:ch.9). The values on both axes are arranged logarithmically, in accordance with human perception of pitch and intervals. For each phoneme, a point in figure 2.6 shows the mean values of F_1 and $F_2–F_1$ for all instances of that phoneme in the sample. An ellipsis shows how the individual instances of each phoneme are distributed around the mean—this is the contour of a bivariate normal distribution model of the data at a level of one standard deviation from the mean. Numeric values are reported in table 2.7.[20]

The high vowels have approximately equal mean values for F_1, as do the mid vowels. Welch's *t*-tests fail to show any effect of backness on mean F_1 for either high vowels ($P \approx 0.57$) or mid vowels ($P \approx 0.27$). Thus vowels with phonemically identical height features are pronounced with approximately equal tongue height. The high back vowels appear to be pronounced more forward in the oral cavity than the mid back vowels and the labiovelar semivowel. There is a notable lack of mid central vowels. The vowel qualities are distributed instead around the edge of the vowel space, and the center remains unutilized (see also section 2.3.10.2).

The long/short pairs of vowel phonemes are close together in terms of formant frequencies. Any differences in mean quality between long and short vowels may be due simply to the noise inherent in the small sample size. It is also possible that there is some systematicity to the quality variation between long and short vowels. Note for instance that the qualities of /i, u, e/ are more central than the qualities of the corresponding long vowels /i·, u·, e·/. The same pattern does not hold however for /a(·), o(·)/.

The qualities of the semivowels appear noticeably less central than any of the vowels: /w/ is apparently more high and back than /u(·)/, and /y/ is apparently more high (and slightly more front) than /i(·)/. A Welch's *t*-test confirms that the mean F_1 value for semivowels /w, y/ is significantly different from the mean F_1 value of the high vowels /i, i·, u, u·/ ($P < 0.001$). The extreme formant values for the semivowels are consistent with the observation that the oral aperture is often close enough to cause some frication during their articulation (see section 2.3.9).

Conversely the quality of the high vowels is noticeably noncardinal.[21] The height of the semivowel /y/ can be taken to represent a cardinally high vocoid, since it is produced so high as to occasionally cause palatal frication, and the high vowels /i(·), u(·)/ have significantly higher F_1 than the semivowels. This is consistent with their representation in the written record, where they are sometimes transcribed with ⟨i, u⟩, but just as often with symbols indicating noncardinal high vowels: ⟨ɪ, ı, ɩ, ʊ, υ, etc.⟩.

Although not evident in the quantitative data, the low vowels /a, a·/ are also off-cardinal. They are not fully open, like a cardinal [a], but are somewhat higher, centering around [ɐ]. This is evident impressionistically from audio recordings. Evidence can also be found in the written record, where phonemic /a(·)/ is sometimes represented as ⟨ʌ⟩ in Haas's notebook and Bright's notebooks (Haas; Bright, c).[22]

Note also the wide vertical distributions of the mid front vowels, and their partial overlap with the distributions of the high front vowels. This is not an artifact of this particular sample, but would appear to be generally true of Patwin. The written record reveals that before Patwin's phonemic inventory was established, multiple researchers had difficulty distinguishing /e(·)/ from /i(·)/.[23] Haas intermittently records both vowels as ⟨ɪ⟩, as in ⟨kíwɪ̀⟩ for /kewe/ 'house', and ⟨łínɪ̀k⟩ for /łinik/ 'nose'. Radin's texts frequently represent both vowels as ⟨ι⟩, as in ⟨dιpi⟩ for /depi/ 'again', and ⟨'ιla´i⟩ for /ʔilay/ 'child' (Radin, c). Conversely Whistler notes that /e, e·/ is often produced lower than cardinal [e] (Whistler, c), though Whistler has confirmed that /e, e·/ may also often sound similar to [ɪ] (pers. comm.). Thus the written archival record and more phonetically informed analyses confirm that Patwin /e, e·/ have a wide range in height, and that their distributions overlap those of /i, i·/.

2.3.10.2. *Vowel Quality in Unstressed Syllables*

It would be natural to suspect that vowel quality may vary in a systematic way depending on whether a vowel is in a stressed or unstressed syllable. Specifically one might expect that vowels in unstressed syllables would be more centralized than vowels in stressed syllables. Some passages in older descriptions might lead to this conclusion (see below). But in Whistler's manuscript, a more trustworthy source on Patwin phonetics, he comments that vowels are "not generally subject to qualitative reduction" (Whistler, c).

To determine whether there are systematic differences in vowel quality between vowels in stressed and unstressed syllables, a small sample of vowels from unstressed syllables was taken from the speech of Lodoga Hill Patwin speaker Oscar McDaniel.[24] As with the other vowel-quality data above, all vowels in this sample are from words uttered in isolation in an elicitation session. Figure 2.7 shows the results, comparing vowel quality in unstressed syllables to vowel quality in stressed syllables. Only short vow-

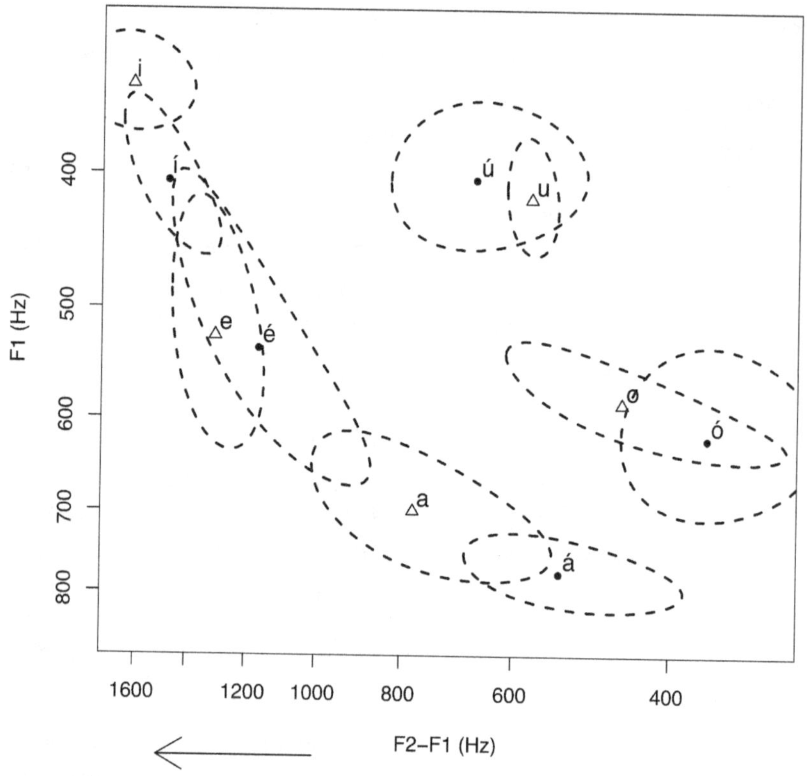

Fig. 2.7. Vowel quality in stressed and unstressed syllables. Mean values of F_1 and F_2–F_1 for each short vowel phoneme, in stressed and unstressed syllables. From words uttered in isolation in an elicitation session by Lodoga Hill Patwin speaker Oscar McDaniel. Vowels from stressed syllables indicated by a filled circle, vowels from unstressed syllables by an unfilled triangle.

els are compared, since all vowels in unstressed syllables are short. The stressed-syllable data is identical to that shown in figure 2.6 and table 2.7. The numerical data for vowels in unstressed syllables is given in table 2.8.

Though vowel quality does vary to some extent in stressed and unstressed syllables, there is no obvious pattern. Unstressed /a, o, i/ are all noticeably more front and high than their stressed counterparts. This could conceivably be explained in terms of hypoarticulation: Unstressed syllables are perhaps characterized by hypoarticulated vowels, where the

Table 2.8. Vowel formant measurements from unstressed syllables

	F_1		F_2		F_2–F_1		
Phoneme							*n*
a	699	55	1475	124	776	148	15
e	524	64	1826	91	1302	91	6
i	345	18	1960	145	1615	145	10
o	585	34	1039	69	453	93	6
u	417	24	992	30	575	22	6

Mean () and standard deviations () measurements for vowel formants from unstressed syllables. From words uttered in isolation in an elicitation session by Lodoga Hill Patwin speaker Oscar McDaniel.

oral cavity does not open as fully as it would for fully articulated vowels (in stressed syllables). It is not clear however why /a, o, i/ should pattern together without /e, u/. The quality of /e, u/ does not vary as much with stress. Moreover /i/ would not generally be expected to be higher and more front in an unstressed environment. It is possible that the differences in figure 2.7 are merely artifacts of the noise inherent in a small data set.

In any case it is clear that vowel-quality distinctions are not neutralized to [ə] in an unstressed environment in this sample, nor are they systematically centralized. The distributions of the five vowel qualities do not cluster in the center of the vowel space in unstressed syllables. This confirms Whistler's observation that Patwin vowels maintain their qualities even in unstressed environments (Whistler, c:B11).

Further confirmation can be found in the written archival record. Few researchers record instances of central vowels ⟨ə, ʌ⟩. Shafer (1961) records several instances of ⟨ə⟩, but many of these are in stressed syllables and even single-syllable words. Shafer's ⟨ə⟩ in fact corresponds to either /a/ or /o/ (and the specific correspondence is often indicated by a subscript ⟨o⟩ or a superscript ⟨a⟩), and cannot be taken to indicate a centralized, stressless vowel. In their notebooks, Haas records many instances of ⟨ʌ⟩ and Bright records some also, all corresponding to /a/ (Haas; Bright, c). Again many of these instances of ⟨ʌ⟩ are in stressed syllables or single-syllable words, and therefore cannot be interpreted as a centralized stressless vowel. Other than in Shafer, Haas and Bright, ⟨ə, ʌ⟩ are extremely rare in the large written archival record of Patwin. Thus the written record also attests to the lack of a process of qualitative reduction by centralization in Patwin vowels.

The descriptions of vowel reduction in de Angulo's and Radin's grammars are unreliable (de Angulo; Radin, b). De Angulo mentions that /i, e, a, o/ sometimes take on a schwa-like quality and are difficult to distinguish, but he gives no examples. He also incorrectly denies the existence of stress in Patwin. Radin describes a bizarre set of vowel-quality changes that he refers to as vowel reduction. Among these changes are /o, o·/ → [a]; /a/ → [o]; and /a·/ → [ɛ]. These changes are not systematic and not attested elsewhere in the literature or in the archival record.

2.3.10.3. Vowel Length

The vowel length distinction in Patwin is one of temporal duration and bears no systematic relation to variation in vowel quality (see section 2.3.10.1). In elicited forms on average, long vowels in stressed syllables are between two and three times as long as short vowels in stressed syllables. In a sample of fifty-eight long vowels and sixty-seven short vowels, all from stressed syllables of words uttered in isolation by Lodoga Hill Patwin speaker Oscar McDaniel, the mean duration of long vowels was 211ms and the mean duration of short vowels was 89ms. Similar ratios were found in smaller samples of stressed long and short vowels from Cortina Hill Patwin speaker Nora Lowell and River Patwin speaker Ida Mitchum, again all from words uttered in isolation in elicitation sessions.[25] Boxplots showing the distribution of durations for short and long vowels for all three speakers are presented in figures 2.8–2.10, and numeric values are in table 2.9.

Note that although long vowels are about twice as long as short vowels on average, still the distributions of the durations of long and short vowels overlap significantly. This is especially visible in the largest sample, taken from the speech of Lodoga Hill Patwin speaker Oscar McDaniel, shown in figure 2.8. In this sample the longest phonemically short vowel is 186ms—over 1.5 times longer than the shortest phonemically long vowel (112ms). Thus although the long/short distinction in Patwin vowels is one of duration, this distinction is not absolute. It is difficult or impossible to determine whether a vowel is long or short if taken out of context.

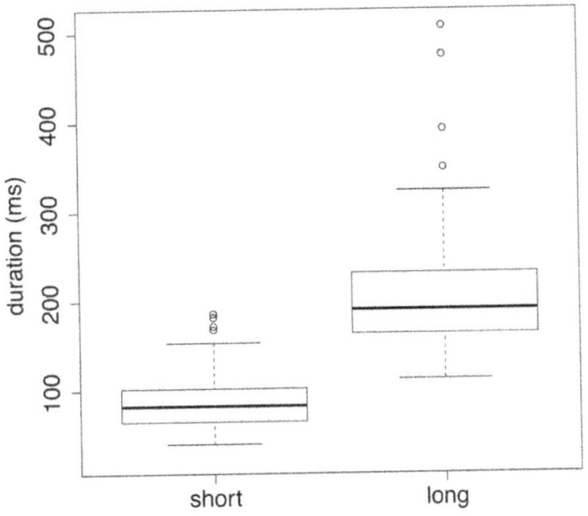

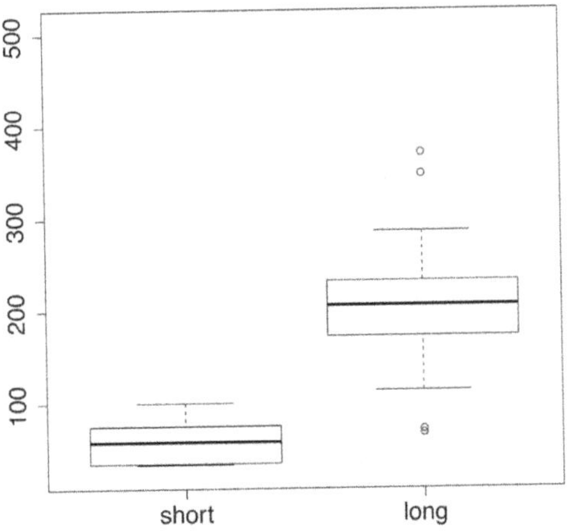

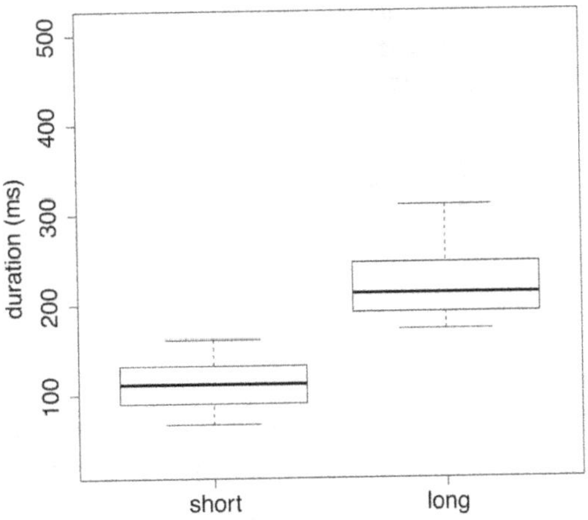

Figs. 2.8–2.10. Durations of long and short vowels, from primary-stressed syllables of words uttered in isolation. 2.8 Oscar McDaniel (Lodoga Hill Patwin); 2.9 Nora Lowell (Cortina Hill Patwin); 2.10 Ida Mitchum (River Patwin).

Table 2.9. Vowel duration measurements

Speaker	Length	μ	σ	n	Ratio V·/V
Oscar McDaniel	V·	211	78	58	2.37
	V	89	32	67	
Nora Lowell	V·	204	78	20	3.40
	V	60	25	6	
Ida Mitchum	V·	219	35	26	1.96
	V	112	28	22	

Means () and standard deviations () from primary-stressed syllables of words uttered in isolation. Measurements shown in milliseconds.

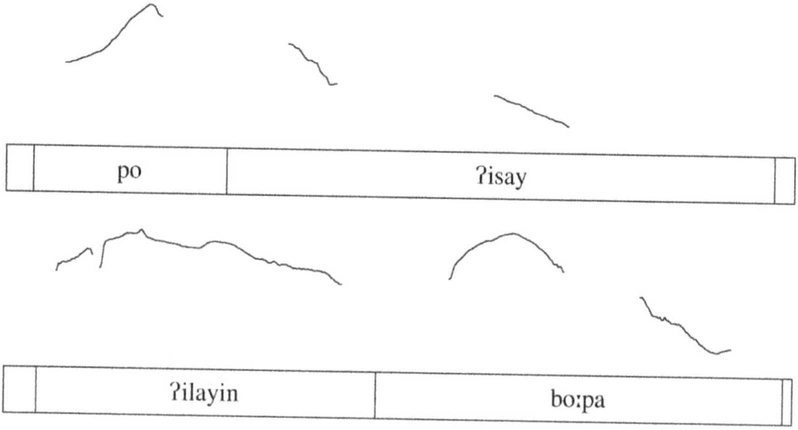

Figs. 2.11 and 2.12. Intonation in elicited questions: 2.11 Hill Patwin *po ʔisay* 'Who is that?' (Oscar McDaniel, HP_L; Ultan, b:6.4:03); 2.12 River Patwin *ʔilayin bo·pa?* 'Do you have children?' (Ida Mitchum, RP; Swadesh and Melton:5:45).

2.4. STRESS AND INTONATION

Stress on a syllable is realized by an increased loudness, raised pitch, and slight lengthening of the syllable.[26] Measurements have not yet been taken to determine the extent of these effects quantitatively. In River Patwin the pitch is raised less markedly than in Hill Patwin, and stressed syllables in River Patwin sometimes have a markedly *lower* pitch than surrounding syllables.

Sentences elicited in isolation generally have final falling pitch, whether they are questions or statements. See figures 2.11 and 2.12, showing the intonation contours of two questions elicited in isolation from Lodoga Hill Patwin speaker Oscar McDaniel and River Patwin speaker Ida Mitchum. A falling pitch can be observed at the end of each utterance. A few instances of questions in River Patwin with rising intonation are noted in the archival record, but this is the exception to the general rule (Ultan, d:7.88, SG; Bright, c:8.G104, SG; Whistler, d:C90, C92, JR). The lack of recorded natural conversations makes it difficult to say whether question intonation would typically be rising in ordinary speech. In texts an utterance in the middle of a connected passage may have a final rising pitch, presumably signaling continuity with the next utterance.

THREE

Phonology

In this chapter the patterns of speech sounds are described.[1] Section 3.1 describes the basic distribution of phonemes, section 3.2 describes the structure of the syllable, and section 3.3 describes the phonological structure of the word and the stem. Section 3.4 describes stress placement and syllable weight. Section 3.5 describes segmental phenomena—how certain phonemes change in specific environments. Section 3.6 describes patterns of reduplication. Finally, section 3.7 describes loanword phonology.

3.1. PHONOTACTICS

All consonant phonemes occur syllable-initially and are contrastive in this environment. On the other hand only a restricted set of consonants may occur syllable-finally. Aspirated and glottalized plosives do not occur in syllable-final position, nor do glottalized affricates. Only the voiceless and voiced series occur in this position.[2] Voiceless stops may have an aspirated release utterance-finally, but this is optional and not contrastive. The glottal stop also does not occur syllable-finally (though see section 3.2.3).

The glottal fricative /h/ is rare in syllable-final position in Hill Patwin but it does occur, as in *behna* 'morning'. /h/ is not attested word-finally in Hill Patwin. In River Patwin syllable-final /h/ is relatively common.[3] For example the agentive nominalizer suffix has an allomorph /-htu/ in River Patwin, which appears after vowels (see section 8.4.3). /h/ is also attested word-finally in River Patwin, as in *ʔih* 'do'. Syllable-final /h/ may vocalize in some cases, causing the preceding vowel to lengthen (see section 3.5.3).

The postalveolar affricate /č/ is infrequent in syllable-final position. In Hill Patwin and South Patwin it may occur word-finally, but not in River Patwin. See section 3.5.4 for a discussion of /č/ deaffricating in syllable-final position.

The rhotic /r/ never occurs word-initially. It occurs only word-internally (*yu·ru* 'to rain') and word-finally (*k'i·r* 'cloud'). It occurs syllable-initially only in intervocalic position. It may occur morpheme-initially—specifically in participles marked with the suffix *-ro*, as in /*tet*^{h}*u·-ro*/ 'swallowing'.

The glottal stop /ʔ/ never occurs syllable-finally, except when it occurs utterance-finally as a prosodic marker (see sections 2.3.7 and 3.2.3). /ʔ/ occurs only morpheme-initially.

The semivowels may be syllable onsets (*we·ł* 'salt'), codas (*lew* 'grass'), or both (*yay*, 'back'). There are no co-occurrence restrictions between semivowels and vowels. Either semivowel may be a syllable onset or coda, regardless of the vowel quality or length in the nucleus. For example in *k'a·y* 'old lady' the syllable has a long vowel in the nucleus and a glide coda.

Any vowel, long or short, can be a syllable nucleus. There are no syllabic consonants.

There are no diphthongs. In syllables with more than one vocalic segment, only one is phonologically a vowel. The others are semivowels phonologically, occupying either the onset or coda of the syllable (though see section 3.2.2).

3.2. THE SYLLABLE

The Patwin syllable template is CV(C). This template is rigidly observed. There are no word-initial consonant clusters, no word-final consonant clusters, and no diphthongs (with the exceptions of the cases discussed in sections 3.2.2 and 3.2.3).

The syllable onset may be any consonant and the syllable nucleus may be any vowel (there are no syllabic consonants). The syllable coda is a more restrictive position. In the coda, contrasts of aspiration and glottalization do not occur. Plosives in the plain and voiced series are both attested in the coda, for instance /p/ in *łúpta* 'drinking soup' (participle) and /b/ in *łébt*^{h}*uro* 'kneeling down', both uttered by Lodoga Hill Patwin speaker Oscar McDaniel in an elicitation session (Ultan, b).[4] The glottal stop also does not occur in the coda. The glottal fricative is rare in codas in Hill Patwin, but relatively common in River Patwin. The occurrence of [č] in codas is somewhat restricted: underlying /č/ often surfaces as [t] (see discussion in section 3.5.4).

There are no co-occurrence restrictions within the syllable. Any nucleus may occur with any onset and any coda, though /i(·)y/ and /u(·)w/ are rare.

3.2.1. Syllable-Preserving Suffix Allomorphy

For some inflectional suffixes on verbs, allomorphy is conditioned by syllable structure constraints. For example the subjunctive suffix has two allomorphs /-m, -mu/.[5] The CV allomorph /-mu/ occurs where the allomorph /-m/ would create a final cluster, thus systematically avoiding violation of the syllable template. Consider (2a) and (2b), both found in Whistler (1977a).[6] In (2a) the subjunctive suffix occurs after a vowel, and takes the default form /-m/. In (2b) the subjunctive suffix occurs after a consonant, and so must take the form /-mu/ to prevent a word-final cluster */lm/.

(2) a. /łahu-m/ [ła.hum] 'look.for-SBJV' [HP_R]

b. /łakal-mu/ [ła.kal.mu] 'play-SBJV' [HP_R]

Similarly the remote past tense suffix has two allomorphs /-n, -ni/.[7] The CV allomorph /-ni/ occurs obligatorily where the allomorph /-n/ would create a final cluster (3a, 3b), or a word-internal CCC cluster (3c), thus avoiding violation of the syllable template. In (3a) the remote past tense suffix occurs word-finally after a consonant, taking the form /-ni/ to prevent a word-final cluster */nn/. In (3b) the suffix occurs before the subjunctive suffix /-m/, and must take the form /-ni/ to prevent a word-final cluster */nm/. In (3c) the remote past tense suffix occurs after a consonant and before the past tense suffix /-sa/, and must take the form /-ni/ to prevent a word-internal cluster */yns/.

(3) a. ⟨hɛnni⟩ /hen-ni/ [hen.ni] 'arrived'
(Ultan, d:6.131, SG) [RP]

b. ⟨ba·nim⟩ /ba·-ni-m/ [ba·.nim] 'did eat?'
(Ultan, d:7.81, SG) [RP]

c. ⟨ʔe·ynɪsa⟩ /ʔe·y-ni-sa/ [ʔe·y.ni.sa] 'bit'
(Ultan, d:6.46, DL) [HP_T]

A different kind of syllable-conditioned allomorphy is found in the finite suffix /-s/ on River Patwin auxiliary stems /boh-/ 'be.AN', /beh-/ 'be.IN', and /čeh-/ 'AUX'.[8] For all other verbs and auxiliaries in Hill Patwin and River Patwin, the suffix /-s/ selects a vowel-final allomorph of the stem (see section 8.1), but the River Patwin auxiliary stems /boh-, beh-, čeh-/ are unusual in that they are always underlyingly consonant-final. Therefore they condition the deletion of the finite suffix to avoid the word-final cluster */hs/, creating surface forms with no overt tense suffix: [boh, beh, čeh].[9,10]

3.2.2. Anomalous Syllables

Table 3.1 shows stems of attested words with anomalous syllables. Each stem is attested as a word on its own, and some are also attested with affixation or in reduplicated forms, as described below. Table 3.1 also shows nonanomalous variants of each word, if attested.

The adjective *layuk* 'good' sometimes takes a form, *layk*, that violates canonical syllable structure. This anomalous stem form, when occurring on its own as a word, could be analyzed as a CVCC syllable /layk/, or as a CVC syllable with a diphthong nucleus /laik/. Neither of these structures is generally licensed in Patwin phonotactics. It may also result in three-consonant clusters, as in *laykʔabes* 'is good', uttered by Lodoga Hill Patwin speaker Oscar McDaniel in an elicitation session (Ultan, b). (In the same session Mr. McDaniel explains that the word *layuk* is the "same thing.")

This anomaly may result from *layuk* being a frequent word. Even when he pronounces the second syllable, Mr. McDaniel says the /u/ very quickly. It is possible that repeated utterances of this word have resulted in the sec-

Table 3.1. Stems of attested words with anomalous syllables

Gloss	Anomalous stem	Nonanomalous counterpart
'good'	*layk*	*layuk*
'scrub jay'	*č'ayt*	*č'ayit*
'queen'	*ma·yn*	*ma·yin*
'shoulder'	*t^hwi·t*	*t^huyit*
'avocet'	*k^hwitk^hwit*	—

ond syllable's nucleus simply disappearing in fast speech and then even in careful speech such as elicited forms.

Snyder points out a similar example, *č'ayč'ayt* 'scrub jay', from River Patwin speaker Sarah Gonzales (Snyder, a:7). This is an onomatopoeic reduplicated form with the anomalous stem /č'ayt/. Whistler elicited the same word from River Patwin speaker Jenny Regalado (Whistler, d:B87). William Bright treats the stem as having a diphthong in his transcription of the same word from River Patwin speaker Ida Mitchum: ⟨č̓áyč̓ait⟩ (Bright, c:2.IM4).[11] Ultan transcribes a nonanomalous form of this same word from River Patwin speaker Sarah Gonzales: ⟨c̓áyc̓àyit⟩ /č'ay-č'ayit/ (Ultan, d:7.41). In its nonreduplicated form (also meaning 'scrub jay') the word is almost invariably given with two, nonanomalous syllables: /č'ayit/ (HP: Ultan, d:6.64; Whistler, d:A91; Bright, c:DL7, MB3, NL143, SL6; RP: Whistler, d:B87). Ultan however transcribes the anomalous one-syllable form, from Lodoga Hill Patwin speaker Oscar McDaniel: ⟨čaɪ̯t⟩ /č'ait/ (Ultan, d:1.48).

A similar example is the more rarely attested stem *ma·yin* 'queen, sister or daughter of chief', which is most often attested in the anomalous form /ma·yn/ (Ultan, d:1.80, OM; McKern 1922:246, TO). Derived forms with this anomalous stem include *mayntu* 'queen' (with the agentive nominalizer /-tu/; Ultan, d:4.62, AN) and *ʔa·k-mayn* 'a bitter, poisonous weed' (literally 'bitter-queen'; Whistler, d:D78, OM; Bright, c:6.NL145, NL).

The anomalous forms of the stems /layuk/ 'good', /č'ayit/ 'scrub jay', and /ma·yin/ 'queen' may be explained with the following generalization: short, unstressed high vowels are optionally deleted in stem-final closed syllables with the onset /y/, where the coda is stem-internal.[12] This may be expressed in the form of a phonological rule as in (4), where "+" represents a morpheme boundary:

(4) [+high, -stress, -long] → Ø / y__C+

Whistler also describes an alternation between the full form *tʰuyit* 'shoulder' (HP_C and HP_R) and an anomalous reduced form that "approximates" *tʰwi·t* in fast speech (Whistler, c:E11). The attested fast form ⟨thwit⟩ [tʰwit] is found once in Whistler's field notebook, from Rumsey Hill Patwin speaker Harry Lorenzo (Whistler, d:F28). It is possible that this putative reduced form is simply a misparsing by a nonnative speaker of the segments in an utterance of *t*ʰ*uyit*. It is of course also possible that /tʰwi(·)t/ is another legitimate anomalous syllable form, in this case with a syllable-initial cluster /tʰw/.

Another attested word with anomalous syllable structure is the onomatopoeic *k*ʰ*witk*ʰ*wit* 'avocet', elicited from Rumsey Hill Patwin speaker Harry Lorenzo (Whistler, d:D31, E54). No nonanomalous counterpart of *k*ʰ*witk*ʰ*wit* is attested.

3.2.3. Extrasyllabic //

The glottal stop may occur optionally in utterance-final position. For instance it occurs frequently in elicitation sessions, following the short, elicited utterances. It also occurs in texts at the end of passages of reported speech, especially when the reported utterance is a command (see for example many examples in Radin, c). This usage of the glottal stop has been called an "emphatic" marker by some authors, and it is often listed alongside other suffixes as if it were itself a suffix (see Morgan 1971; Whistler 1977a, 1981).

However, there is a compelling reason to believe that this utterance-final glottal stop is not an ordinary morpheme: it can occur after consonants, thus systematically creating utterance-final consonant clusters. No other morphemes systematically create violations of the syllable template.

It is therefore most felicitous to analyze the utterance-final glottal stop as a prosodic element—optionally occurring at the end of an utterance but not to be reckoned as a part of its syllabic structure. In other words this glottal stop does not appear to be a part of the preceding word phonologically. Instead it occurs at the end of the utterance, isolated from the preceding word's metrical structure.[13]

Figures 3.1–3.3 show spectrograms of the three elicited utterances with utterance-final glottal stops, to give the reader an idea of how this is realized phonetically. Figure 3.1 shows the glottal stop after a vowel, figure 3.2 shows the glottal stop after a sonorant, and figure 3.3 shows the glottal stop after an obstruent. Note that it is not followed by any vowel. It is merely an audible release of the glottis, sometimes followed by an audible release of breath (most clearly visible in the spectrogram of figure 3.2). Note also that

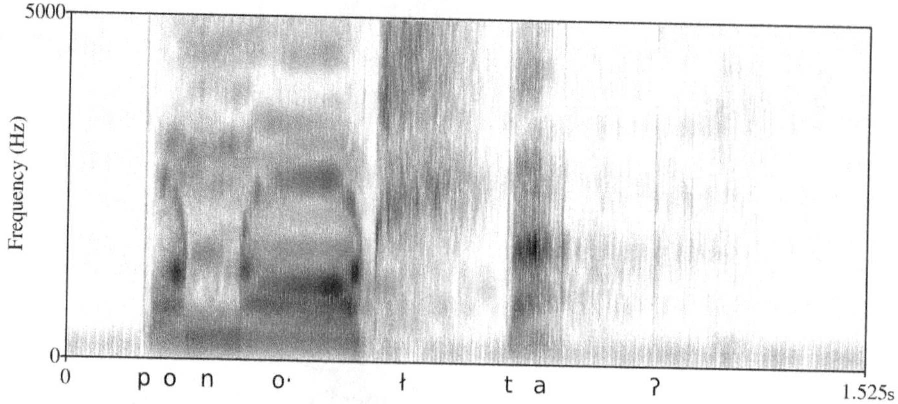
5000
Frequency (Hz)
0
0
p o n o· ł t a ʔ
1.525s

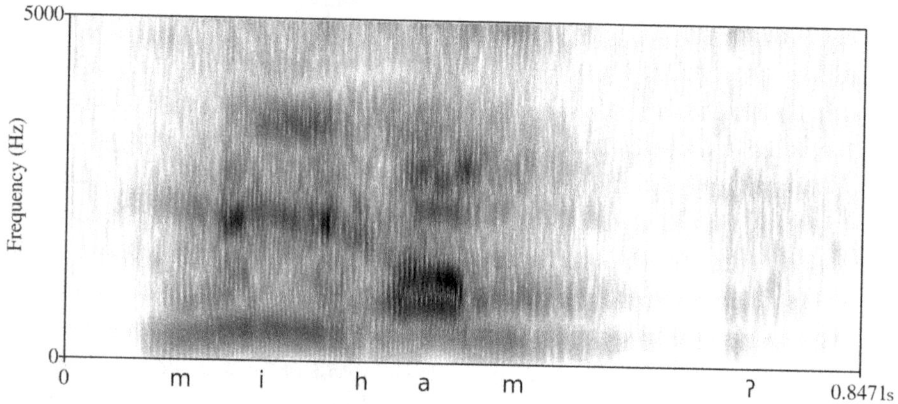
5000
Frequency (Hz)
0
0
m i h a m ʔ
0.8471s

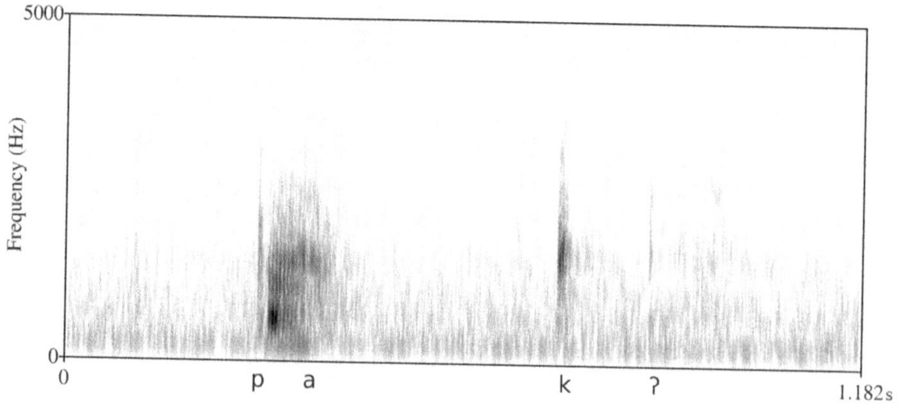
5000
Frequency (Hz)
0
0
p a k ʔ
1.182s

it does not combine with the preceding segment to form glottalized sonorants, creaky-voiced vowels, and so on. The utterance-final glottal stop is always realized as a separate segment at the end of the utterance.

Because the utterance-final glottal stop is a prosodic element, it is glossed in this work with two vertical lines ⟨||⟩, this being the IPA symbol for the end of a major prosodic group. The relationship between utterance-final glottal stop and other prosodic features such as intonation and rhythm is not yet established.

3.3. WORDS AND STEMS

Words may be arbitrarily light, as long as they do not violate syllable structure. For instance the interrogative particle *pa*, a free morpheme, consists of a single open syllable with a short vowel. It is however a function word. It may be that lexical words (as opposed to function words like *pa*) may not be able to be this light, but more detailed lexicographical research is required to confirm this.

In Hill Patwin verb and auxiliary stems must consist of at least one syllable, but otherwise may be arbitrarily light, like the copula /ʔi-/ 'COP' and the verb /ʔu-/ 'to do, to say'. In River Patwin the lightest attested verb and auxiliary stems have either a long nucleus (like /ba·-/ 'to eat') or a single short vowel followed by a consonant (like the copula /ʔih-/).[14] The vast majority of lexical verbs in all dialects are bisyllabic, and some are trisyllabic (Whistler 1981).

Affixes may be arbitrarily light. For example the finite tense marker /-s/ 'FIN' and one of the allomorphs of the objective case /-t/ 'OBJ' both consist of a single obstruent. Additionally, in an analysis allowing phonologically null suffixes, there are phonologically null suffixes, for example on second-

Fig. 3.1. (*opposite top*) Utterance-final glottal stop after a vowel: *pono·ɬta ʔ* 'three' (Ida Mitchum, RP; Swadesh and Melton).
Fig. 3.2. (*opposite middle*) Utterance-final glottal stop after a sonorant: *mi ham ʔ* 'you sit!' (Oscar McDaniel, HP_L; Ultan, b).
Fig. 3.3. (*opposite bottom*) Utterance-final glottal stop after an obstruent: *pak ʔ* 'bone' (Nora Lowell HP_C; Bright, a).

person singular hortative forms (e.g., /ham-Ø/ 'sit-2SG.HORT') and some nominalized forms (e.g., /t'ewe·-Ø/ 'speak-NMLZ'). There are no prefixes of less than a syllable's weight.

Words rarely have more than one long vowel. The only exceptions are derived words, where both the stem and an affix have a long vowel. For example, when the Hill Patwin past tense interrogative suffix /-ta·/ appears on a verb stem that has a long vowel, the resulting word may have two long vowels as in (5a). The process of optional vowel shortening (see section 3.5.1) frequently applies in this situation, however, such that long vowels in affixes become short (5b). Whistler notes that in the speech of Rumsey Hill Patwin speaker Harry Lorenzo, the vowel in /-ta·/ is "short in connected speech" in a stem with a long vowel (Whistler, d:F92, HL).

(5) a. ⟨thıyá·ta·⟩ /tʰiya·-ta·/ 'did call?'
(Whistler, d:G106, HL) [HP_R]

b. ⟨lu·mta⟩ /lu·m-ta·/ → [lu·mta] 'did die?'
(Ultan, d:6.62, DL) [HP_T]

3.4. STRESS ASSIGNMENT AND SYLLABLE WEIGHTS

Stress is sensitive to syllable weight in Patwin, with heavier syllables tending to attract stress, as described below. This description is preliminary, relying primarily on words and sentences elicited in isolation, in the audio and written archival record. A more thorough understanding of audio-recorded connected texts, which are not subject to "list intonation" problems, will aid future descriptions of Patwin stress patterns.

In Hill Patwin there is evidence of three syllable weight classes, which affect stress placement.[15] A syllable with a long vowel or a semivowel coda is heavy. If one of the first two syllables in a word is heavy, that syllable will receive the primary stress. Examples in (6) show heavy syllables attracting stress as first syllables (6a, 6b) and second syllables (6c, 6d).

(6) a. ⟨ɬɔ́·nɷ⟩ [ɬó·.no] 'bee'
(Ultan, d:6.59, DL) [HP_T]

b. ⟨púḁlɛ̀ʰ⟩ [púy.le] 'measles'
(Ultan, d:2.18, OM) [HP_L]

c. ⟨dɒkɒ́·⟩ [do.kó·] 'flint blade'
(Ultan, d:5.36, OM) [HP_L]

d. ⟨k'apa´i⟩ [ka.páy] 'river'
(Radin, c:101/224, AL) [HP_T]

If both of the first two syllables in a word are heavy, either may receive primary stress. This situation arises only in prefixation, reduplication, or compounding, since in no case does a stem begin with two heavy syllables. Examples in (7) show surface forms of /ʔu·y-tʰay/ 'his nephew' with primary stress on the first (7a) and second (7b) syllables.

(7) a. ⟨'u·´it·a`i⟩ [ʔú·y.tʰày] 'his nephew'
(Radin, c:67/194, AL) [HP_T]

b. ⟨u-it·a´i⟩ [ʔu·y.tʰáy] 'his nephew'
(Radin, c:60/187, AL) [HP_T]

A syllable is light if it has a short vowel, and either an obstruent coda or no coda. If the second syllable in a word is light, the first syllable is stressed.

(8) a. ⟨hɛ́liʰ⟩ [hé.li] 'bank'
(Ultan, d:5.14, OM) [HP_L]

b. ⟨wílak⟩ [wí.lak] 'world'
(Whistler, d:F55, HL) [HP_R]

A syllable with a short vowel and a sonorant coda (other than a semivowel) is medium in weight. If the first syllable of the stem is light and the second syllable is medium, then either the first or second syllable may receive primary stress, in free variation. Examples in (9) show freely varying stress in such forms in audio-recorded elicited speech, from Lodoga Hill Patwin speaker Oscar McDaniel.

(9) a. [č'á.lal] ~ [č'a.lál] 'flower'
(Ultan, b:2.3:53–5:06, OM) [HP_L]

b. [ʔú.lum] ~ [ʔu.lúm] 'black basket root'
(Ultan, b:5.0:47–1:11, OM) [HP_L]

Reduplication presents a special case: if the first syllable is in a reduplicant, then the third syllable may receive primary stress, if it is heavy. This is shown in the examples in (10).

(10) a. ⟨witwɪčí́·siṫo⟩ /wič-wiči·si-ṫo/ → [wit.wi.čí·.si.t'o] 'pull more than one'
(Whistler, d:G20, HL) [HP_R]

b. ⟨kaluka·´luhɔn⟩ /kʰalu-kʰa·lu-ho-n/ → [kʰa.lu.kʰá·.lu.hon] 'scattered'
(Radin, c:100/223, AL) [HP_T]

The pattern of stress placement in River Patwin is less certain. Judging from the audio data in Swadesh and Melton's recording, the River Patwin syllable weight system may be simpler than that of Hill Patwin: any syllable with a long vowel or a semivowel coda is heavy, and all other syllable types are light. If one of the first two syllables is heavy, it is stressed, as shown in the examples in (11).

(11) a. [pá·.sa.ni] 'today'
(Swadesh and Melton:20:46, IM) [RP]

b. ⟨chí·li⟩ [čí·.li] 'thorn'
(Whistler, d:B82, JR) [RP]

c. [ła.rá·k] 'star'
(Swadesh and Melton:26:19, IM) [RP]

d. ⟨ṫudúj⟩ [t'u.dúy] 'rock'
(Whistler, d:C79, JR) [RP]

Table 3.2. Tentative syllable weight classes in Hill Patwin and River Patwin

Syllable type	**Hill Patwin**	**River Patwin**
CV·(C)	heavy	heavy
CVY	heavy	heavy
CVS	medium	light
CVO	light	light
CV	light	light

C = consonant, V· = long vowel, V = short vowel, Y = semivowel, S = sonorant, O = obstruent

If neither of the first two syllables are heavy, stress may be realized on either syllable, though with a preference for the first syllable. This variation is shown in the examples in (12).

(12) a. [lá.yuk] ~ [la.yúk] 'clean'
(Swadesh and Melton:53:10, IM) [RP]

b. ⟨k̓ótho, k̓othó⟩ [k'ó.tʰo] ~ [k'o.tʰó] 'crazy'
(Whistler, d:B96, JR) [RP]

The relationship between syllable weight and stress assignment in South Patwin is unclear, because vowel length is only very rarely indicated in South Patwin transcriptions. The syllable weight classes in Hill Patwin and River Patwin are summarized in table 3.2.

3.5. SEGMENTAL PHENOMENA

3.5.1. Vowel Shortening

Although vowel length is contrastive in Patwin (see table 2.4), long vowels are frequently contracted to short vowels, thus neutralizing this contrast. Long vowels are optionally shortened in both connected speech and elicited speech, in all Hill Patwin and River Patwin dialects. (There is very little data on vowel length in South Patwin.) Vowel shortening is well attested in both written and audio materials. Though vowel shortening is optional and may apply in any environment, certain factors increase the likelihood of vowel shortening, as discussed below.

More than one long vowel in a word is dispreferred, especially on adjacent syllables. When a word has more than one long vowel underlyingly, vowel shortening typically applies. For example the third person dual object pronoun in River Patwin can be composed of the root /ʔu·-/ 'third person', the affix /-pe·/ 'dual', and the affix /-t/ 'objective case', making the underlying form /ʔu·pe·t/. However, this pronoun is never attested with two long vowels. The attested forms are [ʔu·pet, ʔupe·t, ʔupet] (e.g., Ultan, d:7.31, SG; Whistler, d:E98, F30, JR).

Function words are especially susceptible to vowel shortening. For example the second person singular subject pronoun *mi·* is sometimes realized with the long vowel [mi·], but by far the most common form of this pronoun is [mi], with a short vowel. Similarly the directional *če·n* 'down' is occasionally attested as [če·n] but most frequently as [čen]. By way of contrast the noun *si·k* 'eagle' is usually realized with a long vowel [si·k].

Long vowels in affixes tend to shorten more than long vowels in stems. For example the past tense interrogative suffix /-ta·/ is usually shortened to [-ta]; whereas the deverbal noun *ba·* 'food' is usually realized with a long vowel [ba·]. Long vowels in prefixed reduplicants also tend to become short vowels, as described in section 3.6.

3.5.2. Rhotic Assimilation

In certain common stems, and before a certain set of suffixes, stem-final /r/ either deletes or assimilates to the immediately following consonant. This can be described as an assimilation (/r/ assimilates to the following consonant) followed by an optional degemination (the resulting geminate optionally becomes a single, short consonant).

The stems that undergo rhotic assimilation include the verbs /har-/ 'go' (13c, 13d, 13g), /wer-/ 'come' (13f, 13h), and /kir-/ 'move with hand' (13e); and the suffixes /-p'ir/ 'reciprocal' (13b) and /-her/ 'passive' (13a). Suffixes that (obligatorily) condition rhotic assimilation in these stems include the participle suffix /-ta(ro)/ (13a, 13b), the remote past suffix /-ni/ (13c), the past tense interrogative suffix /-ta·, te·/ (13d), the hortative suffixes /-le, -se, -di/ (13e),[16] the modal suffixes /-les, -len/ 'can' (13f), the River Patwin conditional suffix /-nini/ (13g),[17] and the South Patwin finite suffix /-t°i/ (13h).[18]

(13) a. /ɬila-her-ta/ → [ɬilahetta] 'shot (PASS)'
(Ultan, b:2.10:13, OM) [HP_L]

b. ⟨múhup̓ita⟩ /muhu-p'ir-ta/ → [muhup'ita]'singing together'
(Whistler, d:A100, OM) [HP_L]

c. ⟨hani⟩ /har-ni/ → [hani] 'went (RPAST)'
(Ultan, d:7.50, SG) [RP]

d. ⟨hat·a·⟩ /har-ta·/ → [hatta·] 'did (he) go?'
(Whistler, d:G49, HL) [HP_R]

e. ⟨pátkile⟩ /pat-kir-le/ → [patkile] 'I'll get (it) out'
(Whistler, d:A72, OM) [HP_L]

f. ⟨w·ɛ´l·ɩs⟩ /wer-les/ → [welles] 'can come'
(Radin, c:57/184, AL) [HP_T]

g. ⟨han nenniʔ⟩ /har-nini ʔ/ → [hanniniʔ] 'if (I) go'
(Bright, c:8.G79, SG) [RP]

h. ⟨Hueti⟩ /wer-t°i/ → [wet(t)i] 'come'
(Arroyo de la Cuesta:24, SC) [SP]

In (13a) rhotic assimilation results in the surface geminate [tt]. In another utterance of the same word, by the same speaker and in the same elicitation session, there is no geminate: [ɬilaheta] 'shot (PASS)' (Ultan, b:2.10:34, OM). This is a good demonstration of the optional degemination that often accompanies rhotic assimilation.

Suffixes that do not condition rhotic assimilation include the second-person nonsingular hortative suffix /-tʰi/ (14a), the subjunctive suffix /-mu/ (14b), and the voice suffixes /-ma/ 'causative' (14c), /-pa/ 'applicative' (14d), and /-me/ 'comitative' (14e). Suffixes historically related to the subjunctive suffix /-mu/ also do not condition rhotic assimilation, for example, /-mele·/ 'negative', /-muʔa/ 'must', and so on.

(14) a. ⟨wɛr̃tʰíʔ⟩ /wer-tʰi ʔ/ → [wertʰiʔ] 'come! (nsg)'
(Ultan, d:2.112, OM) [HP_L]

b. ⟨hàr̃ mu⟩ /har-mu/ → [harmu] 'go (sbjv)'
(Bright, c:3.G15, SG) [RP]

c. /t'oriʔa-p'ir-ma-le/ → [t'oriʔap'irmale] 'I'll stick these together'
(Whistler, d:G26, HL) [HP_R]

d. ⟨harpa⟩ /har-pa/ → [harpa] 'go fetch'
(P. Vallejo, c:21.2) [SP]

e. /har-me-sa/ → [harmesa] 'carried'
(Swadesh and Melton:62:21, IM) [RP]

The inclusive plural hortative suffix /-bu/ optionally conditions rhotic assimilation. For example in (15a) the /r/ is retained but in (15b) the /r/ assimilates to the following /b/ and is deleted.[19]

(15) a. ⟨sidûy sidûy pír̃boʔ⟩ /suduy-suduy-p'ir-bu ʔ/ →
[suduysuduyp'irbuʔ] 'let's play smoke game'
(Bright, c:6.NL81, NL) [HP_C]

b. ⟨hàbúʔ⟩ /har-bu ʔ/ → [habuʔ] 'let's go'
(Bright, c:6.NL116, NL) [HP_C]

3.5.3. /h/ Vocalization

In Hill Patwin underlying /h/ vocalizes syllable-finally in derived environments, such that the fricative [h] does not appear on the surface and the preceding vowel is optionally lengthened. Examples in (16) show the first-conjugation verb *duhu·* 'to pack, to carry (inanimate)', which has two stems. The vowel-final stem /duhu·-/ is found in the citation form (16a) and before the future tense suffix /-t'i/ (16b). The consonant-final stem /duh-/ is found underlyingly before the participle suffix /-taro/ (16c) and before the adverbial participle suffix /-ni/ (16d).[20] Note that the participle suffix, which takes the form /-ro/ after vowels and /-ta(ro)/ after consonants, is /-taro/ in (16c).

This confirms the presence of an underlying stem-final /h/, although no [h] is found in the surface form.

(16) a. ⟨du· ⁻ hu·ˇ⟩ [duhu·]
(Shafer 1961:26, CW) [HP$_{C}$]

b. ⟨duhu·t'is⟩ /duhu·-t'i-s/ → [duhu·t'is]
(Whistler, d:E60, HL) [HP$_{R}$]

c. ⟨du·taro̞⟩ /duh-taro/ → [du·taro]
(Ultan, d:6.83, DL) [HP$_{T}$]

d. ⟨du·ni⟩ /duh-ni/ → [du·ni]
(Whistler, d:E39, HL) [HP$_{R}$]

/h/ vocalization is optional in River Patwin, and underlying /h/ is most frequently retained in the surface form. The examples in (17) show the same verb *duhu·* 'to pack, to carry (inanimate)' in River Patwin. The stem /duhu·-/ is shown as the citation form in (17a), having undergone vowel shortening to surface as [duhu]. In (17b) the stem /duh-/ appears before the participle suffix /-ta/, and in (17c) before the first-person exclusive hortative suffix /-le/. In all of these examples the underlying /h/ appears in the surface forms, even syllable-finally.

(17) a. ⟨dúhu⟩ /duhu/ → [duhu]
(Whistler, d:F4, JR) [RP]

b. /duh-ta/ → [duhta]
(Swadesh and Melton:82:07, IM) [RP]

c. ⟨dúḥle⟩ /duh-le/ → [duhle]
(Whistler, d:C88, JR) [RP]

There are some River Patwin stems that have syllable-final [h], but whose cognates in Hill Patwin never have syllable-final [h], having instead a long vowel in the nucleus of the syllable. Though superficially similar to the synchronic process of /h/ vocalization described above, this variation is best described as dialect variation in the underlying forms. For stems that are never realized with a surface [h], Hill Patwin speakers cannot be expected to infer the existence of some underlying /h/. Thus Hill Patwin and River Patwin have cognate pairs such as the noun *ʔaba·/ʔabah* 'packing basket' (18) and the indefinite numeral *heča·/hičah* 'how many, some' (19). These stems may have a syllable-final [h] in all environments in River Patwin, but never in Hill Patwin, as shown in the examples below. See also the discussion of the auxiliaries *bo·/boh, ʔi/ʔih,* and so on, in section 9.1.

(18) a. ⟨ʔaba·⟩ /ʔaba·/ → [ʔaba·] 'packing basket'
(Whistler, d:F60, HL) [HP$_R$]

b. ⟨ʔabáh⟩ /ʔabah/ → [ʔabah] 'packing basket'
(Whistler, d:F2, JR) [RP]

(19) a. ⟨hetc·a·´m·a⟩ /heča·-ma/ → [heča·ma] 'some'
(Radin, c:98/222, AL) [HP$_T$]

b. ⟨hic^{h}ahma⟩ /hičah-ma/ → [hičahma] 'how many'
(Whistler, d:E8, JR) [RP]

One common stem has a stem-internal syllable-final [h] in both Hill Patwin and River Patwin: *behna* 'morning, next day' (e.g., ⟨bɛhna⟩, Ultan, d:6.123, DL; 7.47, SG).

3.5.4. Deaffrication

In most environments underlying postalveolar affricates /č/ are realized as [t] in syllable-final position. In the examples in (20), verb stems ending in /č/ are followed by consonant-initial suffixes.[21] This puts the underlying /č/ in syllable-final position, where it is realized as [t].

(20) a. ⟨ʔutlɛʔ⟩ /ʔuč-le ʔ/ → [ʔut.le ʔ] 'I'm gonna catch'
(Ultan, d:5.12, OM) [HP$_L$]

b. ⟨ʔɛ́·tmʊʔʊʔ⟩ /ʔe·č-muʔu ʔ/ → [ʔe·t.mu.ʔu ʔ] 'not steal'
(Bright, c:7.NL193, NL) [HP$_C$]

Table 3.3. Words for 'magpie' in the three major dialect groups of Patwin

River Patwin	Hill Patwin	South Patwin	Sources
Ah-chaht´	Ah-´chutch, Ahts-atch	Ahtch-ahtch ('oriole')	(Merriam 1979:124, 125, 127, 249)
a¯tcat`'	a·tc^a·tc¯		(Shafer 1961:22)
ʔác̓at	ʔa·cʔac		(Ultan, d:6.64, 7.41)
ʔác̓át^{h}	ʔáchʔach		(Whistler, d:A91, B79)
ʔá·č̓at	ʔá·č̓ač		(Bright, c:IM15, SL7)
ač̓at^{h}			(Morgan 1971:10)

Forms are given in the orthography found in the source documents.

c. ⟨détta⟩ /deč-ta/ → [det.ta] 'climb'
(Bright, c:1.G140, SG) [RP]

Syllables may end in [č] in some cases, however. In his Patwin phonology manuscript Whistler notes that syllable-final /č/ preceding a glottal-stop onset is retained as [č], as in the following example (from Whistler, c:G9).

(21) /herič-ʔa/ → [he.rič.ʔa] 'sharp'

Words may end in [č] in Hill Patwin and South Patwin, but not in River Patwin, where word-final /č/ is realized as [t]. Compare the words for 'magpie' in table 3.3, which are presented in their original orthography from various written sources.[22] Though details of vowel length, glottal stops, and glottalization are difficult to discern through the noise of the various orthographies, the following conclusion can be drawn from the data: the word is a reduplicated onomatopoeic syllable /ʔač/. Thus the historical source probably ends with /č/. In Hill Patwin and South Patwin the surface form of this word ends with a [č], but in River Patwin the surface form ends with a [t].

In second-person singular hortative forms of verbs (i.e., singular command forms), word-final /č/ changes to [t] in both Hill Patwin and River Patwin (there are no attested relevant examples in South Patwin).[23] The examples in (22) show the verb stems /ʔuč-/ 'catch' and /winič-/ 'get up' used as commands, with word-final /č/ realized as [t].

(22) a. ⟨Oot´⟩ /ʔuč/ → [ʔut] 'catch!'
(Merriam:V72.69) [HP_C]

b. ⟨wìnnít¯⟩ /winič/ → [winit] 'get up!'
(Bright, c:8.G39, SG) [RP]

3.5.5. Deaspiration

Underlyingly aspirated stops change to unreleased stops in syllable-final position, that is, plain stops. This situation arises in CVC reduplication (see section 3.6) for verb stems whose second stem consonant is aspirated: since aspirated consonants are not licensed syllable-finally (see section 3.1), the final consonant of the prefixed reduplicant is deaspirated. For example (23a) shows a CVC reduplication of the verb /yet^{h}e·w-/ 'to dream', in which the aspirated /t^h/ in the reduplicant /yet^h-/ is realized as [t]. Similarly in (23b) the verb /yet^{h}o·/ 'to name' is reduplicated, and the aspirated /t^h/ in the reduplicant /yet^h-/ is realized as [t].

(23) a. ⟨yɛtyɛt^{h}e·wta⟩ /yet^h-yet^{h}e·w-ta/ → [yet.ye.t^{h}e·w.ta] 'dreaming all the time'
(Ultan, d:7.64, SG) [RP]

b. ⟨yɛtyɛt^{h}o·ro⟩ /yet^h-yet^{h}o·-ro/ → [yet.ye.t^{h}o·.ro] 'naming'
(Ultan, d:7.84, SG) [RP]

3.5.6. Vowel Epenthesis

When the /-t/ allomorph of the objective case appears on a consonant-final stem, a vowel is inserted between the stem and the suffix. This vowel is identical in quality to the preceding vowel in the stem and is always short. Examples in (24) show objective /-t/ on the demonstrative stem /ʔew-/ 'this' (24a); on the kinship term /t^{h}a·y-/ 'grandchild, niece, nephew' (24b); and on the proper name /dan-/ 'Don' (24c). In each example a harmonic short vowel appears before the objective suffix, avoiding word-final consonant clusters /wt, yt, nt/.

(24) a. ⟨ʔèwét⟩ /ʔew-t/ → [ʔewet] 'this (OBJ)'
(Bright, c:6.NL77, NL) [HP_C]

b. ⟨u·´itaiyat⟩ /ʔu·y-t^ha·y-t/ → [ʔu·yt^{h}ayat] 'his nephew (OBJ)'
(Radin, c:59/186, AL) [HP_T]

c. ⟨Dónat⟩ /dan-t/ → [danat] 'Don (OBJ)'
(Ultan, d:3.16, OM) [HP_L]

The harmonic vowel before objective case /-t/ appears even when its absence would not cause a violation of syllable structure constraints. Consider (25), where the harmonic vowel [a] appears between the stem /t^ha·y-/ 'grandchild, niece, nephew' and the objective case suffix /-t/.

(25) /ma-t^ha·y-t-in/ → [mat^{h}a·yatin] 'your grandson's place'
(Whistler, d:G95, HL) [HP_R]

Since the locative case suffix /-in/ appears immediately after the objective case suffix, vowel epenthesis is not actually necessary to preserve CV(C) syllable structure.[24] However, the form without the epenthesized vowel is not attested: *[-t^ha·ytin].

3.5.7. South Patwin Nasal Alternation

In South Patwin voiced stops alternate with their homorganic nasal counterparts in certain morphemes. I refer to this process as South Patwin nasal alternation. Some nasal alternation may be observed within single sources, such as the verb forms *boya~moya* 'hunt', both in Curtin (Curtin, b:228), or the ablative suffix forms /-na∗k/~/-da∗k/, both in Vallejo (P. Vallejo, c). Some words vary across sources but do not vary within each source, such as *ba∗* 'eat', in Vallejo (P. Vallejo, c) and Curtin (Curtin, b), versus *ma∗* 'eat', in Arroyo de la Cuesta. Most words do not show evidence of nasal alternation at all, for example 'west' is always *no∗wi* (e.g., Curtin, b:129; P. Vallejo, c:21.3), and 'head' is always *bu∗k* (e.g., Arroyo de la Cuesta:24; Curtin, b:78; Merriam:V76.5).

The Hill Patwin and River Patwin cognates of the ablative suffix and the verb 'eat' are /-na·k/ and *ba·*, respectively. In South Patwin the variant /-da∗k/ of the ablative is a kind of fortition, where a historical nasal is realized as a stop; the variant *ma∗* of 'eat' is a kind of lenition, where a historical stop is realized as a nasal. Thus South Patwin nasal alternation is not a unidirectional historical process of fortition or lenition. Instead the alternation is itself a South Patwin innovation in certain lexemes. Because most words do not show any evidence of nasal alternation, it cannot be definitively concluded that the distinction between voiced stops and nasals is entirely neutralized in South Patwin.

3.6. REDUPLICATION

Reduplication is attested in nouns, verbs, and cardinals, and takes a different form depending on the lexical category of the stem. Reduplication of the entire stem is common in nouns referring to animals, and many reduplicated forms can be found in appendix A of Whistler's (1976) thesis on Patwin animal and plant nomenclature. Examples include *hoshos* 'porcupine' (HP), *loklok* 'red-tailed hawk', *weswes* 'Steller's jay' (HP), *salaksalak* 'swallow' (SP), *mawmaw* 'small pike' (RP), *łupłup* 'worm' (RP), *mene·mene* 'black ant' (HP), and *tu·ktuk* 'mosquito larvae' (HP). Onomatopoeic reduplication in animal names is also common. Examples include *čikči·ki* 'chipmunk' (HP), *to·ttot* 'yellow-breasted chat' (HP), *pulukpuluk* 'mourning dove' (RP), and *č'urumč'urum* 'cricket' (RP).

Partial reduplication occurs in verbs. The most common kind of reduplication on verbs is CVC reduplication, where the first CVC sequence of the stem is reduplicated. Examples include /k'ob-k'obo·li-/ 'to buy many things' (< /k'obo·li-/ 'to buy') and /ƛ'eb-ƛ'e·bi-/ 'to nibble' (< /ƛ'e·bi-/ 'to chip'). CV reduplication is also attested in verbs, as in /hu-hupu·-/ 'to dive repeatedly' (< /hupu·-/ 'to dive'). CVCV reduplication on verbs is also attested, as in /p'et^{h}i-p'et^{h}i-/ 'to hunt frequently' (< /p'et^{h}i-/ 'to hunt'). The form and function of verbal reduplication is discussed in greater depth in section 8.3.1.

Cardinals ('north', 'south', etc.) may be intensified with full reduplication. In Tebti Hill Patwin speaker Anderson Lowell's texts, *nome(·)l-nome(·)l* 'extreme west' is attested, derived from the cardinal stem /nom-/ 'west' + the remote suffix /-e·l/ 'far', with full reduplication (Radin, c:12/148, 21/156, AL).[25] In the same texts *woreltina-woreltina* 'from the very extreme south' is also attested, derived from the cardinal stem /wor-/ 'south' + the remote suffix /-e·l/ + the stative suffix /-ti/ + the prolative case suffix /-na/, with full reduplication (Radin, c:61/188, AL).

3.7. LOANWORDS

In this section phonological issues surrounding loanwords from Spanish and English into Patwin will be discussed, including phoneme correspondences and syllable structure. Spanish loanwords are far more commonly attested than English loanwords. This section expands on Bright and Bright (1959), which is a discussion of loanwords in Patwin that focuses on borrowings from Spanish.

3.7.1. Phoneme Correspondences

Table 3.4 summarizes consonant correspondences in Spanish and English loanwords, expanding on the correspondences listed in Bright and Bright (1959). Spanish /b/ is almost always borrowed as Patwin /w/. The word *baka* 'cow' is a rare exception, attested only by River Patwin speaker Jennie Regalado (see table).[26,27] A far more common form of the same borrowing is *wa·ka*, attested in both Hill Patwin and River Patwin. Spanish /d/ is more highly variable in loanwords. As the onset of a stressed syllable it is generally borrowed as Patwin /d/, as in *wande·ra* 'flag'. In other environments it is borrowed as /t, l, Ø/, with no clear pattern to the variation. Spanish /f/ is always borrowed as Patwin /p/. Spanish /g/ may be borrowed as either Patwin /k/ or /h/, or may be dropped. The Spanish palatal nasal /ñ/ (i.e., [ɲ]) is realized as a sequence of two segments /y/ and /n/, with /y/ generally preceding /n/. For example Spanish *español* 'Spaniard' is borrowed as *paynol* (P. Vallejo, c:21.4), and Spanish *año* 'year' is usually borrowed as *ʔa·yno* (Ultan, d:6.110, DL). However, Lodoga Hill Patwin speaker Oscar McDaniel uses /ny/ in the same word (see table). Spanish /l/ is almost always borrowed as Patwin /l/, but *yihor* 'beans' is an exception attested in both Hill Patwin and River Patwin. Spanish rhotics /r, ɾ/ are generally borrowed as Patwin /r/. The word *lema·te* 'oar' presents an interesting case where the source word *remo* begins with /r/. Since words may not begin with /r/ in Patwin (see above) another phoneme must be used, in this case /l/. English

/v/ is borrowed as Patwin /p/ in the word *sipi* 'sieve'. Spanish and English stress is realized as vowel length in loanwords.

Not mentioned in table 3.4 are consonants that do not significantly change when borrowed. Spanish /p, t, č, k, m, n, s, y, w/ are borrowed as Patwin /p, t, č, k, m, n, s, y, w/. Note that the Spanish voiceless stops are consistently borrowed as plain stops (Bright and Bright 1959). English voiceless stops are sometimes borrowed as aspirated stops (e.g., ⟨kháw⟩ /k^haw/ 'cow', Whistler, d:E4, JR) and sometimes as plain stops (e.g., ⟨píčɪš⟩ /pičis/ 'peach', Ultan, d:6.108, DL). English borrowings are infrequently elicited, so the factors conditioning this variation are not known. Spanish /x/ is always borrowed as Patwin /h/, as in ⟨páreho⟩ *pareho* 'smooth, even' (< *parejo* 'equal', Whistler, d:G109, HL).

Vowels are generally borrowed as the closest corresponding Patwin vowel, but a notable exception is word-final vowels in Spanish loanwords. Here a great deal of variation is found. Examples mentioned in Bright and Bright (1959) include *kaye·na~kaye·no~kayi·nu* 'chicken' (< *gallina*), *ʔawha ~ ʔawho* 'needle' (< *aguja*), and *le·če ~ le·či ~ le·čo* 'milk' (< *leche*).[28] Bright and Bright (1959) speculate that this variation may reflect grammatical alternations in word-final vowels in Spanish, which change depending on the grammatical or biological gender of the referent. This alternation may have been perceived by second-language speakers as a kind of free variation, resulting in freely varying word-final vowels for these words. On the other hand individual speakers tend not to vary in the vowels used for any given word. Detailed lexicographical research may be able to shed more light on this subject in the future.

3.7.2. Syllable Structure in Loanwords

Sources of borrowed words may violate Patwin syllable structure constraints, in which case the form must be altered in some way. A consonant may be deleted, a vowel may be inserted, or some substitution may occur.

Vowel insertion is the most commonly attested strategy, using a vowel of the same quality as the following vocoid. The Spanish word *trigo* 'wheat' is borrowed into Patwin as *tiri·ko~tiri·ku* (e.g., Ultan, d:6.109, DL; Whistler, d:C84, JR). Here the harmonic vowel /i/ is inserted to break up the word-initial cluster /tr/. Similarly the English word *plum* is borrowed into

Table 3.4. Consonant correspondences in Spanish and English loanwords, with examples

Span.	/b/ →	/w/	⟨wʊlsa⟩ /wolsa/ 'pocket' (< *bolsa*; Ultan, d:7.101, SG)
		/b/	⟨báka⟩ /baka/ 'cow' (< *vaca*; Whistler, d:B86, JR)
Span.	/d/ →	/d/	⟨wandé·ra⟩ /wande·ra/ 'flag' (< *bandera*; Whistler, d:A46, OM)
		/t/	⟨só·řto⟩ /so·rto/ 'deaf' (< *sordo*; Whistler, d:F105, HL)
		/l/	⟨siwá·la⟩ /siwa·la/ 'barley' (< *cebada*; Whistler, d:A46, OM)
		Ø	⟨haná·u⟩ /hana·w/ 'cattle' (< *ganado*; Ultan, d:7.104, SG)
Span.	/f/ →	/p/	⟨pá·ha⟩ /pa·ha/ 'belt' (< *faja*; Bright, c:1.IM15, IM)
Span.	/g/ →	/k/	⟨wɔre·ka⟩ /wore·ka/ 'sheep' (< *borrego* 'lamb'; Ultan, d:7.04, SG)
		/h/	⟨haná·u⟩ /hana·w/ 'cattle' (< *ganado*; Ultan, d:7.104, SG)
		Ø	⟨ʔáwhʊ⟩ /ʔawho/ 'needle' (< *aguja*; Bright, c:2.MB7, MB)
Span.	/ñ/ →	/yn/	⟨pujná·l⟩ /puyna·l/ 'dagger' (< *puñal*; Whistler, d:A118, OM)
		/ny/	⟨á·nyʊ⟩ /ʔa·nyo/ 'year' (< *año*; Ultan, d:2.98, OM)
Span.	/l/ →	/l/	⟨pìlá·te⟩ /pila·te/ 'dishes' (< *plato*; Bright, c:9.DL19)
		/r/	⟨yihɔř⟩ /yihor/ 'beans' (< *frijole*; Ultan, d:7.104, SG)
Span.	/r/ →	/r/	⟨só·řto⟩ /so·rto/ 'deaf' (< *sordo*; Whistler, d:F105, HL)
		/l/	⟨lema·te⟩ /lema·te/ 'oars' (< *remo*; Whistler, d:E10, JR)
Eng.	/v/ →	/p/	⟨sípi⟩ /sipi/ (< *sieve*; Whistler, d:F60, HL)

Patwin as *pʰulum*, with the harmonic vowel /u/ inserted to break up the word-initial cluster /pʰl/. The Spanish word *puente* is borrowed into Patwin as *puwento* (Ultan, d:1.110, OM; Ultan, b:4.2:49, OM). Here the epenthetic vowel /u/ matches the quality of the following vocoid /w/.

Other strategies are also attested. In ⟨pá·pʊrty⟩ *pa·purti* (< *property*), the onset cluster /pr/ is simplified by deleting the /r/ (Bright, c:10.DL86, DL). In ⟨Wariente⟩ *waryente* 'liquor' (< *aguardiente*), the word-internal cluster /rdy/ is simplified by deleting the /d/ (P. Vallejo, c:19.7.3). In ⟨somlᴇ·lo⟩ *somle·lo* 'hat' (< *sombrero*), the word-internal cluster /mbr/ is simplified to /ml/. In ⟨yihɔř⟩ *yihor* 'beans' (< *frijole*), the word-initial consonant cluster /fr/ is simplified to /y/.

Some loanwords do not follow normal syllable structure constraints. Lodoga Hill Patwin speaker Oscar McDaniel borrows Spanish *maíz* 'corn' as a single syllable word with two adjacent vocoids (e.g., Ultan, d:2.12; Whistler, d:C10). This word could be analyzed as /mais/ (with a diphthongal nucleus, violating canonical syllable structure) or /mays/ (with a complex coda, also violating canonical syllable structure). Similarly the word ⟨tawnła⟩ 'to town' is attested from Tebti Hill Patwin speaker Daisy Lorenzo, where the root is borrowed from English *town* and followed by the locative case suffix /-ła/ (Ultan, d:6.105). The stem has two adjacent vocoids, such that the word could be analyzed as /taunła/ or /tawnła/, both of which violate canonical syllable structure.

FOUR

Nominals and Nominal Morphology

4.1. INTRODUCTION

There are three morphologically distinct categories of nominals in Patwin: nouns, kinship terms, and pronouns. Syntactically, nominals can function as arguments of the predicate in a clause or as possessors of other nominals (among other things). Semantically, nominals are referring expressions, picking out their referent as an object in the world.

Both nouns and kinship terms are lexical words (as opposed to function words); they can function as nominal arguments in a clause, as complements of adpositions, as possessors of other nominals, and as predicates of nonverbal clauses. Kinship terms can be distinguished from nouns in two ways: (1) Semantically, kinship terms express family relationships such as 'mother', 'elder brother', 'child', and so on, their referents being the people who bear these relations. (2) Morphologically, kinship terms are relatively complex and characterized by a high degree of irregularity, whereas the morphology of nouns is fairly simple. Because of the significant differences in their morphology, nouns and kinship terms are best considered as two separate lexical categories in Patwin.

Pronouns are function words. They may function as stand-alone arguments in a clause, or they may modify another nominal, whether as possessors or demonstrative determiners. Because of the size of the pronoun paradigm and pervasive dialect differences, an accurate account of the pronouns including dialect variation has constituted its own research project. Pronouns are therefore discussed at length in a dedicated chapter (chapter 5).

To these three basic categories of nominals may be added a fourth, derived category: the nominalized verb. Nominalized verbs can host case suffixes like nouns can, but are syntactically and functionally distinct from nouns. Syntactically, some nominalized verbs trigger specialized agreement in possessives, distinct from that of nouns. Functionally, they may be either referring expressions (like nominals) or heads of (subordinate) clauses (like verbs).

4.2. NOUNS

Common nouns in Patwin are the largest class of referring expressions. Three other classes of nominals are morpho-syntactically distinct from common nouns, and will be discussed in separate sections below.

4.2.1. Inflectional Classes

There are two inflectional classes of common nouns: animate and inanimate. These two classes are identifiable by differences in the realization of object marking on the noun. Grammatically inanimate nouns are never realized with object marking, so that their forms are identical whether they are subjects or objects. For example the noun *t^{h}o·k* 'tree' is grammatically inanimate and appears in the same form whether it is the subject (26a) or the object (26b). Grammatically animate nouns take the suffix /-ma/ when used as objects and take no case suffix when used as subjects. For example the noun *čip* 'bird' (HP) is grammatically animate. It appears in its bare form when it is the subject of a clause (27a) and takes the suffix /-ma/ when it is the object (27b).

(26) a. ⟨pi t^{h}ɔ·k sɛkʔas⟩

pi	t^{h}o·k	sekʔa-s
DIST.SG.SBJ	tree	green-FIN

That tree is green.

(Ultan, d:6.61, DL) [HP$_T$]

b. ⟨t^{h}o·k cu WINIS⟩

t^{h}o·k	ču	wini-s
tree	1SG.SBJ	see-FIN

I see a tree.

(Ultan, d:6.38, NeL) [HP$_T$]

(27) a. ⟨cip piła hɛnis⟩

čip piła hene-s

bird DIST.LOC arrive-FIN

A bird is just arriving there.

(Ultan, d:6.25, NeL) [HP$_T$]

b. ⟨wɪnɪs cu cɪpma⟩

wini-s ču čip-ma

see-FIN 1SG.SBJ bird-OBJ

I see the bird.

(Ultan, d:6.63, DL) [HP$_T$]

The instrumental and locative case suffixes also change form depending on the animacy of the stem (see sections 4.6.2.3 and 4.6.2.4).

The grammatical animacy distinction is also reflected in patterns of agreement outside of the nouns themselves. Possessive nominals agree with the possessed noun in animacy (see section 4.6.1.3). Demonstratives used as determiners or as pronouns agree with their referent in animacy (section 5.3.3). The stative auxiliary verb *bo·/be·/boh/beh* 'be' agrees with the subject in animacy (section 9.1.2). Because the two inflectional classes trigger obligatory agreement, they are grammatical "genders" in the sense of Corbett (1991) and Hockett (1958). To avoid confusion with the concept of biological gender, I will refer to the inflectional class of a noun as its *grammatical animacy.*

Grammatical animacy in Patwin is related to semantic animacy in the following way: all nouns referring to animals or people are grammatically animate. Some nouns referring to plants, body parts, and inanimate objects are grammatically inanimate; some are grammatically animate. For example *tʰo·k* 'tree', *sem* 'hand', and *nun* 'bow, gun' are grammatically inanimate; while *sa·l* 'clover', *tu·s* 'face', and *t'usa* 'pestle' are grammatically animate. There are also some pairs of nouns that are formally identical and similar in meaning, but belong to different inflectional classes. For example the inanimate noun *k'odoy* means 'rock' (HP) or 'dirt clod' (RP), while the animate noun *k'odoy* means 'money'; the inanimate noun *no·p* means 'meat' while the animate noun *no·p* means 'deer'. Further lexicographical work is required to obtain full lists of nouns according to inflectional class.

4.2.2. Human Nouns

Nouns referring to humans (e.g., *č'iyak* 'old man', *p'okita* 'woman', etc.) have more complex morphology than other common nouns. While human nouns do not form an entirely separate lexical class like kinship terms do, it is worth commenting on their salient characteristics.

One salient characteristic of human nouns is that they usually inflect for number, whereas other common nouns typically do not (but see section 4.5). This number inflection is marked with a combination of suffixation and irregular changes to the stem itself. The suffixes marking number inflection in human nouns are /-pel/ 'DU' and /-ba/ 'PL' or /-in/ 'PL'. Singular nouns are unmarked. The same stem is used in both the singular and dual, but the stem may change unpredictably in the plural. See table 4.1, where *wi·ta* 'man' has the stem *wiya-* in the plural, *p'okita* 'woman' has the suppletive stem *k'aya-* in the plural, and *k'a·y* 'old woman' does not change in the plural. A full catalog of stem changes in human nouns will necessitate further lexicographical research. See also sections 4.5 and 5.3.2 for more discussion of number marking in nominals.

Another salient characteristic of many (but not all) human nouns is the presence of the suffix /-ta/, which Whistler describes as the "human nominal suffix" (Whistler 1980:200). This suffix appears only on human nouns and only in the singular and dual. It is a part of the stem, appearing before both number and case suffixes. See table 4.1, where *serita* 'young man', *wi·ta* 'man', and *p'okita* 'woman' have this characteristic suffix in the singular and dual.

4.2.3. Noun Citation Forms

In elicitation of nouns, the most common citation form is the subjective case—that is, the bare stem form with no case marking. Sometimes speakers use the object form of animate nouns as a citation form, perhaps to convey information about the noun's inflectional class.

Table 4.1. Selected nouns referring to humans, in singular, dual, and plural

Gloss	Singular	Dual	Plural	Sources
young man	seri-ta	seri-ta-pel	seri-ba	(Bright, c:G127, SG; Whistler, d:G56, HL)
man	wi·-ta	wi·-ta-pel	wiya-ba	(Whistler, d:A6, OM; Bright, c:1.G117, SG)
woman	p'oki-ta	p'oki-ta-pel	k'aya-ba	(Radin, c:43/172, AL; Whistler, d:A56, OM)
old woman	k'a·y	k'a·y-pel	k'a·y-ba	(Ultan, d:3.2, OM)
child	ʔila·y	ʔilay-pel	ʔila·y-in	(Radin, c:17/152, AL; Whistler 1977a:160, 169, NL/HL)

4.3. KINSHIP TERMS

Kinship terms are a well-defined lexical class in Patwin, distinct from common nouns. They are characterized by (a) a special set of bound possessive pronominals, (b) obligatory number marking via suffixation, (c) the occurrence of the absolutive suffix /-·n/, and (d) irregular stem changes associated with both possessive marking and number marking. For discussion of the possessive pronominals see sections 5.3.1.3.3 and 5.3.1.3.4. For discussion of number marking on kinship terms see section 4.5. For discussion of the absolutive suffix see section 4.7. For a thorough catalog of irregular stem changes in kinship terms, as well as a thorough discussion of the semantics of Patwin and Wintuan kinship terms, see Whistler (1980).

4.3.1. Possession of Kinship Terms

One of the identifying characteristics of kinship terms as a lexical class is their use of a special set of bound possessive pronominals, like *ʔuy-* '3SG.POSS$_K$ (his/her)' in (28).

(28) ⟨ʔʊytan⟩
ʔuy-ta-n
3SG.POSS$_K$-father-ABS
his father
(Ultan, d:4.6, AN) [HP$_L$]

These bound possessive pronominals are morphologically related to free pronouns, and are discussed in section 5.3.1.3.3.

Possession of kinship terms can also be expressed with free nominals. In (29a) the kinship term *ne·n* 'mother' is modified by the possessive common noun *p'okitano* 'woman's'. In (29b) the kinship term *tan* 'father' is modified by the possessive kinship term *ne·nčuy* '(my) mother's'. In (29c) the kinship term *tan* 'father' is modified by the possessive pronoun *mipelnomin* 'your (DU)'.

(29) a. ⟨p'okita nonɛ·´n⟩
p'okita-no ne·-n
woman-POSS$_{\text{K-F}}$ mother-ABS
the woman's mother
(Radin, c:51/179, AL) [HP$_{\text{T}}$]

b. ⟨Nan´-choo ĕ-tan⟩ 'Grandfather (mother's father)'
ne·n-ču-y ta-n
mother-RL-POSS$_{\text{K-F}}$ father-ABS
(my) mother's father
(Merriam:V72.2) [HP$_{\text{C}}$]

c. ⟨míp̓ɛlnômɪn tán⟩
mipelnomin ta-n
2DU.POSS$_{\text{K-F}}$ father-RL
your (DU) father
(Ultan, d:4.6, AN) [HP$_{\text{L}}$]

Kinship terms modified by free possessive nominals may also be marked by a coreferential bound possessive pronominal. For example in (30a) the kinship term *tan* 'father' is modified by the possessive kinship term *tačuy* '(my) father's', and also marked with the third-person singular possessive pronominal */ʔuy-/*. Similarly in (30b) the kinship term *tʰa·y* 'grandchild' is modified by the free possessive pronoun *namin* 'my', and also marked with the kinship-relational suffix */-ču/*.[1]

(30) a. ⟨tacuy ʔuytan⟩

ta-ču-y ʔuy-ta-n

father-RL-POSS$_{K\text{-}F}$ 3SG.POSS$_{K}$-father-ABS

my father's father

(Ultan, d:6.13, NeL) [HP$_{T}$]

b. ⟨nâmɪn tʰá·i̯ču⟩

namin tʰa·y-ču

1SG.POSS$_{K\text{-}F}$ grandchild-RL

my grandchild

(Ultan, d:4.6, AN) [HP$_{L}$]

See further discussion of free nominal possessors in section 4.6.1.3.

4.3.2. Kinship Term Citation Forms

In Hill Patwin and River Patwin the citation forms for kinship terms are invariably possessed forms. In other words when a field worker asks the word for "father", the response is always "my father" or some other possessed form of "father". The most commonly used possessive affix is the kinship-relational suffix *-ču*, which tends to imply a first-person referent (see section 5.3.1.3.4).

In South Patwin both possessed forms and nonpossessed stems are given as citation forms with about equal frequency, in every major source (Arroyo de la Cuesta, Vallejo, and Merriam).

4.4. NOMINALIZED VERBS

Verbs can be nominalized with an overt nominalizing suffix or by using the bare nominal stem of the verb. See section 8.1 for a discussion of the nominal stem and section 8.4 for a discussion of nominalization morphology. In this section the resulting nominalized verbs are compared with other nouns morphologically and syntactically.

There are two morphosyntactically distinct types of nominalized verb. The first type is morphologically and syntactically identical to an inanimate noun. The second is morphologically identical to an inanimate noun, but triggers a special agreement in the possessive pronoun.

An example of the first type is *t'e·we* 'language', derived from the verb *t'e·we* 'speak'. Used in this way, *t'e·we* 'language' is identical to an inanimate noun morphologically and syntactically. Example (31a) shows *t'e·we* triggering inanimate agreement in the possessive pronoun *mato* 'your (SG.POSS$_{IN}$)'. Example (31b) shows *t'e·we* triggering inanimate agreement in a relative clause with the inanimate auxiliary *be* 'be (IN)'.

(31) a. ⟨matɷ ṫe·wɛ k̓ayɪscu⟩

mato — t'e·we — k'ayi-s — ču

2SG.POSS$_{IN}$ — language — like-FIN — 1SG.SBJ

I like your language.

(Ultan, d:6.119, DL) [HP$_T$]

b. ⟨súnbe ṫéwe⟩ 'this language here'

[sun — be] — t'ewe

[here — be.IN] — language

the language [that is here]

(Whistler, d:B18, OM) [HP$_L$]

Because this type of nominalized verb is morphosyntactically identical to an inanimate noun, it can be considered an inanimate noun for the purposes of grammatical analysis.

A nominalization of the same verb can be used to illustrate the second type of nominalized verb. When a nominalization of *t'e·we* 'speak' is used as the predicate of a subordinate clause, it triggers a special form of the possessive pronoun unique to this type of nominalized verb. This form of the possessive is glossed POSS$_V$. Example (32) shows *t'e·we* 'speak' used as the predicate of the subordinate clause *na·y t'e·wet'uka* 'until I speak', where *na·y* is the special POSS$_V$ form of the first-person singular possessive pronoun 'my'.

(32) ⟨[. . .] ga·´turobɔ·`ti na·´it'ɛ·`wɛt'uka.⟩

[. . .] — ka·tu-ro — bo·-t^hi

be.hidden-PART — be.AN-2nSG.HORT

[na·y t'e·we-t'uka]
[1SG.POSS$_V$ speak.NMNL-ALL]

[. . .] stay hidden [until I speak].
(Radin, c:102/225, AL) [HP$_T$]

Example (33) shows another nominalized verb *č'o·wi* 'look' used as the predicate of a subordinate clause. This is another example of a nominalized verb triggering the special POSS$_V$ agreement in its possessor—in this case, *ʔu·y* 'his'. It is also an example of a nominalized verb appearing with the morphology of an inanimate noun: the inanimate locative suffix /-ła/.

(33) ⟨čˀo·wi-ła ʔuy, peri-ṫo ʔut.⟩
[č'o·wi-ła ʔuy] peri-t'o ʔut
[look-LOC$_{IN}$ 3SG.POSS$_V$] swallow-INCEP 3SG.OBJ
[When he looked], (the snake) was about to swallow him.
(Whistler 1978:54/56, NL/HL) [HP$_R$]

Note that the nominalized verbs in both (32) and (33) have case suffixes (allative and locative, respectively)—confirmation that these are indeed nominalizations.

Because this second type of nominalized verb triggers a special form of possessive pronoun, this type of nominalized verb must be considered to be its own category of nominal, distinct from nouns, kinship terms, and pronouns. See sections 4.6.1.3 and 5.3.1.3.3 for further discussion of POSS$_V$-type possessors.

4.5. NUMBER MARKING

Kinship terms and pronouns obligatorily inflect for number with a combination of suffixation and irregular stem changes. For kinship terms the number suffixes are /-pel/ 'DU' and /-ba/ 'PL'. For pronouns the suffix allomorphy is significantly more complicated, and is explained in detail in section 5.3.2. The stem changes associated with dual and plural kinship terms are highly irregular (especially in the dual), and are well summarized in Whistler (1980:213 ff.). This summary need not be repeated here, though detailed lexicographical work in the future may increase our understanding of the system.

Common nouns generally do not inflect for number. However, nouns referring to humans typically do. Nonhuman nouns also occasionally inflect for number. In no case is number inflection obligatory for common nouns.

Like kinship terms, common nouns inflect for number using a combination of suffixation and irregular stem changes. The most common number suffixes for nouns are /-pel/ 'DU' (34a) and /-ba/ 'PL' (34b). More rarely /-le·/ 'PL' is used for nouns (34c). In some citation forms the suffix /-ma/ is used for nonsingular nouns, like the plural reference in (34d) and the dual reference in (34e).[2] The choice of plural marker appears to be lexically specified.

(34) Number marking on common nouns

a. ⟨Pe´-pel-wim-pel⟩ /pi*pel win-pel/ 'those two people'
(Merriam:V71.56) [HP_T]

b. ⟨k̓ʌ́yʌ́bʌ̀⟩ /k'aya-ba/ 'women'
(Haas:17, IM/WM) [RP]

c. ⟨cùkûy lè·ǹo⟩ /čukʰu·y-le·-no/ 'bears' ($POSS_{IN}$)'
(Bright, c:1.G125, SG) [RP]

d. ⟨t̓iwí·lma⟩ /t'iwi·l-ma/ 'lot of rattlesnakes'
(Ultan, d:2.72, OM) [HP_L]

e. ⟨ʔú·no sáma⟩ /ʔu·no sa-ma/ 'his eyes'
(Whistler, d:A90) [HP_L]

The stem changes associated with dual and plural inflection in nominals are irregular, and vary by dialect. Detailed lexicographic work will have to be carried out before these stem changes can be fully cataloged. I do not attempt a full description here. Whistler (1980:213 ff.) includes a complete discussion of stem changes in kinship terms. See table 4.1 for some examples of stem changes in common nouns referring to humans.

A special use of number marking is found in terms of address for in-laws. Directly addressing in-laws is traditionally avoided (Kroeber 1932: 272; Whistler 1980:97–98), but nonsingular nominals may be employed when in-law address is necessary. The most commonly reported terms are third-person and second-person plural pronouns (see section 5.5), but plural nouns are sometimes used as well. For example Oscar McDaniel tells Ultan that ⟨lɔ·yba⟩ /lo·y-ba/ means 'lots of girls' or 'girl that son goes with' (Ultan, d:6.67).

4.6. CASE MARKING

Patwin is a heavily dependent-marking language. The grammatical functions of clausal arguments and adjuncts are indexed primarily by case marking (as opposed to agreement marking on the predicate), and possession is typically indicated by case marking on the possessor (as opposed to the head noun). The only exceptions are the hortative mood, in which the verb agrees with the subject in person and number, and kinship terms, where possession is usually indicated with bound pronominals.

Cases usually appear on nominal stems (nouns, kinship terms, and pronouns), but can also appear on nominalized verbs functioning as the predicates of subordinate clauses, where they indicate the relation of the subordinate clause to the matrix clause. Cases are marked with suffixation, rarely accompanied by a change in the form of the stem. There are two major categories of case marking in Patwin, which I call grammatical cases and semantic cases. Grammatical cases indicate core structural functions of nominals in a phrase (subject, object, and possessor); semantic cases have more specific meanings.[3] Each category is discussed below.

4.6.1. Grammatical Cases

There are three grammatical cases in Patwin. The subjective case (SBJ) marks the subject of an independent clause, the objective case (OBJ) marks the direct or indirect object and some adjuncts, and the possessive case (POSS) marks the possessor of another nominal or the subject of a nominalized subordinate clause. These cases are described individually below.

4.6.1.1. *Subjective Case*

A nominal functioning as the subject of a main clause takes no overt case marking. This unmarked case is referred to as the subjective case.[4] In (35a) the subject is *su·l-č'iyak* 'Old Man Eagle', which has no overt case marking. Compare the other nominals in the same example: *ʔa·pakʰe* 'uncle' is marked with the vocative suffix /-kʰe/, and both objects are marked with objective case suffixes, *ne·nčut* 'mother' with /-t/ and *peru·ma* with /-ma/. In (35b) the subject is *silay-k'ay* 'Old Lady Bear', which has no overt case marking. The other nominal in the sentence *no·p-č'iyakma* 'Old Man Deer' is marked for the objective case with /-ma/.

(35) a. ⟨ʔa·pa-khe·, ne·n-ču-t peru·-ma k̓ača·-ro sul-thi-s su·l-č̓iyak.⟩

ʔa·pa-kʰe· ne·n-ču-t peru·-ma k'ača·-ro
uncle-VOC mother-RL-OBJ throat-OBJ cut-PART

sultʰi-s <u>su·l-č'iyak</u>
kill-FIN <u>eagle-old.man</u>

Uncle, <u>Old Man Eagle</u> cut our mother's throat and killed her.
(Whistler 1977a:166/172, NL/HL) [HP_R]

b. ⟨silay-k̓ay sul-thu-ro no·p-č̓iyak-ma.⟩
<u>silay-k'ay</u> sultʰu-ro no·p-č'iyak-ma
<u>bear-old.lady</u> kill-PART deer-old.man-OBJ
<u>Old Lady Bear</u> killed Old Man Deer.
(Whistler 1977a:163/171, NL/HL) [HP_R]

4.6.1.2. *Objective Case*

The objective case is marked with a suffix on kinship terms, pronouns, and animate nouns. On animate nouns the suffix is /-ma/. On kinship terms with the plural suffix /-ba/, the objective case suffix is also /-ma/. On other kinship terms and on proper names, the objective case suffix is /-t/. For pronouns the allomorphy is significantly more complicated, for which see section 5.3.1.2. Grammatically inanimate nouns are not marked for objective case.

There is no morphological distinction between direct and indirect objects, primary and secondary objects, and so on—all of these categories are marked with the objective case. In (36a) the objective case noun *siyama* 'deer' is the patient (direct undergoer) of the action 'hunt'. In (36b) the objective case pronoun *nat* 'me' is the beneficiary of the action 'give'. In (36c) both the patient *kʰudima* 'bird' and the beneficiary *danat* 'Don' are in the objective case. Thus ditransitive verbs like *doyi* 'give' may have two objective case arguments.

(36) a. ⟨cıama boyawuti⟩
siya-ma boya-wuti
deer-OBJ hunt-CERT
hunt deer
(Curtin, b:228) [SP]

b. ⟨nat doyusa⟩
nat doyu-sa
1SG.OBJ give-PAST
He gave it to me.
(Swadesh and Melton:59:43, IM) [RP]

c. ⟨Oscar kʰudima dóyibʊs Dónat⟩
Oscar kʰudima doyibus danat
Oscar kʰudi-ma doyi-bus dan-t
Oscar bird-OBJ give-FIN Don-OBJ
Oscar gave a bird to Don.
(Ultan, d:3.16, OM) [HP$_{L}$]

Nouns functioning as adverbial modifiers to the clause may appear in the objective case. In (37a) the phrase *ʔete·ma sema·no* 'one week (OBJ)' is a temporal adjunct to the clause, indicating the span of time for which the event has persisted.[5] In (37b) the pronoun *pima* 'that (OBJ)' refers not to what was paid nor who was paid, but what was paid *for*.[6]

(37) a. ⟨pɪ ʔilájcʰu čhojú·ro ʔeté·ma ṣɛmá·no⟩

pi	ʔilay-ču	čoyu·-ro	ʔete·-ma	sema·no
DIST.SG.SBJ	child-RL	sick-PART	one-OBJ	week

That baby has been sick for one week.

(Whistler, d:A3, OM) [$\mathrm{HP_L}$]

b. ⟨pi na·t k̓obo·lusa píma⟩

pi	nat	k'obo·lu-sa	pima
3SG.SBJ	1SG.OBJ	pay-PAST	DIST.OBJ

He paid me for it.

(Whistler, d:G71, HL) [$\mathrm{HP_R}$]

4.6.1.3. *Possessive Case*

The possessive case[7] marks the possessor function: nominals that grammatically possess other nominals. The possessive case is also used for the agent in passive constructions and for the subject in nominalized subordinate clauses—functions that may be called "agentive," following Whistler (1980:230ff).

Nominals inflected for the possessive case agree with the possessed word in lexical category (noun vs. kinship term vs. nominalized verb) and in animacy (for nouns). For example (38) shows the word *wi·ta* 'man' used as a possessive in two different contexts: In (38a) the possessed noun *nun* 'gun' is grammatically inanimate, so *wi·ta* takes the inanimate possessive suffix /-no/. In (38b) the possessed noun *ʔilay* 'child' is grammatically animate, so *wi·ta* takes the animate possessive suffix /-nomin/.

(38) a. ⟨wɪtanɷ nún⟩

wita-no	nun
man-POSS_{IN}	gun

the man's gun

(Ultan, d:2.48, OM) [$\mathrm{HP_L}$]

b. ⟨wí·tanɷmɪn ʔɪláḭ⟩

wita-nomin ʔilay

man-POSS$_{AN}$ child

the man's baby

(Ultan, d:2.48, OM) [HP$_L$]

The possessive case suffix thus has four separate form classes, depending on the lexical category and animacy of the possessed nominal. To efficiently indicate these classes in the gloss, subscripts are used: possessors of inanimate nouns are marked POSS$_{IN}$, possessors of animate nouns are marked POSS$_{AN}$, free nominal possessors of kinship terms are marked POSS$_{K\text{-}F}$ (as opposed to the bound possessive pronominals on kinship terms, which are glossed POSS$_K$), and possessors of nominalized verbs (including subjects of nominalized subordinate clauses) are marked POSS$_V$.

Different categories of nominals inflect for possessive agreement in formally distinct ways. For example common nouns take the suffix /-no/ when used as agentive possessives, whereas kinship terms take the suffix /-y/ in this context. Example (39) shows two subordinate clauses. In (39a) the subject of the subordinate clause is a noun, so it is marked with /-no/. In (39b) the subject of the subordinate clause is a kinship term, so it is marked with /-y/.

(39) a. ⟨'ila´ipɛlnɔ hɛne·´La mem paro·´rɔbɛm.⟩

[ʔilay-pel-no hene·-ła]

[child-DU-POSS$_V$ arrive-LOC]

mem paro·-ro be-m

water full-PART be.IN-SBJV

[When the two children arrived] (the basket) was full of water.

(Radin, c:25/129, AL) [HP$_T$]

Table 4.2. Forms of the possessive case suffix

		Possessed			
		Noun		Kinship Term	Nominalized Verb
		Inanimate (POSS$_{IN}$)	Animate (POSS$_{AN}$)	(POSS$_{K\text{-}F}$)	(POSS$_{V}$)
Possessor	Noun	-no	-nomin	-no	-no
	Kinship term	-(t)-no	-(t)-nomin (HP), -min (RP)	-y	-y
	Pronoun	-no, -to	-nomin, -min, -tomin	-nomin, -min, -tomin	-y, -t

b. ⟨la·bečupeléy hene·ła [. . .]⟩

la·be-ču-pele-y hene·-ła [. . .]

older.brother-RL-DU-POSS$_{V}$ arrive-LOC

When my two older brothers came [. . .]

(Whistler, d:G61, HL) [HP$_{R}$]

Table 4.2 summarizes the various forms of the possessive case suffix. The possessive case suffix on common nouns takes the form /-no/ when the possessed nominal is an inanimate noun (POSS$_{IN}$, as in 40a), kinship term (POSS$_{K\text{-}F}$, 40c), or nominalized verb (POSS$_{V}$, 40d); and /-nomin/ when the possessed nominal is an animate noun (POSS$_{AN}$, 40b).[8]

(40) a. ⟨t̓ɪwí·l no sí·⟩

t'iwi·l-no si·

rattle.snake-POSS$_{IN}$ teeth

rattlesnake's fangs

(Whistler, d:A90, OM) [HP$_{L}$]

b. ⟨hú·rnomɪn pú·⟩

hu·r-nomin pu·

salmon-POSS$_{AN}$ eggs

salmon eggs

(Whistler, d:A121, OM) [HP$_{L}$]

c. ⟨sedew ceyakno lá·bèn⟩
sedew-č'iyak-no laben
coyote-old.man-POSS$_{K-F}$ older.brother
Old Man Coyote's older brother
(Bright, c:6.NL127, NL) [HP$_{C}$]

d. ⟨tc'iaknɔ hɛne·´La [. . .]⟩
č'iyak-no hene·ła [. . .]
old.man-POSS$_{V}$ arrive-LOC
When the old man arrived [. . .]
(Radin, c:67/194, AL) [HP$_{T}$]

The possessive case suffix on kinship terms takes the form /-no/ when the possessed nominal is an inanimate noun (POSS$_{IN}$, as in 41a), /-nomin/ in Hill Patwin when the possessed nominal is an animate noun (POSS$_{AN}$, 41b), /-min/ in River Patwin when the possessed nominal is an animate noun (POSS$_{AN}$, 41c), and /-y/ when the possessed nominal is a kinship term (POSS$_{K-F}$, 41d) or nominalized verb (POSS$_{V}$, 41e). Note that on kinship terms, the possessive case suffix may be preceded by the objective case suffix when the possessed nominal is a noun—see below.

(41) a. ⟨ʔá·pačuno dí·hiti⟩
ʔa·pa-ču-no di·hi-ti
grandfather-RL-POSS$_{IN}$ home-ABL
from my grandfather's home
(Whistler, d:G59, HL) [HP$_{R}$]

b. ⟨ne·n-ču-t-nomin ʔana⟩
ne·n-ču-t-nomin ʔana
mother-RL-OBJ-POSS$_{AN}$ head
mother's head
(Whistler 1977a:162/170, NL/HL) [HP$_{R}$]

c. ⟨lá·becumɪn ʔílà·yìn⟩

la·be-ču-min ʔila·y-in

older.brother-RL-POSS$_{AN}$ child-PL

my older brother's children

(Bright, c:8.G107, SG) [RP]

d. ⟨ʔapacuy ʔuynɛn⟩

ʔapa-ču-y ʔuy-nen

grandfather-RL-POSS$_{K\text{-}F}$ 3SG.POSS$_{K}$-mother

my grandfather's mother

(Ultan, d:6.13, NeL) [HP$_{T}$]

e. ⟨ʔuy né· mómhùròʔ ʔúmała [. . .]⟩

ʔuy-ne-y momhu-ro ʔ ʔuma-ła [. . .]

3SG.POSS$_{K}$-mother-POSS$_{V}$ tell-PART || finish-LOC

When their mother finished telling [. . .]

(Bright, c:10.DL107, DL) [HP$_{T}$]

The possessive case suffix on pronouns displays a more complicated set of possessive allomorphy, described in sections 5.3.1.3.1–5.3.1.3.5. Nominalized verbs are not attested in the possessive case.

Double case marking in possessive kinship terms: In Hill Patwin, kinship terms functioning as possessors of nouns optionally take a sequence of two case suffixes: the possessive case suffix /-no/ 'POSS$_{IN}$' or /-nomin/ 'POSS$_{AN}$' may be preceded by the objective case suffix /-t/ 'OBJ'. This is similar to the pattern of double case marking in the semantic cases on all nominals, where the semantic case suffix is optionally preceded by an objective case suffix (see section 4.6.2.1). But unlike in the semantic cases, double case marking in the possessive case is almost entirely limited to kinship terms. Nouns in the possessive case never have an objective case marker. For pronouns in the possessive case, double case marking is attested only on proximal pronouns, and only in Lodoga Hill Patwin (see sections A.2.1 and 5.3.1.3.1).

Example (42b) shows the kinship term *ne·n* 'mother' in possessive case (modifying an animate possessed noun). Note that the objective case suffix /-t/ precedes the animate possessive case suffix /-nomin/. Compare (42a), which is the objective case form of 'mother', also marked with /-t/ 'OBJ'. Similarly (43) shows the kinship term *łabe* 'older brother' in objective case (43a) and possessive case (43b), in this case with an inanimate possessed noun *di·hi* 'home'. In this example also, the possessive suffix on the kinship term is preceded by the objective case suffix /-t/.

(42) Kinship term *ne·n* 'mother' in OBJ and POSS case

a. ⟨ne·n-ču-t⟩ /ne·n-ču-t/ '(our) mother (OBJ)'
(Whistler 1977a: 164/171, NL/HL) [HP_R]

b. ⟨ne·n-ču-t-nomin ʔana⟩
/ne·n-ču-t-nomin ʔana/ '(our) mother's head'
(Whistler 1977a: 162/170, NL/HL) [HP_R]

(43) Kinship term *łabe* 'older brother' in OBJ and POSS case

a. ⟨máłabét⟩ /ma-łabe-t/ 'your older brother (OBJ)'
(Whistler, d:G57, HL) [HP_R]

b. ⟨máłabétno dí·hiła⟩ /ma-łabe-t-no di·hi-ła/ 'to your older brother's home'
(Whistler, d:G59, HL) [HP_R]

The objective case suffix is not obligatory on kinship terms in the possessive case, however, as shown in (41a). Another example is shown in (44a). Here the inanimate possessive case suffix /-no/ is not preceded by an objective case suffix, but follows the stem /ne·n/ 'mother' directly. Compare (44b), where the inanimate possessive suffix /-no/ occurs on the same stem, but with the objective case suffix /-t/ preceding it.[9]

(44) a. ⟨ʔûy nê·n no dí·łà⟩

ʔu·y-ne·n-no	di·-ła
3SG.POSS$_K$-mother-POSS$_{IN}$	home-LOC

her mother's home
(Bright, c: 10.DL113, DL) [HP_T]

b. ⟨mani·tno di·hiła⟩

ma-ni·-t-no di·hi-ła

2SG.POSS$_K$-mother-OBJ-POSS$_{IN}$ home-LOC

to your mother's home

(Whistler, d:G95, HL) [HP$_R$]

Whistler (1977a) analyzes the suffix /-t/ in this context as an archaic remnant of a Proto-Wintuan system of nominal aspect.[10] Whistler (1980) analyzes the /t/ as part of the possessive affix: /-tno/ 'POSS$_{IN}$ (on kinship terms)', /-tnomin/ 'POSS$_{AN}$ (on kinship terms)'. However, given the general tendency of Patwin case suffixes to appear in doubly case marked constructions with the objective case suffix, it seems most felicitous to analyze the /-t/ here as the objective case suffix.

Agentive: Subjects of nominalized subordinate clauses, agents of passivized clauses, and possessors of nominalized verbs are expressed with a special form of the possessive case. In this work this form is called the agentive form of the possessive case and glossed 'POSS$_V$' (for "possessor of a verb"). The distinctive array of possessive case suffix forms associated with the agentive is described as a kind of agreement.

Whistler (1980) tentatively identifies these POSS$_V$ forms as a separate case, which he calls the "genitive" case, as distinct from the "alienable possessive" case, used for possessors of nouns (i.e. POSS$_{IN}$ and POSS$_{AN}$). He also includes the bound possessive pronominals found on kinship terms in the genitive case (Whistler 1980:230). This bipartite division of possessive forms into alienable possessive versus genitive is probably driven by a combination of formal and functional distinctions. Whistler does not recognize a separate category for free possessors of kinship terms (POSS$_{K\text{-}F}$), and in the absence of this category the formal difference between the alienable possessives and the genitive is near categorical (though the two are identical for possessive nouns). Functionally, agentive nominals are not the same as possessive nominals, so a distinction can be made here as well (with the bound pronominals grouped with the former category because of formal similarity).

However, the recognition of a distinct category for free possessors of kinship terms blurs the formal distinction between agents and possessors.

Nouns used as possessors of kinship terms (POSS$_{K-F}$) are formally identical to nouns used as possessors of inanimate nouns (POSS$_{IN}$); pronouns used as possessors of kinship terms (POSS$_{K-F}$) are formally identical to pronouns used as possessors of animate nouns (POSS$_{AN}$); and kinship terms used as possessors of kinship terms (POSS$_{K-F}$) are formally identical to kinship terms used as the agents of subordinate clauses (POSS$_{V}$). Moreover the use of possessive case can be expected in an agentive context: from a crosslinguistic perspective, possessive case is one of the expected cases to mark the subject of a nominalized clause (e.g., Malchukov et al. 2008). And in Penutian languages specifically, agents of passive constructions are typically realized in the possessive case (see Dixon and Kroeber 1919:97; DeLancey and Golla 1997:189 ff.). Therefore for formal, typological, and historical reasons, it seems natural to recognize Patwin agentive nominals as being in the possessive case.

4.6.2. Semantic Cases

The cases described in this section mark nouns as having specific semantic functions in a clause, with roughly the following meanings: comitative /-da/ means '(along) with', instrumental /-sin, -tin/ means 'with' or 'using', locative /-ła, -tin/ means 'at' or 'to', allative /-tuka/ means 'toward', ablative /-ti, -na·k/ means 'from', and prolative /-na/ means 'via'. The meanings of each of these cases are discussed in more detail below. All of these semantic cases are expressed with overt suffixation, only very rarely accompanied by irregular modification to the stem.[11] In addition to their literal meanings, most of the semantic cases are attested with more metaphorical meanings, which are extensions of the literal ones. The polysemy of each suffix is described below. All of the semantic cases are also attested on pronouns, for which see section 5.3.1.4.

4.6.2.1. *Double Case Marking in Semantic Cases*

On animate nouns the semantic cases may optionally follow the objective case suffix /-ma/. In other words semantic case suffixes may optionally select an objective case stem. The resulting forms have two case suffixes, as shown in (45). In (45a) the instrumental /-sin/ follows the objective /-ma/. In (45b) the allative /-tuka/ follows the objective /-ma/ in *tʰasi·matuka* 'to mink'.

(45) Semantic case suffixes co-occurring with OBJ suffix

a. ⟨t̓ará·lmasin⟩
t'ara·l-ma-sin
scraper-OBJ-INS$_{IN}$
with a scraper
(Whistler, d:A114, OM) [HP$_L$]

b. ⟨sɛdɛ´utc'iak' du·´tarɔ ha·´rmem tasi·´matu·`ka⟩

sedew-č'iyak	du·taro	ha·rmem	t^{h}asi·matuka
sedew-č'iyak	duh-taro	ha·r-me-m	t^{h}asi·-ma-tuka
coyote-old.man	carry-PART	go-COM-SBJV	mink-OBJ-ALL

Old Man Coyote took them and carried them back to mink.
(Radin, c:13/148, AL) [HP$_T$]

This double case marking is optional and appears to have no semantic value. Compare (45b) with (46). In (45b) the word *t^{h}asi·matuka* 'to mink' includes an objective case suffix. In (46) the word *t^{h}asi·tuka* 'to mink' has no objective case suffix. Both words have the same root, are used in the same syntactic context, and are spoken by the same speaker.

(46) Semantic case suffixes without objective case suffix
⟨sɛdɛ´utc'iak [. . .] ɛte·´ma kɔ´ltcɩs 'ʊlkitaro ha´rmem tasi·´tuka.⟩
'Old man coyote [. . .] put [them] in a sack and took them to mink.'

sedew-č'iyak	[. . .]	ʔete·ma	k^{h}olčis
sedew-č'iyak		ʔete·-ma	k^{h}olčis
coyote-old.man		one-OBJ	sack

ʔolkitaro	harmem	t^{h}asi·tuka
ʔol-kir-taro	har-me-m	t^{h}asi·-tuka
up-move-PART	go-COM-SBJV	mink-ALL

Old Man Coyote [. . .] picked up one sack and took it to mink.
(Radin, c:5/142, AL) [HP$_T$]

Similarly in pronouns, semantic case suffixes may optionally select either the objective case form or the subjective case form of the stem. See section 5.3.1.4 for examples.

Clear instances of the semantic case suffixes occurring on the objective forms of kinship terms are not forthcoming. This may be due to the fact that the objective suffix for kinship terms is /-t/, and the semantic case suffixes commonly used with kinship terms begin with /t/, which may coalesce with the case suffix. On the other hand one would expect an occasional geminate /tt/ to result in careful speech, and gemination is not attested in this context (even in Radin's texts, where length is liberally indicated for consonants).

Although it is not clear whether semantic case suffixes select objective forms of kinship terms, it *is* clear that semantic case suffixes may select either the absolutive stem of kinship terms (marked with absolutive /-·n/, as in 47a) or the bare stem (47b).[12] The bare stem is more commonly selected. As with nouns and pronouns, there is no clear semantic contribution of the choice of stem form.[13]

(47) Kinship terms in semantic cases, selecting absolutive and nonabsolutive stems

a. ⟨'u·´itama·`nda⟩
ʔu·y-tʰama-·n-da
3SG.POSS$_K$-grandmother-ABS-COM
with his grandmother
(Radin, c:100/223, AL) [HP$_T$]

b. ⟨'u·´itapa t'uka⟩
ʔu·y-tʰapa-t'uka
3SG.POSS$_K$-uncle-ALL
to his uncle
(Radin, c:105/227, AL) [HP$_T$]

Because one of the case markers is semantically vacuous in Patwin double case marking structures, they lie outside of the better-known typologies of double case marking: Dench and Evans (1988:38 ff.), Plank

(1995), and Moravcsik (1995). These typologies document double case marking structures where both markers play some functional or semantic role. A double case marking structure more similar to Patwin is found in many Indic languages (Masica 1991:230 ff.). In these languages there may be multiple "layers" of case marking on nouns: a semantically vacuous "oblique" suffix followed by a semantic case suffix.[14]

The Sierra Miwok languages also have a pattern of double case marking that is similar to the Patwin system. In these languages the semantic case suffixes regularly co-occur with the nominative case suffix /-ʔ/, which contributes no separate semantic or functional meaning in this context (Callaghan 1987:22, 2003, 2014:179 ff.). In Broadbent's description of Southern Sierra Miwok, semantic cases may co-occur with either the nominative suffix /-ʔ/ or the accusative suffix /-y/ (Broadbent 1964:49 ff.). Broadbent mentions no semantic or functional distinction between nominative and accusative case marking in these constructions. This would make double case marking in Southern Sierra Miwok entirely parallel to that in Patwin, where semantic case suffixes may occur with either subjective (i.e., null) or objective case marking, with no semantic or functional distinction coded by this variation.[15]

4.6.2.2. *Comitative Case /-da/ 'with'*

The comitative case suffix /-da/ may carry a true comitative meaning 'with, along with', and it may be used to coordinate nominal expressions. Here I discuss its morphological expression and its usage in comitative contexts. For more about its coordinating function see section 6.6.1. For comitative marking on verbs, see section 8.2.4.4.[16]

The form of the comitative case suffix is invariant, always realized as /-da/. It appears directly on the noun. The comitative case generally marks comitative adjuncts (optional expressions not selected by the verb), such as the comitative-marked kinship term *ʔu·ytʰama·nda* 'with his grandmother' in (48a) and the comitative-marked noun *ʔamoda* 'with friend' in (48b).

(48) a. ⟨nɔp malı·´lıtu' 'u·´itama·`nda bɔm.⟩
nop-ma le·li-tu ʔ
deer-OBJ make-NMLZ$_{AG}$ ||

ʔu·y-tʰama-·n-da	bo-m
3POSS$_{K}$-grandmother-ABS-COM	be.AN-SBJV

Deer-maker stayed with his grandmother.
(Radin, c:100/223, AL) [HP$_{T}$]

b. ⟨ču harátibus tɛntatuka námin ʔámɒda⟩

ču	hara·-t'i-bus	tenta-tuka	namin	ʔamo-da
1SG.SBJ	go-FUT-FIN	town-ALL	1.SG.POSS$_{AN}$	friend-COM

I'm going to town with my friend.
(Ultan, d:4.34, AN) [HP$_{L}$]

Comitative case marking on nominals is optional when the comitative nominal is an argument of the verb (i.e., when the verb has a comitative suffix or an inherently comitative stem). See section 8.2.4.4 for examples of arguments in the comitative case.

Comitative /-da/ also appears on pronoun stems, where it also selects either the subject or object form of the stem. See section 5.3.1.4.

4.6.2.3. *Instrumental Case /-tin, -sin, -win, -in, -kin/ 'with'*

The instrumental case 'with, using' has a few allomorphs, conditioned phonologically and grammatically. On animate nouns (and pronouns), the instrumental case is /-tin/, identical to the locative case (52). On inanimate nouns (and pronouns), there are a number of phonologically conditioned allomorphs. Inanimate stems ending in /h/ or sonorants take the allomorph /-in/, as shown in (49).[17] Stems ending in /k/ take the allomorph /-kin/ or /-in/, in free variation (50). Elsewhere the basic form /-sin/ is found in Hill Patwin and /-win/ in River Patwin (51).

(49) INS on inanimate stems ending in /h/ or sonorants

a. ⟨nu·´hɪn⟩ /nu·h-in/ 'with a boat'
(Radin, c:39/169, AL) [HP$_{T}$]

b. ⟨k'i·´rin⟩ /k'i·r-in/ 'with a cloud'
(Radin, c:58/185) [HP$_{T}$]

c. ⟨łuk̓awɪn⟩ /łuk'aw-in/ 'with a blanket'
(Ultan, d:7.49, SG) [RP]

(50) INS on inanimate stems ending in /k/

a. ⟨ṫókkin⟩ /t'ok-kin/ 'with a stick'
(Whistler, d:A75, OM) [HP_L]

b. ⟨ṫókin⟩ /t'ok-in/ 'with a stick'
(Whistler, d:A101, OM) [HP_L]

c. ⟨'ɔ·´kɪn⟩ /ʔo·k-in/ 'with a basket'
(Radin, c:25/159, AL) [HP_T]

(51) INS on other inanimate stems

a. ⟨khúpat sɪn⟩ /kʰupat-sin/ 'with grapevine root'
(Whistler, d:A74, OM) [HP_L]

b. ⟨pho·-sin⟩ /pʰo·-sin/ 'with fire'
(Whistler 1977a:164/171, NL/HL) [HP_R]

c. ⟨hugɛwɪn⟩ /huke-win/ 'with rain'
(Snyder SF, SG) [RP]

(52) INS on animate stems

a. ⟨kawa·yumatin⟩ /kawa·yu-ma-tin/ 'with a horse'
(Ultan, d:6.90, DL) [HP_T]

b. ⟨ṫɛbimatin⟩ /t'ebi-ma-tin/ 'with an arrowhead'
(Ultan, d:7.50, SG) [RP]

The instrumental case is used for adjuncts with any instrumental-like meaning. It may indicate the tool used for a task (53a, 53b), materials used to make something (53c), a vehicle used for travel (53d), or the particular body part that the agent uses for an activity (53e, 53f).

(53) a. ⟨kučí·yašın čú nɔ́pma k̓ɔ́p̓itɒ⟩

kuči·ya-sin	ču	nop-ma	k'opi-t'o
knife-INS$_{\text{IN}}$	1SG.SBJ	deer-OBJ	cut-INCEP

I'm gonna cut up the deer with a knife.
(Ultan, d:3.18, OM) [HP$_{\text{L}}$]

b. ⟨Kodoi inchu thlelas-aboti⟩

k'odoy-in	ču	ɬila·-sa-boti
stone-INS$_{\text{IN}}$	1SG.SBJ	shoot-PAST-CERT

I flung a stone (at him).
(lit. 'I shot him with a stone.')
(P. Vallejo, c:23.9) [SP]

c. ⟨t̓a·ṣın ʔɔ́k lɛlú·ṛɒ bɛṣ⟩

t'a·-sin	ʔok	lelu·-ro	be-s
dogwood-INS$_{\text{IN}}$	basket	make-PART	be.IN-FIN

The basket is made of dogwood.
(Ultan, d:3.24, OM) [HP$_{\text{L}}$]

d. ⟨nuhın pi cu hara·t̓i⟩

nuh-in	pi	ču	hara·-t'i
boat-INS$_{\text{IN}}$	DECL	1SG.SBJ	go-FUT

I'm gonna go by boat.
(Ultan, d:6.90, DL) [HP$_{\text{T}}$]

e. ⟨chu ná·no sémın píma khori ƛ̓ochú·ro⟩

ču	na·no	sem-in
1SG.SBJ	1SG.POSS$_{\text{IN}}$	hand-INS$_{\text{IN}}$

pima	k^{h}ori	ƛ'oču·-ro
DIST.SG.IN.OBJ	pinole	grab-PART

I picked up that pinole with my hand.
(Whistler, d:B61, OM) [HP$_{\text{L}}$]

f. ⟨kówasin t'áltaro k'ánas⟩

kowa-sin t'al-taro k'ana-s

back-INS$_{IN}$ fall-PART sleep-FIN

He's sleeping on his back.

(Whistler, d:F70, HL) [HP$_R$]

The instrumental case is attested only on nouns and pronouns (see section 5.3.1.4). It is not attested on kinship terms.

4.6.2.4. Locative Case /-ła, -tin/ 'at, to'

The locative case has two basic allomorphs, conditioned by the grammatical animacy of the stem. On grammatically inanimate stems and on nominalized verbs, the locative case suffix is /-ła/. On grammatically animate stems, the locative case suffix is /-tin/, except after /h/, where it takes the form /-in/. (The locative case suffix is thus formally identical to the instrumental case on animate nouns.) The locative case suffix on kinship terms always takes the animate forms /-tin, -in/. Because the form of the suffix indexes information about the inflectional class of the noun, I gloss the form appearing on inanimate stems LOC$_{IN}$ and the form appearing on animate stems LOC$_{AN}$.

Example (54) shows the locative case on animate and inanimate nouns. In (54a) the inanimate noun stem *me·mpu* 'ocean' takes the inanimate form of the locative suffix, /-ła/. In (54b), the animate noun stem *tʰasi·* 'mink' takes the animate form of the locative suffix, /-tin/.

(54) a. ⟨me·´mpuLa hɛ·´nɛbɔm⟩

me·mpu-ła he·ne bo-m

ocean-LOC$_{IN}$ arrive be.AN-SBJV

She got to the ocean.

(Radin, c:94/218, AL) [HP$_T$]

b. ⟨tasi·´tin hɛ´nmɛm⟩

tʰasi·-tin hen-me-m

mink-LOC$_{AN}$ arrive-COM-SBJV

He got them over to mink.

(Radin, c:5/142, AL) [HP$_T$]

Example (55) shows the formal variation in the locative case on animate stems. In (55a) the locative case appears after /h/, and so takes the form /-in/. In (55b) the locative does not immediately follow /h/, and so takes the form /-tin/.[18]

(55) a. ⟨pi·´tupu ʼu´yɪnɔk ʼu´iLahɪn ha·´rmo⟩

pi·tupu ʔuy-ʔonok

then 3SG.POSS$_K$-wife

ʔuy-łah-in ha·r-mu

3SG.POSS$_K$-younger.sibling-LOC$_{AN}$ go-SBJV

Then his wife went to her sister.

(Radin, c:16/151, AL) [HP$_T$]

b. ⟨ʔanuhmatin henta⟩ 'came to the Buttes'

ʔanuh-ma-tin hen-ta

turtle-OBJ-LOC$_{AN}$ arrive-PART

arrived at turtle's place

(Ultan, d:7.27, SG) [RP]

On nouns, pronouns, and kinship terms, the locative case is used to express location. It is used in two semantically related ways in the clause. First, it is used for the static location where the event or situation happens, as in *ku·lła* 'in the shade' in (56a). Second, it is used for the end point or goal of a motion event, as in *kewela* 'into the house' in (56b).[19] The locative is not used to mark either the starting point or source of a motion event (ablative is used instead), or the path of a motion event (prolative is used instead).

(56) a. ⟨népɛl hámta bɔ́·ṣ ku·lła⟩

nepel ham-ta bo·-s ku·l-ła

1EXCL.DU.SBJ sit-PART be.AN-FIN shade-LOC$_{IN}$

We're sitting in the shade.

(Whistler, d:A5, OM) [HP$_L$]

b. ⟨kathit-se·ktu ʔel-hara-s ʔu·no kewe-ła.⟩

katʰit-se·ktu	ʔel-hara-s	ʔu·no	kewe-ła
falcon-chief	in-go-FIN	3SG.POSS$_{IN}$	house-LOC$_{IN}$

Falcon Chief went inside his house.
(lit. 'went inside to his house')
(Whistler 1978:52/55, NL/HL) [HP$_R$]

The locative case may also be used metaphorically to express temporal adjuncts, as in *le·niła* 'in the evening' in (57).

(57) ⟨le·´niLa nu·´hɪn me´m·na ha·´rmu⟩
'In the evening with his canoe he got in the water [. . .]'

le·ni-ła	nu·h-in	mem-na	ha·r-mu
evening-LOC$_{IN}$	boat-INS$_{IN}$	water-PROL	go-SBJV

In the evening, with his boat, he went through the water.
(Radin, c:39/169, AL) [HP$_T$]

Nominalized verbs functioning as heads of adjunct subordinate clauses may also appear in the locative case, marked with /-ła/. See section 9.3.2.

4.6.2.5. *Allative Case /-tuka, -t'uka/ 'toward'*

The allative case suffix has no regularly conditioned allomorphy, always taking the form /-tuka/ or /-t'uka/.[20] The plain and glottalized variants /-tuka/ and /-t'uka/ vary by dialect, speech rate, and possibly by individual. The glottalized variant is attested in Tebti Hill Patwin, Rumsey Hill Patwin, and River Patwin. In his Tebti materials from speaker Anderson Lowell, Radin almost invariably transcribes the glottalized variant. But Ultan transcribes only the plain variant for Tebti speaker Daisy Lorenzo. River Patwin speaker Jennie Regalado uses the glottalized variant in slow speech but the plain variant in quick speech (see note in Whistler, d:F113, G10). But River Patwin speaker Sarah Gonzales is recorded only using the plain variant. Rumsey Hill Patwin speaker Harry Lorenzo uses both variants: see (58b) and (58d). Only the plain variant is attested in Lodoga and Cortina Hill Patwin.

This variation by itself may suggest that the glottalized variant /-t'uka/ is the original form, and that the glottalization is becoming neutralized in quick speech in River Patwin, for some speakers being neutralized entirely. However, the probable cognate of this suffix in Wintu is *čuka·* 'approach (verb)', whose initial /č/ should correspond to Patwin plain /t/ (Shepherd 2005:14, 71). The variation in the allative suffix therefore remains something of a mystery.

The basic sense of the allative case suffix is indicating motion toward something, as in *ʔu·ytʰapat'uka* 'toward his uncle' in (58a). It is also attested in a number of other, semantically related usages. In (58b) the allative *kewetuka* is used in the sense of 'onto the house'—something that is being climbed onto. In (58c) the allative *kewet'uka* 'against the house' is an object being leaned against. In (58d) the allative marks an oblique experiencer argument: *na·t'uka* 'to me' = 'to my perception'.

(58) a. ⟨ha·´rmu 'u·´tapa t'uka [. . .]⟩
ha·r-mu ʔu·y-tʰapa-t'uka [. . .]
go-SBJV 3SG.POSS$_K$-uncle-ALL
He went to his uncle [. . .]
(Radin, c:105/227, AL) [HP$_T$]

b. ⟨chu deces kewetuka⟩
ču deče-s kewe-tuka
1SG.SBJ climb-FIN house-ALL
I'm climbing onto the house.
(Whistler, d:E71, HL) [HP$_R$]

c. ⟨kewetuka ču thókthuro⟩
kewe-t'uka ču tʰoktʰu-ro
house-ALL 1SG.SBJ lean-PART
I'm leaning against the house.
(Whistler, d:G10, JR) [RP]

d. ⟨ʔelé·s ná·ṫuka láykʔam pi⟩

ʔele·-s	na·t'uka	laykʔa-m	pi
NEG-FIN	1SG.ALL	good-SBJV	DIST.SG.SBJ

I am not satisfied with it.
(lit. 'It is not good toward me.')
(Whistler, d:G97, HL) [HP_R]

On nominalized verbs functioning as the heads of subordinate clauses, the allative case can be used to mean 'until'. See section 9.3.2.

4.6.2.6. Ablative Case /-ti,-na·k/ 'from'

The ablative case is used to indicate 'from': nominal expressions representing the origin of an action, or similar roles. There are two formally unrelated ablative suffixes, /-ti/ and /-na·k/.[21] These forms appear to be in a kind of complicated and lexically specified complementary distribution. I therefore analyze them as two allomorphs of the same morpheme, the ablative case suffix.

Forms of the ablative

	-ti	regular
	suna·k	here.ABL
	pina·k	DIST.ABL
	ʔewna·k	PROX.ABL
HP_L	-ti	(only?)
SP	-na*k ~ -da*k	(only)

Distributions of /-ti/ and /-na·k/: In Hill Patwin and River Patwin /-na·k/ occurs only on the distal demonstrative stem *pi* 'that', the proximal locative demonstrative stem *sun* 'here', and the proximal demonstrative stem *ʔew* 'this'. The form *pina·k* 'from there' is attested in Tebti and Rumsey Hill Patwin, as well as River Patwin (e.g., Radin, c:105; Whistler, d:D10,F25). The form *suna·k* 'from here' is attested in Tebti Hill Patwin and River Patwin (e.g., Radin, c:56; Whistler, d:F25; Ultan, d:7.77). The form *ʔewnak* 'from this' is also attested in River Patwin (Merriam:V75.46). On other pronoun stems and on all noun stems, /-ti/ is the marker for the ablative case. (See examples in 60.) In Lodoga Hill Patwin only the /-ti/ variant is attested, even on the distal demonstrative stem *pi* (see 60e). It may be that /-na·k/ is absent from Lodoga entirely, although no ablative forms of the proximal locative pronoun stem *sun* or the proximal demonstrative stem *ʔew* are attested for Lodoga, so this cannot be verified.

In South Patwin only /-na*k/ and /-da*k/ are attested. (The form /-da*k/ results from the /n/~/d/ alternation, which is a characteristic of South Patwin—see section 3.5.7. The length of the vowel is not clear from the South Patwin sources.) These are attested on all nominal stems where the ablative case is attested: pronouns, nouns, and nominalized verbs. For example in (59) the ablative noun *nuyanda*k* 'from the darkness' is marked with /-da*k/, where nouns in Hill and River Patwin would be marked with /-ti/. Ablative /-ti/ is not attested in South Patwin.

(59) ⟨Pal lal wichissut nuyandac.⟩

pal	lal	wičisu-t	nuyan-da*k
and	light	stretch-FIN	darkness-ABL

And he divided the light from the darkness.

(P. Vallejo, c:19.7.6) [SP]

The ablative case is rarely attested on kinship terms but is always the /-ti/ allomorph when it occurs. For example Harry Lorenzo gives Whistler ⟨ʔúytʰapáti⟩ /ʔuy-tʰapa-ti/ 'from his grandfather's place' (Whistler, d:G60, HL).

Functions of the ablative case: The ablative case can function to indicate the literal ablative meaning 'away from', as in *kapayti* 'from the river' in (60a). Another slightly less literal ablative meaning is shown in (60b), where the ablative nominalized verb *tʰono*na*k* 'from dancing' represents an activity that the subject has moved away from. The ablative in (60c) is used to indicate motion 'out of', in the ablative noun *tʰo·biti* 'out of the hole'. The ablative *mayti* 'by the foot' in (60d) indicates the part of the patient's body that is being used to carry out an event.[22] A more metaphorical usage is shown in (60e), where the ablative marks the reason or stimulus for the activity described in the verb: *natti* 'because of me' (lit. 'from me').[23]

(60) a. ⟨pi weré·bus kapájti⟩
pi were·-bus kapay-ti
3SG.SBJ come-FIN river-ABL
He's coming from the creek.
(Whistler, d:A57, OM) [HP_{L}]

b. ⟨Tun-no-nok choo hen´-te⟩ 'I have danced'
tʰono*-na*k ču hen-t°i
dance-ABL 1SG.SBJ arrive-FIN
I am coming from dancing.
(Merriam:V76.63) [SP]

c. ⟨λ̓et tepis tho·biti⟩
ƛ̓et tepi-s tʰo·bi-ti
ground.squirrel emerge-FIN burrow-ABL
The ground squirrel is coming up out of his hole.
(Whistler, d:E71, HL) [HP_{R}]

d. ⟨mayti nat wičí·su⟩
may-ti nat wiči·su
foot-ABL 1SG.OBJ pull.2SG.HORT
Pull me by the foot!
(Whistler, d:F53, HL) [HP_{R}]

e. ⟨nátti pí ṫálabʊs⟩
natti pi t'ala-bus
1SG.ABL 3SG.SBJ fall-FIN
On account of me he fell.
(Ultan, d:4.76, AN) [HP_{L}]

4.6.2.7. *Prolative Case /-na/ 'via'*

The prolative case is invariant in form, always realized as the suffix /-na/. Its basic function is to mark the path of an event. Typical glosses might be 'via', 'along', or 'through'.

The prolative case is used to mark the path of the action, as in *kewena* 'through the house' (61a), or the direction of the action, as in *k^{h}aluna* 'different direction' (61b). It may also mark a static location, as in *wenemna* 'in the middle' in (61c), or the spatial goal of the action, like *k^{h}olčisna* 'into the sack' in (61d).

(61) Spatial uses of prolative case

a. ⟨kewena harʔ⟩

kewe-na har ʔ

house-PROL go.2SG.HORT ||

Go through the house.

(Ultan, d:7.75, SG) [RP]

b. ⟨khálùnàʔ⟩

k^{h}alu-na ʔ

other-PROL ||

different direction

(Bright, c:1.G164, SG) [RP]

c. ⟨[. . .], ʔew ṫusa wenem-na bor-či-ṫi.⟩

[. . .] ʔew t'usa wenem-na borči-t'i

PROX.SG.SBJ pestle middle-PROL break-FUT

[. . .], this pestle will break in the middle.

(Whistler 1977a:159/170, NL/HL) [HP_R]

d. ⟨ṫipa kholčhis-na λ̇op-taro [. . .]⟩

t'ipa k^{h}olčis-na ƛ'op-taro

bread sack-PROL put.in-PART

(He) put acorn bread in a sack [. . .]

(Whistler 1978:54/56, NL/HL) [HP_R]

The prolative can also mark the part of the patient being directly affected by the action. For example in (62a) the prolative *ƛ'ayi·na* 'at the hair knot' is the part of the hair being pierced. This function of the prolative is most often seen marking affected body parts, as in *semna* 'on the hand' in (62b) and *peru·na* 'by the neck' in (62c). In this usage a literal prolative interpretation is possible for some examples (e.g., 'through the hair knot' 62a, 'through the hand' 62b), while in others a literal prolative interpretation is less obvious (62c).

(62) a. ⟨dɔk·o·´ t·i· L'ayi·´na L·iwι´staro⟩

dok'o·	tʰi·	ƛ'ayi·-na	łewis-taro
knife	hair	hair.knot-PROL	pierce-PART

stuck a knife in his hair-knot
(lit. 'knife pierced hair through the hair-knot')
(Radin, c:106/228, AL) [HP_T]

b. ⟨t'ιwí·l nat sémna ʔeyes⟩

t'iwi·l	nat	sem-na	ʔeye-s
rattlesnake	1SG.OBJ	hand-PROL	bite-FIN

The rattlesnake bit me on the hand.
(Whistler, d:F66, HL) [HP_R]

c. ⟨chu nópma k̓ápmaro perú·na⟩

ču	nop-ma	k'ap-ma-ro	peru·-na
1SG.SBJ	deer-OBJ	be.caught-CAUS-PART	throat-PROL

I caught the deer by the neck.
(Whistler, d:B5, OM) [HP_L]

4.7. ABSOLUTIVE SUFFIX

The suffix /-·n/, occurring on kinship terms, is an anomalous suffix. It is called *absolutive* here, following Whistler (1980:201), who calls it the "kin-term absolutive suffix." Formally it is the suffix /-·n/, which conditions length on the preceding segment in certain environments. Functionally, it may be associated with the subjective case. It appears only on subjective case kinship terms and optionally on kinship terms with semantic case suffixes (see section 4.6.2.1).

However, it is an anomalous case suffix in two ways. First it does not appear where a case suffix would be expected to appear. It comes before the relational suffix /-ču/, whereas all other case suffixes come after the relational suffix. Second its pattern of occurrence is highly irregular and subject to a complicated pattern of lexical and grammatical conditioning, as well as dialect variation. The pattern is described in detail in Whistler (1980:201 ff.).

Given the irregular distribution of the suffix and its stem-adjacent position, it may be most felicitous to simply consider this suffix to be a part of the stem of kinship terms, such that lexical entries for kinship terms must simply specify which stem forms end with /-·n/ and which do not.

This "fused /-·n/" analysis is compatible with Whistler's historical reconstruction. Whistler finds that absolutive /-·n/ is old in the Wintuan language family, reconstructing kinship terms with both absolutive and nonabsolutive stems in Proto-Wintuan (e.g., */ʔa·pa-/~*/-apa-n/ 'grandfather', */neh-/~*/-ne·-n/ 'mother'; 1980:263) and Pre-Proto-Wintuan (1980:334). This suggests that while /-·n/ used to be a productive suffix (perhaps related to the Wintu generic aspect suffix—see Shepherd 2005:38), it is now a fossilized part of certain kinship term stems, not a productive element of synchronic Patwin grammar.

4.8. VOCATIVES

Vocatives are nominals used to address the interlocutor. Patwin vocatives may be marked with one of a set of vocative suffixes /-k^he·, -e·, -se·/. There is also a set of special, nonpossessed stems for certain kinship terms that are used as vocatives. Additionally, vocative expressions may be unmarked as such—that is, subjective case nominals can function as vocative expressions. A good discussion of vocative expressions in Patwin can be found in Whistler (1980:216–18), including a comprehensive table of the special vocative kinship stems. Readers interested in individual vocative words should refer to this work. The following sections comment on the grammatical structures used in Patwin vocative expressions.

The vocative suffix: Suffixation is the most formally transparent way of indicating that a nominal is functioning as a vocative. The vocative suffix takes three forms: /-kʰe·, -e·, -se·/. Of these, /-kʰe·/ occurs only on kinship terms. In (63) the kinship stem *ta-* 'father' is marked with the vocative suffix /-kʰe/.[24]

(63) ⟨tákᴇ wɛrʔ⟩

ta-kʰe	wer	ʔ
father-VOC	come.2SG.HORT	‖

Father, come here!
(Ultan, d:4.78, AN) [HP$_{L}$]

Most kinship term stems that can take the vocative suffix take the /-kʰe·/ allomorph, with two exceptions: the stems *nik'a* 'partner, co-spouse' and *p'okse* 'brother's wife' both take the /-se·/ allomorph.[25] Kinship terms marked with the plural suffix /-ba/ also take the /-se·/ allomorph of the vocative suffix, as in *tʰaybase·* 'grandchildren (VOC)' (Whistler 1980:216). Kinship terms marked with the dual suffix /-pel/ take the /-e·/ allomorph of the vocative, as in *te·pele·* 'children (DU.VOC)' (Whistler 1977a:165/168, NL/HL).

Nouns take either the /-se·/ or the /-e·/ allomorph of the vocative suffix. The /-se·/ allomorph occurs after vowels, and the /-e·/ allomorph occurs after consonants (Whistler 1980:217). In (64) the noun *č'uku·y* 'pet' is marked with the vocative suffix /-e·/.

(64) ⟨"sɛla·ˊ'aman hɪma t'e·ˊunɪs· 'i·ˊwɛ," 'ʊm, "namɪntc'uku·ˊye."⟩

"sela·ʔa-ma-n	hima	t'e·w-nis	ʔi·we,"
afraid-CAUS-ADV	always	speak-can	do.2SG.HORT

ʔu-m,	"namin	č'uku·y-e."
say-SBJV	my	pet-VOC

"You are to speak scarily," he said, "my pet."
(Radin, c:38/168, AL) [HP$_{T}$]

Subjective case nominals as vocatives: Nouns and kinship terms in the subjective case (i.e., morphologically unmarked or with the absolutive suffix) can also be used as vocative expressions. In (65), the subjective case noun *č’uku·y* ‘pet’ is used as a vocative expression. Compare (64), where the same noun is marked with the vocative suffix /-e·/ when used in this same function by this same speaker.

(65) ⟨pi·´ropal ’u·´nomɪn tc·ok·u·´ima t’ɛt’ɛpe·´r·mu, ’ɛpa´ɪpi, na·´mɪn tc·oku·´i, sʊna·´k t’e·´wi yaiyo·´tibɔ.”⟩

pi·ropal ʔu·nomin č’uku·y-ma t’et’epir-mu,
then 3SG.POSS$_{\text{AN}}$ pet-OBJ converse-SBJV

“ʔepaypi, na·min č’uku·y,
may.it.be 1SG.POSS$_{\text{AN}}$ pet

suna·k t’e·we yayo·-t’i bo.”
here.ABL speak begin-FUT be.AN

Then he spoke with his pet, “May it be, my pet, that you will begin speaking from here.”
(Radin, c:39/40/169, AL) [HP$_{\text{T}}$]

Some nominals *always* take a subjective case form when used as vocatives. Examples are *tʰay* ‘nephew, grandson’ and *ła·n* ‘younger sibling’, both of which are frequently attested in a vocative function.

Special vocative forms: Some kinship terms also have special, morphologically simplex forms that are used only in the vocative. Example (66) shows two such forms: *tah* ‘father (VOC)’ and *ʔa·p* ‘uncle, grandfather (VOC)’.

(66) a. ⟨tah wɛrʔ.⟩

tah wer ʔ
father.VOC come.2SG.HORT ||

Father, come here!
(Ultan, d:4.78, AN) [HP$_{\text{L}}$]

b. ⟨ʔa·p⟩
ʔa·p
grandfather.voc
Grandfather!
(Ultan, d:7.1a, SG/HH) [RP]

These special forms alternate with forms taking the vocative suffix. Note that the forms *tah* 'father.voc' in (66a) and *takʰe* 'father-voc' in (63) are uttered by the same speaker, and are in fact recorded on the same page of Ultan's notebook.

Taboo avoidance: Directly addressing in-laws and siblings of the opposite sex is traditionally avoided. Vocative forms for these kinship terms are therefore rarely attested. When in-laws and cross-sex siblings are addressed, nonsingular nouns and pronouns in the subjective case are generally used. See sections 4.5 and 5.5.

4.9. ORDER OF MORPHEMES

Case marking comes after number marking. In (67a) the common noun *ʔilay* 'child' is inflected for the plural number and the objective case. In (67b) the kinship term *ne·n* 'mother' is inflected for the dual number and the objective case. Example (67b) is also an example of a kinship term marked with the kinship-relational suffix /-ču/, which always occurs before the number suffix.

(67) a. ⟨ʔɪlayɪnma⟩
ʔilay-in-ma
child-PL-OBJ
children (OBJ) (Ultan, d:6.104, DL) [HP_T]

b. ⟨nɛ´n·tcup'ɛlɛt⟩
ne·nčupelet
ne·n-ču-pel-t
mother-RL-DU-OBJ
my parents (OBJ) (Radin, c:33/164, AL) [HP_T]

In double case marking constructions, the objective case suffix precedes the semantic case suffix or the possessive case suffix. See sections 4.6.2.1 and 4.6.1.3 for examples.

4.10. VERBALIZATION

Verbalization is the process whereby stems that are not inherently verbs are made into verbs. Nominals in Patwin may be verbalized with overt suffixes: /-ho/ derives verbs denoting activities (section 4.10.1), and /-ʔa/ derives verbs denoting states (4.10.2). Verbalization of pronouns is discussed in section 5.4.

4.10.1. Active Verbalizer /-ho/

The active verbalizer suffix /-ho/ 'VBLZ$_A$' turns words from a variety of lexical categories into verbs denoting actions. Some examples are shown in (68). Examples (68a) and (68b) show the suffix /-ho/ deriving the verbs *sasho* 'to look for' and *ha·čeho* 'to chop' from the noun stems *sas* 'eye' and *ha·če* 'axe', respectively.[26] Example (68c) shows the numeral stem *ʔete·* 'one' verbalized with /-ho/ to mean 'gather'. Example (68d) shows the verbalizer /-ho/ on the stem *ʔepaypi*, which is an exclamation used when making a wish or curse. The word *ʔepaypi* can be roughly glossed 'may it be that . . .'; verbalized *ʔepaypiho* means 'to make a curse'. Example (68e) shows the verbalizer /-ho/ on the stem *ʔo·* 'yes, alright', an exclamation indicating agreement.

(68) a. sas-ho·-ro ču
eye-VBLZ$_A$-PART 1SG.SBJ
I looked for (it).
(Swadesh and Melton:35:41, IM) [RP]

b. ha·če-ho-ro
axe-VBLZ$_A$-part
(I) chopped (it).
(Swadesh and Melton:60:21, IM) [RP]

c. ⟨ʔɛte·hɔro⟩
ʔete·-ho-ro
one-VBLZ$_{A}$-PART
gather
(Ultan, d:7.73, SG) [RP]

d. ⟨ʔepáypihos pi⟩
ʔepaypi-ho-s pi
may.it.be-VBLZ$_{A}$-FIN 3SG.SBJ
He made a curse.
(Whistler, d:F48, HL) [HP$_{R}$]

e. ⟨pɪ nat ʔo(·)hos⟩
pi nat ʔo·-ho-s
3SG.SBJ 1SG.OBJ yes-VBLZ$_{A}$-FIN
He agreed with me.
(Whistler, d:G8, JR) [RP]

Formal variation: The verbalizing suffix /-ho/ has a number of allomorphs: /-ho, -ho·, -o, -yo, -so/. Of these, only /-ho, -o/ are strongly attested. /-ho·, -yo, -so/ are attested only on single words. Nevertheless the apparent distribution of all the allomorphs is described below.

After /l/ and /k/ the verbalizing suffix /-ho/ is realized as /-o/. After /y/ it is realized as /-yo/. Whistler (1981:62) describes an additional allomorph /-so/, which is attested only on *tu·so* 'to go first' (< *tu·* 'first'). Elsewhere it is realized as /-ho(·)/. The long allomorph /-ho·/ apparently occurs after stems of the shape CVC (with short vowels), as in *sasho·ro* 'looked for' (see 68a). Elsewhere the vowel is consistently short: /-ho/—even for this same speaker. In some stems the /h/ of the /-ho(·)/ allomorph has coalesced with the preceding consonant to make an aspirated consonant. Example (68) shows several examples of the basic /-ho/ allomorph. Examples of the other allomorphs are shown in (69).

(69) Restricted allomorphs of /-ho/ 'VBLZ$_A$'

a. /-o/ after /l, k/
ʔuselo 'to poison'
(< *ʔusel* 'poison'; Whistler 1981:73) [HP$_L$]

⟨ċóbɒkɒ⟩ *č'oboko* 'beat a drum'
(< *č'obok* 'drum'; Ultan, d:6.103, DL) [HP$_T$]

b. /-yo/ after /y/
sílayyo 'to gather clover'
(< *sílay* 'clover sp.'; Whistler 1977a:159, NL/HL) [HP$_R$]

c. /-so/ after *tu·*
tu·so 'to go first'
(< *tu·* 'first'; Whistler 1981:62) [HP$_R$]

d. /-ho·/ after CVC stem
sasho· 'to look for'
(< *sas* 'eye'; Swadesh and Melton:35:41, IM) [RP]

e. /h/ of /-ho(·)/ coalesces with preceding consonant
yet^{h}o· 'to name'
(< *yet* 'name'; Whistler 1981:53) [HP$_R$]

4.10.2. Stative Verbalizer /- a/

The stative verbalizer /-ʔa/ 'VBLZ$_S$' turns nominals and directional stems into verbs denoting properties, states, or, rarely, actions. The form of the suffix is always /-ʔa/. Example (70) shows three verbs derived with /-ʔa/ reported for Rumsey Hill Patwin in Whistler (1981:70). The first is derived from a noun, the second from a kinship term, and the third from a directional stem.

(70) a. *pakʔa* 'hard' (< *pak* 'bone') [HP$_R$]

b. *ʔonokʔa* 'to have a wife' (< *ʔonok* 'wife') [HP$_R$]

c. *ʔole·lʔa* 'to be way up high' (< *ʔole·l* 'up') [HP$_R$]

The resulting verb may be used as the predicate in a clause, like *sekʔas* 'is green' in (71a). It may also be used as an adjective modifying a noun, as in *sekʔa* 'green' in (71b).

(71) a. ⟨pi tʰɔ·k sɛkʔas⟩
pi tʰo·k sek-ʔa-s
DIST.SG.SBJ tree greenery-VBLZ$_S$-FIN
That tree is green.
(Ultan, d:6.61, DL) [HP$_T$]

b. ⟨sɛ́kka phó·⟩
sek-ʔa pʰo·
greenery-VBLZ$_S$ fire
green light
(Whistler, d:A45, OM) [HP$_L$]

The suffix /-ʔa/ can also be used in a kind of external possessive construction, with the possessor in either objective or subjective case.

(72) a. ⟨čáket yúčinʔas na·t⟩
čaket yučin-ʔa-s na·t
lots enemy-VBLZ$_S$-FIN 1SG.OBJ
I have lots of enemies.
(Whistler, d:G72, HL) [HP$_R$]

b. ⟨ʔelé·s pı k̓ódoyʔamʔú⟩
ʔele·-s pi k'odoy-ʔa-mʔu
NEG-FIN 3SG.SBJ money-VBLZ$_S$-NEG
He has no money.
(Whistler, d:G86, HL) [HP$_R$]

More abstractly, the verbalizer /-ʔa/ can be used to indicate a plurality of referents, as in ⟨thó·ƚʔàròʔ⟩ /tʰo·ƚʔa-ro/ 'mountains' (lit. "having mountain"; Bright, c:1.G145, SG).

4.11. COMPOUND CONSTRUCTIONS

Compound constructions involving nouns are frequent in Patwin, and compounds involving kinship terms, pronouns, and nominalized verbs are also attested.[27] In compound constructions the second root is the head, and the first root modifies the head. Compound constructions are morphologically distinct from possessive constructions, because the modifying noun is morphologically bound to the head in a single derived word and the modifying noun is not marked for the possessive case.

Characters in traditional texts are frequently referred to with noun-noun compounds, where the first element is an animal and the second element is a human noun. Examples of this are shown in (73).

(73) a. ⟨su·l-č̓iyak⟩ /su·l-č'iyak/ 'Old Man Eagle'
(< *su·l* 'eagle' + *č'iyak* 'old man'; Whistler 1977a:166/172, NL/HL) [HP_R]

b. ⟨nó·p ʔèlâypel⟩ /no·p-ʔilay-pel/ 'the two Deer Children'
(< *no·p* 'deer' + *ʔilay* 'child' + /-pel/ 'DU'; Bright, c:1.G160, SG) [RP]

In Hill Patwin, kinship terms may be found in compounds with the directional *ʔol* 'up', denoting what Whistler calls "potential" parents and children (e.g., 1980:110, 113). Potential parents are stepparents and parents' same-sex siblings (i.e., father's brothers and mother's sisters). Potential children are the reciprocal of this: stepchildren, and children of one's same-sex siblings. Thus from Whistler (1980:109): *ʔol-tan* 'stepfather, father's brother' (< *ʔol* 'up' + *tan* 'father') and *ʔol-te·* 'woman's stepchild, woman's sister's child' (< *ʔol* 'up' + *te·* 'woman's child').

A compound of the pronoun *neč'u* 'we (EXCL)' and the noun *win* 'person' is sometimes elicited as a word for 'relatives' in Hill Patwin: ⟨néč̓uwin⟩ (HP_R, Whistler, d:G55, HL); ⟨nèč̓·úwɪn⟩ (HP_L, Bright, c:2.MB12, MB).

Nominalized verbs also appear frequently as the first element in compound constructions with verbs. See section 8.5.

Demonyms: The noun *sel* 'person' is frequently used in Hill Patwin compound words referring to tribes or people living in a certain area. Example

(74) shows *sel* in compounds with a noun (74a), a nominalized verb (74b), a directional (74c), and a cardinal (74d), forming demonyms.

(74) a. ⟨Lol´-sel⟩ /lol-sel/ 'people of Lol'
(< *lo·l* 'tobacco'; Merriam:V71.74) [HP_T]

b. ⟨Tebti-sel⟩ /$t^h ebt^h i$-sel/ 'people of Tebti'
(< $t^h ebt^h i$ 'to flow together'; Kroeber 1932:263)

c. ⟨Chen´sil⟩ /če*n-sel/ 'down people'
(< *če·n* 'down'; Merriam:V71.74) [HP_T]

d. ⟨Poo´-e-sil⟩ /puy-sel/ 'people of the east'
(< *puy* 'east'; Merriam:V71.74) [HP_T]

Demonyms may also be formed with the noun *win* 'person', as in *puy-win* (< *puy* 'east' + *win* 'person'; Whistler 1980:29). The nouns *sel* and *win* may also be attested together in a compound construction: ⟨'Klet´-sil win´⟩ /ƛ'et-sel-win/ 'people of Klet' (< *ƛ'et* 'ground squirrel' + *sel* 'person' + *win* 'person'; Merriam:V72.76).

Toponyms: The noun *di·hi* 'home' is frequently used in Hill Patwin and River Patwin compound words referring to tribes and villages. The names of the three contemporary federally recognized Patwin tribes are all compounds with *di·hi*: Cachil Dehe (< *kačil* 'net fisherman' + *di·hi* 'home'), Klet-sel Dehe (< *ƛ'et* 'ground squirrel' + *sel* 'person' + *di·hi* 'home'), and Yocha Dehe (< *yo·ča* 'spring' + *di·hi* 'home').

FIVE

Pronouns

The Patwin pronoun paradigm is rich in the categories it distinguishes. There are three grammatical persons (first, second, third), three grammatical numbers (singular, dual, plural), and nine cases: three grammatical cases (subjective, objective, possessive) and six semantic cases. Within the third person, personal pronouns are distinct from demonstratives in Hill Patwin and River Patwin. There is a clusivity distinction in the dual and plural (inclusive vs. exclusive), a distal/proximal distinction and an animacy distinction (animate vs. inanimate) in the demonstratives, and possibly a distributive/collective distinction in the second-person nonsingular possessives. For pronouns in the possessive case, there is agreement with the animacy of the possessed head and with the lexical category of the possessed head (noun vs. kinship term vs. nominalized verb). Additionally there is a set of bound possessive pronominals that appear on kinship terms.

Pronouns and demonstratives comprise a natural class of forms in Patwin. They belong to the same inflectional paradigm (i.e., they inflect for number and case in the same way). They also have a similar syntactic distribution. Both personal pronouns and demonstratives may be used either on their own as pronouns or as modifiers of nouns (i.e., determiners).

The Patwin pronoun paradigm is characterized by a high degree of analyticity. Most Patwin pronouns consist of three clearly identifiable elements: (a) the root, which indicates grammatical person and clusivity (and possibly distributiveness), (b) a number suffix, and (c) a case suffix. However, the morphemes bearing these meanings vary in their forms across and within the various dialects of Patwin.

Some details of Patwin pronouns have been published—most notably the description of Hill Patwin kinship possessive pronominals in Whistler's dissertation (1980:205 ff.) and some Hill Patwin and River Patwin pronouns in Shepherd's Proto-Wintuan reconstruction (2005:42 ff.). The full Patwin paradigm has not been previously described.

This chapter begins with a set of tables showing the full pronoun paradigm (section 5.1), and continues with discussions of the morphology and dialect variation observed in this paradigm. Section 5.2 discusses pronoun roots; section 5.3 discusses suffixes. This is followed by discussions of verbalization (section 5.4), in-law address forms (5.5), and doubled subject pronouns (5.6). Paradigms of attested forms for individual dialects can be found in the appendix.

5.1. TABLES OF FORMS

The Patwin pronoun paradigm is shown in tables 5.1–5.6.[1] Following the paradigms are discussions of the morphology and dialect variation found in the pronoun system.

The letters to the right of each form indicate which dialects are associated with it. Due to spatial constraints the dialect abbreviations are different in tables 5.1–5.4 than they are elsewhere in this work, as follows: P for all Patwin dialects; H for Hill Patwin; R for River Patwin; S for South Patwin; H_T for Tebti Hill Patwin, H_R for Rumsey Hill Patwin, and so on; and S_V for Vallejo's South Patwin. Because the kinship possessive pronominals (POSS_K) and the agentive pronouns (POSS_V) are always the same in form, I have collapsed them into one category for these tables, labeled genitive (GEN, see section 5.3.1.3.3 below). Similarly I have collapsed the animate possessive series (POSS_{AN}) together with the free kinship possessive series ($\text{POSS}_{K\text{-}F}$), since these series are identical in the pronouns (see section 4.6.1.3).

Long vowels shown in tables 5.1–5.6 are frequently shortened, both in fast speech and in elicited forms. As function words pronouns are especially susceptible to optional vowel shortening, as described in section 3.5.1.

Table 5.1. Attested first-person pronouns in the grammatical cases

	SBJ		OBJ		POSS$_{IN}$		POSS$_{AN}$		GEN	
1SG	ču·	P	na·-t	H,R	na·-no	H,R	na·-min	H,R	na·-y	H,R
			ču·-t	S	na·-nu	$H_{T,C,R}$,R			ču·-y	S
					ču·-no	S				
					ču·-n	S				
					ču·-do	S				
1DU.INCL	p'e-pel	H,R	p'e-pel(e)-t	H,R	p'e-pele·-no	$H_{T,C,R}$,R	p'e-pele·-no-min	$H_{T,C}$	p'e-pel(e)-y	H,R
			p'e-pe·-t	R	ʔe-pele·-no	H_C			ʔe-pel(e)-y	H_R,R,S
					p'e-pel-no	$H_{L,T}$	p'e-pel-no-min	$H_{L,T}$		
							p'e-pele·-min	H_R,R		
							ʔe-pele·-min	H_R		
1PL.INCL	p'e-le·	P	p'e-le·-t	H,R	p'e-le·-no	H,R	p'e-le·-no-min	H,S	p'e-le·-y	P
							p'e-le·-min	H_T,R		
1DU.EXCL	ne-pel	H,R	ne-pel(e)-t	H,R	ne-pele·-no	H_T,R	ne-pele·-no-min	H_T	ne-pel(e)-y	H,R
			ne-pe·-t	R	ne-pel-no	$H_{L,T,C}$,R	ne-pel-no-min	$H_{L,T}$		
							ne-pele·-min	R		
1PL.EXCL	ne-č'u·	P	ne-č'u·-t	$H_{L,T}$,R	ne-č'u·-no	$H_{L,T}$,R	ne-č'u·-no-min	$H_{L,T}$,S	ne-č'u·-y	H,R
			ne-č'u·-m	S_V	ne-č'u·-nu	S	ne-č'u·-min	H_L,R	(ne-č'u·)	H_T
					te-č'u·-nu	S				
1PL.?	ču*-y	S_V	ču*-y(a)-m	S_V	ču*-y-no	S_V				
			(ču*-m)	S_V						

Table 5.2. Attested second-person pronouns in the grammatical cases

	SBJ		OBJ		$POSS_{IN}$		$POSS_{AN}$		GEN	
2SG	mi·	P	mi·-t	H, S	ma·-to	P	ma·-to-min	P	ma·	P
	(ʔu·)	S_V	mi·-s	R	ma·-to-no	R, S	ma·-to-no-min	S_V	mat	H, S
			(ma-t)	S	ma·-to-k	H_R, R			mi	H_R
					ma·-to-m	S_V				
					ma·-to-n	S_V				
2DU	mi·-pel	P	mi·-pel(e)-t	H, R	mi·-pele·-no	H_T			mi·-pel(e)-y	H
			mi·-pe·-t	R	mi·-pel-no	$H_{L,T,C}$	mi·-pel-no-min	$H_{L,T}$		
							mi·-pele·-min	R		
					ma·-pele·-no	$H_{T,C}$, R	ma·-pele·-no-min	H_T	ma·-pel(e)-y	H, R
					ma·-pel-no	$H_{L,T}$, R	ma·-pel-no-min	H_L		
							ma·-pele·-min	R		
2PL	mi·-le·	P	mi·-le·-t	H, R	mi·-le·-no	H, S	mi·-le·-no-min	$H_{L,T}$, S	mi·-le·-y	$H_{T,C}$
							mi·-le·-min	H_L		
					ma·-le·-no	P	ma·-le·-no-min	$H_{L,T}$	ma·-le·-y	$H_{L,T}$, R
							ma·-le·-min	H_L, R		

Table 5.3. Attested third-person pronouns in the grammatical cases

	SBJ		OBJ		$POSS_{IN}$		$POSS_{AN}$		GEN	
3SG	pi·	P	ʔu·-t	P	ʔu·-no	P	ʔu·-no-min	H, S	ʔu·-y	P
					ʔu·-nu	$H_{L,C}$	ʔu·-nu-min	$H_{T,C}$		
							ʔu·-min	R		
3DU	pi·-pel	P	ʔu·-pel(e)-t	H, R	ʔu·-pele·-no	H_T, R			ʔu·-pel(e)-y	H, R
			ʔu·-pe·-t	R	ʔu·-pel-no	H, R	ʔu·-pel-no-min	$H_{L,T}$		
							ʔu·-pele·-min	R		
3PL	pi·-le·	P	ʔu·-le·-t	H, R	ʔu·-le·-no	H, R	ʔu·-le·-no-min	$H_{L,T}$	ʔu·-le·-y	H, R
					ʔu·-le·-n	H_L	ʔu·-le·-min	H_R, R		
PROX.SG	ʔew	P	ʔe· (IN)	H	ʔewe-no	H_C, R	ʔewe-min	R	ʔew(e)-y	H_R
			ʔe·-s (IN)	R	ʔew(e)-t-no	H_L				
			ʔew(e)-t (AN)	H, R	ʔewe	R				
DIST.SG	pi·	P	pi·-ma (IN)	H, R	pi·-no	H_T	pi·-no-min	H_T	pi	H_T
			pi·-t (AN)	H, R						
			pi·-m	S_V						
PROX.DU	ʔew-pel	H, R	ʔew-pel(e)-t	H_T						
DIST.DU	pi·-pel	P	pi·-pel(e)-t	H_L	pi·-pel-no	H_T	pi·-pel-no-min	H_T	pi·-pel(e)-y	R
							pi·-pele·-min	R		
PROX.PL	ʔew-le·	P	ʔew-le·-t	H_T	ʔew-le·-t-no	H_L			ʔew-le·-y	H_R
DIST.PL	pi·-le·	P	pi·-le·-t	H_L	pi·-le·-no	P	pi·-le·-no-min	H_T, S	pi·-le·-y	H_T, S
			pi·-le·-m	S						

Table 5.4. Attested pronouns in the semantic cases

	COM		INS		LOC		ALL		ABL		PROL	
1SG	na·-da	H,R					na·-t-tuka	$H_{L,R}$	na·-t-ti	H_L		
	na·-t-da	H_T					na·-t-t'uka	H_T				
	na·y-da	H_T					na·-t'uka	H_R				
	ču·-da	S										
1DU												
1PL.INCL							p'e-le·-t'uka	H_R				
1PL.EXCL	ne-č'u·-da	H_L										
1PL?											ču*-y-na-m	S_V
2SG	mi·-da	H					mi·-t-tuka	H_L				
	mi·-s-da	R										
2DU												
2PL												

3SG	ʔu·-da	$H_{L,T}$,R			ʔu·-tin	H_T	ʔu·-tuka	H_L	ʔu·-t-ti	H_L		
	ʔu·-t-da	R					ʔu·-t-t'uka	H_T				
3DU	ʔu·-pel-da	H_L,R			ʔu·-pele·-tin	H_T						
3PL	ʔu·-le·-da	H_T,R										
PROX.SG			ʔew-sin (IN)	H	ʔew-ła	P	ʔew-tuka	H_L	ʔew-nak	R,S	ʔew-na	$H_{L,T}$
			ʔew-ma-tin (AN)	R								
DIST.SG	pi·-da	R	pi·-sin	H	pi·-ła	P	pi·-tuka	$H_{L,T}$	pi·-nak	P	pi·-na	H,R
							pi·-t-tuka	H_T	pi·-ti	H_L		
							pi·-t'uka	H_T				
PROX.DU												
DIST.DU	pi·-pel-da	H_L										
PROX.PL	ʔew-le·-da	H_T										
DIST.PL												

Table 5.5. Personal and impersonal indefinite pronouns in the grammatical cases

	SBJ	OBJ	POSS_{IN}	POSS_{AN}	POSS_{V}
Personal	po·	po·-t	po·-no	po*-no-min (HP)	po·-y (HP)
Impersonal	pe· (HP&SP)	pe· (HP&SP)	pe·-no		
	pe·s (RP)	pe·s (RP)			
		pe·-ma (HP var.)			

Table 5.6. Other attested indefinite pronouns

- pe·- (impersonal)
  - pe·yła 'when' (LOC, HP&RP)
  - pe·sin 'with what' (INS)
  - pe·na 'where' (PROL)
- he·- (locational)
  - he·ła 'where' (LOC)
  - he·tuka 'to where' (ALL)
  - he·t'uka 'to where' (ALL, HP_T)
  - he·ti 'from where' (ABL, HP)
  - he·nak 'from where' (ABL, SP)
  - he·na 'where' (PROL)
- heke- 'which' (HP&RP)
  - heke 'which'
  - heketta 'which' (RP)
  - hekeła 'where' (LOC)
  - heketi 'from where' (ABL)
- heče- 'which' (SP_V)
  - heče 'which, how' (?)
- heka- 'where' (HP&RP)
  - heka 'where' (static)
  - hekapel 'which' (DU?)
- hečew- ? (SP_V)
  - hečew 'where'
  - hečewła 'when' (?)

5.2. ROOTS

The root is the first element in each pronoun, followed by a number suffix (which is null in the singular) and then a case suffix (which is null in the subjective case). The root of the pronoun indicates its grammatical person (first, second, or third person). For nonsingular pronouns in the first person, the root also indicates clusivity: inclusive pronouns refer to a set of people including both the speaker and the hearer; exclusive pronouns refer to a set of people including the speaker but not the hearer. In the third person the root differentiates personal pronouns ('she', 'them', etc.) from demonstratives ('that', 'these', etc.) and indefinites ('who', 'something', etc.). Each category of root is discussed individually in the following sections.

Allomorphs of 1SG	
na·-	HP, RP
ču·-	SP
Suppletive form (HP, RP)	
ču·	'1SG.SBJ'

5.2.1. First-Person Singular Root /na·-, ču·-/ '1SG'

Attested forms of first-person singular pronouns are shown in the first rows of tables 5.1 and 5.4. In Hill Patwin and River Patwin the allomorph of the first-person singular root with the widest distribution is /na·-/. This is the form of the root of all first-person singular pronouns except in the subjective case, where the suppletive pronoun *ču·* is found instead. In South Patwin the allomorph /na·-/ is entirely absent. The form /ču·-/ is the only form of the first-person singular root in South Patwin, and occurs in all cases. It may also be the root of the first-person plural series with the stem /ču*y-/, attested in Vallejo's South Patwin (see section 5.2.4).

Shepherd reconstructs Proto-Wintuan first-person pronoun root */ne-/, saying that the vowel change to Patwin /na·-/ arose by analogy with second-person /ma·-/ (2005:56).

5.2.2. Inclusive Root /p e-/ '1INCL'

The inclusive root /p'e-/ has two variants: /p'e-/ and /ʔe-/. The /p'e-/ variant is by far more commonly attested. The /ʔe-/ variant is attested only in the dual, in *ʔepeleno* '1DU.INCL.POSS$_{IN}$' (HP$_{C}$), *ʔepelemin* '1DU.INCL.POSS$_{AN}$' (HP$_{R}$), and *ʔepeley* '1DU.INCL.POSS$_{K}$' (HP$_{R}$, RP, SP). All of these forms also have corresponding /p'e-/ forms attested in the same dialect, except in South Patwin. It is possible that /ʔe-/ is the only inclusive root in South Patwin, since glottalized consonants debuccalizing to glottal stops is a common sound change found in South Patwin (Shepherd 2005:19). However, with only one inclusive pronoun attested in South Patwin, its form cannot be identified with certainty.

Shepherd reconstructs */p'e-/ as the Proto-Wintuan inclusive root (2005:56).

5.2.3. Exclusive Root /ne-/ '1EXCL'

The exclusive root is always /ne-/. Shepherd reconstructs the first-person root in Proto-Wintuan as */ne-/, giving rise to both the Patwin exclusive root /ne-/ and the Patwin first-person singular root /na·-/ (2005:56).

5.2.4. First-Person Plural in Vallejo's South Patwin /ču*(y)-/ '1PL'

A series of pronouns in Vallejo's South Patwin material (SP$_{V}$) has a stem like /ču*y-/ or /ču*-/ and is glossed as a first-person plural series. This series is shown at the bottom of table 5.1 and in the pronoun *ču*ynam* in table 5.4. It is probable that the root of these pronouns is first-person /ču·-/ and that the /-y/ is acting as a pluralizer. The first-person series with the stem /ču*y-/ exists alongside the exclusive series with the stem /neč'u·-/ in SP$_{V}$. No clear instances of the inclusive series with /p'e-, ʔe-/ is attested in SP$_{V}$, though this series is attested in Merriam's SP. The /ču*y-/ stem is not attested with an inclusive meaning in SP$_{V}$.

Allomorphs of second person

mi·-	SBJ, OBJ, semantic
ma·-	SG.POSS
mi·- ~ ma·-	NSG.POSS

5.2.5. Second-Person Roots /mi·-, ma·-/

The second-person pronouns are shown in tables 5.2 and 5.4. The two forms of the second-person root are /mi·-/ and /ma·-/. For some pronouns the distribution of these two forms is grammatically conditioned. In the subjective case the root is always /mi·-/ (except for a few mentions of a suppletive form *ʔu** '2SG.SBJ' in Vallejo's SP, which may be errors). In the objective case the root is almost always /mi·-/.[2] The semantic cases (COM, ALL, ABL) also always have /mi·-/ as the root. In singular possessive pronouns the second-person root is always /ma·-/ (except in one attested instance of the unexpected pronoun *mi* '2SG.POSS$_V$', from Rumsey Hill Patwin speaker Harry Lorenzo).

In the nonsingular possessive pronouns the roots /mi·-/ and /ma·-/ are both attested, and appear to have different meanings. However, the nature of the semantic distinction is not clear.

Ultan pursues an analysis where the distinction between /ma·-/ and /mi·-/ in nonsingular possessive pronouns is one of distributiveness: in his field notebooks, working with Lodoga Hill Patwin speaker Amelia Nunes and Tebti Hill Patwin speaker Daisy Lorenzo, second-person nonsingular possessive pronouns with the /mi·-/ root are sometimes accompanied by a note indicating that they carry the meaning of "each" (i.e., distributive). For example Ultan elicited the following near-minimal pair from Daisy Lorenzo:

(75) Distinction between /ma·-/ and /mi·-/ roots

a. ⟨mapɛlnɑ nʊn ʔɪs pi⟩

mapelno	nun	ʔi-s	pi
2DU.POSS$_{IN}$	gun	COP-FIN	DIST.SG.SBJ

That's your (DU) gun.

(Ultan, d:6.117, DL) [HP$_T$]

b. ⟨mɪpɛlnɑ nʊ ʔɪs ʔew⟩

mipelno	nu[n?]	ʔi-s	ʔew
2DU.POSS$_{IN}$	gun	COP-FIN	PROX.SG.SBJ

These are your guns (two boys and two guns).

(Ultan, d:6.117, DL) [HP$_T$]

Working with Lodoga Hill Patwin speaker Oscar McDaniel, however, Ultan notes that the /ma·/-rooted *mapelnomin* '2DU.POSS$_{AN}$' is distributive in meaning and carries the meaning of "each," a notation that Ultan accompanies with a question mark (Ultan, d:1.105, OM). Even Ultan's notes from Daisy Lorenzo, immediately following the minimal pair shown above, show that the meaning distinction between /mi·-/ and /ma·-/ roots is not clear: Ms. Lorenzo calls *mapelno* and *mipelno* (2DU.POSS$_{IN}$) the "same thing," likewise for *maleno* and *mileno* (2PL.POSS$_{IN}$; Ultan, d:6.117, DL). Further Hill Patwin examples (76)–(78) show how tenuous the connection between the second-person root and distributiveness is.

(76) Distributive pronouns with /ma·-/

a. ⟨mapʰɛlnɔ yɛt⟩ /mapelno yet/ 'your (DU) names'
(Ultan, d:1.82, OM)

b. ⟨mālé·nɔ̀ yɛ̀t⟩ /male·no yet/ 'your (PL) names'
(Ultan, d:1.84, OM)

(77) Distributive pronouns with /mi·-/

a. ⟨mɪpɛlnomɪn ɷnɷk⟩ /mipelnomin ʔonok/ 'your (DU) wives'
(Ultan, d:1.96, OM)

b. ⟨mɪpɛlnomɪn łân⟩ /mipelnomin łan/
'your (2) brothers' ("each have brother")
(Ultan, d:1.116, OM)

(78) Non-distributive pronoun with /ma·-/
⟨mapelɛne·´tɪn⟩
/mapele[y]ne·tin/ 'your (DU) mother (SG)'
(Radin, c:27/159, AL)

Harry Lorenzo offers Whistler another explanation, explaining that *mile·no* '2PL.POSS$_{IN}$' is used only when referring to an in-law of the opposite sex, whereas *male·no* is the "ordinary word" for second-person plural inanimate possessives (Whistler, d:F76).[3] This may be the case for Mr. Lorenzo or for his dialect (Rumsey Hill Patwin, which does not have a great number of second-person nonsingular possessive pronouns attested), but it is very unlikely that this is the case in all of Patwin. If *mile·no* and /mi·-/ roots in general are used only for addressing in-laws, we would not expect to see them attested so widely in the archival record, nor to be always glossed simply 'your'.

Thus it seems likely that there is some meaningful distinction between the /mi·-/ and /ma·-/ roots for second-person nonsingular possessives, but it is not clear what this distinction is.

Shepherd reconstructs both */mi-/ and */ma-/ as second-person roots in Proto-Wintuan, with a similar pattern of variation to that described here for Patwin /mi·-/ and /ma·-/ (2005:56).

5.2.6. Third-Person Personal Pronouns / u·-, pi·-/

Tables 5.3 and 5.4 show a series of personal pronouns (glossed with '3') distinct from series of proximate and distal demonstratives ('PROX', 'DIST'). Though the distinction between third-person personal pronouns and demonstratives has not been previously described for Patwin, there is ample evidence to show that the personal pronouns are distinct in Hill Patwin and River Patwin. Third-person personal pronouns are difficult to discern since they are formally similar to demonstratives—in fact they are identical to distal demonstratives in the subjective case. However, there is a strong pattern of usage that shows a functionally distinct set of third-person personal pronouns.

3rd-person personal roots	
ʔu·-	regular form
pi·-	SBJ

Third-person subject pronouns glossed in English as personal pronouns invariably have the root /pi·-/ (identical with the distal demonstrative series), never /ʔew-/ (PROX). For nonsubject third-person pronouns glossed in English as personal pronouns, the root is almost invariably /ʔu·-/ (a special form used only for third-person personal pronouns), not /pi·-/ (DIST) nor /ʔew-/ (PROX). On the other hand pronouns with the root /ʔew-/ are only very rarely glossed with a personal pronoun, and the same is true of nonsubject pronouns with the root /pi·-/. Thus of the three roots /ʔu·-, ʔew-, pi·-/, we can make the following statements for Hill Patwin and River Patwin:

(79) a. /ʔu·-/ is used only for personal pronouns

b. /ʔew-/ is used only as a proximal demonstrative

c. /pi·-/ is shared between two series:

i. In the subjective case, /pi·-/ is used both as a personal pronoun and as a distal demonstrative

ii. In nonsubject cases, /pi·-/ is used only as a distal demonstrative

The distinction between personal pronouns and demonstratives extends also to the semantic cases. Table 5.7 shows that third-person semantic case pronouns with personal reference use the third-person personal pronoun root /ʔu·-/, as in *ʔu·tt'uka* 'toward him' and *ʔutti* 'from him'. Third-person semantic case pronouns with impersonal deictic reference on the other hand use the demonstrative roots /ʔew-/ 'PROX', /pi·-/ 'DIST', or *sun* 'here'.

Note that the distinction between third-person personal pronouns and demonstratives is not merely an animacy distinction, as the proximal and distal demonstratives reflect animacy distinctions separately. See section 5.3.3.

The existence of third-person personal pronouns would be more obvious if there were systematic syntactic or morphological differences between personal pronouns and demonstratives. However, demonstratives in Patwin inflect in the same way as personal pronouns. From a morphological perspective both demonstratives and personal pronouns inflect for almost the same set of cases using the same set of suffixes.[4] From a syntactic perspective both personal pronouns and demonstratives can be used either on their own as referring expressions or as modifiers of nouns (determiners). Therefore the strongest evidence that can be expected to differentiate personal pronouns from demonstratives in the third person is the kind of pattern of usage that we do see here: one series (personal pronouns) used for personal reference and other series (demonstratives) used for impersonal deictic functions.

Table 5.7. Third-person personal pronouns and demonstratives in the semantic cases

	Form	Gloss	Source
ALL	ʔu·tt'uka	'toward him'	(Radin, c:54/103, AL)
	ʔewtuka	'this way'	(Whistler, d:A22, OM)
	pituka	'there, that way, toward that'	(Whistler, d:A57, OM)
	sunt'uka	'[toward] here'	(Radin, c:24/97, AL)
ABL	ʔutti	'from him'	(Whistler, d:B73, OM)
	piti	'because of that'	(Whistler, d:B52, OM)

In South Patwin there is no strong evidence for the existence of third-person personal pronouns as a class distinct from demonstratives. Both the distal and proximal forms are attested for subjective case personal reference, for example ⟨eule⟩ /ʔewle*/ 'these, they' (P. Vallejo, c:24.11); ⟨Ā´-oo⟩ /ʔew/ 'He (him, she, or her)' (Merriam:V76.56); ⟨eú⟩ /ʔew/ 'he, she, it' (P. Vallejo, c:21.8). Moreover, the distal series with the root /pi·-/ is used for third-person personal possessive pronouns in Vallejo's South Patwin materials. These forms do not occur sparsely as in Hill Patwin and River Patwin, but are used exclusively, with no attestation of plural possessive pronouns having the expected personal root /ʔu·/. Thus although there are *formal* analogs of the Hill Patwin and River Patwin third-person personal pronouns (i.e., pronouns with the root /ʔu·-/) and demonstrative pronouns (i.e., pronouns with the roots /ʔew-, pi-/), there is no semantic evidence in South Patwin for a distinction between personal pronouns and demonstratives in the third person.

A noteworthy form in the South Patwin archive is found in Curtin's untranslated conjugation of the verb *ba·* 'to eat' in his 1884 wordlist (Curtin, b). Here the phrase ⟨upılka babot⟩ occurs, which may be the only instance in the entire Patwin archive of a subjective case pronoun with the root /ʔu·-/. The source provides no information besides the Patwin form in a rough and phonetically unreliable orthography, but if this is indeed a subjective case pronoun with the root /ʔu·-/, it is significant enough to mention here. A tentative gloss is given in (80).

(80) ⟨upılka babot⟩

ʔu-pel-k°a ba⁎-bot

3?-DU.SBJ-*k°a* eat-CERT?

They two are eating.

(Curtin, b:228) [SP]

It may also be that ⟨upıl⟩ in (80) represents the dual proximal demonstrative pronoun *ʔewpel*.

5.2.7. Demonstrative Roots

The two basic demonstrative roots are proximal /ʔew-/ 'PROX' and distal /pi·-/ 'DIST', as shown in tables 5.3 and 5.4. These two roots are discussed in sections 5.2.7.1 and 5.2.7.2. Section 5.2.7.3 describes the additional locative demonstrative *sun* 'here'.

Proximal roots (HP & RP)

ʔew-	regular
ʔe·-	IN (SG.OBJ only)

5.2.7.1. Proximal Roots /ʔew-, ʔe·-/ 'PROX'

In Hill Patwin and River Patwin proximal demonstrative roots take in two forms: /ʔew-/ and /ʔe·-/.

The form /ʔe·-/ has a restricted distribution, occurring only in the singular inanimate objective forms *ʔe·* 'PROX.SG.OBJ.IN' (HP) and *ʔe·s* 'PROX.SG.OBJ.IN' (RP). The corresponding animate form in both Hill Patwin and River Patwin is *ʔewet* 'PROX.SG.OBJ.AN', with the regular root /ʔew-/. This animacy contrast can be seen in examples (89) and (90). Since the root /ʔe·-/ occurs only in this function, and since it is in semantic contrast in this environment with the root /ʔew-/, these two forms must be considered distinct morphemes. However, this animacy distinction is not realized outside of the objective singular, and the root /ʔe·-/ is not found outside of this environment. The inanimate root /ʔe·-/ is not attested in South Patwin, but this may be an issue of data sparsity.

Shepherd reconstructs the proximal root in Proto-Wintuan as */ʔe-/ or */ʔew-/ (2005:56).

5.2.7.2. *Distal Root /pi·-/* 'DIST'

The distal demonstrative root is always /pi·-/. In the subjective case the distal demonstratives are not formally distinct from the third-person personal pronouns. Shepherd reconstructs the Proto-Wintuan distal root with two allomorphs: */pi-/ (in the subjective case) and */pu-/ (in other cases; 2005:56).

5.2.7.3. *Proximal Locative* sun *'here'*

Another demonstrative is proximal locative *sun* 'here', robustly attested in all dialects. Examples are shown in (81).

(81) a. ⟨pi sún bó·mɛlɛ́s⟩

pi	sun	bo·-mele-s
3SG.SBJ	here	be.AN-NEG-FIN

He's not living here.

(Whistler, d:A76, OM) [HP_L]

b.

sun	ču	di·hu-ro
here	1SG.SBJ	dwell-PART

I live here.

(Swadesh and Melton:42:57, IM) [RP]

c. ⟨Mattom yulé wereto sun.⟩

matom	yule	were-t'o	sun
$2SG.POSS_{IN}$	kingdom?	come-INCEP	here

[May] your kingdom come here.

(P. Vallejo, i) [SP]

The difference in meaning between *sun* 'here' and *ʔewła* 'PROX.LOC' is not clear.

Sun can be inflected for specific locative cases, like the prolative, allative, and ablative forms in (82). *Sun* is not attested with overt marking for the locative case (/-ła, -tin/).

(82) a. ⟨píleʔ ṣúnaʔ wɛré·buṣ⟩

pile suna were·bus
pile sun-na were·-bus
3PL.SBJ here-PROL come-FIN
They're coming back this way.
(Whistler, d:A7, OM) [HP$_L$]

b. ⟨cʊ´nt'uka we·r'⟩

sun-t'uka wer ?
here-ALL come ||
Come here!
(Radin, c:24, AL) [HP$_T$]

c. ⟨sunak ʔu·t hariʔ⟩

sun-nak ʔu·t hari ?
here-ABL 3SG.OBJ take.AN ||
Take him away from here!
(Ultan, d:7.77, SG) [RP]

In South Patwin a possessive pronoun *suno* is attested, possibly an inflection of this same proximal locative root.

(83) ⟨Súno onoc⟩

sun-no ʔonok
here-POSS wife
his wife
(P. Vallejo, c:25.11) [SP]

5.2.8. Indefinite Roots

Indefinite pronouns are used for any indefinite reference. In a noninterrogative context, they are used to refer indefinitely to some referent: 'someone', 'something', 'somewhere', 'anyone', 'anything', and so on. In an interrogative context the same pronouns can be used as question words: 'who', 'what', 'where', and so on. In a negative context the same pronouns can be used to mean 'no one', 'nobody', and so on. Example (84) shows the personal indefinite pronoun *po* 'who' used in interrogative (84a), positive declarative (84b), and negative declarative (84c) contexts.

(84) a. ⟨po wérebo?⟩
po were-bo ?
who.SBJ come-Q ||
Who is coming?
(Bright, c:1.G137, SG) [RP]

b. ⟨po wéttacey⟩
po wetta če·
po wer-ta čeh-s
who.SBJ come AUX-FIN
Someone is coming.
(Bright, c:1.G137, SG) [RP]

c. ⟨ʔele·-s po hen-muʔu.⟩
ʔele·-s po hen-muʔu
NEG-FIN who.SBJ arrive-NEG
No one is here.
(Whistler 1977a:168/172, NL/HL) [HP$_R$]

Table 5.5 shows the indefinite pronouns attested in the grammatical cases (SBJ, OBJ, POSS) in every dialect. There are two indefinite pronoun roots attested in the grammatical cases: personal /po·-/ 'who, someone' and impersonal /pe·-/ 'what, something'. The examples in (85) show indefinite pronouns in the subjective, objective, and possessive cases.

(85) a. ⟨ná·no perú·ła pé· bé·s⟩
na·no peru·-ła pe· be·-s
1SG.POSS$_{IN}$ throat-LOC what.SBJ be.IN-FIN
Something is in my throat.
(Whistler, d:A41, OM) [HP$_L$]

b. ⟨pe· pipel du·ni harasay⟩

pe·	pipel	du·ni	harasay
pe·	pipel	duh-ni	hara-say
what.OBJ	3DU.SBJ	carry-ADV	go-Q

What are they carrying?

(Whistler, d:E39, HL) [HP$_R$]

c. ⟨ʔéw pa pó·no⟩

ʔew	pa	po·no
PROX.SG.SBJ	Q	who.POSS$_{IN}$

Whose is this?

(Whistler, d:F26, JR) [RP]

Indefinite pronouns outside of the grammatical cases are shown in table 5.6, grouped by root. The examples in (86) show these pronouns in interrogative contexts. The impersonal root /pe·-/ is attested in the locative and instrumental cases: *pe·yła* 'when' (86a) and *pe·sin* 'with what' (86b). Note that locative case *pe·yła* means 'when' rather than 'where'.[5] The meaning 'where' is most commonly expressed by *he·ła*, a locative case pronoun with the root /he·-/ (86c). The root /he·-/ is also attested in all of the other locational cases: allative *he·t(')uka* 'to where' (86d), ablative *he·ti* and *he·nak* 'from where' (86e), and prolative *he·na* 'along where' (86f). The stems /heke-/ (HP, RP) and /heče-/ (SP) mean 'which' in their bare forms (86g). The locative case *hekeła* 'where' is also attested in both Hill Patwin and River Patwin (86h), the ablative case *heketi* 'from where' in Hill Patwin (86i). The River Patwin form *heketta* 'which' has an unknown suffix (86j). The pronoun *heka* 'where' is attested in both Hill Patwin and River Patwin (86k).

(86) a.

pe·yła	pa	p'ele	hara·-t'i
when	Q	1PL.INCL.SBJ	go-FUT

When will we go?

(Swadesh and Melton:2:52, IM) [RP]

b. ⟨ʔút pé·sin mi théptej⟩

ʔut	<u>pe·-sin</u>	mi	t^hep-te·
3SG.OBJ	<u>what-INS</u>	2SG.SBJ	hit-Q.PAST

<u>What</u> did you hit him <u>with</u>?

(Whistler, d:B10, OM) [HP_L]

c. ⟨Héthla mi canamta?⟩

<u>he*-ła</u>	mi	k'ana-mt°a
<u>where-LOC</u>	2SG.SBJ	sleep-PAST.Q

<u>Where</u> did you sleep?

(P. Vallejo, c:23.3) [SP]

d. ⟨mi hará·ṫisaj hétuka⟩

mi	hara·-t'i-say	<u>he-tuka</u>
2SG.SBJ	go-FUT-Q	<u>where-ALL</u>

<u>Where</u> are you going to travel?

(Whistler, d:A95, OM) [HP_L]

e. ⟨Hā´-te me hen´-tah⟩

<u>he·-ti</u>	mi	hen-ta
<u>where-ABL</u>	2SG.SBJ	arrive-Q.PAST

<u>Where</u> did you come <u>from</u>?

(Merriam:V73.71) [HP_R]

f. ⟨hé·na pi k'ʌpayłaʔ t'állmoʔ⟩

<u>he·-na</u>	pi	kapay-ła	ʔ
<u>where-PROL</u>	3SG.SBJ	river-LOC	‖

t'al-mu	ʔ
fall-SBJV	‖

<u>Whereabouts</u> did he fall in the river?

(Bright, c:1.G135, SG) [RP]

g. ⟨Hek´-kĕ-is-si mah-tah-min choo´-choo⟩
heke ʔi-say matomin ču*ču
which COP-Q 2SG.POSS$_{AN}$ dog
Which is your dog?
(Merriam:V70.71) [HP$_L$]

h. ⟨hékeła bo·bo pi⟩
hekeła bo·bo pi
heke-ła boh-bo pi
which-LOC be.AN-Q 3SG.SBJ
Where is he?
(Whistler, d:F26, JR) [RP]

i. ⟨Hek-ket-te me hen´-ne-si⟩
heke-ti mi hene-say
which-ABL 2SG.SBJ arrive-Q
Where did you come from?
(Merriam:V70.71) [HP$_L$]

j. ⟨hɛkɛtta⟩ /heketta/ ‘which one?’
(Ultan, d:7.19, SG/HG) [RP]

k. ⟨l·e´niLa ka´ktc’iak, “hɛka ’ɪla´i”ʊm?”⟩
le·ni-ła kak-č’iyak, “heka ʔilay?” ʔu-m
evening-LOC raven-old.man where child say-SBJV
In the evening Old Man Raven said, “Where is the child?”
(Radin, c:28/160, AL) [HP$_T$]

The roots /he·-, heke-, heka-, heče-, hečew-/ are all related historically and cognate with the Wintu interrogative roots /hE-, hek(e)-/.[6] Wintu /hE-/ and Patwin /he·-/ are directly cognate, as are Wintu /hek(e)-/ and Patwin /heke-/. South Patwin /heče-/ is derived from */heke-/, the /k/ having fronted to /č/ (a common historical sound change in Patwin—see Shepherd 2005). South Patwin /hečew-/ is probably derived from South Patwin /heče-/, though the source of the /w/ is unknown.

The Patwin impersonal indefinite root /pe·-/ 'something' is cognate with the Wintu impersonal indefinite root /pe·-/ 'something', although this is not mentioned in Shepherd (2005). See Pitkin (1985:412) for some Wintu indefinite pronouns with this root. The Patwin personal indefinite root /po·-/ 'someone' does not have a formal analog in Wintu. This is a Patwin innovation, possibly related to the animacy distinction in the auxiliary verbs *be·*/*bo·* (although the distinction between /pe·-/ and /po·-/ is not exactly one of grammatical animacy).

5.3. SUFFIXES

Suffixes on pronouns mark case and number, as described in sections 5.3.1 and 5.3.2. In demonstratives, case suffixes reflect animacy distinctions in the objective and instrumental cases, as described in section 5.3.3. A South Patwin suffix /-k°a/ of uncertain function is discussed in section 5.3.4.

5.3.1. Case Suffixes

Case is regularly indicated by suffixation. The case suffix is the final suffix, following the root and the number suffix.

5.3.1.1. *Subjective Case*

The subjective case is regularly unmarked in pronouns, as it is in other nominals (see section 4.6.1.1). Note that in tables 5.1–5.3 the subjective case forms (in the first column) have no case suffix (although the nonsingular forms are marked with dual or plural number suffixes).[7] Shepherd reconstructs the subjective case in Proto-Wintuan as unmarked as well (2005:58).

Another notable regularity of the subjective case pronouns is that they are rarely attested ending with long vowels, even in cases where the final vowel is optionally long. For example *ču·* '1SG.SBJ' and *p'ele·* '1PL.INCL.SBJ' are most frequently attested as [ču] and [p'ele]. It may be that subject pronouns, being the most frequently uttered, are especially subject to the general pattern of vowel length contraction described in section 3.5.1.

Allomorphs of OBJ	
-t	regular
-s	RP *mis, ʔe·s*
-ma	*pi·ma, pe·ma*
-m	SP_V

Suppletive form	
ʔe·	'PROX.SG.OBJ.IN' (HP)

5.3.1.2. Objective Case

The objective case suffix has the allomorphs /-t, -s, -ma, -m/. The /-t/ allomorph is the most common in pronouns, attested in every dialect, every number, and every person, on personal pronouns, demonstratives, and indefinite pronouns.[8] It is also the regular form of the object marker on kinship terms (Whistler 1980:229). Shepherd reconstructs */-t/ as the objective case marker for most pronouns in Proto-Wintuan (2005:58). The other allomorphs have more restricted distributions within the Patwin pronoun paradigm and are described below.

The /-s/ allomorph of the objective case occurs only in River Patwin, on the second-person singular pronoun *mis* 'you' and on the the proximal singular inanimate demonstrative *ʔe·s* 'this'. *Mis* is a conservative form in River Patwin, appearing also in Wintu and Nomlaki, and reconstructed for Proto-Wintuan (Shepherd 2005:58). Hill Patwin and South Patwin have replaced the */-s/ marking with the regular pronoun objective suffix /-t/ in the corresponding pronoun *mi·t*.

In the pronouns the /-ma/ allomorph is attested only on the distal demonstrative *pi·ma* 'DIST.SG.OBJ.IN' (HP and RP) and on the indefinite pronoun *pe·ma* 'what.OBJ' (HP). On animate nouns /-ma/ is the regular object marker in Hill Patwin and River Patwin, and is attested in South Patwin as well. Shepherd reconstructs */-ma/ as an objective case marker in Proto-Wintuan, related to the Northern Wintuan objective case suffixes /-m, -um/, but does not reconstruct any Proto-Wintuan pronouns with /-ma/ (2005:124).

The /-m/ allomorph is attested only in Vallejo's South Patwin materials. The South Patwin objective pronouns gathered by Merriam have only the /-t/ allomorph. There may be a dialect difference at play here: Vallejo specifically records the Suisun dialect, and it is not known what dialect Merriam records.[9] It is interesting also to note the formal similarity between South Patwin objective-case /-m/ and the Northern Wintuan objective case marker /-m, -um/. This suggests that */-m/ is a better reconstruction of the Proto-Wintuan objective suffix than Shepherd's */-ma/, and that /-ma/ 'OBJ' may be an innovation in (northern) Patwin.

The demonstrative *ʔe·* 'PROX.SG.OBJ.IN' is a suppletive form occurring only in Hill Patwin. The corresponding River Patwin form is *ʔe·s*, marked with the /-s/ allomorph of the objective case. See section 5.3.3 for a discussion of the significance of these pronouns in terms of grammatical animacy. The impersonal indefinite pronouns *pe·* (Hill Patwin and South Patwin) and *pe·s* (River Patwin) do not differentiate subjective from objective case.

Two of the allomorphs of the objective case suffix /-t/ and /-ma/, usually in complementary distribution, are contrastive in the distal singular demonstratives. *Pi·ma* is used for grammatically inanimate referents, and *pi·t* for grammatically animate referents. See section 5.3.3 for further discussion.

5.3.1.3. Possessive Case

The possessive case suffix on pronouns varies in form depending on the grammatical animacy and lexical category of the possessed nominal. Section 5.3.1.3.1 describes the morphology of the possessive case suffix when the possessed nominal is an inanimate noun (POSS_{IN}); section 5.3.1.3.2 describes the morphology of the possessive case suffix when the possessed nominal is an animate noun (POSS_{AN}); and section 5.3.1.3.3 describes the morphology of "genitive" forms—that is, agentive pronouns and possessive pronominals on kinship terms. For a discussion of the possessive case and agreement with possessed nominals in general, see section 4.6.1.3.

Primary allomorphs of POSS$_{IN}$	
-no	regular
-to	2SG
Other variants	
-nu	
-n	
-do	(SP only)
-tok	(2SG, in HP$_R$ & RP only)
-to-no	(2SG, in RP & SP only)
-tom	(2SG, in SP only)

5.3.1.3.1. Inanimate Possessives

Inanimate possessive pronouns (POSS$_{IN}$) are pronouns in the possessive case, used when the possessed nominal is a grammatically inanimate noun. The inanimate possessive suffix varies quite a bit in its attested forms, but the two most well attested allomorphs are /-no/ and /-to/. The basic pattern is that /-to/ occurs in the second-person singular (*ma·to*) in every dialect, and /-no/ occurs elsewhere. The suffix /-no/ is thus the regular form. Outside of the pronoun system it is also the form that marks nouns and some kinship terms as possessors of inanimate nouns. The form **mano* is never attested, nor does the allomorph /-to/ occur outside of the second-person singular. Shepherd reconstructs roughly this same pattern of allomorphy for Proto-Wintuan: */-to/ for 2SG (and maybe 1SG) and */-no/ elsewhere (2005:59–60).

Other forms are attested scattered throughout various dialects; these will be discussed briefly below. They are never the only forms attested for any given environment, but are always in seemingly free variation with one of the more common forms /-no, -to/.

The most widespread of these alternate forms is /-nu/, attested at least once in every dialect. For example the form *na·nu* '1SG.POSS$_{IN}$' is attested in Tebti, Cortina, and Rumsey Hill Patwin, and in River Patwin. In Lodoga Hill Patwin Merriam elicits the form *ʔu·nu* '3SG.POSS$_{IN}$', though this is the only /-nu/ form attested for the well-documented Lodoga Hill Patwin dialect. Vallejo gives *neč'unu* and *teč'unu* '1PL.EXCL.POSS$_{IN}$' for South Patwin.

Although some amount of error is to be expected in vowel transcriptions, /-nu/ is so widely attested that it is probably best to consider it really distinct from the regular form /-no/. However, /-no/ and /-nu/ always appear to be in free variation with one another. For every attested pronoun ending with /-nu/, a corresponding pronoun with /-no/ is always attested in the same dialect, often by the same speaker.

Another allomorph similar in form to the regular /-no/ is /-n/, attested in Lodoga Hill Patwin *ʔulen* '3PL.POSS$_{IN}$' as well as in SP$_V$ *ču*n* '1SG.POSS$_{IN}$' and *maton* '2SG.POSS$_{IN}$'. This may simply be a contracted form of /-no/ used in fast speech, and is attested occasionally outside of the pronoun system as well.

The pronoun *matok* '2SG.POSS$_{IN}$' is attested in Rumsey Hill Patwin and River Patwin, possibly with a more specific meaning than *mato* '2SG.POSS$_{IN}$'. Another form similarly extended with a suffix /-k/ is attested in River Patwin: kinship-relational suffix allomorph /-čuk/ (see section 5.3.1.3.4). The significance of the /-k/ suffix is not known.

The pronoun *matono* '2SG.POSS$_{IN}$' is also widely attested in River Patwin (in Ultan, Bright, and Merriam) and South Patwin (Vallejo), being a second-person singular form where the regular /-no/ occurs after the 2SG allomorph /-to/.

In South Patwin various versions of the Lord's Prayer and the Angelic Salutation from Vallejo contain the form *matom* 'thy/your', for 'thy name', 'thy kingdom', 'thy will', and 'thy womb' (P. Vallejo, a, c:19.8, e, g, i; N. Vallejo, b). Other versions of these same texts by the same author use a variety of other forms for 'thy' in these same phrases: *mato, mat, maton, matonomen*, or *matomen* (P. Vallejo, a, c:19.2, 19.4, 19.6, h). There is no noticeable pattern to this variation; we may safely call all of these forms free variants in Vallejo's South Patwin.

Merriam attests a South Patwin form *čudo* '1SG.POSS$_{IN}$', with the suffix /-do/ representing the regular phonological alternation between /n/ and /d/ in South Patwin (see section 3.5.7).

Double case marking: While the possessive suffix usually attaches directly to the stem ({root} + {number suffix}), there are two attested proximal demonstrative forms in Lodoga Hill Patwin where the possessive suffix /-no/

follows the objective case suffix /-t/ in a double case marking construction: *ʔewetno* /ʔew-t-no/ 'PROX.SG.POSS$_{IN}$' (Ultan, d:3.30, OM; 4.38, AN) and *ʔewletno* /ʔew-le-t-no/ 'PROX.PL.POSS$_{IN}$' (Ultan, d:3.38, OM). These are the only inanimate possessive proximal demonstratives attested in Lodoga Hill Patwin, and may represent the regular pattern. I analyze this /-t/ as an objective case suffix, such that this construction mirrors the double case marking structures on kinship terms in the possessive case (see section 4.6.1.3). It may also be related to the Wintu particular aspect marker /-t/ found on Wintu pronouns and possibly Wintu kinship terms (Whistler 1980:255). Shepherd points to reflexes of the Proto-Wintuan sequence */-t-no/ in third-person pronouns in Wintu and Nomlaki as well, suggesting that this /-t/ may be a retention from a Proto-Wintuan objective or inalienable possessive suffix */-t/ (2005:60).

Allomorphs of POSS$_{AN}$

-min	HP & RP
-no-min	HP & SP
-to-min	2SG
-to-no-min	2SG SP var.

5.3.1.3.2. Animate Possessives

Animate possessive pronouns (POSS$_{AN}$) are pronouns in the possessive case used when the possessed nominal is a grammatically animate noun. Free pronouns functioning as possessors of kinship terms (POSS$_{K\text{-}F}$) are formally identical to the animate possessive series. There are four attested forms of the animate possessive suffix: the simplex form /-min/, the two-part forms /-no-min, -to-min/ (comprising the inanimate possessive suffixes /-no, -to/ followed by the simplex animate possessive form), and the three-part form /-to-no-min/.

The second-person singular animate possessive is *ma·tomin* in every dialect, using the two-part /-to-min/ possessive marking. In South Patwin the form *ma***tonomin* 'your (2SG.POSS$_{AN}$)' is also attested, with the three-part /-to-no-min/ marking. As with inanimate possessive pronouns, /-to/ is only attested in the second-person singular.

Outside of the second-person singular, River Patwin uses the simplex form /-min/ (e.g., *p'ele·min* '1PL.INCL.POSS$_{AN}$', *mipelemin* '2DU.POSS$_{AN}$', *ʔu·min* '3SG.POSS$_{AN}$'). South Patwin uses the two-part form /-no-min/ exclusively, and Hill Patwin varies freely between the simplex /-min/ and the two-part /-no-min/. The two-part marking is more frequently attested in Hill Patwin, but there appears to be no difference in meaning between the two.[10]

The first-person singular is invariably *na·min* 'my (1SG.POSS$_{AN}$)', with the simplex /-min/, in Hill Patwin and River Patwin. The form **na·nomin* with the two-part suffix /-no-min/ is not attested. No first-person singular animate possessive is attested for South Patwin.

5.3.1.3.3. Genitives

Subjects of nominalized subordinate clauses and agents of passive clauses appear in a special form of the possessive case signaling their agentive function (glossed 'POSS$_{V}$'; see section 4.6.1.3). Possession for kinship terms is typically expressed with bound kinship-possessive pronominals glossed 'POSS$_{K}$' (see section 4.3.1). The only systematic formal difference between the POSS$_{V}$ pronouns and the POSS$_{K}$ pronominals is that whereas the former are free pronouns, the latter are bound pronominals. See (87), where the form /ʔu·y/ is a bound pronominal prefix in (87a) and a free agentive pronoun, the subject of the nominalized subordinate clause, in (87b).

(87) a. ⟨'u·´inɛn⟩

ʔu·y-nen

3SG.POSS$_{K}$-mother

his mother

(Radin, c:35, AL) [HP$_{T}$]

b. ⟨kal·ubʊ·´ma dɪpi·´ L·ahi·´ hara·´La 'u·i p'amala´i we·´rmu [. . .]⟩

[kʰalu	bo·-ma	depi	łahi·	hara·-ła	ʔu·y	]	p'amalay	wer-mu
[other	be.AN-OBJ	again	seek.NMNL	go-LOC	3SG.POSS$_{V}$	]	bobcat	come-SBJV

[When he went looking for something else], bobcat came [. . .]

(Radin, c:37/167, AL) [HP$_{T}$]

Since kinship-possessive pronominals are bound forms, they are not strictly speaking pronouns, nor do they have case in a technical sense (since they are markers in a head-marking construction rather than dependent-marked free forms). However, they naturally have a place within the Patwin pronoun paradigm, because they share the roots and number suffixes of the pronouns, and because their forms are systematically related to agentive pronouns. In fact since the forms of kinship-possessive pronominals and agentive pronouns are identical except for their boundedness, they can be thought of as one class of forms. When referring to them together I will refer to them as *genitive* (GEN) forms, following Whistler (1980).[11]

Allomorphs of GEN	
-y	regular
Suppletive forms	
mat, ma·	'2SG.GEN'
pi	'3SG.GEN' (infrequent)

The regular suffix for the genitive is /-y/, in every dialect. There are no allomorphs of this suffix, but there are a few suppletive genitive forms.

The most commonly attested suppletive genitive forms are *ma* and *mat,* both second-person singular forms. These are widely attested both as kinship-possessive pronominal prefixes and as agentive pronouns. The regular 2SG.GEN form **ma·y* is not attested. The allomorphy between /mat-/ and /ma-/ as pronominal prefixes is lexically conditioned, although the latter allomorph is roughly associated with alveolar-initial stems (see Whistler 1980:206).

Outside of the pronoun system, the genitive suffix /-y/ also occurs on kinship terms (Whistler 1980:211). Genitive kinship terms can function both as agentive nominals (POSS_{V}) and as free possessors of other kinship terms ($\text{POSS}_{\text{K-F}}$). See sections 4.6.1.3 and 4.3.1.

Shepherd reconstructs a similar pattern to Patwin's for Proto-Wintuan: second-person and first-person singular genitives take the suffix */-t/ (as in Patwin *mat* '2SG.GEN') and other genitive forms take the suffix */-r/, from which Patwin /-y/ 'GEN' derives (2005:59). Paradigm leveling has occurred in Patwin, such that the potential form **na·t* '1SG.GEN' is not attested. The first-person singular genitive in Patwin is always *na·y*.

5.3.1.3.4. Kinship-Relational Suffix

The kinship-relational suffix /-ču/ 'RL' occurs as a suffix on kinship terms and expresses the general concept of relation, often implying first-person singular possession. It is not always used with first-person singular referents, however, so cannot be properly described as an allomorph of the first-person singular kinship-possessive pronominal *nay*. See (88), where /-ču/ is used with a third-person possessor (indicated by the free pronoun *ʔu·nomin* '3SG.POSS$_{AN}$').

(88) ⟨ʔú·nomin tá·chu⟩ 'that's his father'

ʔu·nomin	ta·-ču
3SG.POSS$_{AN}$	father-RL

his father

(Whistler, d:B21, OM) [HP$_L$]

The kinship-relational suffix also does not have a formally corresponding agentive pronoun, unlike all of the true kinship-possessive pronominals. However, the suffix is in a mutually exclusive relationship with the other possessive pronominals and performs the same function of indicating possession, albeit abstractly.

The kinship-relational suffix has two well understood allomorphs: /-ču/ (in all dialects) and /-ku/ (in River Patwin, on the stems *na* 'mother' and *ʔa·ma* 'grandmother'). A handful of other attested forms may be inflected variants of /-ču/, with uncertain functions: /-čis/ (HP$_T$), /-čuk, -čey, -ko/ (RP), /-čuy/ (SP). (The case of the kinship term is a suffix occurring after the kinship-relational suffix. See Whistler 1980:195 ff. and section 4.9.)

The kinship-relational suffix is formally similar, but not identical, to the first-person pronoun root /ču·-/ (see section 5.2.1). The vowel in the kinship-relational suffix is always short, and the kinship-relational form is a suffix, unlike the first-person root. The two are probably historically related.

5.3.1.3.5. Free Possessive Pronouns with Kinship Terms

The most common means of expressing the possessor of a kinship term is with a bound pronominal, but free nominals, including pronouns, are occasionally attested as possessors of kinship terms as well. They may be the only exponent of possession for the kinship term, or they may appear along with a coreferential bound pronominal. See section 4.3.1. The form of free pronouns functioning as possessors of kinship terms is identical to the form of pronouns functioning as possessors of animate nouns.

Semantic cases

-da	COM
-sin, -tin	INS
-ła, -tin	LOC
-t(')uka	ALL
-na·k, -ti	ABL
-na	PROL

5.3.1.4. *Semantic Cases*

The semantic cases are all marked by suffixes. The semantic cases themselves are regular, taking the same forms as they do on common nouns but with less variation in form. (See section 4.6.2 for a discussion of the semantic cases on nouns.)

Dialect variation for the semantic case suffixes on pronouns is as follows. For the ablative South Patwin uses the /-na·k/ allomorph while Hill Patwin and River Patwin use /-ti/. For the allative Tebti Hill Patwin varies between /-tuka/ and /-t'uka/, while other dialects use the former.

The instrumental and locative cases vary in form according to the animacy of their referent. For inanimate referents the instrumental case suffix is /-sin/ and the locative case suffix is /-ła/. For animate referents both the instrumental and locative case suffixes are /-tin/. Indefinite pronouns always take the inanimate allomorphs of the instrumental and locative case suffixes.

As with nouns and kinship terms, semantic case suffixes may select either the bare stem or objective stem of the pronoun. When the objective stem is selected, the resulting pronoun has two case suffixes: the objective suffix followed by a semantic case suffix. See section 4.6.2.1 for a discussion of this double case marking generally.

5.3.2. Number

The number suffix regularly occurs directly on the root of definite pronouns and demonstratives, and is followed by the case suffix. There is no number marking on indefinite pronouns.

5.3.2.1. *Singular*

The singular number is regularly unmarked in pronouns, as in other classes of nominals. See tables 5.1–5.4, where the singular pronouns have no overt number suffix (though the nonsubjective forms have case suffixes). The only pronoun that is arguably overtly marked for singular is *ču·* '1SG.SBJ'—a single morpheme expressing its person, number, and case synthetically. The singular number is also unmarked in Proto-Wintuan (Shepherd 2005:57).

Forms of the dual suffix

SBJ:	-pel	
OBJ:	-pel	(HP, RP)
	-pe·	(RP)
POSS$_{IN}$:	-pel	(HP$_L$, HP$_T$, RP)
	-pele·	(HP$_T$, HP$_C$, HP$_R$, RP)
POSS$_{AN}$:	-pel	before /-no-min/
	-pele·	before /-min/
GEN:	-pel	

5.3.2.2. *Dual*

The dual suffix in pronouns has three allomorphs: /-pel, -pele·, -pe·/. In the subjective case the dual is always /-pel/ in every dialect. In the objective case the dual is always /-pel/ in Hill Patwin.[12] In River Patwin objective pronouns the dual varies between /-pel/ and /-pe·/, the latter resulting in the characteristic syncopated River Patwin dual object pronouns *p'epe·t* '1DU.INCL.OBJ', *nepe·t* '1DU.EXCL.OBJ', *mi·pe·t* '2DU.OBJ', and *ʔu·pe·t* '3DU.OBJ'.

River Patwin speakers Sarah Gonzales and Hazel Hanes (Gonzales) are attested producing both the long and syncopated forms, but Jennie Regalado produces only the syncopated forms. Ms. Regalado attributes this difference to age: she tells Whistler that people in older generations say the longer forms with /-pel/, but that she uses the syncopated /-pe·/ forms (Whistler, d:F34). There are no attested dual objective pronouns in South Patwin.

For inanimate possessives there is some dialect variation in the dual suffix. Lodoga Hill Patwin consistently uses /-pel/ in this environment, creating the sequence /-pel-no/. Cortina Hill Patwin consistently uses /-pele·/, creating the sequence /-pele·-no/. The only attested dual inanimate possessive in Rumsey Hill Patwin, *p'epeleno* '1DU.INCL.POSS$_{IN}$', also uses /-pele·/. In Tebti Hill Patwin and River Patwin, the dual suffix shows variation in the inanimate possessive forms. In Tebti Hill Patwin /-pel/ is the most widely attested, occurring in the forms *p'epelno* '1DU.INCL.POSS$_{IN}$', *nepelno* '1DU.EXCL.POSS$_{IN}$', *mipelno* '2DU.POSS$_{IN}$', *mapelno* '2DU.POSS$_{IN}$', *pipelno* 'DIST.DU.POSS$_{IN}$', and *ʔupelno* '3DU.POSS$_{IN}$', collectively attested by Nelson Lowell, Daisy Lorenzo, and Anderson Lowell. However, /-pele·/ is also attested by two of the same speakers (*mipeleno, mapele·no, ʔupeleno, ʔupele·no*—Daisy Lorenzo and Anderson Lowell). In River Patwin the /-pele·/ allomorph is more common, but the /-pel/ form is also attested. River Patwin speaker Sarah Gonzales uses both in free variation.

For animate possessives the variation in the dual suffix is driven primarily by morphological context rather than dialect variation. Before the simple animate possessive suffix /-min/, only /-pele·/ is attested. Before the two-part /-no-min/, the allomorph /-pel/ is highly preferred. The only place where /-pele·-no-min/ is attested is Cortina Hill Patwin ⟨Pep-pel´-le no´-min⟩ *p'epelenomin* '1DU.INCL.POSS$_{AN}$' (Merriam:V72.57) and in the series of animate possessive personal pronouns reported in Radin's grammar, which may or may not have been directly elicited from Cortina Hill Patwin speaker Fred Gonzales (Radin, b). It is possible that Cortina Hill Patwin generally allows the /-pele·-no-min/ sequence, but *p'epelenomin* is the only attested dual animate possessive form definitely attested in Cortina Hill Patwin.

Dual pronouns are sparsely attested in the semantic cases. The form *ʔupelda* '3DU.COM' is attested in Lodoga Hill Patwin and River Patwin, *pipelda*

'DIST.DU.COM' is attested in Lodoga Hill Patwin, and *ʔupeletin* '3DU.LOC$_{AN}$' is attested in Tebti Hill Patwin.

The pronoun *hekapel* 'which' is remarkable for being an indefinite pronoun with what appears to be the dual number suffix. This is the only apparent example of an indefinite pronoun with an overt number suffix. Unfortunately it is attested in isolation with the gloss 'which', and no more can be said about its meaning: ⟨Hek-kah´-pel⟩ 'which' (Merriam:V70.53).

Outside of pronouns, the dual suffix occurs on kinship terms and optionally on a small set of human or culturally significant nouns, but not on nouns in general. Only the form /-pel/ is attested outside of the pronoun system. See section 4.5.

For Proto-Wintuan pronouns, Shepherd reconstructs */-pel/ before vowels and */-pele/ before consonants (2005:57).

Forms of the plural

-le·	regular
-č'u·	EXCL
-y ~ -Ø	1st-person SP$_{V}$

5.3.2.3. *Plural*

The plural suffix on pronouns is /-le·/ except in the first-person exclusive, where it is /-č'u·/ (forming the first-person exclusive plural stem /neč'u·-/). Shepherd reconstructs a Proto-Wintuan plural suffix */-le·/, and speculates that the Patwin /-č'u·/ allomorph may be related to the Patwin first-person singular pronoun *ču·* (2005:56, 57).

A series of pronouns in Vallejo's South Patwin with a stem like /ču*y-/ may contain an additional form of the plural: /-y/. See discussion in section 5.2.4.

In nouns and kinship terms the plural may be marked with one of a number of allomorphs /-ba, -in, -le·, -ma/—see section 4.5.

PROX.SG.OBJ *animacy*

ʔe·	IN (HP)
ʔe·s	IN (RP)
ʔewet	AN (HP&RP)

DIST.SG.OBJ animacy	
pi·ma	IN (HP&RP)
pi·t	AN (HP&RP)

Instrumental case animacy	
-sin	IN (HP&RP)
-(ma)tin	AN (HP&RP)

5.3.3. Animacy in Demonstratives

There is a limited animacy distinction in the Hill Patwin and River Patwin demonstratives, attested only in the singular objective case and in the instrumental case.[13]

In the proximal singular objective, the pronouns *ʔe·s* (RP) and *ʔe·* (HP) are used for inanimates. For both dialects *ʔewet* is the form used for animates. The animacy is thus coded in both the root (/ʔe·-/ for inanimates, /ʔew/ for animates) and in the objective case suffix (/-s, -Ø/ for inanimates, /-t/ for animates). This animacy contrast can be seen in Hill Patwin (89) and in River Patwin (90).[14]

(89) *ʔe·/ʔewet* contrast in Hill Patwin

a. ⟨ʔé· wílak yalú·ro⟩

ʔe·	wilak	yalu·-ro
PROX.SG.OBJ.IN	world	leave-PART

He left this country.

(Whistler, d:A56, OM) [HP_L]

b. ⟨mi cɛlí·ʔ ʔewɛt pé·soma⟩

mi	čeli·	ʔ	ʔewet	pe·so-ma
2SG.SBJ	own.AN	||	PROX.SG.OBJ.AN	money-OBJ

You keep this money!

(Ultan, d:6.56, DL) [HP_T]

(90) *ʔe·s/ʔewet* contrast in River Patwin

a. ⟨ʔe·s ba·ro har!⟩

ʔe·s	ba·-ro	har
PROX.SG.OBJ.IN	eat-PART	go

Eat this and go!

(Whistler, d:G66, JR) [RP]

b. ⟨chu déčet'i ʔewet mi·ma⟩

ču	deče-t'i	ʔewet	mi·-ma
1SG.SBJ	climb-FUT	PROX.SG.OBJ.AN	tree-OBJ

I'm going to climb that tree.

(Whistler, d:F33, JR) [RP]

Similarly in the distal singular objective forms, *pi·ma* is inanimate and *pi·t* is animate. Here, two objective case suffixes /-t, -ma/ that are ordinarily allomorphs in complementary distribution are used to effect a semantic contrast.

In the impersonal series of indefinite pronouns (see table 5.5), the set of objective case forms is superficially similar to the set of forms seen in the proximal demonstratives: River Patwin uses *pe·s*, while Hill Patwin and South Patwin use *pe·*. An alternate Hill Patwin form has the objective case overtly marked with /-ma/. However, unlike in the definite demonstratives, there is no evidence that the use of *pe·(s)* versus *pe·ma* correlates with grammatical animacy. In the impersonal pronouns, *pe·ma* is attested only in Hill Patwin, and is merely a rare variant of the commonly attested *pe·*. Example (91) shows examples of both *pe·* and *pe·ma* being used as objects of the same verb in the same syntactic context (interrogative). The verb *čeme·* 'to have (IN)' is used only when the grammatical object is inanimate, so both *pe·* and *pe·ma* must refer to inanimates in these examples.

(91) a. ⟨Pā-me´ chem´ me-si⟩

pe·	mi*	čeme-say
what.OBJ	2SG.SBJ	have.IN-Q

What do you have?

(Merriam:V72.67) [HP_C]

b. ⟨pé·ma píła chemé·saj⟩
pe·ma piła čeme·-say
what.OBJ DIST.LOC have.IN-Q
What do (you) have there?
(Whistler, d:B118, OM) [HP_L]

Pronouns in the instrumental case also mark an animacy contrast, using the suffix /-sin/ for inanimate referents and /-tin/ for animate referents, as in nouns (see section 4.6.2.3). The contrast is shown in (92).

(92) a. ⟨[. . .] 'ɛ·´ucɪn Lila·'' [. . .]⟩
ʔew-sin łila· ʔ
PROX-INS_{IN} shoot.2SG.HORT ||
[. . .] shoot with them [. . .]
(Radin, c:53/181, AL) [HP_T]

b. ⟨ʔéwmatin ló·sthunan⟩
ʔew-ma-tin lo·stʰu-nan
PROX-OBJ-INS_{AN} rub-REFL
you rub this on yourself (lit. 'rub yourself with this')
(Whistler, d:F33, JR) [RP]

There is no evidence of an animacy distinction in South Patwin demonstratives, either in the objective case or in the instrumental case.[15] As with other aspects of South Patwin, the lack of an attested animacy distinction in the demonstratives may simply be due to the sparsity of the data.

5.3.4. South Patwin /-k°a/

In the South Patwin sources, pronouns seeming to end in a suffix /-k°a/ are frequently attested. Some of these forms from the Vallejo materials are given in (93), showing the original written form, the probable phonemic content, and the original gloss.

(93) a. ⟨Chu-ca⟩ /čuk°a/ 'I myself'
(P. Vallejo, c:19.9.1,26.1)

b. ⟨Nechuca⟩ /neč'uk°a/ 'we'
(P. Vallejo, c:24.11,26.1)

c. ⟨Mica⟩ /mik°a/ 'thou'
(P. Vallejo, c:26.1)

d. ⟨Miléca⟩ /mile*k°a/ 'you'
(P. Vallejo, c:26.1)

e. ⟨píca⟩ /pi*k°a/ 'he'
(P. Vallejo, c:19.9.1)

f. ⟨picá⟩ /pik°a/ 'that one'
(P. Vallejo, c:19.3.4)

g. ⟨picá⟩ /pik°a/ 'that'
(P. Vallejo, d:2)

While South Patwin pronouns with /-k°a/ are most frequently attested in the Vallejo materials, they also appear in other sources. Example (94a) shows an example from Curtin's 1884 word list. A particularly interesting example is (94b) from Rumsey Hill Patwin speaker Harry Lorenzo, giving Whistler an example of how Dixon South Patwin sounds. That Chairman Lorenzo's chosen example of South Patwin has one of these /-k°a/ forms is some indication of how salient they are as a feature of this dialect.[16] There are no instances of pronouns with /-k°a/ in Merriam's South Patwin vocabulary (Merriam:V76).

(94) South Patwin pronouns with /-k°a/

a. ⟨batcuka⟩
ba·-t <u>ču-k°a</u>
eat-FIN <u>1SG.SBJ-*k°a*</u>
<u>I</u> am eating. [no gloss given in source]
(Curtin, b:228) [SP]

b. ⟨ču kʰa wáno wí·tinak˺ ʔíbot⟩

ču-k°a	wano	wi·ti-nak	ʔi-bot
1SG.SBJ-*k°a*	also	man.VBL?-ABL?	COP-CERT?

I am a man, too.

(Whistler, d:G100, HL) [SP]

It is not known what the /-k°a/ element corresponds to outside of South Patwin, so the phonetics cannot be exactly reconstructed. The most phonetically reliable source containing this element is Whistler's notebook, which contains only one instance, however, and that from a speaker of a different dialect (94b). In Whistler the vowel is short, so I tentatively assume that the vowel is generally short. Whistler transcribes the consonant as an aspirated ⟨kʰ⟩, but notes that the aspiration is light. The laryngeal category of the consonant therefore cannot be determined with certainty.

This /-k°a/ is not the irrealis particle *ka*, though the two may be related. It is plausible that such a particle could frequently occur as a second-position element in South Patwin clauses, encliticizing to pronouns to create the forms in question. But the irrealis particle is associated with uncertainty, and there is no evidence that the /-k°a/ pronouns have such a meaning in South Patwin. The functional mismatch here forces us to conclude that these elements are not the same. See section 9.2.3 for a discussion of the irrealis particle.

5.4. VERBALIZATION

Patwin is unusual in that the demonstrative roots and indefinite pronoun roots can be used as verb roots. Both the proximal and distal demonstrative roots are attested as verb roots, with meanings like 'do like that'. Some attested verbal demonstrative forms have explicit verbalizing morphology, such as the verbalizing suffix /-ʔu/ 'VBLZ'.[17] Others are simply demonstrative roots or demonstrative pronouns used as verbs with no overt verbalizing morphology. The attested demonstrative roots forming the bases of these verbal forms are /ʔew-/ 'PROX' and /pi·-/ 'DIST'. The indefinite roots /pe·-/ (impersonal) and /heče-/ 'which' (SP) are also attested forming the bases of verbs.

Proximal root as a verb: For Hill Patwin Whistler attests an explicitly verbalized proximal form where the proximal root /ʔew-/ is verbalized with /-ʔu/. An example from Oscar McDaniel (HP$_{L}$) is shown in (95a), where *ʔewʔule* is the main verb in an independent hortative clause. Another Hill Patwin example of the verbalized proximal demonstrative /ʔew-ʔu-/ is shown in (95b) from Tebti Hill Patwin speaker Anderson Lowell. Here the verb *ʔewʔuro* is in the participle form and refers anaphorically to the action described in the previous clause.

(95) a. ⟨chu ʔéwʔule⟩

ču	ʔew-ʔu-le
1SG.SBJ	PROX-VBLZ-1EXCL.HORT

I'm gonna do this way.
(Whistler, d:C18, OM) [HP$_{L}$]

b. [...] ⟨'ɛu 'uro lɔ·´rmu t'o´n·ima wi·´tama he·´rema.⟩

[...]	ʔew-ʔu-ro	lo·r-mu	t'oni-ma
[...]	PROX-VBLZ-PART	hand.to-SBJV	ball-OBJ

wi·ta-ma	he·re-ma
man-OBJ	reach-OBJ

[...] [he] did like this and handed the ball to the man who was reaching.
(Radin, c:50/178, AL) [HP$_{T}$]

For River Patwin both Whistler and Ultan attest a verbal proximal demonstrative with an unchanging stem /ʔewu-/ 'to do like this'. In (96a) *ʔewus* is the main verb of the clause, inflected for tense. In (96b) the same verb appears in the adverbial participle form *ʔewun,* modifying the main verb *ʔih* 'do'. River Patwin speaker Ida Mitchum gives Swadesh another form of this verb, with the verbalizing suffix /-ʔu/ and no audible /w/, in the participle form *ʔeʔu·ro* 'doing like this' (96c).

(96) a. ⟨pi ʔewʊs⟩

pi ʔewu-s

3SG.SBJ PROX.VBL-FIN

He is doing like that.

(Ultan, d:7.31, SG&HG) [RP]

b. ⟨ʔéwun ʔíh⟩

ʔewu-n ʔih

PROX.VBL-ADV do

Do it this way!

(Whistler, d:F24, JR) [RP]

c. ču· ʔe-ʔu·-ro ʔi-sa

1SG.SBJ PROX-VBLZ-PART do-PAST

I did it this way.

(Swadesh and Melton:18:33, IM) [RP]

The River Patwin verbal demonstrative stem /ʔewu-/ may be historically derived from an explicitly verbalized form like Hill Patwin /ʔew-ʔu-/, or it may be a reduced form of /ʔew-ʔu-/ appearing in fast speech.

The form /ʔew-/ is possibly attested as a verb root in South Patwin. The possible attestations are given in (97), with the original form and gloss first, followed by a probable parse in standard orthography and probable gloss.

(97) a. ⟨eurobé⟩ 'around'

ʔew(u?)-ro be*

PROX.VBL-PART be.IN

being like this

(P. Vallejo, c:26.12) [SP]

b. ⟨Eú si⟩ 'Look here.'

ʔew(u?)-se

PROX.VBL-1DU.INCL.HORT

Let's (do like) this! (P. Vallejo, c:28.2) [SP]

These South Patwin forms are to be taken with a few grains of salt, as the original glosses clearly do not express a verbal demonstrative meaning. But the forms suggest a verb with a stem like /ʔew(ʔu)-/, and the glosses are at least compatible with a situation where a speaker used a verbal demonstrative that was taken to mean something else by Vallejo.

Distal root as a verb: The distal root /pi·-/ is also attested as a verb, both with (98) and without (99) verbalizing morphology. In (98) *piʔule* is the main verb in an independent hortative clause. In (99) the verb *pi·ła* is the head of an adjunct clause, appearing in a nominalized form with the locative case suffix /-ła/.

(98) ⟨chu píʔule⟩

ču	pi-ʔu-le
1SG.SBJ	DIST-VBLZ-1EXCL.HORT

I'm gonna do that.

(Whistler, d:C18, OM) [$\mathrm{HP_L}$]

(99) ⟨pi·´La ’u·´i sɛdɛ ´u we·´rmu⟩ [...] ‘There a coyote was coming along [...]’

pi·-ła	ʔu·y,	sedew	wer-mu [...]
DIST.VBL-LOC	3SG.POSS$_V$	coyote	come-SBJV

As he was doing like that, a coyote came [...]

(Radin, c:38/168, AL) [$\mathrm{HP_T}$]

Example (99) shows the distal verbal demonstrative in its most common function: anaphoric reference to a situation described in a previous clause. Verbal demonstratives with an anaphoric function are common in Radin's texts from Anderson Lowell ($\mathrm{HP_T}$), serving as "clause linkers" integrating the present clause with the preceding story (Radin, c). They are attested in a variety of forms typical of subordinate verbs: participles with /-ro/ ‘PART’, adverbial expressions with /-n/ ‘ADV’, and nominalized forms with /-ła/ ‘locative case’.[18] In the following examples from the Radin texts, the situation described in preceding clauses is given in square brackets. In (100a) the participle form *pi·ro* ‘do like that and ...’ functions as a clause-linker indicating a sequence of events: it refers back to what the protagonist has just done before he proceeds with the action described in the clause. The form *pi·ła* in (100b) functions as a clause-linker indicating simultaneity or a sequence of events (nominalized verbs in /-ła/ can be used with either meaning). The form *pi·n* in (100c) functions as an adverb of manner meaning 'in that way' (or [doing-like-that]-ly), anaphorically referring to the preceding description of how the agents tricked a wolf into sinking into some mush. It should be emphasized that the glosses in (100) are my own. Radin gives only vague translations of these clause-connective verbal demonstratives, using words like "so," "then," "thus," and so on.

(100) a. [He told the wild animals to remain hidden.]

⟨pi·´ropal pi wılak'arobɛ·´t'uka ha·´rmo.⟩

pi·-ro	pal	pi	wilak-ʔa-ro
DIST-PART	now	3SG.SBJ	valley-VBLZ-PART

be·-t'uka	har-mu
be.IN-ALL	go-SBJV

He did like that and then he went toward the opening.

(Radin, c:103/225, AL) [HP$_T$]

b. [He threw something away.]

⟨pi·´ro dıpi ha·´rmu pi·´La 'u·i nɔp we·´rmu⟩

pi·-ro	depi	ha·r-mu.
DIST-PART	again	go-SBJV

pi·-ła	ʔu·y	nop	wer-mu [. . .]
DIST-LOC	3SG.POSS$_V$	deer	come-SBJV

He did that and went again. When he did that a deer came.

(Radin, c:37/167, AL) [HP$_T$]

c. [They made hot mush and the wolf sank into it.]

⟨pi·n pilɛ pal sɛwɔ·´m 'ut·.⟩

pi·-n	pile	pal	sewo·-m
DIST-ADV	DIST.PL.SBJ	now	bury-SBJV

ʔut.

PROX.SG.OBJ.AN

In that way (doing-like-that-ly) they then buried him.

(Radin, c:70/197, AL) [HP_T]

Indefinite roots as verbs: The impersonal root /pe·-/ 'what, something' is attested forming the base of a verb with a meaning like 'to do what' in all three major dialect groups, in a variety of forms: /pe·-/, /pe·ʔu-/, /pe·w-/ (HP), and /pe·hi-/ (RP). River Patwin /pe·hi-/ is a stem of the third conjugation, varying between /pe·hi-/ and /pe·hu-/ depending on its morphological environment (see section 8.1). Example (101) shows examples of each of the verbs derived from indefinite pronouns.

In (101e) I take it that Bright's ⟨péyhʊroʔ⟩ is phonemically /pe·huro/—that is, /e·/ rather than /ey/. Though Bright consistently transcribes this verb with ⟨y⟩, no other River Patwin source does. In Swadesh and Melton's recording, River Patwin speaker Ida Mitchum clearly articulates the stem /pe·hu-/. I take it that this ⟨y⟩ is a product of Bright's analysis, not a feature of the stem.

Turning to the stems /pe·ʔu-/ and /pe·w-/—these stems are so phonetically similar that one of them might be a mishearing of the other. Specifically /pe·w-/ might be a mishearing of the morphologically transparent /pe·ʔu-/, where the impersonal root /pe·/ is verbalized by the affix /-ʔu/ 'VBLZ'. However, I analyze /pe·ʔu-/ and /pe·w-/ as two separate stems, with morphophonological evidence: in (101c) the stem /pe·w-/ selects the /-ni/ allomorph of the adverbial participle suffix, which occurs only after consonants. In (101b) and (101f) the stem /pe·ʔu-/ selects the /-ro/ allomorph of the participle suffix, which occurs only after vowels. I take this as evidence that the two stems are phonologically distinct.

The form of the South Patwin verb is ambiguous in (101f); it could be /pe*ʔun/ or /pe*yun/. I assume the stem is /pe*ʔu-/, since /-ʔu/ is known to be a verbalizing suffix and since the stem /pe·ʔu-/ is attested in Hill Patwin.

In (101a) the inceptive verb *pe·t'o* 'in order to do what' is used to ask about the motive of an activity, and may be translated "why." In (101e) the participial verb *pe·huro* 'doing what' is used to ask about the reason for an event (or lack thereof); it may also be translated "why." It forms a clause chain with the following verb. A literal translation might be, "Doing what, mother has not arrived." In (101c) and (101f) the verbs *pewni* and *pe∗ʔun* are marked with the adverbial participle suffix /-n, ni/. They function as manner adverbs: 'how', or literally 'doing-what-ly'. In (101b) and (101d) the verbs *pe·ʔuro* and *pe∗hibo* are main verbs meaning 'to do what'. Note that while all of the examples in (101) are semantically questions, three of them (101a, 101b, and 101e) have no overt morphological interrogative marking. Instead the indefinite verb stems themselves contribute the interrogative meaning.

(101) a. ⟨pe·-t̉o mat ʔe·če?⟩

pe·-t'o	mat	ʔe·če
do.what-INCEP	2SG.POSS_V	steal.NMNL

Why did you steal?
(Whistler 1978:53/55, NL/HL) [HP_R]

b. ⟨pe·´'uro mipɛ·´l, pe· t'ɔtu·´ro?⟩
'What's the matter, are you short of anything.'

pe·-ʔu-ro	mipel,	pe·	t'otʰu·-ro
what-VBLZ-PART	2DU.SBJ	what.OBJ	lack-PART

What are you doing—are you short of anything?
(Radin, c:4/141, AL) [HP_T]

c. ⟨pew̥ni mi bɷ·say⟩

pew-ni	mi	bo·-say
do.what-ADV	2SG.SBJ	be.AN-Q

How are you getting along?
(Ultan, d:6.64, DL) [HP_T]

d. ⟨Pās-mē pa-hē-bo⟩

pe·s	mi∗	pe∗hi-bo
what.OBJ	2SG.SBJ	do.what-Q

What are you doing?
(Merriam:V75.67) [RP]

e. ⟨péyhʊroʔ nàkhû hiǹmìlé·roʔ⟩
pe·hu-ro ʔ na-k^{h}u hen-mele·-ro ʔ
do.what-PART || mother-RL arrive-NEG-PART ||
Why has mother not come home?
(Bright, c:1.G159, SG) [RP]

f. ⟨Pey un mi ibo?⟩
pe*ʔu-n mi ʔi-bo
what-VBLZ-ADV 2SG.SBJ do-Q
How are you?
(P. Vallejo, c:23.4) [SP]

In Cortina Hill Patwin and South Patwin, additional indefinite verb stems are attested: /heku-/ (HP$_C$) and /hečeʔu-/, /heče-/ (SP). The South Patwin stems are related to the South Patwin indefinite pronoun *heče* 'which'. The Cortina Hill Patwin stem is formally similar to the Hill Patwin indefinite pronoun stem /heke-/ 'which', and may be a contracted form of */hekeʔu-/, though this form is not attested in the archive. Because these verbs are related to pronouns meaning 'which', they are here glossed 'to do which'—although their meaning is not clearly distinct from the 'to do what' verbs described above. Examples are shown in (102).

(102) a. ⟨ilai t̓cait mato-min keku-n bo-say⟩
ʔilay č'ayt matomin heku-n
child scrub.jay 2SG.POSS$_{AN}$ do.which-ADV

bo-say
be.AN-Q

How is your young scrub jay?
(de Angulo:113, FG) [HP$_C$]

b. ⟨Hechewru mi thleinan-mita⟩

heče-ʔu-ro mi łey-nan-mit°a

which-VBLZ-PART 2SG.SBJ lie-REFL-PAST.Q

How did you lie down?

(P. Vallejo, c:23.3) [SP]

c. ⟨Hechén bómi⟩

heče-n bo* mi

do.which-ADV be.AN 2SG.SBJ

What do you mean?

(P. Vallejo, c:28.2) [SP]

Inflected pronouns as verbs: Demonstrative pronouns inflected for a semantic case may also be attested as verbs. Example (103) is a possible instance of this from Anderson Lowell (HP_T). The first word is a verb in the participle form (marked with /-ro/) whose stem appears to be /pina·k-/ 'DIST.ABL' followed by the verbalizer /-ʔu/ or the verbalizer /-ho/.

(103) ⟨pɩna·´koro wɛrɛs· po· ’ʋm⟩

"pina·k-[ʔu?/ho?]-ro were-s pʰo·," ʔu-m.

DIST.ABL-VBLZ-PART come-FIN fire say-SBJV

"The fire is coming from there," he said.

(Radin, c:19/154, AL) [HP_T]

Discussion: It is typologically rare for demonstrative pronoun roots to be used as verbs. Diessel's (1999) typology of demonstratives does not mention demonstratives used in this way. Dixon (2003) does include "verbal demonstratives" as a category in his typology of demonstratives, but describes only Boumaa Fijian (ISO code for Fijian: fij) and Dyirbal (dbl) as having verbal demonstratives with similar semantics to the Patwin verbal demonstratives (i.e., 'do like this'). Unlike the verbal demonstratives Dixon describes for Fijian and Dyirbal, which are specialized verb forms, the Patwin verbal demonstratives are clearly morphologically related to their nominal demonstrative counterparts.

Although the use of demonstrative roots as verbs seems to be globally rare, the phenomenon may be locally common. Pitkin identifies the Wintu verb *ʔun* 'to do or be thus' as having the demonstrative root *ʔu* 'that' (Pitkin 1985:810). The Wintu forms *pi ʔuni* and *ʔew ʔuni* (Pitkin 1985:811) may be similar verbs based on the Wintu demonstrative roots *pi* and *ʔew*, although Pitkin does not identify them as such. A similar structure is also mentioned for neighboring Nisenan in Eatough (1999:42): *myjaa* 'do thus [v.]', based on the demonstrative root *my* 'that'. A study of demonstrative verbs in this geographical area may prove to be fruitful.

5.5. IN-LAW ADDRESS FORMS

Because of a social taboo, direct address of parents-in-law and children-in-law is traditionally avoided (Kroeber 1932:272; Whistler 1980:97–98). If one needs to address an in-law, a nonsingular pronoun is typically used.[19]

The most frequently used forms for this purpose are the third-person plural personal pronouns. Oscar McDaniel (HP_L) tells Ultan and Whistler that the third-person plural pronoun *pile* 'they' is used to address one's father-in-law or son-in-law (Ultan, d:2.2; Whistler, d). In the objective case, McDaniel gives Ultan and Whistler the third-person plural pronoun *ʔule·t* 'them' for 'father-in-law, son-in-law, [and] sister-in-law' (Ultan, d:2.66; Whistler, d:C63).

Harry Lorenzo (HP_R) describes a more complicated system in which the distal plural pronoun *pile* is used to address in-laws of the same sex whereas the second-person plural pronoun *mile* is used for in-laws of the opposite sex. Mr. Lorenzo also explains that the inanimate possessive form *mile·no* is used for cross-sex in-law speech whereas the /ma/-rooted *male·no* would be the normal second-person plural inanimate possessive pronoun (Whistler, d:F76; and see section 5.2.5).

Daisy Lorenzo (HP_T) tells Ultan that the dual pronoun *pipel* 'they two' is used to address an in-law (Ultan, d:1.112).

5.6. DOUBLED PRONOUNS

There are a few attestations of subject pronouns occurring twice in the same clause. One of them immediately follows the verb, coming after all of the suffixes that attach to the verb. The doubling of the subject pronoun, and the fact that one of the pronouns invariably occurs immediately after the verb in these cases, suggests that the postverbal pronoun may be functioning as an agreement marker. See examples in (104), where I tentatively analyze the postverbal pronoun as a clitic expressing agreement with the subject.

(104) a. ⟨Pal mi henébo mi⟩

pal mi hene· bo=mi

now 2SG.SBJ arrive be.AN=2SG.SBJ

You have arrived. (a greeting)

(Kroeber, b:202.34, JS) [HP_L]

b. ču k'ati-s=ču

1SG.SBJ full-FIN=1SG.SBJ

I'm full.

(Ultan, b:14:33, OM) [HP_L]

SIX

Nominal Modifiers and the Noun Phrase

A number of elements may modify a nominal in Patwin: pronouns, adjectives, numerals, quantifiers, relative clauses, and possessors. Possessors are discussed in section 4.6.1.3. Other modifiers of nominals are discussed in this chapter. Coordination of nominals is discussed in section 6.6.

Usually a head nominal and its modifiers are adjacent and can be thought of as a syntactic constituent of a clause. I call such a constituent a noun phrase and refer to its core noun, kinship term, or pronoun as the head nominal. Typically the head noun is the final element in the noun phrase. Noun phrases without head nominals are also common in Patwin, and discontinuous noun phrases are attested. See section 6.7 for a discussion of the theoretical implications of these departures from prototypical noun phrase structure.

When present, the head nominal of the noun phrase under discussion is shown in bold in the examples throughout this chapter. Relative clauses are bracketed with square brackets.

6.1. PRONOUNS AS MODIFIERS

Pronouns (both demonstratives and personal pronouns) can function as modifiers to other nominals. In this usage they have the function of determiners, adding a deictic meaning to the noun phrase.

In (105a) the demonstrative *pi* 'that' functions as a modifier of the kinship term *matapan* 'your grandfather'. In (105b) the demonstrative *pima* 'that (OBJ.IN)' functions as a modifier to the noun *t'ok* 'wood'. In (105c) the personal pronoun *ʔut* 'him' functions as a modifier of the noun *wi·tama* 'man'.

(105) a. ⟨saltu ʔi-s čʼiyak, pi ma-tapan.⟩

saltu	ʔi-s	č'iyak,	pi
saltu	COP-FIN	old.man	DIST.SG.SBJ

ma-tapan
2SG.POSS$_{K}$-grandfather

The old man is a *saltu*, that **grandfather of yours.**
(Whistler 1978:53/55, NL/HL)

b. ⟨píma ṫok ċałú·ro⟩

pima	**t'ok**	č'ału·-ro
DIST.SG.OBJ.IN	**wood**	split-PART

(He is) splitting that **wood.**
(Whistler, d:A113, OM) [HP$_{L}$]

c. ⟨ʔūt wī·tāmā č^{h}ū bω̄kt^{h}úlɛ̀⟩

ʔut	**wi·ta-ma**	ču	bokt^{h}u-le
3SG.OBJ	**man-OBJ**	1SG.SBJ	hit-1EXCL.HORT

I'm gonna hit that **man.**
(Ultan, d:2.4, OM) [HP$_{L}$]

Pronouns appear in the objective case when the head nominal is in the objective case (as in 105b and 105c) and the subjective case otherwise. Note that pronouns are marked for the objective case regardless of the grammatical animacy of the head nominal, although inanimate noun heads are not themselves marked for objective case (like *t'ok* 'wood' in 105b).

Although pronouns can appear in possessive or semantic cases when used on their own as noun phrases (see chapter 5), they do not appear in the possessive case or in semantic cases when modifying other nominals as determiners. Example (106a) shows the distal subjective demonstrative *pi·* modifying the noun *wi·tano* 'man', which is in the possessive case. Example (106b) shows the proximal subjective demonstrative *ʔew* modifying the noun *k'enisin* 'with cooking basket', which is in the instrumental case.

(106) a. ⟨pi· wi·tano hene·ła lómibosa⟩

pi·	**wi·ta-no**	hene·-ła	lomi-bosa
DIST.SG.SBJ	**man-POSS_V**	arrive-LOC	happy-HAB

(I'm) happy when that **man** comes.
(Whistler, d:G60, HL) [HP_R]

b. ⟨mi láhuta· ʔew k̓énisin.⟩

mi	lahu-ta·	ʔew	**k'eni-sin**
2SG.SBJ	cook-Q.PAST	PROX.SG.SBJ	**cooking.basket-INS**

Did you cook with this **basket**?
(Whistler, d:G37, HL) [HP_R]

6.2. ADJECTIVES

Many of the words used as adnominal adjectives in Patwin are derived from verbs. Example (107) shows the word *watwa·ti* 'red' (HP_L) used as an adnominal adjective (107a) and as a sentential predicate (107b). The presence of verbal morphology (/-ro/ 'PART' in 107b), the stem ablaut (varying between /watwa·ti-/ and /watwa·tu-/), and the characteristic CVC reduplication in the stem (although the stem /wa·ti-/ is not attested independently) all show that *watwa·ti* 'red' is a verb stem.

(107) a. ⟨watwa·ti kɛ́wɛl⟩

watwa·ti	**kewel**
red.NMNL	**house**

red house
(Ultan, d:3.24, OM) [HP_L]

b. ⟨piła kɛ́wɛl watwâ·túro⟩

piła	kewel	watwa·tu-ro
DIST.LOC	house	red-PART

That house is red.
(Ultan, d:3.24, OM) [HP_L]

In (107a) *watwa·ti* appears in its nominal stem form (i.e., ending with /i/), but this is not true of all verbs used as adnominal adjectives. First conjugation verbs used as adnominal adjectives almost always appear in their consonant-final participial stem form: for example, ⟨bɛn sía⟩ /ben siya/ 'big buck' (Whistler, d:A27, OM). The vowel-final nominal stem form is attested also, but uncommonly: for example, ⟨bɛne·´ba⟩ /bene· ba/ 'big feast' (Radin, c:19/153, AL). In River Patwin, participle forms may be used as adjectives: for example, ⟨bɛ́nta hayʊʔ⟩ /ben-ta hayu ʔ/ 'big dog' (Bright, c:8.G58, SG). The choice of stem form for verbs used as adnominal adjectives is erratic, seemingly varying by word and dialect.

There are also a few words that are inherently adjectives, and that are not derived from verbs. Examples are *layuk* 'good' and *k'uču*y 'small'. Such a class of words may be an innovation in Patwin, as adjectives are not present in Wintu (Pitkin 1984).

Although many adnominal adjectives are derived from verbs, they are morphosyntactically distinct from relative clauses. Specifically, adnominal adjectives (whether derived from verbs or not) are never marked for the objective case, whether their referent is animate or inanimate. For example, in (108a) the adjective *watwa·ti* 'red' is not marked for objective case, although it modifies the objective case noun *hawma* 'fox'. In (108b) the adjective *be*ne* 'big' is not marked for objective case, although it modifies the objective case noun *t*^{h}*i·rma* 'fish'. In (108c) the adjective *k'uču*y 'small' is not marked for the objective case, although it modifies the objective case noun *č'a·li* 'light' (which itself is unmarked for the objective case, because it is grammatically inanimate). And in (108d) the adjective *benta* 'big' is not marked for the objective case, although it modifies the objective case noun *hayuma* 'dog'.

(108) a. ⟨watwá·ti háwma ču łilá·bʊs⟩

watwa·ti	**haw-ma**	ču	łila·-bus
red	**fox-OBJ**	1SG.SBJ	shoot-FIN

I shot a red **fox**.

(Ultan, d:3.6, OM) [HP$_L$]

b. ⟨Bin´-ne tēr mah oo´-choo-sah pe´⟩

be∗ne	**t^{h}i·r-ma**	ʔu·ču-sa	pi
big	**fish-OBJ**	catch-PAST	3SG.SBJ

He caught a big **fish**.

(Merriam:V72.67) [HP$_C$]

c. ⟨pi·´ka sɛdɛ´utc'iyak nɔmɛlnɔmɛl k'utci tc'a·´li wɩ´n·mu.⟩

pi·	ka	sedew-č'iyak	nomel-nomel
3SG.SBJ	IRR	coyote-old.man	REDUP-west

k'učuy	**č'a·li**	win-mu
small	**light**	see-SBJV

Old Man Coyote saw a small **light** in the far west.

(Radin, c:21/156, AL) [HP$_T$]

d. ⟨ʔìláyʔìláytʌʔ béntʌ hayʊʔmʌʔ wɩnntʌʔ ṣálmʌtɩnʔɛl⟩

ʔilay	ʔilayta	ben-ta	**hayu-ma**
little	child	big-PART	**dog-OBJ**

win-ta	sal-ma-tin	ʔel
see-PART	clover-OBJ-LOC$_{AN}$	in

The little girl saw a large **dog** in the clover field.

(Bright, c:8.G58, SG) [RP]

Adjectives standing on their own as noun phrases are marked for the objective case if they refer to an animate object, as in (109a). Adjectives standing on their own referring to inanimate objects are not marked for objective case, as in (109b).

(109) a. Q: What kind of fox did you shoot?

A: ⟨watwa·tíma⟩

watwa·ti-ma

red-OBJ

A red one.

(Ultan, d:3.6, OM) [HP$_L$]

b. ⟨layuk were!⟩

layuk	were
good	come.COM.IN

Bring good (wood)!

(Whistler 1977a:160/170, NL/HL) [HP_R]

6.3. NUMERALS

This section discusses numerals—first the morphosyntactic structures associated with numerals used as modifiers of nouns (section 6.3.1), then the structure of the number system itself (section 6.3.2).

6.3.1. Morphology and Syntax

In their citation forms and in the subjective case, most cardinal numerals ('one', 'two', 'three', etc.) end with the cardinal suffix /-ta/ 'CARD', like *ʔete·ta* 'one' in (110a). Some cardinal numerals never take the cardinal suffix—see section 6.3.2. In the objective case, numerals end with the objective case suffix /-ma/ 'OBJ', replacing the cardinal suffix /-ta/ (110b, 110c). Like pronouns, numerals are marked for the objective case regardless of the animacy of the head nominal. (Inanimate nouns are not themselves marked for the objective case, like *kʰolčis* 'sack' in 110c.)

(110) a. ⟨ʔɛté·ta k̓odój⟩

ʔete·-ta	**k'odoy**
one-CARD	**dollar**

one **dollar**

(Whistler, d:A31, OM) [HP_L]

b. ⟨ʔɛtᴇ·ma kɒdɔ́·yma ʔut˺ ču dɔ́yibʊs⟩

ʔete·-ma	**k'odo·y-ma**	ʔut	ču	doyi-bus
one-OBJ	**dollar-OBJ**	3SG.OBJ	1SG.SBJ	give-FIN

I gave him one **dollar**.

(Ultan, d:4.34, AN) [HP_L]

c. ⟨ɛt·e·´ma kɔ·´ltcɪs· tɪp'umɛm.⟩
ʔete·-ma **kʰolčis** tepu-me-m
one-OBJ **sack** emerge-COM-SBJV
He went out with one **sack**.
(Radin, c:2/139, AL) [HP_T]

The stem of the numeral without a suffix functions as a multiplicative ('once', 'three times', etc.) like *ʔete* 'once' in (111).[1]

(111) ⟨hánịṣačù píła ʔétɛʔ⟩
hanisa ču piła ʔete ʔ
har-ni-sa ču piła ʔete ʔ
go-RPAST-PAST 1SG.SBJ there once ||
I went there once.
(Ultan, d:4.72, AN) [HP_L]

Numerals modifying semantic case nominals sometimes appear in the subjective case, and sometimes in the objective case. In (112a) the comitative case noun *p'okitada* 'with women' is modified by the numeral *pampata* 'two', which appears in the subjective case with the cardinal suffix /-ta/. In (112b) the instrumental case noun *yirin* 'with a leg' is modified by the numeral *ʔete·ma* 'one', which appears in the objective case with the suffix /-ma/. Such constructions are rarely attested, so the factors conditioning the form of the numeral are not known.

(112) a. ⟨pa´mpata p'ɔki·´tada cɔ´itʊm.⟩
pampa-ta **p'oki·ta-da** soytʰu-m
two-CARD **woman-COM** lie-SBJV
He lay down with the two **women**.
(Radin, c:106/228, AL) [HP_T]

b. ⟨ʔeté·ma jɪrín ƛódthoyƛódthoyta⟩
ʔete·-ma **yir-in** ƛ'odtʰoy-ƛ'odtʰoy-ta
one-OBJ **leg-INS** REDUP-hop-PART
He's hopping on one **leg** (of a human).
(Whistler, d:C9, OM) [HP_L]

When numerals appear on their own as noun phrases without a head nominal, they may host semantic case suffixes themselves, which appear after the cardinal suffix /-ta/. In (113) the numeral *ʔete·tała* 'at one place' is in the locative case.

(113) ⟨'ɛte·´taLa bɛnɛ·´ba'am⟩
'At one place (where) there was a big feast'.
ʔete·-ta-ła bene· ba-ʔa-m
one-CARD-LOC big food-VBLZ$_S$-SBJV
At one place there was a big feast.
(Radin, c:19/153, AL) [HP$_T$]

6.3.2. Numeral System

The Patwin numeral system was addressed in a conference presentation by Ken Whistler (Whistler 1979).[2] Because some of the information on Hill Patwin and River Patwin numerals in this section derives from Whistler (1979), specific archival sources are not given for some forms. This section expands on Whistler (1979), with information about variation in Hill Patwin and River Patwin, and with South Patwin numerals found in archival materials, as described below. Some information about the Patwin numeral system has also been published in Dixon (1909) and Golla (2011).

The Hill Patwin and River Patwin numerals 'one' to 'ten' are shown in table 6.1. The numerals 'one' to 'four' have simplex stems. The numeral stems /ʔetesem-/ 'five' and /pampasem-/ 'ten' are etymologically related to *sem* 'hand', prepended with /ʔete·-/ 'one' and /pampa-/ 'two' respectively. The stems /serpo·ɬ-/ 'six' and /pan(ʔ)emu·s-/ 'eight' are related to /pono·ɬ-/ 'three' and /ʔemu·s-/ 'four' respectively, with value doubling indicated by *ser* 'crosswise, in two directions, twice' and *panom* 'twice' respectively. The stems /serpote·-/ 'seven' and /panem(e)te·-/ 'nine' are related to /serpo·ɬ-/ 'six' and /pan(ʔ)emu·s-/ 'eight' respectively, iterated with a suffix related to /ʔete·-/ 'one'.[3] Note that Grimes River Patwin has divergent forms for 'four' and 'eight' with /h/ in place of the more common /s/, and a divergent form for 'seven' with /e/ rather than the more common /o/. In 'eight' and 'nine' the segments shown in parentheses are not always attested, but the source of this variation is not known. All of the forms and reconstructions in table

Table 6.1. Hill Patwin and River Patwin numerals 1–10

1	ʔete·-ta		
2	pampa-ta		
3	pono·ɬ-ta		
4	ʔemu·s-ta, ʔemu·h-ta (RP_G)		
5	ʔetesem-ta	<ʔete·-sem	'1-hand'
6	serpo·ɬ-ta	<ser-pono·ɬ	'crosswise-3'
7	serpote·-ta, serpete·-ta (RP_G)	<serpo·ɬ-ʔete·	'6-1'
8	pan(ʔ)emu·s-ta, pan(ʔ)emu·h-ta (RP_G)	<panom-ʔemu·h	'twice-4'
9	panem(e)te·-ta	<panʔemu·h-ʔete·	'8-1'
10	pampasem-ta	<pampa-sem	'2-hand'

Table 6.2. South Patwin numerals 1–10

1	ʔet-ta		
2	pápa-ta		
3	ponóɬ-ta		
4	ʔemu(h)-ta		
5	ʔetesem	<ʔete·-sem	'1-hand'
6	k'ačéta		
7	kalapá-ta		
8	panomúya	<panom-ʔemu·h-ta	'twice-4-CARD'
9	kenete·la		
10	papasem huyá	<papa-sem	'2-hand'

6.1 are from Whistler (1979), except for the divergence of the Grimes dialect and the optionality of the segments in 'eight' and 'nine'.The South Patwin numerals from 'one' to 'ten' are significantly different, as shown in table 6.2.[4] As in the other dialects, 'one' to 'four' have simplex stems. In South Patwin, 'six', 'seven', and 'nine' also have simplex stems, not etymologically related to the other dialects' forms. There are two words for 'ten': *papasem* is the independent word for 'ten', being the only word to appear as a citation form for that number. *Huyá* is the combining word for 'ten', found only as an element of larger numerals (see below). In *panomúya* 'eight' the stem and cardinal suffix have merged, with the /t/ in the suffix undergoing lenition

Table 6.3. Multiples of 10

	HP	RP	SP
10	pampasem-ta	pampasem-ta	papasem
20	ʔetek'ay(i)	ʔetek'ayi	panom papasem papata papasem panom huyá papata huyá ʔemú(h)sem
30	ponłara	ponłara łeymat(in) pampak'ayi	ponół papasem ponoł huya
40	ʔemus pampasem-ta	pampak'ayi	ʔemú(h) papasem
50	ʔetesem pampasem-ta	łeymat(in) połk'ayi	ʔétsem pápsem
60	serpoł pampasem-ta	połk'ayi	k'ačeta pápsem
70	serpote· pampasem-ta	łeymat(in) ʔemuhk'ayi	
80	panʔemus pampasem-ta	ʔemuhk'ayi	
90	panʔemuste·ta pampasem-ta	łeymat(in) ʔetesemk'ayi	
100	pampasem(ta) pampasemta depi ʔete·ta senta panom ʔetesem pampasem	ʔetesemk'ayi	(ʔeta) papasem papasem huyá papasem

to /y/ (compare HP and RP *pan(ʔ)emu·sta*). In *k'ačéta* 'six', the /ta/ is never separated from the stem, even in constructions for 'sixty' and 'six hundred', where the stem would be expected to appear on its own (see below). I therefore analyze *k'ačéta* as a simplex form, with no cardinal suffix. Numbers ending in /sem/ (< *sem* 'hand') do not take the cardinal suffix in South Patwin, unlike in the other dialects. This suggests that these numbers may not be true numerals from a morphological perspective in South Patwin. Finally, the stems /ʔet-/ 'one' and /pápa-/ 'two' are reduced in South Patwin compared to their Hill Patwin and River Patwin cognates /ʔete·-, pampa-/.

Table 6.3 shows forms for multiples of ten in the three major dialect groups, with Hill Patwin and River Patwin forms mostly from Whistler (1979) and South Patwin forms from archival sources.[5] The number 'twenty' is *ʔetek'ay(i)* in Hill Patwin and River Patwin, derived from *ʔete·* 'one' + *k'ayi* 'walk' (?). *K'ayi* is also the basis of other multiples of twenty in River Patwin: *pampak'ayi* 'forty', *połk'ayi* 'sixty', *ʔetesemk'ayi* 'one hundred', and so on.

'Thirty', 'fifty', 'seventy', and 'ninety' in River Patwin are expressed in relation to the next multiple of 20: *łeymat(in) połk'ayi* 'fifty' = *łeymat(in)* 'set aside from' + *połk'ayi* 'sixty'; and *łeymat(in) ʔetesemk'ayi* 'ninety' = *łeymat(in)* 'set aside from' + *ʔetesemk'ayi* 'one hundred'. These numbers are not attested with the cardinal suffix /-ta/ (except *ʔetek'ayta* 'twenty' optionally in Lodoga Hill Patwin), and thus may be morphologically distinct from true numerals. The numeral *ponłara* 'thirty' is in both Hill Patwin and River Patwin, derived from *ponoł* 'three' + *hara* 'go' (Whistler 1979). In Hill Patwin, multiples of ten between forty and ninety may be expressed with a multiplicative numeral followed by the number 'ten'. Thus, *ʔemus pampasemta* 'forty' = *ʔemus* 'four times' + *pampasemta* 'ten'. It is not known whether this pattern extends above 'one hundred'. Multiples of ten in South Patwin are relatively regular, and may all be composed of a numeral, with no cardinal suffix, followed by one of the words for 'ten': *papasem* or *huyá*. In some South Patwin forms, *papasem* is attested in a contracted two-syllable form, *papsem*.

For numerals higher than twenty that are not multiples of ten, Hill Patwin and River Patwin use the following structures (as described in Whistler 1979): the last multiple of ten is stated, with the cardinal suffix /-ta/ (114a), or the inanimate locative case suffix /-ła/ (114b), or neither (114c). This is followed by a numeral from 'one' to 'nine'. Hill Patwin also uses this pattern for the numerals 'eleven' to 'nineteen' (see examples in 115). Note that the expressions for multiples of ten may comprise multiple words, as in *ʔemus pampasemta* 'forty'.

(114) a. ⟨ʔɛtɛsɪm pʌmpʌsɪmta ʔɛte·ta⟩
[ʔetesem pampasem-ta] ʔete·-ta
[fifty -CARD] one-CARD
fifty-one
(Bright, c:7.NL178, NL) [HP$_C$]

b. ⟨ʔᴇmuṣ pampasɛmła ʔᴇte·ta⟩
[ʔemus pampasem-ła] ʔete·-ta
[forty -LOC] one-CARD
forty-one
(Ultan, d:6.5, NeL) [HP$_T$]

Table 6.4. River Patwin numerals 11–19

11	lu·mete·-ta	<lu·mu-ʔete·	'die-1'
12	panłomi	<panom-łomi	'twice-put'
13	panłomite·-ta	<panłomi-ʔete·	'12-1'
14	łoti		'bad'?
15	ponosem-ta	<pono·ł-sem	'3-hand'
16	posete·-ta	<ponosem-ʔete·	'15-1'
17	posepampa	<ponosem-pampa	'15-2'
17 or 18	posepano	<ponosem-panom	'15-twice'
		<ponosem-panoł	'15-3'
19	posemu·-ta	<ponosem-ʔemu·h	'15-4'
18	panweli	<pan-weli	'twice-subtract'
19	yayweli	<yay-weli	'back-subtract'

Source: Whistler (1979).

c. ⟨ʔέmʊs pʌmpʌsɪm εte·tʌ⟩
[ʔemus pampasem] ʔete·-ta
[forty] one-CARD
forty-one
(Bright, c:7.NL177, NL) [HP$_{C}$]

(115) a. ⟨Pom-pă-sem´-tah em-moos-stă⟩
pampasem-ta ʔemu*s-ta
ten-CARD four-CARD
fourteen
(Merriam:V71.1, AT) [HP$_{T}$]

b. ⟨pampasemła ʔetesemta⟩
pampasem-ła ʔetesem-ta
ten-LOC five-CARD
fifteen
(Whistler, d:D13, HL) [HP$_{R}$]

River Patwin numerals 'eleven' to 'nineteen' are significantly more complicated, as shown in table 6.4. A set of numerals 'sixteen' to 'nineteen' begins with /pose/, derived from *ponosem* 'fifteen', reduced to /pose/: *posete·ta* 'sixteen' (15+1), *posepampa* 'seventeen' (15+2), *posepano* 'eighteen' (15+3), and *posemu·ta* 'nineteen' (15+4).[6,7] Two alternate forms for 'eighteen' and 'nineteen' are subtractive, taking 'twenty' as their reference value: *yayweli* < /yay-weli/ 'back-subtract (from 20)', and *panweli* < /panom-weli/ 'twice-subtract (from 20)'. The word attested for 'fourteen' is *łoti*, meaning 'bad', which may indicate a taboo. The numeral *panłomi* 'twelve' is derived from /panom/ 'twice' + /łomi/ 'put'.[8] The numeral *lu·mete·ta* 'eleven' is derived from /lu·mu/ 'die' + /ʔete·/ 'one', thus iterating from 'ten'. The numeral *panłomite·ta* 'thirteen' iterates from *panłomi* 'twelve'.

In South Patwin various patterns are attested in Vallejo's word list (Vallejo, c) for numbers above 'ten' that are not multiples of ten. The most common pattern is for numerals to be composed of a multiple of ten, followed by a numeral in the range 'one' to 'nine', including the cardinal suffix, followed by /be/. I tentatively analyze this /be/ as the auxiliary verb *be* 'be.IN'.[9,10] Examples of this pattern are shown in (116).

(116) a. ⟨papasem papatabe⟩

papasem	papa-ta	be
ten	two-CARD	be.IN

twelve

(P. Vallejo, c:23.12) [SP]

b. ⟨papasem emutabe⟩

papasem	ʔemu(h)-ta	be
ten	four-CARD	be.IN

fourteen

(P. Vallejo, c:23.12) [SP]

c. ⟨ponol papasem ponoltabe⟩

[ponol	papasem	]	ponoł-ta	be
[thirty		]	three-CARD	be.IN

thirty-three

(P. Vallejo, c:24.4) [SP]

The numerals 'fifteen' and 'twenty' are sometimes attested in base-five forms in Vallejo's South Patwin, derived from *sem* 'hand'. These forms are shown in (117).

(117) a. ⟨ponoltasem⟩
ponoł-ta-sem
three-CARD-hand
fifteen
(Mason) [SP]

b. ⟨ponoLsem⟩
ponoł-sem
three-hand
fifteen
(Mason) [SP]

c. ⟨emusem⟩
ʔemu(h)-sem
four-hand
twenty
(P. Vallejo, c:23.11) [SP]

Finally the word *wanó* 'also' may be used to compose numbers in Vallejo's South Patwin. In this pattern *wanó* is always last, but the other elements may be in any order.

(118) a. ⟨papasem etesem wanó⟩
papasem ʔetesem wanó
ten five also
fifteen
(P. Vallejo, c:23.12) [SP]

b. ⟨panompapasem eta wanó⟩

[panom	papasem]	ʔet-ta	wanó
[twenty	]	one-CARD	also

twenty-one

(P. Vallejo, c:23.12) [SP]

c. ⟨papata huyá wanó⟩

papata	huyá	wanó
two	ten	also

twelve

(P. Vallejo, c:4.1) [SP]

In addition to the definite numerals discussed above, there is an indefinite numeral *hičahta* (RP) *heča·ta* (HP) 'how many, some, few'. Example (119a) shows *hičahta* in the subjective case, with the cardinal suffix /-ta/. Note that nominals that can take plural morphology appear in the plural when modified by *hičahta*, like *ʔilayin* 'children' in (119a). Example (119b) shows *hičahma* in the objective case, taking the objective case suffix /-ma/ in place of the cardinal suffix /-ta/. Example (119c) shows that object marking on *hičahta* is optional. In (119c), *hičahta* takes its citation form with the cardinal suffix /-ta/, although the noun it modifies is in the objective case.

(119) a. ⟨hìcáhtaʔ ʔélàyìn bobo sʊn⟩

hičahta	**ʔilayin**	bobo	sun
hičah-ta	**ʔilay-in**	boh-bo	sun
how.many-CARD	**child-PL**	be.AN-Q	here

How many **children** are here?

(Bright, c:1.G133, SG) [RP]

b. ⟨hic^{h}ahma mi jo·mam⟩

hičah-ma	mi	yo·ma-m
how.many-OBJ	2SG.SBJ	lost-SBJV

How many did you lose?

(Whistler, d:E8, JR) [RP]

c. ⟨hìcáhtaʔ thí·rmaʔ pi ʔótmʊʔ⟩

hičahta	**tʰi·rma**	pi	ʔutmu
hičah-ta	**tʰi·r-ma**	pi	ʔuč-mu
how.many-CARD	**fish-OBJ**	3SG.SBJ	catch-SBJV

How many **fish** did he catch?

(Bright, c:1.G133, SG) [RP]

6.4. QUANTIFIERS

6.4.1. Collective *čaket* 'all'

The collective quantifier *čaket* refers to a referent or a group of referents as a collectivity (120a–120c) or an entirety (120d). It is variously glossed 'all' (120a, 120d), 'a lot' (120b), or in negative contexts 'any' (120c).

(120) a. ⟨chu píma ṫók ċopó·bus cháketma⟩

ču	pima	**t'ok**	č'opo·-bus	čaket-ma
1SG.SBJ	DIST.OBJ.IN	**wood**	chop-FIN	all-OBJ

I chopped all that **wood**.

(Whistler, d:B72, OM) [HP$_{L}$]

b. ⟨wɪnis chu chaket winma were·ma⟩

wini-s	ču	čaket	**win-ma**	were·-ma
see-FIN	1SG.SBJ	all	**person-OBJ**	come-OBJ

I see a lot of **people** coming.

(Whistler, d:D11, HL) [HP$_{R}$]

c. ⟨ʔele·s pi čáketma ḱáyumʔu⟩

ʔele·-s	pi	čaket-ma	k'ayu-mʔu
NEG-FIN	3SG.SBJ	all-OBJ	like-NEG

He doesn't like any (of them).

(Whistler, d:G39, HL) [HP$_{R}$]

d. ⟨pi·´La tcakɛt wilak lɪ´btoro.⟩
pi·ła čaket **wilak** libtʰu-ro
do.like.that-LOC all **world** sink-PART
Thus, all the **world** was drowned.
(Radin, c:8/144, AL) [HP_T]

Čaket can also modify pronouns, as in ⟨chákeṭ p̓éle⟩ /čaket p'ele/ 'all of us' (Whistler, d:E49, HL) or ⟨píle? caket⟩ /pile ? čaket/ 'they all' (Bright, c:1.G165, SG).

In the objective case *čaket* is optionally marked with the objective case suffix /-ma/. In (120a) *čaketma* modifies the object *t'ok* 'wood' and takes the objective suffix. In (120b) *čaket* modifies the object *winma* 'people', but does not take the objective suffix. This also applies to *čaket* standing on its own as a noun phrase: in the objective case, it may be marked with /-ma/, as in (121a) or not (121b).

(121) a. ⟨t'ú·lus cáketma mi⟩
t'u·lu-s čaket-ma mi
spill-FIN all-OBJ 2SG.SBJ
You spilled all of it.
(Whistler, d:F13, JR) [RP]

b. ⟨chákhɛtʰ mis dójule⟩
čaket mis doyu-le
all 2SG.OBJ give-1EXCL.HORT
I'll give you all of it.
(Whistler, d:B80, JR) [RP]

When modifying nouns in semantic cases, *čaket* appears in its bare stem form, for example, ⟨chaket k̓odojła⟩ /čaket k'odoy-ła/ 'where all the rocks are' (Whistler, d:D13, HL).

Used on its own as a noun phrase or as the head of a noun phrase, *čaket* may be inflected for the possessive case. In (122a) it appears in the inanimate form of the possessive case (/čaketno/), being the possessor of the noun *kewel* 'house'. In (122b) it appears in the agentive form of the possessive case (also /čaketno/) as the subject of a nominalized subordinate clause.

(122) a. ⟨milέ·nɔ čákεtnɔ kέwεl ʔisέ·⟩

'is that your folks' house (all you guys?)'

mile·no	čaket-no	**kewel**	ʔi-sey
2PL.POSS$_{IN}$	all-POSS$_{IN}$	**house**	COP-Q

Is that you all's house?

(Ultan, d:4.84, AN) [HP$_L$]

b. ⟨ču lómis čáketno láyukʔaro hará· ʔéwsani⟩

'I'm satisfied with everything the way it went today.'

ču	lomi-s	[čaket-no
1SG.SBJ	happy-FIN	[all-POSS$_V$

layuk-ʔa-ro	hara·	ʔewsani	]
good-VBLZ$_S$-PART	go	today	]

I'm happy with [everything going well today].

(Whistler, d:G97, HL) [HP$_R$]

On its own as a noun phrase, *čaket* is also attested with locative case marking, ⟨tcakε·´tLa⟩ /čaket-ła/ (Radin, c:100/223, AL), and with prolative case marking, ⟨chaketna⟩ /čaket-na/, glossed 'all over' (Whistler, d:E65, HL).

6.4.2. Distributive *halihali* 'all kinds'

The distributive quantifier *halihali* means 'all kinds', implying a heterogeneous set of different types of referents. It is never marked for the objective case, whether it modifies an inanimate noun (123b) or an animate noun (123c), or whether it stands alone as a single-word noun phrase (123d).

(123) a. ⟨halé·hali k̓eré·n p̓éthi píła bo·s⟩

hali·hali	k'ere·n	**p'et^{h}i**	piła	bo·-s
all.kinds	small	**game.animal**	DIST.LOC	be.AN-FIN

All kinds of small **game** are there.

(Whistler, d:A39, OM) [HP$_L$]

b. ⟨[. . .] ba· halihali titc'o·´m pɪn·a.⟩

'he put all kinds of food therein.'

[. . .]	**ba·**	halihali	tič'o·-m	pina
	food	all.kinds	put.in-SBJV	DIST.PROL

[. . .] put all kinds of **food** through (the hole he had made).

(Radin, c:7/144, AL) [HP$_T$]

c. ⟨[. . .] pipel thúptù hʌnim hali hali p'étima⟩

[. . .]	pipel	tupt^{h}u	hanim
	pipel	tupt^{h}u	har-ni-m
	3DU.SBJ	look.at	go-RPAST-SBJV

halihali	**p'et^{h}ima**
halihali	**p'et^{h}i-ma**
all.kinds	**game.animal**

[. . .] they went to look at all kinds of **animals.**

(Bright, c:10.DL108, DL) [HP$_T$]

d. ⟨pal 'ɛ·´tcɪmu haleha·´le [. . .]⟩

pal	ʔe·če-mu	haliha·li	[. . .]
then	steal-SBJV	all.kinds	

Then he stole everything [. . .]

(Radin, c:41/171, AL) [HP$_T$]

Halihali is attested with possessive case marking. For example in the relative construction ⟨halihali·´nɔ dɪ´ktihɪm⟩ /halihali·-no dikt^{h}i-hem/ 'everything that was burned up', the word *halihali·no* is in the agentive form of the possesive case, being the subject of a nominalized clause (Radin, c:25/159, AL).

Halihali is sometimes attested with a long vowel in the second syllable (as in 123a), the third syllable (123d), or the fourth syllable (previous paragraph). It is not clear what conditions the presence or absence of length. Further lexicographical work may reveal some pattern of dialect variation.

6.4.3. *a·na* 'much'

The word *ʔa·na* is a quantifier in Hill Patwin meaning 'much', 'many', 'lots', 'too much', or 'too many'. Example (124) shows a number of examples of *ʔa·na* modifying nouns. Object marking is optional on *ʔa·na,* as shown by its presence in (124a) and its absence in (124b). In both of these examples *ʔa·na* is modifying an animate noun that is the object of the sentence. Plural marking on the noun modified by *ʔa·na* is also optional, as shown by its presence in (124c) and its absence in (124d). In these examples *ʔa·na* is modifying nouns with human referents, which may take plural morphology (see section 4.2.2), but only in (124c) does that morphology occur.

(124) a. ⟨ʔa·nama ṫaka·ma ṫakis pi⟩
ʔa·na-ma **t'aka·-ma** t'aki-s pi
much-OBJ **acorn-OBJ** pound.acorns-FIN 3SG.SBJ
She's pounding a lot of **acorns.**
(Whistler, d:E39, HL) [HP$_R$]

b. ⟨ʔá·na ƛ̓étma ƛ̓ilú·ro⟩
ʔa·na **ƛ̓et-ma** ƛ̓ilu·-ro
much **ground.squirrel-OBJ** roast-PART
roasting lots of **ground squirrels**
(Whistler, d:C40, OM) [HP$_L$]

c. ⟨Ah´-nah we-ab´-bah⟩
ʔa·na **wiya-ba**
much **man-PL**
many **men**
(Merriam:V71.58) [HP$_T$]

d. ⟨Ah´-nah po´-ke-tah⟩
ʔa·na **p'okita**
much **woman**
many **women**
(Merriam:V73.58) [HP$_R$]

In Lodoga Hill Patwin *ʔa·na* may also function as a clausal quantifier, modifying a verb. Example (125) shows two instances of this usage.

(125) a. ⟨pi nat ʔá·na k̓ájabuṣ⟩

pi	nat	<u>ʔa·na</u>	k'aya-bus
3SG.SBJ	1SG.OBJ	<u>much</u>	like-FIN

He likes me.

(Whistler, d:A76, OM) [HP$_L$]

b. ⟨á·na k^{h}ó· p̓ɔ́r̃man t^{h}úbumabʊṣ⟩

<u>ʔa·na</u>	k^{h}o·	p'orma-n	t^{h}ubu-ma-bus
<u>much</u>	skunk	bad-ADV	smell-CAUS-FIN

The skunk smells <u>pretty</u> bad.

(Ultan, d:3.8, OM) [HP$_L$]

An etymologically related word in South Patwin is a verb. It is attested in a tensed form ⟨anti⟩ /ʔan-t°i/ (P. Vallejo, c:26.12); in its participle form ⟨antaṟa⟩ /ʔan-taro/ (Barrett, b), ⟨Ahn´-tar´-ro⟩ /ʔa∗n-taro/ (Merriam: V76.58); and in its bare stem form ⟨Ah´-nah⟩ /ʔa∗na/ (Merriam:V76.43). In River Patwin a verb *ʔana* is also attested once, with the finite suffix /-s/: ⟨ʔanʌṣ⟩ /ʔana-s/ (Bright, c:3.G34, SG).

The word *mu·nču* is also attested as a quantifier meaning 'much', 'many', 'lots', and so on in Hill Patwin and River Patwin. It is borrowed from non-standard Spanish *muncho*.

6.5. RELATIVE CLAUSES

A relative clause is a nominalization, referring to an entity that is also an argument of the relative clause's predicate. A relative clause may function as a modifier of a head nominal, or it may stand on its own as a referring expression. In the examples in this section I will render head nominals in boldface, when present, and enclose relative clauses with square brackets.

6.5.1. Morphological Marking

Relative clauses are headed by nominalized verbs. The verbs may appear in a bare nominal stem form, or they may take overt relativizing suffixes /-hVm/ 'REL' (HP, SP), /-sem/ 'REL' (RP), or the oblique relativizer /-sok/ (HP) 'REL$_{OBL}$'.[11]

The vowel in /-hVm/ is short and assimilates to the preceding vowel in quality, but generally remains nonhigh. Thus after /a, a·/ the suffix is /-ham/; after /e, e·, i, i·/ the suffix is /-hem/; and after /o, o·, u, u·/ the suffix is /-hom/. Forms with high vowels are occasionally attested, but not in phonetically reliable sources. The vowels in River Patwin /-sem/ and Hill Patwin /-sok/ are invariant. All of the relativizing suffixes /-hVm, -sem, -sok/ select the nominal stem of the verb to which they attach (see section 8.1).

6.5.2. Order in the Relative Construction

The relative clause is usually ordered after the head nominal, as in (126a), where the head *sululatayma* 'roadrunner' precedes the relative clause *ʔuču·ma t'asalay-ma* 'catching a lizard'. However, the opposite order is also attested (126b), as are head-internal relative constructions (126c). Headless relative constructions are frequent (126d).

(126) a. ⟨wınis chu sululatajma ʔuchu·ma ṫasalajma⟩

wini-s ču **sululatay-ma** [ʔuču·-ma
see-FIN 1SG.SBJ **roadrunner-OBJ** [catch-OBJ

t'asalay-ma]
lizard-OBJ]

I see a **roadrunner** [catching a lizard].
(Whistler, d:D31, HL) [HP$_R$]

b. ⟨cu·´nak hara·´ham·a maLa·´t ca´n·tc'iak cʊ´ltıs⟩
'From here go, old man sun has killed your brother.'
[su·nak hara·hamma]
[su·nak hara·-hVm-ma]
[here.ABL go-REL-OBJ]

maƚa·t	san-č'iyak
ma-ƚa·-t	san-č'iyak
2SG.POSS$_K$-brother-OBJ	sun-old.man

sult^{h}is
sult^{h}i-s
kill-FIN

Old Man Sun killed **your brother**, [who was going from here].
(Radin, c:55/183) [HP$_T$]

c. ⟨[. . .] 'ɔpɛle pat ba·´ yalɛhɪm tɛpu·´robam.⟩

[. . .]	[ʔupeley	pat	**ba·**	yalihem	]
	[ʔupeley	pat	**ba·**	yali-hVm	]
	[3DU.POSS$_V$	outside	**food**	leave-REL	]

tepu·ro bam.
tepu·-ro ba-m.
emerge-PART eat-SBJV

[. . .] he came out and ate the **food** [that they had left out].
(Radin, c:30/161, AL) [HP$_T$]

d. ⟨na·y k̓obo·lisɛm nat werepaʔ⟩

[na·y	k'obo·li-sem	]	nat
[1SG.POSS$_V$	pay-REL	]	1SG.OBJ

were-pa ʔ
bring-APPL ||

[What I paid for], bring it to me!
(Ultan, d:7.106, SG) [RP]

The verb tends to be final in the relative clause, but not always. For example in the relative clause in (126a) the verb *ʔuču·ma* 'catching' appears before its object *t'asalayma* 'lizard'.

6.5.3. Relativized Functions

Relative clauses are semantically unlike other clauses: where normal clauses describe an event, relative clauses refer to an object. For example the independent clause (127) describes an event of seeing: someone (*ču* 'I') sees something (*ʔi·ma* 'acorns') somewhere (*ʔewet mi·ła* 'in this tree'). Compare this to the relative construction (128): this phrase refers not to an event, but to an entity—that which is seen.

(127) ⟨chu wínis ʔí·ma ʔéwet mí·ła⟩

ču	wini-s	ʔi·-ma
1SG.SBJ	see-FIN	acorns-OBJ

ʔewet	mi·-ła
PROX.SG.OBJ	tree-LOC

I see acorns in this tree.
(Whistler, d:F20, JR) [RP]

(128) ⟨piʔ mápèlè wìnní·hèm thó·kła ʔòlél⟩ [. . .]

pi	ʔ	[mapeley	wini·hem
pi	ʔ	[mapeley	wini·-hVm
DIST.SG.SBJ	‖	[2DU.POSS$_V$	see-REL

tʰo·kła	ʔolel	] [. . .]
tʰo·k-ła	ʔolel	]
tree-LOC	up	]

That [which you see up in the tree] [. . .]
(Bright, c:10.DL110) [HP$_C$]

It can be said that the relative clause in (128) relativizes on its object: the referent of the clause (that which is seen) would be the grammatical object of the verb *wini·hem* 'seeing', if it were expressed.

Patwin relative constructions may relativize on the subject, on the object, or on a locative. Example (129a) shows a relative clause relativizing on a subject (the one who did the stealing). Example (129b) shows a relative clause relativizing on a grammatical object that is semantically the direct object (that which was stolen). Example (129c) shows a relative clause relativizing on a grammatical object that is semantically the indirect object (the one who was stolen from). Example (129d) shows a relative clause relativizing on a locative (the place where they were).

(129) a. ⟨ba· 'ɛ·´tcɛhɛm wi·´ta⟩

[ba·	ʔe·čehem	]	**wi·ta**
[ba·	ʔe·če-hVm	]	**wi·ta**
[food	steal-REL	]	**man**

the **man** [who stole the food]
(Radin, c:46/174, AL) [HP$_T$]

b. ⟨ʔûy ʔɛ́·cɛhɪm łúbe⟩

[ʔuy	ʔe·čehem	]	**łube**
[ʔuy	ʔe·če-hVm	]	**łube**
[3SG.POSS$_V$	steal-REL	]	**property**

the **property** [that he stole]
(Bright, c:10.DL82, DL) [HP$_T$]

c. ⟨'u·´i 'ɛ·´tcehɛm win·⟩

[ʔu·y	ʔe·čehem	]	**win**
[ʔu·y	ʔe·če-hVm	]	**win**
[3SG.POSS$_V$	steal-REL	]	**people**

the **people** [from whom he was stealing]
(Radin, c:42/172, AL) [HP$_T$]

d. ⟨'uitɛsba·´ nobɔ·´hɔm kɛ´wɛLa ha·´rmu.⟩
'To the house where his mother-in-law lived they went.'

[ʔuyt'esbano	bo·hom	]
[ʔuy-t'es-ba-no	bo·-hVm	]
[3SG.POSS$_K$-in.law-PL-POSS$_V$	be.AN-REL	]

kewełа ha·rmu
kewe-ła ha·r-mu
house-LOC go-SBJV

They went to the **house** [where his in-laws lived].
(Radin, c:68/194, AL) [HP$_{T}$]

To relativize on instrumentals and comitatives in Hill Patwin, the verb of the relative clause is marked with the oblique relativizer /-sok/ 'REL$_{OBL}$', which can also mark relativization on locatives.[12] Example (130) shows relativization on instrumental, comitative, and locative arguments using /-sok/.

(130) a. ⟨múhiṣɷ<k ƛ̓ałî·⟩
[muhi-sok] **ƛ̓ałi·**
[sing-REL$_{OBL}$] **singing.sticks**
singing sticks [for singing]
(Ultan, d:3.12) [HP$_{L}$]

b. ⟨wɪtí·lisok⟩
[witi·li-sok]
[run-REL$_{OBL}$]
something you run with
(Whistler, d:B113, OM) [HP$_{L}$]

c. ⟨'a·Lacɔk pi·´ma⟩
[ʔa·ła-sok] pi·ma
[set-REL$_{OBL}$] DIST.SG.OBJ.IN
that (place) [where (Old Man Sun) sets]
(Radin, c:58/185, AL) [HP$_{T}$]

Relativization on instrumentals and comitatives is not attested in River Patwin or South Patwin.

There are no attested instances of relativizing on possessives (the man [whose dog I see]) or objects of comparison (the man [who I am taller than]). It is not known whether these structures are strictly impossible in Patwin, or whether they have simply never been attested. Possessives and objects of comparison are the farthest categories down Keenan and Comrie's relativization accessibility hierarchy, so it is plausible that this type of relativization is impossible in Patwin (Keenan and Comrie 1977).

There are no pronouns representing the relativized argument within a Patwin relative clause: no relative pronouns (the man [whom I see]) and no resumptive pronouns (the man [that I see him]). This means that the relativized function is not represented within the relative clause except in head-internal constructions, where it is expressed as a lexical noun (like *kučuyma* 'bird' in 131).

(131) ⟨nay kucuyma wɪnɪsɛm⟩
[nay **kučuy-ma** wini-sem]
[1SG.POSS$_V$ **bird-OBJ** see-REL]
the **bird** [that I saw]
(Ultan, d:7.51, SG) [RP]

6.5.4. Case and Number Marking on the Relative Construction

Case and number marking may appear either on the head of the relative construction, on the verb of the relative clause, or both. The distribution of this marking is described in this section.

A relative clause is marked for objective case with /-ma/, if the referent is animate. In (132a) the grammatical object *nop-ʔilayma* 'deer children' is animate, and is the head nominal of a relative construction. Therefore both this head nominal and the relative clause modifying it are marked with the objective case /-ma/. In (132b) the grammatical object *ʔaba·* 'basket' is inanimate. Neither this noun nor the relative clause modifying it are marked with the objective case suffix.

(132) a. ⟨phóke mɪn cìyák łìllʌ́s nop ʔìlâymaʔ mê·m tètímaʔ⟩
p'okimen-č'iyak łila-s
garter.snake-old.man shoot-FIN

nop-ʔilay-ma	ʔ	[me·m	tet^{h}i-ma	]	ʔ
deer-child-OBJ	||	[water	drink-OBJ	]	||

Old Man Garter Snake shot the **deer children**, [who were drinking water].

(Bright, c:6.NL91, NL) [HP$_{C}$]

b. ⟨ca´ntc'iak ɛt·ɛsɛ·´ma 'a·´ba·` hiLi paro·´nbɛ t'a´lmu.⟩

san-č'iyak	ʔetesem-ma	**ʔaba·**	[hiłi·
sun-old.man	five-OBJ	**basket**	[bead

paro·-n	be	]	t'al-mu
full-ADV	be.IN	]	bet-SBJV

Old Man Sun bet five **baskets** [full of beads].

(Radin, c:51/179, AL) [HP$_{T}$]

In the semantic cases the verb of the relative clause takes a case suffix only if there is no head nominal. In (129d), the relative construction is in the locative case. This is indicated by the locative suffix /-ła/ on the head nominal, but the relative clause itself is unmarked for case. Compare (133), another relative construction in the locative case. This relative construction has no head nominal, so the locative case suffix /-ła/ appears directly on the relative clause.

(133) ⟨hɛ´n·mu k'ainɔ bo·´hɔmLa⟩

henmu	[k'ayno	bo·homła	]
hen-mu	[k'ay-no	bo·-hVm-ła	]
arrive-SBJV	[old.woman-POSS$_{V}$	be.AN-REL-LOC	]

(He) came [to where the old woman lived].

(Radin, c:56/184, AL) [HP$_{T}$]

Only headless relative constructions are attested in the possessive case, where they are marked with a possessive case suffix, as in (134).

(134) ⟨lʋmuho´mnu t'ɛ´c·pa⟩
'the dead man's mother-in-law'
[lumuhomnu] t'esba
[lumu-hVm-nu] t'es-ba
[die-REL-POSS$_{K\text{-}F}$] in.law-PL
(the one) [who had died's] in-laws
(Radin, c:60/187, AL) [HP$_T$]

A relative clause whose referent is plural is optionally marked with the suffix /-ba/ 'PL', as in (135).

(135) ⟨tcakɛt wɪn· dɪktihɪ´mba⟩
čaket **win** [dikt^{h}ihem<u>ba</u>]
čaket **win** [dikt^{h}i-hVm-<u>ba</u>]
all **person** [burned.up-REL-<u>PL</u>]
all the **people** [who got burnt]
(Radin, c:26/159, AL) [HP$_T$]

6.6. NOMINAL COORDINATION

This section describes the three basic strategies for coordinating nominals: use of the comitative case suffix /-da/, use of coordinating particles *ʔiro* and *ʔan*, and simple juxtaposition. Nominal coordination with the clause connector /=ʔu/ is also attested, for which see section 9.6.

6.6.1. Coordination with Comitative /-da/

The comitative case suffix /-da/ is commonly used to coordinate nominals in Hill Patwin and River Patwin. Each nominal expression that is coordinated is usually marked with the comitative case, as in the examples in (136). In (136a) the nouns *sududay* 'titmouse' and *č'o·ka* 'bluebird' are coordinated, both marked with the suffix /-da/. Similarly in (136b) the nouns *t^{h}i·r* 'fish', *siya* 'buck', and *k^{h}ay* 'goose' are coordinated with the suffix /-da/; together they are the object of the verb *doyus* 'give'. Note that in (136b) the coordinands are not marked with the objective case suffix /-ma/, although they are grammatically animate nouns and although the objective and comitative case suffixes may in principle co-occur. Thus object marking is optional for nominals coordinated with the comitative case /-da/, just as it is for any nominal in a semantic case. (See section 4.6.2.1 for a discussion of double case marking in semantic cases.)

(136) a. ⟨cududa´ida tc'o·´kada pipɛl hoya'u wɩ´n·mu w·ere·´ma.⟩

'Cudaida and bluejay saw them coming from afar.'

sududay-da	č'o·ka-da	pipel	hoyaʔu
titmouse-COM	bluebird-COM	3DU.SBJ	already

win-mu	were·-ma
see-SBJV	come-OBJ

Titmouse and bluebird, they had already seen those who were coming.

(Radin, c:58/185, AL) [HP$_T$]

b. ⟨č⁼u ut^h t^{h}i·řda siyada k^{h}ayda t⁼ɔyus⟩

ču	ʔut	t^{h}i·r-da	siya-da
1SG.SBJ	3SG.OBJ	fish-COM	buck-COM

k^{h}ay-da	doyu-s
goose-COM	give-FIN

I gave him a fish, a buck, and a goose.

(Snyder, b:SG) [RP]

Sometimes only one coordinand is marked with /-da/, as in the examples in (137). In both of these examples only the final coordinand is marked with /-da/; the preceding coordinands are unmarked.[13]

(137) a. ⟨yɛl bɛ·´hɛna'o k'a·´ip'ɛl tc'ia´kda hɛ´n·mu⟩

'The next morning the two of them, the old woman and the old man, got over there'

yel	behna=ʔu	k'a·y-pel
behind	tomorrow=CONN	old.woman-DU

č'iyak-da	hen-mu
old.man-COM	arrive-SBJV

And the next morning, the two old women and the old man arrived [. . .]
(Radin, c:31/162, AL) [HP_T]

b. ⟨kʊcui tʊsʊʔ loklokdaʔ hʌttʌ́ʔ⟩
'a bird + squirrel + hawk went.'

kučuy	tʰusu	ʔ	loklokda	ʔ
kučuy	tʰusu	ʔ	loklok-da	ʔ
bird	squirrel	‖	red.tailed.hawk-COM	‖

hatta	ʔ
har-ta	ʔ
go-PART	‖

A bird, a squirrel, and a red-tailed hawk went.
(Bright, c:8.G98, SG) [RP]

6.6.2. Coordinating Particles: *iro, an*

Rarely, free particles serve to coordinate nominals. In Lodoga Hill Patwin the coordinating particle *ʔiro* is attested, as in (138a) and (138b). The form *ʔiro* may be derived from the participle form of the copula *ʔi*. In Vallejo's South Patwin, the coordinating particle ⟨an⟩ *ʔan* is attested for nominal coordination, as in (138c). The historical source for *ʔan* is unknown, though it does bear a strong resemblance to English *and*.

(138) a. ⟨p̉ípel p̉ókete ʔíɾoʔ wí·ta hέnta bo· haɾá·buṣ⟩

pipel	p'okita	ʔiro	wi·ta
3DU.SBJ	woman	and	man

hen-ta	bo·	hara·-bus
arrive-PART	be.AN	go-FIN

A man and a woman were here but they're going.
(Whistler, d:A8, OM) [HP_L]

b. ⟨ná·no nók̓oma ʔíro nún⟩

na·no	nok'o-ma	ʔiro	nun
1SG.POSS$_{IN}$	arrow-NSG	and	bow

my bow and arrows
(Whistler, d:A104, OM) [HP$_L$]

c. ⟨[. . .] winíto winímatoy an yoknitoy⟩

[. . .]	wini-t'o	winimatoy	ʔan	yoknitoy
	see-INCEP	living	and	dead

[. . .] to judge the living and the dead
(P. Vallejo, c:19.9.2) [SP]

6.6.3. Juxtaposition

Some nominal coordination has no overt marking at all and is expressed by simple juxtaposition of the nominals. In (139a), the compound nouns *san-č'iyak* 'Old Man Sun' and *kat^{h}it-sektu* 'Falcon Chief' form a coordinated structure, together comprising the subject of the sentence. Similarly in (139b) the nouns *k^{h}osolma* 'lungs' and *p^{h}u·ruma* 'heart' are coordinated, together comprising the object of the sentence. In both examples there is no overt marking of the coordination.

(139) a. ⟨ca´ntc'iak katɛtts'ɛ·´ktu ha·´ta ha·´m·u.⟩

san-č'iyak	kat^{h}it-se·ktu	ha·r-ta	ha·m-mu
sun-old.man	falcon-chief	go-PART	sit-SBJV

Old Man Sun and Falcon Chief went and sat down.
(Radin, c:53, AL) [HP$_T$]

b. ⟨yel-ti-taro, khosol-ma phu·ru-ma ʔetek-ła phem-taro.⟩

yelti-taro	k^{h}osol-ma	p^{h}u·ru-ma
backwards-PART	lungs-OBJ	heart-OBJ

ʔetek-ła	p^{h}em-taro
one.side-LOC	grasp-PART

Backwards, holding (our) lungs and hearts out to one side.
(Whistler 1977a:164/171, NL/HL) [HP$_R$]

6.7. HEADLESS AND DISCONTINUOUS NOUN PHRASES

Generally, a noun phrase has a core nominal element (the head nominal), and its modifiers are adjacent to it, coalescing into a syntactic constituent that I have called the noun phrase. However, this prototypical situation does not always hold in Patwin: noun phrases without head nominals are common in Patwin.[14] Elements of the noun phrase may also be displaced from the rest of the noun phrase, resulting in a discontinuous noun phrase. These departures from the prototypical structure of a noun phrase suggest that the head nominal and its modifiers may in fact be syntactically separate constituents. Examples of headless and discontinuous phrases are discussed here, and the theoretical implications for Patwin grammar are briefly explored.

Headless noun phrases: The examples in (140) show noun phrases without head nominals.

(140) a. ⟨pi cháketma cheme·s⟩
pi čaket-ma čeme·-s
3SG.SBJ all-OBJ have.IN-FIN
He has lots, he has it all.
(Whistler, d:E63, HL) [HP$_{R}$]

b. ⟨εt·e·´ta di·´hυm⟩
ʔete·ta di·hu-m
one wake.up-SBJV
One of them woke up.
(Radin, c:106/228, AL) [HP$_{T}$]

Discontinuous noun phrases: The examples in (141) show discontinuous noun phrases. In (141a) and (141b) the determiners *pi* 'that' and *ʔut* 'him' are separated from their head nominals *ču·ču* 'dog' and *su·l-č'iyakma* 'Old Man Eagle', respectively. In (141c) the head nominal *ʔilayma* 'child' is separated from its possessor *namin* 'my'. In (141d) the head nominal *č'elo·ma* 'jackrabbit' is separated from the modifying relative clause *hamta boma* 'that was sitting'. Example (141a) shows a discontinuous noun phrase functioning as a subject, while the other examples in (141) show discontinuous noun phrases functioning as objects.

(141) a. ⟨pi nát chú·chu ʔejé·bus⟩

pi	nat	**ču·ču**	ʔeye·-bus.
DIST.SG.SBJ	1SG.OBJ	**dog**	bite-FIN

That **dog** bit me.
(Whistler, d:A60, OM) [HP_L]

b. ⟨sul-thu-se ʔut, nok̓o-sak-ma lelu·-ro, su·l-č̓iyak-ma.⟩

sultʰu-se	ʔut	nok'o-sak-ma
kill-1DU.HORT	3SG.OBJ	stone-spear-OBJ

lelu·-ro	**su·l-č'iyak-ma**
make-PART	**eagle-old.man-OBJ**

Let's kill that **Old Man Eagle** (by) making a stone spear.
(Whistler 1977a:166, 172, NL/HL) [HP_R]

c. ⟨ʔilayma cu namın bamaⁿs⟩

ʔilay-ma	ču	namin	ba-ma-s
child-OBJ	1SG.SBJ	1SG.$POSS_{AN}$	eat-CAUS-FIN

I'm feeding my **baby**.
(Ultan, d:6.39, NeL) [HP_T]

d. ⟨hámta bóma pál ču łilá·bʊs čɛló·ma⟩
'the rabbit was sitting + I shot him'

[ham-ta	bo-ma	]	pal	ču
[sit-PART	be.AN-OBJ	]	now	1SG.SBJ

łila·-bus	**č'elo·-ma**
shoot-FIN	**jackrabbit-OBJ**

I shot the **jackrabbit** [that was sitting].
(Ultan, d:2.94, OM) [HP_L]

The examples in (141) are representative of discontinuous noun phrases in Patwin in general, in that in every case one element of the phrase is displaced to the periphery of the clause. In most instances of discontinuous noun phrases, one element is on the left periphery of the clause specifically. Noun phrases like this may be a kind of focus construction, bringing a particular aspect of a referent into focus by displacing it to the periphery of the clause.[15]

Discussion: The fact that noun phrases may be lacking heads, and that their various elements may be dispersed across the clause, suggests that the noun phrase may not be a valid unit of syntactic analysis for Patwin. Moreover, noun phrases are not the only phrases that may be discontinuous in Patwin. Example (142a) shows a discontinuous adverbial clause *mat . . . yorihem monʔan* 'like you told', with the subordinate subject *mat* 'you' separated from the rest of the clause. Example (142b) shows a discontinuous complement clause *mat . . . weret'i* 'that you would come', with the subject of the matrix clause occurring inside of it.

(142) a. ⟨mat cu yorihem mónʔan ʔis⟩

mat	ču	yorihem	monʔan
mat	ču	yori-hVm	monʔa-n
2SG.POSS$_V$	1SG.SBJ	direct-REL	be.like-ADV

ʔis
ʔi-s
do-FIN

I'm doing (it) like you told (me).
(Whistler, d:F41, F78, HL) [HP$_R$]

b. ⟨mat tcu wiri-ti halu-nisa⟩

mat	ču	were-t'i	halu-nisa
2SG.POSS$_V$	1SG.SBJ	come-FUT	think-HAB

I thought you would come.
(de Angulo: 112, FG) [HP$_C$]

Therefore Patwin may be well suited to a syntactic analysis with a nontraditional approach to phrase structure.

One analysis would consider Patwin to be a nonconfigurational language, in the sense of Hale (1983).[16] Under such an analysis individual elements of the noun phrase are separate constituents, creating a characteristic multibranching "flat structure" for the clause. Case marking indicates which elements are to be attached to which functional roles. For example in (141a) *pi* 'that' and *ču·ču* 'dog' may be separate constituents, each mapping onto the agent function of the predicate *ʔeye·bus* 'bites', by virtue of the fact that they are both in the subjective case. Such an analysis is roughly schematized in (143). In this rough schematic tree structure N is the label for any nominal element (including nouns and pronouns), and case is represented by subscript 'SBJ' for subjective and 'OBJ' for objective.

(143)

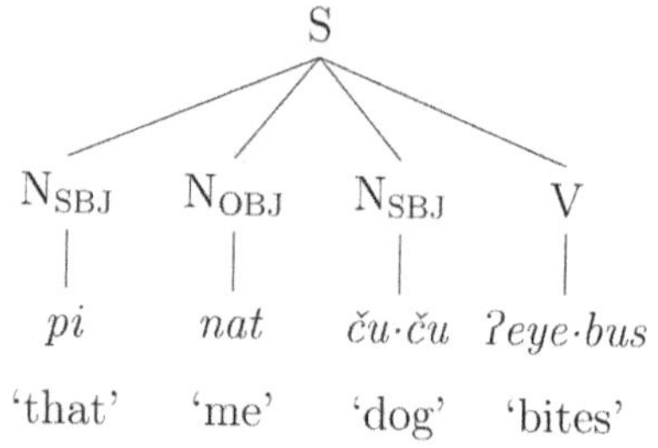

On the other hand the fact that nominal modifiers do normally occur adjacent to the head nominal suggests that the noun phrase may be a useful unit of analysis. A noun and its modifiers do generally coalesce into a contiguous group that for descriptive purposes may be called a noun phrase. The concept of the noun phrase could be regularly applied to Patwin syntax by appealing to a family of theories that allows discontinuous expressions: in theories allowing discontinuous constituency (crossing lines in a syntactic tree), the concept of a constituent can be applied even to discontinuous elements. The basic configurational structure is still retained in the syntactic tree's dominance relations (e.g., Ojeda 2006; Steele 1987). A rough sketch of such a tree for the sentence in (141a) is shown in (144). Here the words *pi* 'that' and *ču·ču* 'dog' are interpreted as the subject of the sentence by virtue of the fact that they form a syntactic constituent NP, which is the sister of the VP.[17]

(144)

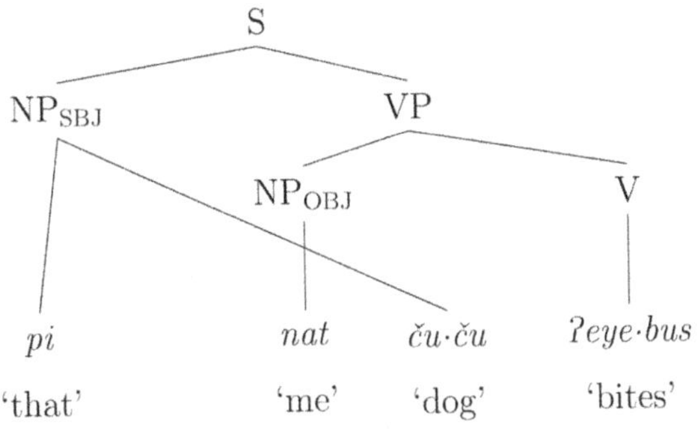

Both the nonconfigurational analysis and the discontinuous constituent analysis fit with the Patwin data, at least insofar as Patwin syntax is currently understood. The nonconfigurational analysis has the benefit of analyzing modifiers as nounlike constituents in their own right, which accords well with the possibility of these modifiers occurring on their own without a head nominal. On the other hand the head nominal is an important concept in Patwin grammar: the presence or absence of a head nominal has implications for case marking on adjectives, and the grammatical animacy of the head nominal triggers agreement within the noun phrase and throughout the clause—even if the head nominal is not overtly stated. The discontinuous constituent analysis has the benefit of identifying the head nominal in the constituent structure as the element that projects the noun phrase in the constituent structure. On the other hand the concepts of a head nominal and agreement can be accounted for outside of the constituent structure (Falk 2001; Sag, Wasow, and Bender 2003).

SEVEN

Directionals and Cardinals

Directionals and cardinals are closed classes of words with spatial meanings. Cardinals refer to the cardinal directions north, south, east, and west. Directionals refer to spatial concepts like "inside," "on top," "behind," and "downstream."

Directionals and cardinals are similar in that both may function as locative adjuncts to the clause without explicit locative case marking, like *če·n* 'down' in (145a). Nominals must be marked with the locative case in order to function as locative adjuncts, like *keweła* 'to the house' in (145b).

(145) a. ⟨har? ce·n⟩

har	ʔ	<u>če·n</u>
go.2SG.HORT	‖	<u>down</u>

Go <u>down</u>.
(Ultan, d:7.74, SG) [RP]

b. ⟨keweła har?⟩

<u>kewe-ła</u>	har	ʔ
<u>house-LOC</u>	go.2SG.HORT	‖

Go <u>to the house</u>.
(Ultan, d:7.75, SG) [RP]

Directionals and cardinals are also similar in that both may occur with the remote suffix /-e·l/ and the stative suffix /-ti/, as described below. Both directionals and cardinals may also be intensified with full reduplication.

However, directionals and cardinals are structurally distinct: only directionals take the movement suffix /-pa/.[1] Only cardinals take the second-degree remote suffix /-na/ (in Grimes River Patwin). Only in cardinals can both the remote suffix /-e·l/ and the stative suffix /-ti/ occur in the same word. Directionals are commonly attested in compound constructions with verbs, whereas cardinals are not.[2] Directionals also may take a nominal complement, whereas cardinals do not.

The following sections discuss the morphosyntax of directionals (7.1) and cardinals (7.2).

7.1. DIRECTIONALS

Directionals occur in two basic stem forms: bound forms, which are morphologically simplex forms occurring in compound constructions, and free forms, which may be used as independent words. Table 7.1 summarizes the attested forms for directionals.[3]

Three of the directionals always have the same stem form whether they

Table 7.1. Bound and free stem forms of directionals

Bound forms	**Free forms**
čen- 'down'	če·n 'down'
	čen-ti 'below'
	čen-pa 'downstream'
yel- 'back, after'	yel-e·l 'last'
	yel-ti 'behind'
	yel-pa 'back'
	yel-in 'back' (HP_L)
ʔol- 'up'	ʔol-e·l 'up'
	ʔol-pa 'upstream'
tu·- 'first'	tu· 'first'
	tu·-pa 'in front, before'
k^{h}al- 'away' (HP)	k^{h}al-e·l 'far' (HP&SP)
k^{h}ay- 'away' (RP)	
daw- 'out'	daw-pa 'in front'
ʔel- 'in'	ʔel 'inside'
pat- 'out'	pat 'outside'
panti 'on top'	panti 'on top'

are bound or free: /ʔel/ 'in, inside', /pat/ 'out, outside', and /panti/ 'on top'. The directionals /ʔol/ 'up', /yel/ 'back', /kʰal/ 'away' (HP), and /daw/ 'out, in front' must take the suffixes /-ti, -pa, -e·l, -in/ to be used as independent words, as shown in table 7.1 (the functions of these suffixes will be discussed below). The directionals /če·n/ 'down' and /tu·/ 'first' may occur in either suffixed or non-suffixed forms when used as independent words. The River Patwin directional /kʰay/ 'away' is attested only in compound constructions, and has no corresponding free form in River Patwin.

The examples below show the directionals *ʔel* 'in' and *pat* 'out' used as bound and free forms. In (146a) the directional *ʔel* 'in' is compounded with the verb *łeye·* 'to put', to create the predicate *ʔel-łeye·* 'to put in'. In (146b) the same directional is used as an independent word. It has an adverbial function in the clause, specifying the location where the activity takes place. In (147a) the directional *pat* 'out' is compounded with the verb *kiri* 'to move with the hand', creating the predicate *pat-kiri* 'to take out with the hand'. In (147b) the same directional is used as an independent word. It has an adverbial function in the clause, specifying the spatial goal of the activity.

(146) a. ⟨[. . .] 'o·´pɛlɛt 'ɛlL·e-e·´ro bɩ´l·pam.⟩
[. . .] ʔupelet ʔel-łeye·-ro bil-pa-m
3DU.OBJ in-put-PART burn-APPL-SBJV
[. . .] (they) put them in and set it on fire.
(Radin, c:71/197, AL) [HP$_T$]

b. ⟨ʔɛ́lču k̓aná·bʊṣ kEwɛ́lła⟩
ʔel ču k'ana·-bus kewel-ła
in 1SG.SBJ sleep-FIN house-LOC
I sleep inside the house.
(Ultan, d:2.114, OM) [HP$_L$]

(147) a. ⟨mi hójʔo mátomin ƛ̓áłima pátkɩrisáj⟩
mi hoyʔo matomin ƛ'ałi-ma
2SG.SBJ already 2SG.POSS$_{AN}$ rattle-OBJ

pat-kiri-say

out-move-Q

Did you get your rattle out already?

(Whistler, d:A94, OM) [HP_L]

b. ⟨harʔ pat⟩

har	ʔ	pat
go.2SG.HORT	||	out

Go outside!

(Ultan, d:7.74, SG) [RP]

Suffixes on directionals: The independent stems of some directionals have suffixes /-ti, -pa, -e·l, -in/, which are unique to directionals and cardinals. These suffixes are discussed individually below.

The stative suffix /-ti/ 'STAT' is attested in /čen-ti/ 'below' and /yel-ti/ 'behind', as well as on cardinals (see section 7.2).[4,5] For the directional /če·n/, the suffix carries a stative meaning. Without the suffix, *če·n* means 'down', referring to the direction of a movement. With the suffix, *čenti* means 'below' or 'bottom', referring to a static location. It is also associated with a stative meaning in *yelti* 'behind', in opposition to other suffixed forms of this directional *yelpa* 'back' and *yelin* 'back' (HP_L).

The movement suffix /-pa/ 'MOVT' is attested in /čen-pa/ 'downstream', /ʔol-pa/ 'upstream', /yel-pa/ 'back', and /tu·-pa/ 'in front, before'. It is associated with a stream-direction meaning in *čenpa* and *ʔolpa*, and plausibly with a directional meaning in /yelpa/. Its semantic contribution to *tu·pa* is less obvious, since this directional is used to refer to a static location.

The remote suffix /-e·l/ 'REM' is attested in /kʰal-e·l/ 'far' (in HP and SP), /yel-e·l/ 'last', and /ʔol-e·l/ 'up', and is attested productively on cardinals in all dialects.[6] It signifies remoteness, deriving *yele·l* 'last' from /yel-/ 'behind', *kʰale·l* 'far' from /kʰal-/ 'away', and remote cardinals (see section 7.2). Its semantic contribution to *ʔole·l* 'up' is not clear; there is no nonremote form of /ʔol/ for comparison.

The suffix /-in/ is unique to Lodoga Hill Patwin. It is attested only in the directional /yel-in/ 'back', and almost always followed by the allative case suffix /-tuka/ in the word *yelintuka* 'backward'. Thus it may signify direction of motion, standing in opposition to the stative suffix /-ti/ in Lodoga Hill Patwin.

Case marking: Used as independent words, directionals may be marked with a spatial case /t(')uka/ 'ALL', /-ti/ 'ABL', or /-na/ 'PROL'. Example (148) shows the directional *ʔel* in each of these three cases: allative *ʔeltuka* 'into the inside' (148a), ablative *ʔelti* 'from inside' (148b), and prolative *ʔelna* 'around inside' (148c).

(148) a. ⟨piłí·rohɷs t̉ɔ·kuma ʔɛltuka⟩

piłi·roho-s   t'o·ku-ma   ʔel-tuka

blow.cold-FIN   cold-CAUS   in-ALL

The cold (wind) is blowing in.

(Ultan, d:6.50, NeL) [HP_T]

b. ⟨L·u´tLa 'ɛlha·´ram 'ɛ´l·ti s·ɩ´n·pɛ ko·´pɛcɩn la·´tmero [. . .]⟩

łu·t-ła   ʔel-ha·ra-m   ʔel-ti   sinpe

dance.house-LOC   in-go-SBJV   in-ABL   door

ko·pe-sin   la·t-me-ro   [. . .]

root-INS   wrap-COM-PART

They went into the dance house and tied the door with grapevine root from the inside [. . .]

(Radin, c:40/170, AL) [HP_T]

c. ⟨ʔɛ́lnaču k̓ayí·bʊs⟩

ʔel-na   ču   k'ayi·-bus

in-PROL   1SG.SBJ   walk-FIN

I'm walking around inside (the house).

(Ultan, d:2.114, OM) [HP_L]

Case suffixes may also appear on directionals with the locational suffixes /-ti/ 'STAT' (149a), /-pa/ 'MOVT' (149b), /-e·l/ 'REM' (149c), and /-in/ (149d). The case suffix always follows the locational suffix.

(149) a. ⟨cɪp téwtaro haras tho·k centina⟩

čip tew-taro hara-s t^ho·k <u>čen-ti-na</u>

bird fly-PART go-FIN tree <u>down-STAT-PROL</u>

The bird is flying <u>under</u> the tree.

(Whistler, d:E71, HL) [HP_R]

b. ⟨ʔɷlpaťuka har̃ʔ⟩

<u>ʔol-pa-t'uka</u> har ʔ

<u>up-MOVT-ALL</u> go ||

Go <u>upstream</u>.

(Ultan, d:7.18, SG) [RP]

c. ⟨ɔlɛ´lt'uka pɔ· L·e·´pam⟩ 'and shot the fire'

<u>ʔol-e·l-t'uka</u> p^ho· łe·y-pa-m

<u>up-REM-ALL</u> fire put-APPL-SBJV

He shot the fire <u>upward</u>.

(Radin, c:24/158, AL) [HP_T]

d. ⟨yɛ́lɪntuka hará·bus⟩

<u>yel-in-tuka</u> hara·-bus

<u>back-*in*-ALL</u> go-FIN

(He) went <u>backward</u>.

(Whistler, d:A28, OM) [HP_L]

Complements: Directionals used as independent words may optionally have a nominal complement, as in the examples in (150). In (150a) the directional *panti* 'on top' takes the noun complement *ki·lakma* 'Kilak'.[7] In (150b) the directional *yelti* 'behind' takes the pronoun complement *nat* 'me'. In (150c) the directional *tu·pa* 'before' takes the nominalized clause *san tepi* 'sun emerging' as a complement. In (150d) and (150e) the directional *ʔel* takes the noun complements *kolła* and *keweła*. The complement typically occurs before the directional (150a–150d), but may occur after (150e). The complement generally occurs in the objective case (150a, 150b), but complements in the locative case are attested, especially with *ʔel* 'in' (150d, 150e).

(150) a. ⟨kɩ·´lakma pa´nti t'u·l 'ʊm.⟩

ki·lak-ma	panti	t'u·lu-m
Kilak-OBJ	on.top	pour-SBJV

(He) poured (it) on top of Kilak.
(Radin, c:66/193, AL) [HP_T]

b. ⟨pónołta win nat yélti bo·s⟩

ponołta	win	nat	yelti	bo·-s
three	person	1SG.OBJ	behind	be.AN-FIN

There are three people behind me.
(Whistler, d:F69, HL) [HP_R]

c. ⟨sʌ́n t̳ɛ̀pì tú·pà⟩

[san	tepi	]	tu·pa
[sun	emerge.NMNL	]	before

before sun rise
(Bright, c:7.NL225, NL) [HP_C]

d. ⟨[. . .] tùdûy łêytaʔ kolłaʔel⟩

[. . .]	t'uduy	łe·y-ta	ʔ	kol-ła	ʔel
	stone	put-PART	‖	mouth-LOC	in

[. . .] (they) put a stone in (her) mouth.
(Bright, c:1.G162, SG) [RP]

e. ⟨pi ʔɛlkeweła bo·⟩

pi	ʔel	kewe-ła	bo·
pi	ʔel	kewe-ła	boh-s
3SG.SBJ	inside	house-LOC	be.AN-FIN

He's inside the house.
(Ultan, d:7.75, SG) [RP]

Table 7.2. Stems for cardinal directions

Gloss	Stem I	Stem II
'north'	way	wa·ri way (HP_T) wa· (RP_G)
'south'	wor	wori wor (HP_T)
'east'	puy	pu·ri puy (HP_T) pu· (RP_G)
'west'	nom	no·wi

7.2. CARDINALS

Cardinal stems take two forms, referred to here as stem I and stem II. Stem I is the same in every dialect: /way/ 'north', /wor/ 'south', /puy/ 'east', and /nom/ 'west'. Stem II varies by dialect. In Lodoga Hill Patwin, Cortina Hill Patwin, and South Patwin, the forms of stem II are /wa·ri/ 'north', /wori/ 'south', /pu·ri/ 'east', and /no·wi/ 'west'. These are also the forms for stem II in Colusa River Patwin (RP_C). In Grimes River Patwin (RP_G) two of the stem II forms are contracted: /wa·/ 'north' and /pu·/ 'east'. In Tebti Hill Patwin stem II is identical to stem I for /way/ 'north', /wor/ 'south', and /puy/ 'east'. In all dialects stem II of 'west' is /no·wi/. These stem forms are summarized in table 7.2.

The suffixes appearing on cardinals select a specific stem. For example the remote suffix /-e·l/ 'REM' selects stem I of the cardinal to which it attaches, and the remote suffix /-na/ 'REM2' selects stem II. In the absence of suffixes the choice of stem may indicate degrees of remoteness in some dialects (see below). Both stems are attested as citation forms, but stem I is more commonly elicited.

Degrees of distance: Degrees of remoteness are signaled by the suffixes /-e·l/ 'REM' and /-na/ 'REM2', or by choice of stem form. Indication of degrees of remoteness varies by dialect, and is not well documented for most

Table 7.3. Degrees of remoteness in cardinals

Dialect	Near	Far	Farther
RP_C	{stem I}	{stem II}	{stem I}-e·l
RP_G	{stem I}	{stem I}-e·l	{stem II}-na
HP_R	{stem I}	{stem I}-e·l	
HP_L	{stem II}	{stem I}-e·l	{stem I}

dialects. The systems in the more robustly documented dialects are shown in table 7.3; the patterns of suffixation and stem choice are described in the following paragraphs.

The remote suffix /-e·l/ 'REM' selects stem I of the cardinal to which it attaches and always appears immediately adjacent to the root. It is frequently attested in all dialects and is associated with an increased degree of remoteness compared to the unmarked stem. For example Rumsey Hill Patwin speaker Harry Lorenzo gives ⟨nom⟩ /nom/ for 'west' and ⟨nomé·l⟩ /nom-e·l/ for 'west, way over west, far off to the west' (Whistler, d:F53).

The remote suffix /-na/ 'REM2' signifies a further degree of remoteness (e.g., ⟨pú·na⟩ /pu·-na/ 'way back east'; Bright, c:1.G160, SG), and is also used to refer to the sides of houses (e.g., ⟨wá·na⟩ /wa·-na/ 'north side [of the house]'; Bright, c:1.G160, SG). It is attested infrequently in River Patwin and more rarely in Hill Patwin. It generally selects stem II of the cardinal to which it attaches, though it is attested selecting stem I in Colusa River Patwin, Lodoga Hill Patwin, and Cortina Hill Patwin. The remote suffixes /-e·l/ 'REM' and /-na/ 'REM2' never co-occur in the same word.

The choice of stem also signals degree of remoteness in some dialects. In Colusa River Patwin, Merriam describes stem I as 'near', stem II as 'farther', and forms with the remote suffix /-e·l/ as 'farthest' (Merriam:V75, 38). The reverse is attested in Lodoga Hill Patwin, where both Oscar McDaniel and Merriam's informants use stem I to indicate a high degree of remoteness and stem II for nearby reference (Merriam:V70, 38; Whistler, d:C4).

Full reduplication of the cardinal, including any suffixes, may be used to indicate extreme remoteness in Tebti Hill Patwin speaker Anderson Lowell's texts, as in (151).

(151) ⟨nɔmɛ·ˊlnɔmɛ·ˋl, ʼa·ˊpatcutɪn, tcu hɛˊn·ɪsa.⟩

'Toward the extreme west there I went uncle.'

nome·l-nom-e·l	ʔa·pa-ču-t-in	ču
REDUP-west-REM	uncle-RL-OBJ-LOC	1SG.SBJ

hen-ni-sa
arrive-RPAST-PAST

I came to my uncle in the extreme west.

(Radin, c:12/148, AL) [HP_T]

Stative suffix: The stative suffix /-ti/ 'STAT' follows the remote suffix /-e·l/, and is not attested without the remote suffix (though the remote suffix may occur without /-ti/).[8] It is attested in citation forms for cardinals in South Patwin: ⟨Wi-yelˊ-te, War-relˊ-te, Pooˊ-yelˊ-te, No-melˊ-te⟩ /waye·lti, wore·lti, puye·lti, nome·lti/ 'north, south, east, west' (Merriam:V76.38). It is also attested before the ablative suffix /-nak/ in South Patwin, as shown in the word *waye*ltinak* 'from the north' in (152a). The stative suffix is only infrequently attested in River Patwin and Hill Patwin, where it always occurs before a spatial case suffix /t'uka/ 'ALL' (152b) or /na/ 'PROL' (152c).

(152) a. ⟨Wayeltinac chu henti⟩

way-e*l-ti-nak	ču	hen-t°i
north-REM-STAT-ABL	1SG.SBJ	arrive-FIN

I come from the north.

(P. Vallejo, c:23.8) [SP]

b. ⟨wákwàk t'ʊ̀kút'ʊ̀kú ʔʊ́nò łʊ́pòhóroʔ nùmɛ́ltı̀t'ʊ̀ká⟩

wakwak	t'ukut'uku	ʔuno
crane	neck	3SG.$POSS_{IN}$

łupoho-ro	ʔ	nom-el-ti-t'uka
stick.out?-PART	||	west-REM-STAT-ALL

Crane stuck out his neck toward the west.

(Bright, c:1.G162, SG) [RP]

c. ⟨w·ɔrɛl tɩ·´na⟩
wor-e·l-ti*-na
south-REM-STAT-PROL
from the south
(Radin, c:66/192, AL) [HP_T]

Demonym suffix: The demonym suffix /-i·n/ signifies reference to people and selects stem I of the cardinal to which it attaches. For example *puyi·n* means 'people to the east' (e.g., Ultan, d:6.13O, SG; Whistler, d:E83, JR) and *wayin* means 'people to the north' (Merriam:V72.76). These terms may describe tribes or ethnic groups, including Patwin tribes (as described by others). The suffix /-i·n/ is probably etymologically related to the noun *win* 'person'.

Case suffixes: The case suffixes attested on cardinals are allative /-t(')uka/, ablative /-ti, na·k/, and prolative /-na/. They are attested immediately after the stem (153a), following remote suffixes /-e·l/ and /-na/ (153b, 153c) and following the stative suffix /-ti/ (152b, 152c).

(153) a. ⟨k̓ɩ·r puytuka haras⟩
k'i·r puy-tuka hara-s
cloud east-ALL go-FIN
Clouds are moving east.
(Whistler, d:D10, HL) [HP_R]

b. ⟨wɔrɛ´lti w·ɔlɛ·´La ha·´t·a [. . .]⟩
'From the south there at the burrowing-hole they came [. . .]'
worelti wole·ła ha·tta
wor-el-ti wole·-ła ha·r-ta
south-REM-ABL burrow-LOC go-PART
From the south (they) came to the burrow [. . .]
(Radin, c:66/192, AL) [HP_T]

c. ⟨pículu wánnat'ʊkaʔ wìtí·luroʔ⟩

pičulu	wa-na-t'uka	ʔ	witi·lu-ro	ʔ
then?	north-REM2-ALL	‖	run-PART	‖

Then (she) ran northward.

(Bright, c:1.G172) [RP]

When appearing directly on the stem, case suffixes almost always select stem I, as in (153a). However, the ablative suffix /-nak/ is attested after stem II in Tebti Hill Patwin: ⟨no·´wɪnak·⟩ /no·wi-nak/ 'from the west' (Radin, c:98/222, AL).

EIGHT

The Verb and Verbal Morphology

The verb in Patwin is the locus of much of the semantic and grammatical information in the clause. The verb root—that is, the single morpheme at the heart of the verb—expresses the activity or state described in the clause. Suffixes express various categories of tense, aspect, mood, voice, and syntactic category. Reduplication and other changes to the stem express event and participant plurality.

The following sections describe the morphology of the verb stem (section 8.1), verbal suffixes (section 8.2), the expression of event and participant plurality (section 8.3), nominalization (section 8.4), and verb compounding (section 8.5).

8.1. THE VERB STEM

The Patwin verb stem is the best described area of Patwin grammar, being described in depth for Rumsey Hill Patwin in Whistler (1981). Whistler discusses Rumsey Hill Patwin verb-stem canons and the systematic formal variation in verb stems known as ablaut. Whistler addresses only Rumsey Hill Patwin, however, so some description of the other dialects here will not be redundant. Moreover Whistler's description of stem ablaut can be simplified for a presentation more appropriate in a descriptive grammar.

Patwin verb stems vary systematically in form, conditioned by the suffix appearing directly after the stem. Nonsuffixed stems ("bare stems") also occur, in which case different forms of the stem carry different meanings. For example consider the verb *muhi* 'to sing', whose stem takes one of two forms /muhi-, muhu-/. The subjunctive mood suffix /-m(u)/ and the applicative suffix /-pa/ condition the stem form /muhu-/ (which I will call the "hortative stem" of *muhi*), yielding /muhu-m/ 'sing-SBJV' and /muhu-pa/ 'to sing for'; whereas the future suffix /-t'i/ conditions the stem form /muhi-/

(the "nominal stem" of *muhi*), yielding /muhi-t'i/ 'will sing'. The bare hortative stem functions as a singular command form (second-person singular hortative): *muhu* 'sing! (SG)', and the bare nominal stem can function as a noun: *muhi* 'song'. Compare the verb *hama·* 'to sit', whose stem takes one of three forms in Hill Patwin: /hama·-, hama-, ham-/. The subjunctive and applicative suffixes condition the hortative stem form /ham-/, yielding /ham-mu/ 'sit-SBJV' and /ham-pa/ 'to sit on, to press down'; whereas the future suffix conditions the nominal stem /hama·-/, yielding /hama·-t'i/ 'will sit'. The bare hortative stem functions as a singular command form: *ham* 'sit! (SG)', and the bare nominal stem can function as a noun: *hama·* 'chair'. Different form-classes of stems such as the hortative stem and the nominal stem are here referred to as *stem classes* (following Whistler 1981).

Different verbs vary in different ways across stem classes, such that it is possible to identify three major conjugational classes of verb stems: consonant-stem verbs (which end in a consonant in some stem classes); unchanging-stem verbs (which always end in a vowel of unchanging quality); and *i*-stem verbs (which end in /i(·)/ or /u(·)/, depending on stem class). Stems in these three conjugational classes are here referred to as stems of the first, second, and third conjugation, respectively.[1] Within each of these major conjugational classes, there are two minor conjugational classes: long (the stem-final vowel is long in some contexts) and short (the stem-final vowel is never long).[2] The list in (154) schematizes the major and minor conjugational classes, noting the salient characteristics of each class.

(154) Conjugational classes of the Patwin verb

I. First conjugation verb stems (formally "consonant stems")

Hortative and participial stem forms are consonant-final; other stems have a final vowel of the same quality as the stem-internal vowel.

<u>long:</u> The final vowel in the nominal stem is long (only in HP).

<u>short:</u> The final vowel in the nominal stem is short.

II. Second conjugation verb stems (formally "unchanging stems")

The stem is vowel-final, and does not change in the different stem classes.

<u>long:</u> The final vowel is long.

<u>short:</u> The final vowel is short.

III. Third conjugation verb stems (formally "*i*-stem" verb stems)

Nominal and agentive stems end with /i(·)/; other stems end with /u(·)/.

long: HP: The final vowel in the participial stem is long /u·/; all other stem-final vowels are short.

RP: The final vowel is long in the nominal and participial stems; all other stem-final vowels are short.

short: The final vowel is always short.

The variation between and within conjugational classes in Patwin is limited to the stem-final vowel, which may be called the characteristic vowel of the stem. An additional fourth conjugation, present in River Patwin, is always consonant-final, as described below. The fourth conjugation may also be present in South Patwin, but is not present in Hill Patwin. See section 9.1.2.

8.1.1. Hill Patwin

The Hill Patwin system of verb stem ablaut is summarized in table 8.1. The data in this table is derived from the description in Whistler (1981), but the structure has been changed to reflect a more form-oriented approach. Table 8.1 shows the three major conjugational classes and their subclasses, and the five stem classes for each of these conjugational classes. The stem classes are here named *nominal, agentive, past, hortative, and participial.* These names are given only for the purpose of referring to these classes and should not be interpreted as describing semantic or functional features of the stems. The stem classes are purely formal in nature and do not themselves bear any semantic or functional information. For example verbs with stems in the hortative stem class are not all in the hortative mood.

Table 8.1 also shows the suffixes associated with each of the stem classes. For example the subjunctive suffix /-mu/ selects a stem of the hortative stem class. The forms and functions of the suffixes themselves will be discussed separately below.

For a list of Rumsey Hill Patwin verb stems in each conjugational class, see Whistler (1981).

Table 8.1. Verb stem classes in Hill Patwin

			First conjugation		**Second conjugation**		**Third conjugation**	
			Long	Short	Long	Short	Long	Short
Nominal stem	-t'i	'FUT'	XV·	XV	XA·	XA	X*i*	X*i*
	-t'o	'INCEP'						
	-bosa	'HAB'						
	-boti/beti	'CERT'						
	-hVm	'REL'						
Agentive stem	-s	'FIN'	XV	XV	XA·	XA	X*i*	X*i*
	-tu	'NMLZ$_{AG}$'						
	-sok	'REL$_{OBL}$'						
Past stem	-sa	'PAST'	XV	XV	XA·	XA	X*u*	X*u*
	-say	'Q'						
Hortative stem	-ta·	'PAST.Q'	X	X	XA·	XA	X*u*	X*u*
	-ni	'RPAST'						
	hortatives							
	-mu	'SBJV'						
	-les, -len	'can'						
	-čin	'lest'						
	-mut^{h}ere	'might'						
	-mute·	'might.PAST'						
	-muʔa/ma	'must'						
	voice							
	-mele·	'NEG'						
	-muʔu	'NEG'						
	-ka(m)	'CONC'						
Participial stem	-taro	'PART'	X	X	XA·	XA	X*u*·	X*u*
	-ni	'ADV'						

Whistler's description of Hill Patwin verb stem ablaut: Whistler (1981) describes nine stem classes for each verb, some of which always have the same form. This is because he analyzes the stems as morphemic, in the sense that they must have a specific form and a specific meaning. For example, assuming that stems must be morphemic, it makes sense to say that the "absolutive" and "future" stems (Whistler's Ia and Ib) are distinct stems. Although the absolutive and future stems have the same form for every verb, they are associated with different grammatical functions: the absolutive stem is used in nominalizations (deverbal nominals and nominalized subordinate verbs), whereas the future stem is used in tensed main clauses associated with the morphosyntactic property [+FUT] 'future tense'.

However, there is no compelling reason to posit distinct stem classes that are formally identical based on semantic differences alone. In general the suffixes occurring after the stem can be conceptualized as bearing the semantic and functional information associated with any given form of a verb; the stem need only bear the kind of lexical semantic information generally associated with verb roots (i.e., information about the event denoted by the verb). Stem classes are therefore not analyzed as morphemic here. Rather they are taken as purely formal morphological classes ("morphomic" in the sense of Aronoff 1994 and Bermúdez-Otero and Luís 2016). Whistler's formally identical stem classes can therefore be collapsed, such that only five stem classes need be recognized for Hill Patwin, as shown in table 8.1.

The nominal stem in table 8.1 subsumes Whistler's "absolutive" and "future" stems (Ia and Ib); the agentive stem in table 8.1 is the same as Whistler's "-s stem" (Ic); the past stem in table 8.1 is the same as Whistler's "-sa stem" (II); the hortative stem in table 8.1 subsumes Whistler's "imperative," "hortatory," "modal," and "subjunctive" stems (III, IVa, IVb, and IVc); and the participial stem in table 8.1 is the same as Whistler's participial stem (V).

8.1.2. River Patwin

River Patwin stem classes and conjugational classes have not been previously described. A survey of verbs was therefore conducted in the major available archival materials: Whistler's field notebooks with speaker Jennie Regalado (Whistler, d), Ultan's field notebooks with speakers Sarah Gonzales and Hazel (Gonzales) Hanes (Ultan, d), and Swadesh's audio-recorded elicitation session with speaker Ida Mitchum (Swadesh and Melton). Some other sources were surveyed as well: Bartlett's short word list with speaker H. B. Brown, McKern's two ethnological papers with data from speaker Thomas Odock (McKern 1922, 1923), Shafer's published word list with speaker Jim Perdue (Shafer 1961), and Haas's short word list with speakers Ida and William Mitchum. Another potential source is Morgan's (1971) masters thesis on River Patwin morphology and phonemics. However, Morgan's analysis of verb stem ablaut is based on the description in de Angulo's unpublished grammar, which is a description of Cortina Hill Patwin. Her analysis is therefore misleadingly interwoven with Hill Patwin structure and could not be used for the present survey.

The River Patwin ablaut system is broadly similar to that of Hill Patwin, but has some salient differences. River Patwin ablaut is summarized in table 8.2. All three of the major conjugational classes are present in Hill Patwin and River Patwin: consonant stems, unchanging stems, and *i*-stems. But unlike Hill Patwin, River Patwin has only one conjugational class of consonant-stem verbs (i.e., verb stems of the first conjugation). There is no class of consonant-stem verbs with a characteristic long vowel in the nominal stem. The pattern of vowel length in the long third conjugation class is also different between the two dialects: the characteristic vowel is long in both the nominal and participial stems.

A small fourth conjugation in River Patwin comprises only the auxiliaries *boh* 'be.AN', *beh* 'be.IN', and *ʔih* 'COP', which are all unchanging stems ending in the consonant /h/, and the irregular auxiliary *čeh*, which has two stem forms: /čeh-/ (nominal, agentive, and past stems) and /čel-/ (hortative and participial stems). Fourth conjugation stems are thus characterized by being always consonant-final underlyingly. Although the stem-final /h/ is not always present in surface forms due to optional /h/ vocalization (see section 3.5.3), its presence in the underlying forms of these auxiliaries has morphological implications. The /h/ conditions consonant-following allomorphs of certain suffixes, and it conditions the suppression of the finite suffix /-s/. See section 9.1 for further discussion of the morphology of River Patwin auxiliary stems.

Some of the suffixes shared between Hill Patwin and River Patwin select different stem classes. The suffixes /-t'i/ 'FUT' and /-t'o/ 'INCEP' select the nominal stem in Hill Patwin but the agentive stem in River Patwin. (In other words, there are no attested future or inceptive forms in River Patwin third-conjugation stems with a long characteristic vowel /i·/.)

The finite suffix /-s/ selects the agentive stem in Hill Patwin but the past stem in River Patwin. (In other words, third-conjugation stems selected by

/-s/ have /i/ as a characteristic vowel in Hill Patwin but /u/ as a characteristic vowel in River Patwin.)

The characteristic vowels of the nominal and participial stems of the long third conjugation verbs are particularly prone to vowel shortening (see section 3.5.1). Therefore the boundary between the nominal stem and the agentive stem cannot be established with certainty from the archival record, nor can the boundary between the hortative stem and the participial stem. For the classification of suffixes in table 8.2, I have included in the nominal stem group only those suffixes that are attested with a long vowel for at least one third-conjugation verb stem. There are no third-conjugation verb stems attested with a long characteristic vowel in the future or inceptive forms, so the suffixes /-t'i/ 'FUT' and /-t'o/ 'INCEP' are identified as belonging with the agentive stem group. However, it may be that the long-vowel variants are grammatical and simply unattested, in which case these suffixes select the nominal stem, as in Hill Patwin.

Further lexicographical work will be required to produce a list of River Patwin verbs categorized by conjugational class.

8.1.3. South Patwin

As with the rest of South Patwin grammar, the verbal ablaut system of South Patwin cannot be described with a great deal of confidence. But in spite of the sparse and inconsistent data, the basic outline of the system can be discerned, and is sketched in table 8.3.

All three of the major conjugation classes are clearly present; their formal variation is analogous to that found in Hill Patwin and River Patwin. The first conjugation can be seen in stems like /wini*- ~ win-/ 'to see', for example ⟨Winí⟩ /winí*/ 'to see' versus ⟨winley⟩ /win-le/ 'let me see' (P. Vallejo, c:22.2, 28.3). Thus, as in Hill Patwin and River Patwin, South Patwin stems of the first conjugation vary in form between a consonant-final morph and a vowel-final morph whose final vowel is qualitatively identical to the preceding vowel. The second conjugation can be seen in stems like /ʔot°o*-/ 'to kiss', for example ⟨otó⟩ /ʔot°ó*/ 'to kiss' versus ⟨Otóléý⟩ /ʔot°ó*-le/ 'I am going to kiss' (P. Vallejo, c:26.4). Thus, as in Hill Patwin and River Patwin, stems of the second conjugation in South Patwin are characterized by always being vowel-final regardless of the following

Table 8.2. Verb stem classes in River Patwin

			First conjugation	**Second conjugation**		**Third conjugation**		**Fourth conjugation**
				Long	Short	Long	Short	
Nominal stem	-sem	'REL'	XV	XA·	XA	X*i*·	X*i*	X
Agentive stem	-bo/be	'Q'	XV	XA·	XA	X*i*	X*i*	X
	-t'i	'FUT'						
	-t'o	'INCEP'						
	-tu	'NMLZ$_{AG}$'						
Past stem	-s	'FIN'	XV	XA·	XA	X*u*	X*u*	X
	-sa	'PAST'						
Hortative stem	-ni	'RPAST'	X	XA·	XA	X*u*	X*u*	X
	hortatives							
	-mu	'SBJV'						
	-len	'can'						
	-čin	'lest'						
	voice							
	-mele·	'NEG'						
	-mur	'NEG'						
	-kam	'CONC'						
	-nini	'COND'						
Participial stem	-ta/ro	'PART'	X	XA·	XA	X*u*·	X*u*	X
	-ni	'ADV'						

suffix. This characteristic vowel does not have to have the same quality as the preceding vowel, though it may. The third conjugation can be seen in stems like /t'oki- ~ t'oku-/ 'to be ill', for example ⟨Tóki⟩ /t'óki/ 'ill' versus ⟨tócuma⟩ /t'óku-ma/ 'make ill' (P. Vallejo, c:22.8, 23.2). Thus, as in Hill Patwin and River Patwin, third-conjugation verb stems in South Patwin end with an /i(·)/ or /u(·)/ depending on the following suffix. The auxiliaries *boh* and *beh* may belong to an unchanging, consonant-final stem class like the fourth conjugation in River Patwin, but the evidence is slim. See discussion in section 9.1.2.

One verb shows what appears to be an alternation between /i/ and /o/ as the final vowel: /t'opelti, t'opelto/ 'arise' (both forms are attested in P. Vallejo, c:23.3). Although no other verbs in this *i/o* conjugation are verifiably attested, and in spite of the fact that this conjugation seems to be absent from Hill Patwin and River Patwin, its existence is plausible and is not necessarily an artifact of a messy data source. The system of verb-stem ablaut described for Wintu in Pitkin (1984:72 ff.) is considerably more complicated than the system found in Patwin in terms of variation in the quality of the characteristic vowel. It is therefore plausible that South Patwin may have retained one of the many additional conjugational classes that probably existed in Proto-Wintuan (although this *i/o* class has no identical counterpart in Wintu). This *i/o* stem shows the same pattern of variation as the more common *i*-stem verbs of the third conjugation, except that where typical *i*-stems have a final /u/, this verb has a final /o/.

Establishing the South Patwin stem classes is problematic, but some clear patterns can be observed. Some suffixes can be reliably associated with certain patterns of stem variation; these are assigned to named stem classes in table 8.3. Inceptive /-t'o/ and many bare-stem citation forms pattern together as the *nominal* stem class, selecting the vowel-final allomorphs of first-conjugation verb stems and /i/-final allomorphs of third-conjugation verb stems. This stem class is comparable in form to the nominal and agentive stem classes in Hill Patwin and River Patwin. Hortative suffixes, valence-changing suffixes, subjunctive /-mu/, negative /-mele*/, and participle /-taro/ pattern together as the *hortative* stem class, selecting the consonant-final morph of first-conjugation verb stems and the /u/-final morph of third-conjugation verb stems. This stem class is comparable in form to the hortative and participial stem classes in Hill Patwin and River Patwin. The hortative stem in its bare form is also a common citation form for South Patwin.

One common suffix /-t°i/ 'FIN' is almost always associated with the consonant-final morph of consonant-stem verbs, but is associated with both /i/-final and /u/-final morphs of third-conjugation verb stems. There is no suffix in Hill Patwin or River Patwin that is associated with this pattern of stem variation. I have assigned this suffix to its own stem class: the *finite* stem class. It is possible that the suffix /-t°i/ is actually two different suffixes, one of which selects the nominal stem (resulting in the observed /i/-final third-conjugation stems) and the other selecting a past or horta-

Table 8.3. Verb stem classes in South Patwin

			First conjugation	Second conjugation	Third conjugation
Nominal stem	-t'o	'INCEP'	XV	XA	X*i*
	-boti/beti	'CERT'			
Hortative stem	hortatives		X	XA	X*u*
	-m	'SBJV'			
	voice				
	-mt°i	'FIN?'			
	-mit°a	'Q.PAST'			
	-mit°at	'PAST?'			
	-mele*	'NEG'			
	-taro	'PART'			
Finite stem	-t°i	'FIN'	X	XA	X*i* ~ X*u*
Set 1	-sa	'PAST'	XV	XA	?
Set 2	-net	'RPAST'	X	XA	?
	-ni	'PAST'			
	-ni	'ADV'			
Set 3	-t	'RPAST'	?	XA	X*u*
	-tk°a	?			
Set 4	-say	'Q'	?	XA	?
	-t'i	'FUT'			
	-hVm	'REL'			

tive stem (resulting in the observed /u/-final third-conjugation verbs). However, there is no noticeable semantic distinction to support this two-suffix analysis. The suffix /-t°i/ is the South Patwin analog of Hill Patwin and River Patwin /-s/ 'FIN', being used with ongoing actions and states in the present and past, and this meaning is uniform across /i/-final and /u/-final third-conjugation verb stems.

Many suffixes cannot be definitively associated with one stem class or another. These are suffixes that are not attested with consonant-stem verbs, or not attested with *i*-stem verbs. These suffixes are shown in table 8.3 in sets according to their patterns of attestation.

One stem class present in both Hill Patwin and River Patwin is not definitively present in South Patwin: the past stem, characterized by vowel-final stems of the first conjugation and /u/-final stems of the third conjugation. This stem class may or may not exist in South Patwin. If it does, the past-tense suffix /-sa/ and the interrogative /-say/ are the most likely suffixes to select it, based on their class affiliation in Hill Patwin and River Patwin. However, there is not enough evidence to verify this association for South Patwin.

Table 8.3 shows the patterns identifiable in the South Patwin record, but there are a few exceptions to the patterns shown in the table. The finite suffix /-t°i/ is generally associated with the consonant-final morph of verbs in the first conjugation (/hen/ 'arrive', /k'ak/ 'burn', /yur/ 'rain', etc.), but it is also attested with the vowel-final morph of a verb in the same conjugation: /humu/ 'fat'.[3] Similarly the negative suffix /-mele*/ generally selects the consonant-final morph for verbs in the first conjugation (/ʔet/ 'steal', /har/ 'go', /yok/ 'die'); but for one verb, 'to see', both morphs are attested with /-mele*/: /win ~ wini/ (P. Vallejo, c:22.2, 26.10, 29.5; Merriam:V76.71).

List of South Patwin verbs: The verbs in the South Patwin archival record are listed in (155) according to their probable conjugational class. As with all South Patwin data, the emergent picture is somewhat vague. The problems with identifying the forms of the South Patwin verb stems shown in (155) are discussed here.

Distinctions of glottalization and aspiration are not represented in the South Patwin archive, so these features must be reconstructed based on Hill Patwin and River Patwin cognates. Where cognates could not be found in Hill Patwin or River Patwin and the laryngeal state of an obstruent is not known, a superscript circle follows the obstruent.[4] It should be noted that the data in Mason's word list cast a somewhat troubling shadow over this comparative enterprise. Mason is the only researcher to indicate glottalization for South Patwin. In some cases the patterns of glottalization attested in Mason line up with forms in the other dialects: SP (Mas.) ⟨k'ana´⟩ /k'aná/ 'sleep' (compare HP and RP /k'ana·/, e.g., in Whistler 1981; Haas); SP (Mas.) ⟨kol⟩ /kol/ 'mouth' (compare HP and RP /ko·l/, e.g., in Whistler, d; Haas). However, the glottalization indicated in Mason does not always line up with what we might expect based on cognates in Hill Patwin and River Patwin. For instance Mason gives ⟨t'ai⟩ /t'ay/ for 'cousin', which is /tʰay/ in HP; and ⟨tewe⟩ /tewe/ for 'speak', which is /t'ewe/ in HP and RP. Comparative evidence from Hill Patwin and River Patwin is probably better evidence for laryngeal state than Mason's short list (for which nonnative speaker Platon Vallejo was the linguistic consultant), but the conflict here is another good reminder that these reconstructions should be taken with a grain of salt.

The lists in (155) show South Patwin verbs not only by their major conjugational class, but also by subgroups based on attested stress on the final vowel. Assuming a general similarity between the South Patwin ablaut system and the other dialects' systems, minor conjugational classes may be differentiated partly based on the length of the stem-final vowel. (See schematic in 154 above.) However, vowel length is only rarely represented in the South Patwin archive. Stress on vowels is frequently represented, constituting some indirect evidence for vowel length. Only stress is indicated in (155) unless a long vowel has been clearly indicated in the record. For example the bare nominal stem of the verb for 'to speak' is rendered ⟨umúú⟩ ('name') in Vallejo (P. Vallejo, a:1)—an indication that the final vowel is long, that is, /ʔumú·/.[5]

A further complication is that stress is not necessarily always represented in the archival record—nor can we expect that all verb stems with potentially long characteristic vowels will be attested in forms that reveal this length. Therefore the verb stems in (155) have been classified according to whether they are *sometimes* attested with a stressed final vowel (an indication that this vowel may be long in some inflections), or whether they are *never* attested with a stressed final vowel (some indication that they may have systematically short final vowels).

In some cases forms attested in different South Patwin sources are clearly formally distinct. For example the verb 'want' is given as *ʔoyé* in Vallejo (cognate with RP *ʔoyaʔa* 'want'); whereas in Merriam we find *k'ayú* (cognate with HP *k'ayi* 'want'). Such differences between sources may represent dialect differences within South Patwin. Where two sources show different forms of verb stems, they are represented separately in (155) with the source author indicated in parentheses.

In addition to the three major conjugational class categories, (155) also shows attested irregular verb stems and attested verbs that cannot be definitively assigned to any one conjugational class. The verb *ʔi* 'do' has an irregular hortative form /ʔiwe/, as it does in Hill Patwin (see section 8.2.2.1).

(155) Attested SP verbs grouped by conjugational class

I. First conjugation (consonant stems)

a. Consonant stems with stressed final vowels attested

hará/ha(r) 'go'; *hené/hen* 'arrive, come'; *kirí/kir* 'take, catch'; *łalá/łal* 'smell (INTR)'; *tʰepé/tʰep* 'hit'; *tʰonó/tʰon* 'dance'; *weré/we(r)* 'come'; *winí/win* 'see'; *yurú/yur* 'rain'

b. Consonant stems with only unstressed final vowels attested

ʔana/ʔan 'plenty, lots'; *hete/het/ʔet* 'steal, rob'; *humu/hum* 'fat'; *mutu/mut* 'hear, listen'; *yoko/yok* 'die'

c. Consonant stems attested only in consonant-final form

bohil 'have'; *ham* 'sit'; *k'ak* 'hot, burn'; *łakal* 'play, fun'; *łey* 'lay down, put down'; *t'al* 'fall'; *liwt°iw* 'ask'; *t°emel* 'buy'; *yuduk* 'pity' (Vallejo); *yunuk* 'pity' (Arroyo de la Cuesta)

II. Second conjugation (unchanging stems)

a. Unchanging stems with stressed final vowels attested

ʔelé 'absent, NEG'; *ʔerá* 'cold'; *ʔolí* 'hear'; *ʔot°ó* 'kiss'; *ʔoyé* 'want, desire' (Vallejo); *ʔúmu/ʔú·mu/ʔumú/ʔumú·* 'speak, name, hear'; *ʔupú* 'say'; *bá* 'eat' (Vallejo); *bolá* 'drink'; *čerú* 'finish, create'; *hiná* 'bear, bring forth'; *k'aná* 'sleep'; *k°ané* 'dislike'; *k°owé* 'deceive'; *lomó* 'kill' (Vallejo); *lumó* 'kill' (Merriam); *łelá* 'shoot'; *łeyá* 'give'; *má* 'eat' (Arroyo de la Cuesta); *moyá* 'fish'; *sirí* 'copulate'; *tʰiyá* 'call, bring, let out'; *t'ewé* 'speak'; *t'uyú* 'closed'; *t°erá* 'fly'; *weré* 'bring'; *werí* 'bring'; *witilú* 'run'; *yet(ʔ)á* 'name'; *yulé* 'govern'

b. Unchanging stems with only unstressed final vowels attested

ʔolpʰuru 'breathe, expire'; *čoyi* 'sick'; *čuro* 'not know' (Merriam); *čuru* 'not know' (Vallejo); *hari* 'take'; *ƚ°ami* 'drunk'; *monʔa* 'similar, like'; *nóha* 'angry'; *watʰi* 'cry'

III. Third conjugation (*i*-stems)

a. *i*-stems with stressed final vowels attested

bolí/bolú 'drunk'; *č°eyí/č°eyú* 'break, bend, tear to pieces'; *doyí/doyú* 'give'; *lelí/lelú* 'gentle, smooth, even, slow, sorrowful'; *łomi/łomú* 'keep, guard'; *łotí/łotú* 'bad'; *meč°i/meč°ú·* 'dislike'; *pisí/pisú/ʔísu* 'make, do'; *tepí/tepú* 'emerge, give birth, flow, beget'; *t'óki/t'óku/t'okú* 'sick'; *t'umi/t'umú* 'hazy, misty'; *t°ač°í/t°ač°u* 'cut, divide'; *t°alí/t°alu* 'good'; *yalí/yalú* 'leave'; *yori/yorú* 'command'

b. *i*-stems with only unstressed final vowels attested

hawiri/hawinu [sic] 'fast'; *kosi/kosu* 'angry'; *lewtʰi/lewtʰu* 'throw'; *łattʰi* 'tie'; *łattʰi* 'yell, halloo'; *muk°i/muk°u* 'cloudy'; *wičisi/wičisu* 'pull, lead, rescue, divide'

c. *i/o*-stem

t'opelti/t'opelto 'rise'

IV. Irregular verbs

ʔi/ʔiwé 'do'; *bo(h)* 'be.AN'; *be(h)* 'be.IN'

V. Verbs of uncertain conjugational class

ʔałá 'to be noon'; *ʔená/ʔeni* 'defecate'; *ʔeyí* 'bite'; *ʔonókt°i* 'marry a woman'; *bakó* 'count'; *beré* 'hungry'; *bot'u* 'smoke'; *č'iyá* 'old'; *č'odi* 'crawl (?)' (in Vallejo: ⟨tchoditi⟩ 'horse'); *č°apá* 'sweat'; *č°ayi* 'shy, modest'; *č°elu/č°alu* 'pretty'; *č°eyú* 'bend'; *č°iru* 'admire'; *č°urt°i* 'shriveled'; *č°urú* 'blessed'; *dowu* 'lie down'; *halí* 'think'; *háre* 'go away'; *helélu* 'hug'; *heró* 'help'; *hobó* 'happen'; *katu* 'full'; *kattʰú* 'open'; *kʰonó* 'dry'; *k'ayú* 'want' (Merriam); *k'ayú* 'walk'; *k'omo* 'wide, open'; *k°irí* 'remember'; *lep°é* 'punish'; *lubú* 'kiss'; *łewi* 'sting, prick'; *łompa/łowt°i* 'jump'; *łubúko* 'suck'; *ƛ'eye* 'laugh'; *ƛ°ahú* 'awake'; *ƛ°ayi* 'sing'; *ƛ°ok°aw* 'hide'; *ƛ°omú(r?)* 'paint'; *mok°ú* 'black'; *morí* 'unripe'; *noki* 'ripe'; *pʰúro* 'rest'; *p'iłí* 'gather'; *p°ok°ósu* (Vallejo)/*p°ok°óso* (Merriam) 'strike, hit'; *seté* 'burp'; *seyi* 'tired'; *sit°o* 'smell (TRANS)?' (⟨shitomati⟩ 'it stinks'); *soru/sóru* 'listen'; *sowki* 'wash, bathe'; *soyó* 'walk'; *súyi/suyí* 'suck'; *tehóm(a)* 'give birth, be born?'; *toyó* (Vallejo)/*toyu* (Arroyo de la Cuesta) 'stop, finish'; *tʰanó* 'win'; *t'ú·nu/t'umi* 'urinate, sweat'; *t°ač°i* 'hot'; *t°awá* 'sew'; *t°ayá* 'blind'; *walu* 'burn'; *werú* 'come along'; *yelé* 'wait'; *yetʰé* 'dream'; *yetʰó* 'brave'; *yik°á* 'hollow, empty'

8.2. VERBAL SUFFIXES

A verb may have zero or more suffixes, with no distinct upper limit.

The Patwin verb has four positionally defined categories of suffixes, as shown in table 8.4. A few derivational suffixes always appear immediately adjacent to the root, and may be called *root-bound suffixes*. All other derivational suffixes may appear on any stem, whether adjacent to the root or with one or more intervening derivational suffixes. These suffixes may be called *medial suffixes*. There may be more than one medial suffix. Almost all inflectional suffixes must occur at the end of the verb, and may be called *final suffixes*.

Table 8.4. Maximal structure of the verb

reduplication, compounding	**root**	root-bound suffix	medial suffixes	prefinal suffix	final suffix

The future tense /-t'i/ and the remote past tense /-ni/ are *prefinal suffixes*. They appear after the derivational suffixes, but may be followed by an additional inflectional suffix. Because final suffixes are not obligatory, prefinal suffixes may be the last suffix in a verb.

Root-bound and medial suffixes are verb-like, in that they are subject to the patterns of ablaut described in section 8.1. These suffixes therefore must be assigned to a conjugation. The reflexive suffix /-nana/ for example is a stem of the first conjugation, realized as /-nana/ before the past-tense suffix /-sa/, and as /-nan/ before the participle suffix /-ta(ro)/. The semelfactive suffix /-t^{h}i/ on the other hand is a stem of the third conjugation, realized as /-t^{h}i/ before the past-tense suffix /-sa/ and /-t^{h}u/ before the participle suffix /-ro/. Most derivational suffixes are stems of the second conjugation—that is, they do not vary in form.

Prefinal and final suffixes are not subject to patterns of verbal ablaut, but they may change form depending on their phonological environment. For example the subjunctive suffix is realized as /-m/ after vowels and /-mu/ after consonants. Prefinal and final suffixes may also be invariant in form, like past-tense /-sa/.

8.2.1. Tense and Aspect Suffixes

Patwin verbs distinguish four categories of tense. They may be marked for the past tense (/-sa/ 'PAST' HP and RP; /-ni/ 'PAST' SP), the remote past tense (/-ni/ 'RPAST' HP and RP; /-t, -net/ 'RPAST' SP), or the future tense (/-t'i/ 'FUT'), or they may be marked with a nonspecific tense suffix (/-s, -t°i/ 'FIN'). Interrogative suffixes also distinguish past from nonpast: /-say/ 'Q' versus /-ta·, -te·/ 'Q.PAST' (HP) or /-bo, -be/ 'Q' versus /-mu/ 'SBJV' for past interrogatives (RP). A small number of aspectual suffixes are also attested: inceptive /-t'o/ 'INCEP', habitual /-bosa/ 'HAB' (HP), and resultative /-či/ (HP).

Forms of FIN

-s	HP, RP
-t°i	SP
-bus, -bes	HP_L variants

8.2.1.1. Finite Declarative /-s, -t°i, -bus, -bes/ 'FIN'

The finite suffix 'FIN' takes the form /-s/ in Hill Patwin and River Patwin, and /-t°i/ in South Patwin. It is a final suffix, and selects the agentive stem (HP), the past stem (RP), or the finite stem (SP) of the verb to which it attaches. In Lodoga Hill Patwin the additional forms /-bus, -bes/ occur alongside /-s/, selecting the nominal stem of the verbs to which they attach, as described below.

The semantic contribution of the suffix is difficult to identify. In Hill Patwin and River Patwin, /-s/ has been identified as present tense (de Angulo:22; Morgan 1971:55; Whistler 1977a:174), past tense (Bright, b:5.23), "indefinite present" tense (Radin, b:34), unmarked or neutral tense (Whistler 1978:57, 1986:63), and noninceptive aspect (Whistler 1981:84). Indeed /-s/ can appear in a variety of temporal and aspectual contexts. It is used for events in the recent past (156a), the present (156b), the immediate future (156c), and the future (156d). It is used for completed events (156a), ongoing events (156b), and for the inception of events (156c).

(156) a. ⟨p'ŏkìtà hìnnís⟩

p'okita hene-s̲

woman come-F̲I̲N̲

A woman came.

(Bright, c:6.NL115, NL) $[HP_C]$

b. puči-s̲ ču ʔ

be.well-F̲I̲N̲ 1SG.SBJ ||

I am well.

(Bright, a:1.5:02, NL) $[HP_C]$

c. ʔo· hara-s ču
alright go-FIN 1SG.SBJ
Goodbye. (lit. 'Alright, I'm going.')
(Swadesh and Melton:1:39, IM) [RP]

d. ⟨worɛl t'ʋka tcu hara·´tɪs⟩
worel-t'uka ču hara·-t'i-s
south-ALL 1SG.SBJ go-FUT-FIN
I'm going to go to the south.
(Radin, c:100/223, AL) [HP$_T$]

This variety of tenses and aspects suggests that Whistler's (1978; 1986) description of the finite suffix is best: a suffix that makes the verb finite and marks the clause as declarative, but that contributes no specific tense or aspect information.[6] It does however stand in a kind of opposition to the more specific declarative past-tense suffixes (/-sa/ 'PAST', /-ni, -net/ 'RPAST', etc.) and therefore carries a nonpast implication. Although verbs with the finite suffix are sometimes offered as translations of events in the very recent past (generally earlier the same day), they are not used for events in the remote past or even the relatively recent past (yesterday).[7] Similarly the finite suffix stands in opposition to the more specific future tense suffix /-t'i/ in River Patwin, and could be said to carry a nonfuture implication (though it may be used for the near future, as in 156c). The finite suffix does not carry a nonfuture implication in Hill Patwin, where it is often found together with the future suffix /-t'i/, as described above. In South Patwin the formal distinction between /-t°i/ 'FIN' and /-t'i/ 'FUT' is murky.

South Patwin /-t°i/: The form of the finite suffix in South Patwin is /-t°i/. It selects the finite stem of the verb to which it attaches, a stem class unique to this suffix (see table 8.3). It is characterized by the consonant-final allomorph of first-conjugation stems (157a) and an alternation in the third conjugation between /i/-final stems (157b) and /u/-final stems (157c). This alternation in the third conjugation seems to be semantically vacuous. After vowels the suffix may be realized as /-t/.

(157) a. ⟨Pitch-oot win-te⟩

pi	čut	win-t°i
3SG.SBJ	1SG.OBJ	see-FIN

He sees me.
(Merriam:V76.59) [SP]

b. ⟨Tokiti⟩
t'oki-t°i
sick-FIN
(He) is sick.
(P. Vallejo, c:22.8) [SP]

c. ⟨Taluti⟩ 'Bien'
t°alu-t°i
good-FIN
Good.
(Arroyo de la Cuesta:24, SC) [SP]

Because sources for South Patwin do not indicate aspiration or glottalization, the laryngeal series of the consonant in /-t°i/ is not known. The finite suffix /-t°i/ and the future suffix /-t'i/ are transcribed identically in South Patwin sources, causing some ambiguity in source interpretation.

The etymology of the finite suffix /-t°i/ is not known. It may be related to the future tense /-t'i/.

Lodoga Hill Patwin /-bus, -bes/: Lodoga Hill Patwin has two unique allomorphs of 'FIN': /-bus, -bes/. Both select the nominal stem of the verb to which they attach. The allomorph /-bus/ is used when the subject is a grammatically animate noun, a personal pronoun, or a kinship term. The allomorph /-bes/ is used when the subject is a grammatically inanimate noun or demonstrative. See examples of /-bus/ or /-bes/ from three different Lodoga Hill Patwin speakers in (158).

(158) a. č'iw łeye·-bes
hail fall-FIN
It's hailing.
(Ultan, b:3:09, OM) [HP_L]

b. ⟨Me naht´ win-ne´-bus⟩
mi nat wini·-bus
2SG.SBJ 1SG.OBJ see-FIN
You see me.
(Merriam:V70.59) [HP_L]

c. ⟨p̓akít́ibuṣču ʔɛ·⟩
p'aki-t'i-bus ču ʔe·
hammer-FUT-FIN 1SG.SBJ PROX.IN.SG.OBJ
I'm going to hammer this.
(Ultan, d:4.12, AN) [HP_L]

The meanings of /-bus, -bes/ are indistinguishable from the meaning of the other form of the finite suffix, /-s/, which is also present in Lodoga Hill Patwin. Its distribution also partially overlaps with /-s/, with no discernible distinction in meaning. For example Oscar McDaniel gives both *ču k'atis* and *ču k'atibus* for 'I'm full' (Ultan, b:13:53–14:33). There are some distributional differences between the two, however. For instance the negative auxiliary *ʔele·* and the negative suffix /-mele·/ take only /-s/, and are never inflected with /-bus/ or /-bes/. On the other hand the future-tense suffix /-t'i/ takes only /-bus/ or /-bes/, and is never inflected with /-s/. I therefore analyze /-s, -bus, -bes/ to be allomorphs of the finite declarative suffix in Lodoga Hill Patwin whose distributions partially overlap.

The forms /-bus, -bes/ are clearly derived from the auxiliary verbs *bo·*/*be·* 'be' + /-s/ 'FIN', but are formally and distributionally distinct from this historical source. The vowel quality in /-bus/ is distinctly /u/ rather than /o/, and the vowel is never long either in /-bus/ or /-bes/. Moreover Lodoga Hill Patwin /-bus, -bes/ are bound and never stressed, whereas *bo·* and *be·* are free auxiliary verbs that may be stressed. Unlike *bo·* and *be·*, Lodoga

Hill Patwin /-bus, -bes/ never occur in constructions with participles (section 9.1.2.2) or as auxiliary verbs for nonverbal predicates. (In these environments Lodoga Hill Patwin uses the free auxiliary verbs *bo·* and *be·* like other dialects do.) Furthermore, in spite of the fact that /-bus/ and /-bes/ are derived from two separate morphemes, the two parts are no longer independent—in other words */-bu/ is not a suffix in Lodoga Hill Patwin independent of /-s/. Because of these differences it is best to consider /-bus/ and /-bes/ to be allomorphs of the finite suffix, unique to Lodoga Hill Patwin—in spite of their obvious historical source.

Null marking in River Patwin: In River Patwin the auxiliaries *boh* 'be.AN', *beh* 'be.IN', and *čeh* 'AUX' do not occur with an overt finite suffix. The finite suffix may occur underlyingly (and is so analyzed here), but is elided in the surface form to avoid the word-final cluster */hs/. (See discussion in section 3.2.1.) These stems are attested with a suffix of the form /-s/, but this is the short allomorph of past-tense /-sa/ and always signifies the past tense specifically.

8.2.1.2. Past Declarative /-sa/ 'PAST'

The past-tense declarative suffix /-sa/ is attested in all Patwin dialects. In Hill Patwin and River Patwin it selects the past stem of the verb to which it attaches. It is in semantic contrast with the remote past tense (see below). In Hill Patwin and River Patwin it is a final suffix, but in South Patwin it is attested only before the suffix of certainty /-boti, -woti/ 'CERT' (see section 8.2.2.8). Example (159) shows examples of the past-tense suffix from each of the major dialect groups.[8]

(159) a. ⟨ʔéw sınó·l chu k̓aná·sa⟩

ʔew	sino·l	ču	k'ana·-<u>sa</u>
PROX.SG.SBJ	night	1SG.SBJ	sleep-<u>PAST</u>

I slept last night.

(Whistler, d:A109, OM) [HP_L]

b. ⟨le·ni pi piʔuro bɛssa⟩

le·ni	pi	piʔuro	bessa
le·ni	pi	piʔu-ro	beh-sa
yesterday	DIST.SG.SBJ	do.that-PART	be.IN-PAST

It was that way yesterday.

(Ultan, d:7.97, SG) [RP]

c. ⟨Chu masahuoti⟩ 'Yo comí'

ču	ma-sa-woti
1SG.SBJ	eat-PAST-CERT

I ate.

(Arroyo de la Cuesta:24, SC) [SP]

In Hill Patwin and South Patwin this suffix always takes the form /-sa/. In River Patwin it may be optionally shortened to /-s/ after vowels. This means that the formal distinction between the past-tense suffix /-sa/ and the finite suffix /-s/ is optionally neutralized in River Patwin. Both suffixes select the same stem class of the verbs to which they attach, making the resulting verb forms systematically identical. An alternative analysis that presents itself is that the form /-s/ in River Patwin might always be the finite suffix, which simply is used for past-tense reference alongside the past-tense suffix /-sa/. However, the shortened allomorph /-s/ of the past-tense suffix is formally differentiated from the finite suffix in one set of River Patwin verbs: the auxiliaries *boh* 'be.AN', *beh* 'be.IN', and *čeh* 'AUX', which are not attested with an overt finite suffix. These verbs are formally unusual in that they are underlyingly consonant-final /boh-, beh-, čeh-/ before all suffixes. The finite suffix therefore does not appear in the surface forms of these verbs, to avoiding the word-final cluster */hs/ (see example 160a and section 3.2.1). The past-tense suffix is not subject to this same constraint, even in the form /-s/. Therefore the forms [bo(·)s, be(·)s, če(·)s] are attested in River Patwin, but only in the past tense (as in 160b). When the past tense takes the form /-s/ on River Patwin auxiliaries *boh, beh,* and *čeh* 'AUX', the stem-final /h/ is vocalized, as described in section 3.5.3.

(160) a. ⟨pa· pi piʔuro bɛh⟩

pa·	pi	piʔu-ro	beh
pa·	pi	piʔu-ro	beh-s
now	DIST.SG.SBJ	do.that-PART	be.IN-FIN

It's that way now.

(Ultan, d:7.97, SG) [RP]

b. ⟨le·ni pi piʔuro bɛs⟩

le·ni	pi	piʔuro	bes
le·ni	pi	piʔu-ro	beh-sa
yesterday	DIST.SG.SBJ	do.that-PART	be.IN-PAST

It was that way yesterday.

(Ultan, d:7.97, SG) [RP]

8.2.1.3. Interrogative /-say, -sey/, /-bo, -be/ 'Q'

A clause may be marked as a question with an interrogative suffix on the verb. In Hill Patwin this suffix takes the form /-say/ or /-sey/. It is a final suffix, and selects the past stem of the verb to which it attaches. The variation between /-say/ and /-sey/ is geographically determined (see below). In River Patwin the interrogative suffix takes the form /-bo/ or /-be/. This is a final suffix, and selects the nominal stem of the verb to which it attaches. The variation between /-bo/ and /-be/ is conditioned by the animacy of the subject (see below). In South Patwin both /-say/ and /-bo, -be/ are attested, but the latter is more common.

The interrogative suffix is used in present contexts (161) and in future contexts in combination with the future tense suffix /-t'i/ (162). In Hill Patwin it is also attested in past contexts (163), though the past-tense interrogative /-ta·, -te·/ may be used also (see section 8.2.1.4). In River Patwin the subjunctive suffix is used to mark past-tense interrogatives (see section 8.2.2.2). In South Patwin the suffix /-mit°a/ is used to mark past-tense interrogatives (see section 8.2.1.6).

(161) a. ⟨mi hárasaj⟩

mi hara-say
2SG.SBJ go-Q
Are you going?
(Whistler, d:A84, OM) [HP_L]

b. ⟨pi· thʊ̀lí·boʔ⟩

pi· tʰuli·-bo ʔ
3SG.SBJ swim-Q ||
Is he swimming right now?
(Bright, c:8.G85, SG) [RP]

c. ⟨pé pi yetábo⟩

pe* pi* yeta*-bo
what 3SG.SBJ be.named-Q
What is his name?
(P. Vallejo, c:28.2) [SP]

(162) a. ⟨mi hará·ṫisaj⟩

Mi hara·-t'i-say
2SG.SBJ go-FUT-Q
Are you gonna go?
(Whistler, d:A95, OM) [HP_L]

b. ⟨bɛhna mi tʰɪ·rma ba·ṫibo⟩

behna mi tʰi·r-ma ba·-t'i-bo
morning 2SG.SBJ fish-OBJ eat-FUT-Q
Will you eat fish tomorrow?
(Ultan, d:7.81, SG) [RP]

(163) ⟨mi hójʔo mátomin ƛ'áłima pátkɪrisáj⟩

mi hoyʔo matomin ƛ'ałi-ma
2SG.SBJ already $\text{2SG.POSS}_{\text{AN}}$ rattle-OBJ

pat-kiri-say
out-move.with.hands-Q

Did you get your rattle out already?
(Whistler, d:A94, OM) [HP$_L$]

In Vallejo's South Patwin material, /-say/ is attested marking relative clauses (164a) and with an optative sense expressing a wish (164b).[9] These functions may be Vallejo's own extensions of the function of the interrogative /-say/, expanded to cover construction types that he did not know or could not recall. The use of /-say/ for relative clauses in particular is likely a calque: using interrogative elements in relative clauses is characteristic of English and Spanish, but not attested in Patwin outside of Vallejo's material. However, /-say/ is not attested in South Patwin with its basic interrogative function.

(164) a. ⟨Nechunu Tan olelbosai mattono umuu hé-ébosai!⟩
neč'unu **tan** [ʔolel bo-say]
1PL.EXCL.POSS$_{IN}$ **father** [above be.AN-Q]

matono ʔumu· he· bo-say
2SG.POSS$_{IN}$ name praise be.AN-Q

Our **father**, [who art above], may your name be praised!
(P. Vallejo, c:19.4.3) [SP]

b. ⟨Nechunu Tan, olelbe, talibosai matono yet.⟩
neč'unu tan ʔolel be
1PL.EXCL.POSS$_{IN}$ father above be.IN

[t°ali bo-say matono yet]
[good be.AN-Q 2SG.POSS$_{IN}$ name]

Our father who art above, [may your name be good].
(P. Vallejo, c:29.4) [SP]

Forms of the interrogative suffix

-say	HP_L, HP_C, HP_R, SP
-sey	HP_L, HP_T
-bo	RP, SP (AN)
-be	RP, SP (IN)

Formal variation: There are two etymologically unrelated forms of the interrogative suffix: /-say, -sey/ in Hill Patwin and South Patwin, and /-bo, -be/ in River Patwin and South Patwin.

In Hill Patwin and South Patwin the variation between /-say/ and /-sey/ depends on dialect. The /-say/ variant is most widespread, attested for Lodoga, Cortina, and Rumsey Hill Patwin, and for South Patwin (see above). The suffix /-sey/ occurs in Tebti Hill Patwin (165a, 165b). Lodoga Hill Patwin speaker Amelia Nunes varies between /-sey/ (165c) and /-say/ (165d), tending toward /-sey/. Other Lodoga Hill Patwin data shows only /-say/.

(165) a. ⟨he·´ti mi hɛnɛse·´⟩
he·ti mi hene-sey
where.ABL 2SG.SBJ arrive-Q
Where do you come from?
(Radin, c:34/165, AL) [HP_T]

b. ⟨láykʔan mi bosey⟩
laykʔa-n mi bo-sey
good-ADV 2SG.SBJ be.AN-Q
How are you? (lit. 'Are you well?')
(Ultan, d:6.81, DL) [HP_T]

c. ⟨pêɒnimi bɒsé·⟩
pew-ni mi bo-sey
do.what-ADV 2SG.SBJ be.AN-Q
How are you?
(Ultan, d:4.6, AN) [HP_L]

d. ⟨hɛ́kɛ mílɛ ṫɛwɛṣaɪ̦⟩
heke mile t'ewe-say
which 2PL.SBJ speak-Q
What language do you speak?
(Ultan, d:4.32, AN) [HP_L]

The suffix /-sey/ is sometimes transcribed as /-se·/ (always in Radin, sometimes in Ultan) and sometimes as /-sey/ (always in Bright, usually in Ultan). This apparent variation may be caused by researchers' native languages being English, where the phoneme /e/ is typically realized as the diphthong [eɪ], phonetically similar to Patwin /ey/. Then again, it may be a real point of variation. I transcribe this variant always as /-sey/, since the most phonetically reliable source for this affix (Ultan) usually transcribes it this way.

In RiverPatwin and South Patwin the variation between /-bo/ and /-be/ is conditioned by the animacy of the verb's subject. If the subject is animate, the interrogative suffix takes the form /-bo/, as in (161b) and (162b). If the subject is inanimate, the interrogative suffix takes the form /-be/, as in (166), where the subject is the inanimate noun *botok* 'tree'.

(166) ⟨boṫɷk be·be ṗiła⟩
botok be·-be piła
tree be.IN-Q DIST.LOC
Is there a tree there? (Ultan, d:6.133, SG) [RP]

8.2.1.4. *Hill Patwin Past Interrogative /-ta·, te·/ 'Q.PAST'*

The past interrogative suffix is a final suffix, and selects the hortative stem of the verb to which it attaches. It is attested in all dialects of Hill Patwin, but not outside of Hill Patwin. The variation between /-ta·/ and /-te·/ is geographically determined (see below). This suffix indicates that the clause is in the past tense and that the clause is interrogative. Example (167) shows the suffix in Cortina and Rumsey Hill Patwin.

(167) a. ⟨pò héntâ⟩

po	hen-ta*
who	arrive-Q.PAST

Who came in?

(Bright, c:6.NL115, NL) [HP_C]

b. ⟨he·-ła mi horu-ta·, thay?⟩

he·ła	mi	horu-ta·	tʰay
where	2SG.SBJ	be.saved-Q.PAST	grandson

Where were you saved, grandson?

(Whistler 1978:55/56, NL/HL) [HP_R]

Forms of the past interrogative

-ta·	HP_C, $HP_{T\text{-}Tebti}$, HP_R
-te·	HP_L, $HP_{T\text{-}Lol}$

Formal variation: The variant /-ta·/ is found in Cortina Hill Patwin and Rumsey Hill Patwin (see 167). Lodoga Hill Patwin uses /-te·/, as shown in (168).

(168) a. ⟨mi múhuté·⟩

mi	muhu-te·
2SG.SBJ	sing-Q.PAST

Did you sing?

(Whistler, d:A99, OM) [HP_L]

b. ⟨Hā´-too-kah pe hat-tā⟩

he·tuka	pi	hatte·
he·tuka	pi	har-te·
where.ALL	3SG.SBJ	go-Q.PAST

Where did he go?

(Merriam:V70.70) [HP_L]

Within the Tebti dialect there is some subdialectal variation. Although Tebti proper uses /-ta·/, the Lol subdialect of Tebti Hill Patwin uses /-te·/.

See example (169), showing a Tebti and Lol rendering of the same phrase by Daisy Lorenzo (Ultan, d:6.74).

(169) a. ⟨mʊnʊkta⟩ /munuk-ta/ 'was it sweet?' (Tebti)
b. ⟨mʊnʊktɛ⟩ /munuk-te/ 'was it sweet?' (Lol)

This is a particularly interesting dialectical distinction, as the Tebti and Lol dialects are generally not regarded as being distinct. They are grouped together as Lake County Hill Patwin in Whistler (1980), and as Tebti Hill Patwin in Whistler (1976) and in this work. Merriam does distinguish between Lol (Merriam's Lol´-sel) and Tebti (Chen´-po-sel) in some of his work: see the regions marked "19m (Chen´-po-sel)" and "19n (Lol´-sel)" in Heizer (1966:map 5). Merriam (1977:174), however, combines the two groups, describing the Lol´-sel as a "band of Chen'-po-sel'," though noting that they were regarded as separate tribes by the people themselves.

Anderson Lowell consistently uses /-te·/ in the texts gathered by Radin, suggesting that he speaks the Lol subdialect of Tebti Hill Patwin.

(170) ⟨cʊna´k· mi he·´t'uka ha·´nitɛ?⟩

sunak	mi	he·t'uka	hanni<u>te</u>
sunak	mi	he·t'uka	har-ni-<u>te·</u>
here.ABL	2SG.SBJ	where.ALL	go-RPAST-<u>Q.PAST</u>

Where did you go from here?
(Radin, c:97/221, AL) [HP$_{T}$]

Forms of the remote past	
-ni	after consonants
-n	after vowels (optional in HP)

8.2.1.5. *Remote Past Tense /-ni/ 'RPAST'*

The prefinal suffix /-ni/ 'RPAST' in Hill Patwin and River Patwin marks an event occurring in the remote past. It selects the hortative stem of the verb to which it attaches.

In Hill Patwin /-ni/ is always followed by one additional inflectional suffix: /-sa/ 'PAST' (171a) for declaratives or /-ta·, -te·/ 'Q.PAST' (171b) for interrogatives.[10] In River Patwin it may be the last suffix on a verb (171c), or it may be followed by an inflectional suffix. In the example in (171d) /-ni/ is followed by the subjunctive suffix /-m/, functioning as an interrogative marker.

(171) a. ⟨chu mútnisa ʔut múhɪma tú·be⟩

ču	mut-<u>ni</u>-sa	ʔut	muhi-ma
1SG.SBJ	hear-<u>RPAST</u>-PAST	3SG.OBJ	sing-OBJ

tu·be
long.ago

I heard him singing a long time ago.
(Whistler, d:E51, HL) [HP_R]

b. ⟨mi mútnita· ʔut múhima tu·be⟩

mi	mut-<u>ni</u>-ta·	ʔut	muhi-ma
2SG.SBJ	hear-<u>RPAST</u>-Q.PAST	3SG.OBJ	sing-OBJ

tu·be
long.ago

Did you hear him singing a long time ago?
(Whistler, d:E51, HL) [HP_R]

c. ⟨cu kawa·yuma ʔɛtni⟩

ču	kawa·yuma	ʔet<u>ni</u>
ču	kawa·yu-ma	ʔeč-<u>ni</u>
1SG.SBJ	horse-OBJ	steal-<u>RPAST</u>

I stole a horse.
(Ultan, d:7.70, SG) [RP]

d. ⟨tʰi·rma mi ba·nim⟩

tʰi·r-ma	mi	ba·-<u>ni</u>-m
fish-OBJ	2SG.SBJ	eat-<u>RPAST</u>-SBJV

Did you eat fish?
(Ultan, d:7.81, SG) [RP]

In River Patwin and optionally in Hill Patwin, the remote past takes the form /-n/ in environments where this does not cause a syllable structure violation. The form /-n/ occurs finally after vowels (172b), and prefinally before CV suffixes (172a). In prefinal position before suffixes consisting of a single consonant, the allomorph /-ni/ is obligatory, avoiding word-final consonant clusters (like before subjunctive /-m/ in 171d above).

(172) a. ⟨pɪma cu p̓akunsa hoya⟩

pima	ču	p'aku-n̲-sa	hoya
DIST.SG.OBJ.IN	1SG.SBJ	nail-<u>RPAST</u>-PAST	long.ago

I nailed it long ago.

(Ultan, d:6.22, NeL) [HP_T]

b. ⟨yɛtʰo·n pi ʔut⟩

yetʰo·-n̲	pi	ʔut
name-<u>RPAST</u>	3SG.SBJ	3SG.OBJ

He named him.

(Ultan, d:7.84, SG) [RP]

The temporal boundary between events marked with past /-sa/ and events marked with remote past /-ni/ varies by speaker and maybe by dialect. Tebti Hill Patwin speaker Nelson Lowell says that he uses ⟨łilansa⟩ /łila-n-sa/ 'shot (RPAST)' for an event happening one year earlier; and ⟨łila·sa⟩ /łila·-sa/ 'shot (PAST)' for an event happening one day, one week, or one month earlier (Ultan, d:6.41). Tebti Hill Patwin speaker Daisy Lorenzo describes a similar division, using the remote past for events occurring a "year, 2 y[ea]rs, or 2–3 months" in the past (Ultan, d:6.46). On the other hand River Patwin speaker Sarah Gonzales says that she uses ⟨wɪnni⟩ /win-ni/ 'saw (RPAST)' for an event happening two or three days earlier, and ⟨wínɪsa⟩ /wini-sa/ 'saw (PAST)' for an event happening one day earlier (Ultan, d:7.38).

A cognate of /-ni/ 'RPAST' is attested in South Patwin, but it is a general past-tense marker rather than a remote past-tense marker. See section 8.2.1.6. Shepherd (2005) does not mention the suffix /-ni/, and no obvious Wintu cognate presents itself. The subordinating suffix of simultaneity {n} 'while' may be a candidate, but the semantics are not close enough to be a definite match. Tarpent describes a set of resemblant forms in more northerly Penutian languages that may point to an ancient source for Patwin /-ni/: the Coast Tsimshian and Southern Tsimshian (Tsimshianic; British Columbia; tsi) particle *na(h)* 'past, alienated possession, restrictiveness'; Chinook (Chinookan; Oregon; chh) *ni(g)-* 'indefinite, non-remote past (3 days to 1 year)' and *na(l)-* 'yesterday'; and Coos (Coosan; Oregon; csz) *ni:k!wa* 'use to be, past tense' and *ni:k!wá:li:* 'yesterday' (1997:86).

8.2.1.6. Past Tense in South Patwin

A number of different suffixes are found in South Patwin referring to the past tense. The past declarative /-sa/ has already been mentioned (see example 159c). It is not attested on a third-conjugation stem in South Patwin, so its stem-class selection cannot be stated with certainty. It selects the vowel-final variant of first-conjugation stems in South Patwin, as in Hill Patwin and River Patwin, so it may select a past stem in South Patwin, analogous to the other dialects (though such a stem class is not definitely attested in South Patwin—see section 8.1.3).

Another past-tense suffix /-ni/ is attested, cognate with the remote past-tense suffix in Hill Patwin and River Patwin. In South Patwin the suffix /-ni/ is not limited to the remote past, as demonstrated in (173), where the verb *henni* 'arrived' refers to an event in the recent past. South Patwin /-ni/ selects consonant-final stems of verbs in the first conjugation, and would probably select /u/-final stems of verbs in the third conjugation, though third conjugation verbs with /-ni/ are not attested.

(173) ⟨Houte, henimi!⟩

howte(?)	hen-<u>ni</u>	mi
welcome	arrive-<u>PAST</u>	2SG.SBJ

Ah, you've come!

(P. Vallejo, c:24.8) [SP]

The suffix /-t/ apparently marks the remote past in South Patwin, as in ⟨Pisú-t⟩ /pisu-t/ 'created' and ⟨Téhomat⟩ /te∗homa-t/ 'gave birth', in the contexts of the Christian creation and the birth of Jesus, respectively

(P. Vallejo, c:19.9.1). It selects the /u/-final stem of verbs in the third conjugation, suggesting that it selects the hortative stem of the verb to which it attaches.

Another South Patwin form denoting remote past tense is ⟨-net⟩ /-net/—probably derived from a combination of the past-tense suffixes /-ni/ and /-t/. This suffix occurs three times in Vallejo's translation of the Apostle's Creed, referring to activities carried out in the remote past: ⟨Yoknet⟩ /yok-net/ 'died', ⟨Thleynet⟩ /łe⁎y-net/ 'buried (put, placed)', ⟨Hánnet⟩ /har-net/ 'went' (P. Vallejo, c:19.9.2). It selects the consonant-final stem of verbs in the first conjugation, suggesting that it selects the hortative stem of the verb to which it attaches.

A past-tense interrogative suffix /-mit°a/ is attested in Vallejo's South Patwin material, varying in form between /-mit°a/ and /-mt°a/. The form /-mit°a/ occurs after consonants (174a) and /-mt°a/ occurs after vowels (174b).

(174) a. ⟨Hechewru mi thleinan-mita⟩

heče-ʔu-ro	mi	łey-nan-<u>mit°a</u>
which-VBLZ-PART	2SG.SBJ	lie-REFL-<u>PAST.Q</u>

How did you lie down?

(P. Vallejo, c:23.3) [SP]

b. ⟨Hethla mi canamta?⟩

he⁎ła	mi	k'ana-<u>mt°a</u>
where	2SG.SBJ	sleep-<u>PAST.Q</u>

Where did you sleep?

(P. Vallejo, c:23.3) [SP]

The form /-mit°a/ may be composed of two separate suffixes: a prefinal suffix /-mi, -m/ and a suffix /-t°a/, but their individual meanings are not clear. Though /-mi, -m/ is plausibly related to the subjunctive /-mu, -m/ in its interrogative function, a similar form /-mt°i/ is attested a few times, and only in noninterrogative contexts, as in (175). The /-t°i/ in this suffix is probably related to South Patwin finite suffix /-t°i/, but the function of the /-m/ here is not clear.

(175) ⟨Himá thlotumti pibo wita!⟩

hima	łotu-mt°i	pi	bo	wita
always	bad-?	DIST.SG.SBJ	be.AN	man

This man is always bad.
(P. Vallejo, c:21.7) [SP]

Another similar suffix /-mit°at/ is attested twice—once in a past declarative context (176a) and once in a past interrogative context (176b). Like /-mit°a/ it seems to take the form /-mit°at/ after consonants and /-mt°at/ after vowels. Though the meaning of /-mit°at, -mt°at/ is obscure, the form is interesting: if it is composed of the prefinal suffix /-mi, -m/ followed by two suffixes /-t°a/ and /t/, this suggests that South Patwin may have two prefinal suffix positions.

(176) a. ⟨Olpurumtat⟩
ʔol-pʰuru-mt°at
up-breathe-?
He expired.
(P. Vallejo, c:21.10) [SP]

b. ⟨Pémi hetmitat⟩

pe·	mi	hetmit°at
pe·	mi	heč-mit°at
what.OBJ	2SG.SBJ	steal-?

What did you steal?
(P. Vallejo, c:25.7) [SP]

The suffixes /-mit°a, -mt°i, -mit°at/ all select the hortative stem of the verb to which they attach.

8.2.1.7. Future Tense /-t'i/ 'FUT'

The future tense suffix is /-t'i/. It is a prefinal suffix, selecting the nominal stem (HP) or the agentive stem (RP) of the verb to which it attaches. Its possible attestations in South Patwin are all on verbs of the second conjugation, so it is not known which stem it selects in South Patwin.[11]

The future tense suffix may be followed by an inflectional suffix—generally the finite suffix (177a) or the interrogative suffix (177b). It may also be used without a following suffix, as in (177c).[12]

(177) a. ⟨chu bá·ṫibus péła pá·sani⟩
ču ba·-t'i-bus peyła pa·sani
1SG.SBJ eat-FUT-FIN when today
I will be eating sometime today.
(Whistler, d:A82, OM) [HP_L]

b. ⟨Kle´-lah-te-si⟩
łila-t'i-say
shoot-FUT-Q
Is he going to shoot?
(Merriam:V73.69a) [HP_R]

c. ⟨he·ła pa cu k̓ana·ṫi⟩
he·ła pa ču k'ana·-t'i
where Q 1SG.SBJ sleep-FUT
Where am I going to sleep?
(Ultan, d:6.94, DL) [HP_T]

In River Patwin only the interrogative suffix /-bo, -be/ is attested after the future tense suffix (178a). The finite suffix /-s/ is not attested after the future tense suffix in River Patwin. In noninterrogative environments the future tense suffix is always the last suffix on the verb (178b).

(178) a. ⟨hámaṫi bo mi⟩
hama-t'i-bo mi
sit-FUT-Q 2SG.SBJ
Are you going to sit?
(Ultan, d:6.131, SG) [RP]

b. ⟨ɫıla·ṫi ᵗšu⟩

ɫila·-t'i ču

shoot-FUT 1SG.SBJ

I'm gonna shoot.

(Ultan, d:6.130, SG) [RP]

The etymology of /-t'i/ is unknown. It may be related to the South Patwin finite suffix /-t°i/ (section 8.2.1.1) and to the inceptive suffix /-t'o/ (section 8.2.1.8).

8.2.1.8. *Inceptive /-t'o/ 'INCEP'*

The inceptive suffix /-t'o/ is present in every Patwin dialect. It is a final suffix, and selects the nominal stem of the verb to which it attaches.

When a verb marked with /-t'o/ is the main verb in a sentence, it expresses an inceptive aspect, referring to an event's beginning. It usually refers to a near-future event, that is, an event that is about to begin (179). However, it can also refer to an activity that has just begun (180) or to the inception of an activity in the more distant past (181).

(179) a. ⟨chu pima no·p ṫıpili ṫo ʔis⟩

ču pima no·p t'ipili-t'o ʔi-s

1SG.SBJ DIST.OBJ.IN meat cook.in.ashes-INCEP COP-FIN

I'm gonna cook that meat in ashes.

(Whistler, d:E34, HL) [HP_R]

b. ⟨Yu-roo´-to-it´-te⟩

yuru·-t'o ʔi-t°i

rain-INCEP COP-FIN

It is going to rain.

(Merriam:V76.73) [SP]

(180) ⟨hará·tɔ cu ʔɪs⟩

hara·-t'o ču ʔi-s

go-INCEP 1SG.SBJ COP-FIN

I'm going right now (already started going).

(Ultan, d:6.28, DL) [HP_T]

(181) a. ⟨lɛncul cu hárato ʔisaʔ [. . .]⟩
lenčul ču hara-t'o ʔi-sa
yesterday 1SG.SBJ go-INCEP COP-PAST
I was going to go yesterday [. . .]
(Ultan, d:6.28, DL) [HP_T]

b. ču· hara-t'o ʔih-sa
1SG.SBJ go-INCEP COP-PAST
I was ready to go.
(Swadesh and Melton:58:33, IM) [RP]

When the main verb in a sentence is marked with inceptive /-t'o/, it is almost always accompanied by the copula *ʔi/ʔih*, as in all of the examples above. However, it is occasionally attested on a main verb without the copula, as in (182).

(182) ⟨hójomaʔ chu łéwɪsito·⟩
hoyo-ma ʔ ču łewisi-t'o
sucker-OBJ || 1SG.SBJ gig-INCEP
I'm gonna gig a sucker.
(Whistler, d:A18, OM) [HP_L]

Verbs with inceptive /-t'o/ also appear in subordinate clauses. In one common construction, subordinate inceptive clauses have no copula and express a purposive 'in order to' meaning (183a) or a 'lest' meaning (183b). In these constructions no inceptive meaning is present.

(183) a. ⟨wi·´ta mɔl·ɔk malɛ·´lihɪm di·´La hɛ´n·mu ba·´ 'ɛ·´tcɛt·ɔ.⟩
wi·ta molok-ma le·li-hem di·ła
man effigy-OBJ make-REL home.LOC
hen-mu [ba· ʔe·če-t'o]
arrive-SBJV [food steal-INCEP]

The man who had made the effigy came [in order to steal food].
(Radin, c:41/171, AL) [HP_T]

b. ⟨piʔum ʔurboʔ tʰɪri·ciṫo mi⟩

piʔum	ʔur	bo	ʔ
piʔu-m	ʔur	boh	ʔ
do.thus-SBJV	nothing	be.AN	‖

[tʰiri·čit'o	mi	]
[tʰiri·či-t'o	mi	]
[afraid-INCEP	2SG.SBJ	]

Don't do that, [you might get scared]. (i.e., lest you get scared)
(Ultan, d:7.67, SG) [RP]

Verbs marked with /-t'o/ may also appear in subordinate clauses where an inceptive or near-future meaning is present. In (184a) the subordinate inceptive clause functions as an argument of the verb *huspayus* 'wish'. In (184b) the verb marked with /-t'o/ is part of a conditional clause. The copula in the subordinate clause here takes the River Patwin subordinating conditional suffix /-nini/ 'if'.[13]

(184) a. ⟨húspayus ču layuk ṗeley bo·t'o⟩

huspayus	Ču	[layuk	p'eley
huspayu-s	Ču	[layuk	p'eley
wish-FIN	1SG.SBJ	[good	1PL.INCL.POSS$_V$

bo·t'o	]
boh-t'o	]
be.AN-INCEP	]

I wish [we will be well].
(Whistler, d:F123, JR) [RP]

b. ⟨mi haraṫo ʔinini ċupa·ro yaluʔ⟩ 'Finish that before you go! (leave it finished!)'

[mi	harat'o	ʔinini	]	č'upa·ro
[mi	hara-t'o	ʔih-nini	]	č'upa·-ro
[2SG.SBJ	go-INCEP	COP-COND	]	finish-PART

yalu ʔ
yalu ʔ
leave ||

[If you're going to go], finish (that) and leave.
(Ultan, d:7.63, SG) [RP]

Another function for inceptive /-t'o/ is found in Vallejo's translation of the Ten Commandments. Here /-t'o/ is used with an optative sense, as a translation of English "shall." This may be a calque from English, where "shall" is used for both future time reference and with an optative sense.

(185) ⟨Hima mica lomómeleto⟩
hima mi-k°a lomo·-mele-t'o
always 2SG.SBJ-*k°a* kill-NEG-INCEP
Thou shalt not kill.
(P. Vallejo, c:29.5) [SP$_{V}$]

8.2.1.9. *Hill Patwin Habitual Declarative /-bosa/* 'HAB'

The suffix /-bosa/ on a verb expresses a habitual or continuative aspect, often translated "always," "all the time" (186a), or "never" in negative environments (186b). It is a final suffix, and selects the nominal stem of the verb to which it attaches. It is attested in all dialects of Hill Patwin.

(186) a. ⟨hımaʔarɷ ʔe·yɛbɷṣa ʔʊt⟩
himaʔaro ʔe·ye-bosa ʔut
always bite-HAB 3SG.OBJ
He bites him all the time.
(Ultan, d:6.46, DL) [HP$_{T}$]

b. ⟨tcu 'a·´na p'ıt'ʋ·´m 'ɛle·´bɔca [. . .]⟩
ču ʔa·na p'et^{h}u-m ʔele·-bosa [. . .]
1SG.SBJ much hunt-SBJV NEG-HAB
I have never done much hunting [. . .]
(Radin, c:107/229, AL) [HP$_{T}$]

Etymologically /-bosa/ is clearly derived from the auxiliary *bo·* 'be.AN', with a suffix. This is probably the past-tense suffix /-sa/ 'PAST', though it may be derived from a nominalizing suffix /-s/ fused to the stative verbalizer *ʔa* 'VBLZ_S'.[14] However, in synchronic Patwin grammar the suffix /-bosa/ is functionally and formally distinct from the past-tense auxiliary *bo·sa*, and should be considered its own grammatical element.

In Lodoga Hill Patwin: The suffix /-bosa/ occurs repeatedly in an especially idiosyncratic construction in Lodoga Hill Patwin: /-s-ʔa-bosa/. In this construction the verb is nominalized with the finite suffix /-s/ 'FIN' (see section 8.4.2), verbalized with the stative verbalizer *ʔa* 'VBLZ_S', and inflected with /-bosa/ 'HAB'. Like the simple suffix /-bosa/ in other Hill Patwin dialects, this construction refers to habitual or continuative events, whether in the past (187a) or the present (187b). The suffix /-bosa/ is not attested in Lodoga Hill Patwin outside of this construction. Lodoga Hill Patwin speaker Amelia Nunes is recorded using a variant form of the suffix /-busa/, as in (187c), formally analogous to the Lodoga Hill Patwin finite suffix /-bus/.

(187) a. ⟨pi nun lɛ́lɪṣʔábɒṣa⟩
pi nun leli-s-ʔa-bosa
3SG.SBJ gun make-FIN-VBLZ_S-HAB
He used to make guns.
(Ultan, d:2.52, OM) [HP_L]

b. ⟨cú ʔut ḱáymɛ́lɛ ʔabɒ́ṣa⟩
ču ʔut k'ay-mele-s-ʔa-bosa
1SG.SBJ 3SG.OBJ like-NEG-FIN-VBLZ_S-HAB
I hate him. (lit. 'I never like(d) him.')
(Ultan, d:5.20, OM) [HP_L]

c. ⟨pi mʊ́yʔan bɔ́ṣʔabʊṣaʔ⟩
pi muyʔa-n bo-s-ʔa-busa
3SG.SBJ angry-ADV be.AN-FIN-VBLZ_S-HAB
He's cranky all the time.
(Ultan, d:4.74, AN) [HP_L]

8.2.1.10. *Hill Patwin Habitual Interrogative /-bota/*

The suffix /-bota/ is the interrogative counterpart of the habitual declarative suffix /-bosa/. It is not strongly attested, being found only in texts from Cortina Hill Patwin speaker Fred Gonzales in de Angulo's grammar, as in (188).

(188) ⟨pe mi ut tatci-bo-ta⟩

pe	mi	ʔut	tači-<u>bota</u>
what.OBJ	2SG.SBJ	3SG.OBJ	feed-<u>HAB.Q</u>

What do you feed him?
(de Angulo: 114, FG) [HP$_C$]

De Angulo analyzes /-bota/ as a bound auxiliary /-bo/ + the past interrogative /-ta/, but this is not synchronically correct. Like its declarative counterpart /-bosa/, /-bota/ may be etymologically related to a past-tense suffix, but is not semantically a past-tense marker. The sentence in (188) is in the present tense, for example, being a question about a blue jay that the interlocutor is regularly feeding.

8.2.1.11. *Hill Patwin Resultative /-či/*

The Hill Patwin resultative suffix /-či/ expresses a state resulting from the activity described in the verb. For example, the stem /daka·-/ 'to burn something' may be marked with /-či/ to make the verb /dak-či-/ 'to be burnt' (Ultan, d:5.13, OM). Similarly the stem /k^hoba·-/ 'to cut something' may be marked with /-či/ to make the verb /k^hob-či-/ 'to be cut off' (Whistler, d:F97, HL).

The suffix /-či/ is a root-bound suffix of the third conjugation, having two allomorphs /-či, -ču/. The vowel is always short. The suffix /-či/ attaches directly to the final consonant of the root, with no intervening vowel. Shepherd reconstructs Proto-Wintuan completive */-k/, giving rise to Wintu completive /-k/ and Patwin /-či/ (2005:33).

8.2.2. Mood

Patwin mood suffixes include the hortative series, the subjunctive /-mu/, the suffixes /-les, -len, -le/ 'can', the suffix /-čin/ 'lest', and suffixes expressing epistemic modality: tentative inference /-mutʰere/ and /-mute·/ 'might', confident inference /-ma/ and /-muʔa/ 'must', and certainty /-boti, -beti/ 'CERT'. Each of these is discussed individually below.

8.2.2.1. Hortatives

The hortative suffixes are the only suffixes that agree with the verb's subject in person and number. All hortative suffixes are final suffixes, and select the hortative stem of the verb to which they attach. The paradigm of hortative suffixes is shown in table 8.5. First-person exclusive and third person do not differentiate among singular, dual, and plural referents. For example note the use of /-le/ '1EXCL.HORT' for singular reference "I" in (190e) and dual reference "we" in (190f). The inclusive series differentiates dual /-se/ from plural /-bu/ (singular inclusive is not semantically possible). The second person differentiates only singular /-Ø/ and nonsingular /-tʰi/. The second-person singular hortative has no overt suffix, such that a second-person singular hortative is formally a bare verb in its hortative stem form (189).

(189) ⟨la´ikan tcɛl'.⟩

layk?a-n   <u>čel</u>   ʔ

good-ADV   <u>travel.2SG.HORT</u> ||

Travel well!

(Radin, c:98/222, AL)   [HP_T]

The hortative mood is associated with a variety of related functions: commands (in the second person—see 190a), hortatives (190b), cohortatives ("let's . . . ," with inclusives—see 190c), optatives (in the third person—see 190d), and the near future (190e, 190f).

Table 8.5. Hortative suffixes

			Number		
			SG	DU	PL
Person	1	EXCL	-le	-le	-le
		INCL		-se	-bu
	2		-Ø	-t^hi	-t^hi
	3		-di	-di	-di

(190) a. ⟨ba·-thi ʔe·!⟩
ba·-t^hi ʔe·
eat-2nSG.HORT PROX.SG.OBJ.IN
Eat this!
(Whistler 1977a:161/170, NL/HL) [HP_R]

b. ⟨la·´iyɔk k'ana·´ti⟩
layuk k'ana·-t^hi
good sleep-2nSG.HORT
Sleep well!
(Radin, c:105/227, AL) [HP_T]

c. ⟨ʔut kaho·se⟩
ʔut kaho·-se
3SG.OBJ hide-1DU.INCL.HORT
Let's hide him.
(Ultan, d:7.73, SG) [RP]

d. ⟨p̓ɒkitama ʔut yɔr̩ʔadiʔ⟩
p'okita-ma ʔut yorʔa-di ʔ
woman-OBJ 3SG.OBJ work-3HORT ||
Let that woman work.
(Ultan, d:2.90, OM) [HP_L]

e. ⟨píma jét ƛ'újule⟩

pima yet ƛ'uyu-le

DIST.SG.OBJ.IN name write-1EXCL.HORT

I'm gonna write that word down.

(Whistler, d:C36, OM) [HP_L]

f. ⟨tu· nepel ʔi-le.⟩

tu· nepel ʔi-le

first 1EXCL.DU.SBJ do-1EXCL.HORT

We'll go first.

(Whistler 1977a:162/170, NL/HL) [HP_R]

Both /-le/ '1EXCL.HORT' and /-bu/ '1PL.INCL.HORT' have infrequent variants with /-da/: /-leda, -buda/. What conditions this variation is not clear. Whistler notes /-da/ may be cognate with the Wintu first-person singular suffix /-da/ (Whistler, d:D101). In South Patwin the form /-lena/ is also attested, showing South Patwin's characteristic /d/ ~ /n/ alternation (191c).

(191) a. ⟨o·, t'ihitulɛda' 'u·t· [. . .]⟩

ʔo· t'ihitu-leda ʔu·t

alright ask-1EXCL.HORT 3SG.OBJ

All right, I will ask him [. . .]

(Radin, c:4/141, AL) [HP_T]

b. ⟨hen-thi te·-pel-e·, č̓elow-ho-bu-da.⟩

hen-tʰi te·-pel-e·

arrive-2NSG.HORT child-DU-VOC

č'elow-ho-buda

rabbit-VBLZ-1PL.INCL.HORT

Come here, children! Let's go rabbit-hunting together!

(Whistler 1977a:165/171, NL/HL) [HP_R]

c. ⟨Chu maleina⟩ 'Yo Comere'
   ču ma-lena
   1SG.SBJ eat-1EXCL.HORT
   I will eat.
   (Arroyo de la Cuesta:24, SC) [SP]

The second-conjugation verb /ʔi·/ 'to do, to use' is irregular in the second-person singular hortative in Hill Patwin and possibly in South Patwin. In this environment /ʔi·/ takes the form /ʔi·we/. Example (192a) shows an instance of *ʔi·we* from Lodoga Hill Patwin. Example (192b) shows the possible attestation of *ʔiwe* in South Patwin, from one of Vallejo's translations of the Lord's Prayer. (The structure of this example is unclear—particularly the use of a subjective case pronoun 'we' for the object 'us'.) The corresponding verb in River Patwin is a regular stem of the fourth conjugation (unchanging consonant stem), always taking the form /ʔih/. The second-person singular hortative of this verb is regular, as in (192c).

(192) a. ⟨Dep´-pe-e´-wĕ⟩
   depi ʔi*we
   again do.2SG.HORT
   Do it again.
   (Merriam:V70.73) [HP_L]

b. ⟨Yalum eleiwé nechu⟩ [. . .]
   yalu-m ʔele ʔiwe neč'u [. . .]
   leave-SBJV NEG do.2SG.HORT 1PL.EXCL.SBJ?
   Lead us not [. . .] (lit. 'do not leave we'?)
   (P. Vallejo, c:29.4) [SP]

c. ⟨ʔéwun ʔíh⟩
   ʔewu-n ʔih
   do.this-ADV do.2SG.HORT
   Do it like this!
   (Whistler, d:F24, JR) [RP]

The second-conjugation verb /piʔu-/ 'to do that' is irregular in the second-person hortative in River Patwin. Its stem takes the form /piʔu·we-/ in both singular (193a) and nonsingular (193b) imperative forms.

(193) a. ⟨piʔ ʔú·weʔ⟩
pi̇ʔu·we ʔ
do.that.2HORT ||
Do it (SG).
(Bright, c:1.G115, SG) [RP]

b. ⟨piʔ ʔú·wètìʔ⟩
piʔu·we-tʰi ʔ
do.that.2HORT-2nSG.HORT ||
Do it (nSG). (Bright, c:1.G115, SG) [RP]

South Patwin has an additional hortative suffix /-bi ~ -mi/, attested for second-person hortatives with first-person objects. Tentatively I gloss this form '2>1HORT'.

(194) a. ⟨Heróbi⟩
hero·-bi
help-2>1HORT
Help me.
(P. Vallejo, c:25.1) [SP]

b. ⟨'Klā-ah´-be mem⟩
łeya·-bi mem
give-2>1HORT water
Give me a drink.
(Merriam:V76.69) [SP]

Of previous descriptions of Patwin grammar, only de Angulo recognizes the hortative suffixes as a set, calling them the "volitional mode" (de Angulo:19). Radin calls hortative suffixes "hortatory," except for the first-person exclusive /-le/ ("volitional future") and /-tʰi/ ("imperative"; Radin, b:34 ff.). This is consistent with the most common uses of each suffix, though it does not show the unity of the system. Bright groups /-se, -bu, -di/ together as "imperatives," and calls /-le/ a future tense marker (Bright, b:10 ff.). Whistler (1981) calls the second-person hortatives "imperatives," reserving the term "hortative" for the first-person and third-person suffixes.

8.2.2.2. *Subjunctive /-mu/* 'SBJV'

The subjunctive is a final suffix, and selects the hortative stem of the verb to which it attaches. It takes the form /-mu/ after consonants and /-m/ after vowels, in Hill Patwin and River Patwin. The subjunctive suffix is not attested in South Patwin after consonants, so only the /-m/ form is definitely attested.

The subjunctive has a wide range of functions, all of which imply an opposition to an indicative mood. The subjunctive is used in a variety of negative constructions (see section 9.4). In River Patwin the subjunctive marks questions in the past and remote past tense, as in (195).

(195) a. ⟨ċupá·mmi⟩

č'upa·-m	mi
finish-SBJV	2SG.SBJ

Did you finish it?
(Whistler, d:B91, JR) [RP]

b. ⟨pile hɔya t^{h}ɪ·rma ba·nim⟩

pile	hoya	t^{h}i·r-ma	ba·-ni-m
3PL.SBJ	previously	fish-OBJ	eat-RPAST-SBJV

In the old days, did they eat fish?
(Ultan, d:7.81, SG) [RP]

The subjunctive is also used to mark information as hearsay (196a), in opposition to declarative tense markers (like /-s/ 'FIN' in 196b) and inferentials (like *ka* 'IRR' + /-mte/ 'might.PAST' in 196c). The examples in (196) are all from Tebti Hill Patwin speaker Daisy Lorenzo, and the glosses are presented exactly as they appear in the source document (Ultan, d:6.92).

(196) Hearsay (subjunctive), declarative, and inferential sentences (Ultan, d:6.92, DL)

a. ⟨pi ʔiro bom⟩

pi	ʔi-ro	bo-m
3SG.SBJ	do-PART	be.AN-SBJV

he did it (hearsay – someone told us) [HP_T]

b. ⟨pi ʔiro bɒs⟩

pi	ʔi-ro	bo-s
3SG.SBJ	do-PART	be.AN-FIN

he must have done it. (you know it) [HP_T]

c. ⟨pika ʔɪmte⟩

pi	ka	ʔi-mte
3SG.SBJ	IRR	do-might.PAST

he did it (we think) [HP_T]

Tebti Hill Patwin speakers Anderson Lowell and Daisy Lorenzo use the subjunctive as the narrative voice in traditional stories (197).[15] In this function the subjunctive is sometimes accompanied by explicit quotative or hearsay markers like *ʔupu* 'it is said' (197c).

(197) a. ⟨w·a´it'ʋka ha·´rmo.⟩

way-t'uka	ha·r-mu
north-ALL	go-SBJV

He went toward the north.
(Radin, c:16/151, AL) [HP_T]

b. ⟨kàtìt séktumaʔtasî pʌl wí·nmò̀ʔ⟩ 'Hawk Chief weasel saw'

katʰit-sektu-ma	ʔ	tʰasi·	pal	wi·n-mu	ʔ
falcon-chief-OBJ	‖	mink	now	see-SBJV	‖

Mink saw Falcon Chief.
(Bright, c:9.DL69, DL) [HP_T]

c. ⟨pi·´La ’upu tasi·´ mu·´hi tu·´yʊm [. . .]⟩

pi·-ła	ʔupu	t^hasi·	muhi	toyu-m [. . .]
do.thus-LOC	it.is.said	mink	song	stop-SBJV

Then Mink stopped singing [. . .]

(Radin, c:11/146, AL) [HP_T]

The subjunctive may also mark subordinate clauses expressing purpose (198).

(198) ⟨t’e̱nam hale⟩

t’enam	hale
t’ena-m	har-le
defecate-SBJV	go-1EXCL.HORT

I am going to defecate.

(Shafer 1961:30, CW) [HP_C]

Given the wide array of nonindicative meanings associated with the subjunctive, it is unsurprising that it has been described in a variety of different ways. De Angulo calls it "andative-purposive" (de Angulo:31); Radin calls it "progressive," "negative," and the "aorist participle" (Radin, b:36), Bright calls it "interrogative" (Bright, b:5.9); Morgan identifies it as a negative marker (1971:27); and Whistler calls it "negative/subjunctive mood" (1977a:174), "general subjunctive mood" (1978:57), and "subjunctive" (1986: 63 ff.). Its use in periphrastic negative constructions is universally recognized.

Patwin subjunctive /-mu/ is cognate with Wintu dubitative /-m/. Shepherd reconstructs Proto-Wintuan */-m/ 'dubitative, subjunctive' from these (2005:33).

8.2.2.3. *Ability: /-les, -len, -le/ 'can'*

A somewhat obscure set of modal suffixes /-les, -len, -le/ attested in River Patwin and Hill Patwin have similar functions and may be either historically related suffixes or inflections of the same suffix synchronically. These suffixes select the hortative stem of the verb to which they attach, and are invariant in form. They are glossed 'can' in this work. A sketch of the attested forms and functions of these suffixes in Hill Patwin and River Patwin follows. However, these suffixes are not frequently enough attested for a detailed understanding of their functions or distributions.

Hill Patwin /-les, -len/: In Hill Patwin both /-les/ and /-len/ are attested, though /-les/ is far more common. Both are final suffixes. The suffix /-len/ is attested on verbs accompanied by the copula *ʔi*, with a meaning like "should."

(199) a. ⟨pi pi ʔut táčulen ʔi hóyaʔu⟩
pi pi ʔut taču-len ʔi hoyaʔu
3SG.SBJ DECL 3SG.OBJ feed-can COP already
He should have fed him already.
(Whistler, d:F67, HL) [HP$_R$]

b. ⟨nɔ·´pma milɛ cʊltulɛ·´n·ʼi.⟩
no·p-ma mile sultʰu-len ʔi
deer-OBJ 2PL.SBJ kill-can COP
You should kill deer!
(Radin, c:108/231, AL) [HP$_T$]

The suffix /-len/ is also attested in Hill Patwin without an auxiliary verb, with a meaning like "able to."

(200) a. ⟨mʊ̀hʊ̀lénpìcùʔ⟩
muhu-len pi ču ʔ
sing-can DECL 1SG.SBJ ||
I am able to sing.
(Bright, b:5.7) [HP]

b. ⟨mʊ́hʊ lén(pa mí)⟩
muhu-len pa mi
sing-can Q 2SG.SBJ
Will you sing?
(Bright, c:6.NL103) [HP$_C$]

The suffix /-les/ is more commonly attested than /-len/ in Hill Patwin. In Tebti Hill Patwin speaker Anderson Lowell's texts (Radin, c), it usually occurs on a subordinate verb and in an imperative context (i.e., the matrix verb is a second-person hortative). The subordinate clauses themselves can be considered purposive subordinate clauses ("do this in order to X"). Their association with imperative contexts suggests a somewhat directive meaning ("do this and do that"). For example, in (201a), the matrix verb *ha·ri* 'take (go.COM.AN)!' is in the second-person hortative form (used for commands), and the /-les/-marked verb *ba·les* 'can eat' is the subordinate verb. This is /-les/ functioning to mark a purposive subordinate clause in an imperative environment: "Take gopher so that you can eat." In (201b) the verb *p^ho·holes* 'can make fire' is subordinate to the verb *di·hu* 'get up!', which has imperative force. The resulting construction may mean something like "get up and make a fire!" (where *p^ho·holes* is an additional directive) or "get up to make a fire!" (where *p^ho·holes* has a purposive interpretation).[16]

(201) a. ⟨k'a·´imada ha·´ri ba·´lɪc·.⟩ 'Take some gopher that you might eat it.'

k'a·y-ma-da	ha·ri	ba·-les
gopher-OBJ-COM	take.AN.2SG.HORT	eat-can

Take some gopher so that you can eat.

(Radin, c:13/149) [HP$_T$]

b. ⟨tc'i´yak'e·` di·´hu pɔ·´hɔlɪs.⟩ 'The old man got up, built the fire, and then went to sleep.'

č'iyak-e·	di·hu	p^ho·ho-les
old.man-VOC	awake.2SG.HORT	make.fire-can

Old man, get up and make a fire!

(Radin, c:14/150, AL) [HP$_T$]

Example (202) is similar to the examples in (201), but the matrix verb is the semantically bleached verb *ʔi·we ('do!')*. Here the matrix verb contributes an imperative force, but all specific semantic meaning is left to the subordinate clause marked with /-les/.

(202) ⟨bano·´n hıma·´ sɛla·´ʼaman t'e·´ulɛs· ʼi·´wɛ⟩ 'loudly all the time and fear-inspiring are you to speak.'

bano·-n hima· sela·ʔa-ma-n t'e·w-les ʔi·we

loud-ADV always fear-CAUS-ADV speak-can do.2SG.HORT

You should always speak loudly and frighteningly.

(Radin, c:37/167, AL) [HP$_{T}$]

Finally, /-les/ may occur on the main verb in the clause. In this case it seems to have a mild imperative force.

(203) ⟨nay k̓ačak̓ača-ma-ro yali-hem ʔil-les.⟩

nay k'ača-k'ača-ma-ro yali-hem ʔil-les

1SG.POSS$_{V}$ REDUP-cut-CAUS-PART leave-REL use-can

You can use my extra old frayed one.

(Whistler 1977a:159/170, NL/HL) [HP$_{R}$]

River Patwin /-len(ta), -le/: In River Patwin only /-len/ and /-le/ are attested (not /-les/). The form /-len/ appears to be a prefinal suffix, always followed by the participle suffix /-ta/ and never accompanied by the copula. The construction is glossed with the modal meaning 'can' or 'able to', and in the present tense. It is elicited both for declaratives (204a) and interrogatives (204b), with no differentiating marking. It is attested only in the speech of Sarah Gonzales.

(204) a. ⟨mòhú lénntàcù⟩

muhu-len-ta ču

sing-can-PART 1SG.SBJ

I am able to sing.

(Bright, c:1.G138, SG) [RP]

b. ⟨mi t̓ewlɛnta na·nɷ t̓e·wɛ⟩

mi t'ew-len-ta na·no t'e·we

2SG.SBJ speak-can-PART 1SG.POSS$_{IN}$ language

Can you speak my language?

(Ultan, d:7.52, SG) [RP]

The River Patwin suffix /-le/ marks purposive subordinate clauses, like Hill Patwin /-les/. It often marks purposive subordinate clauses in imperative environments (205a), but unlike Hill Patwin /-les/ it is also attested in nonimperative environments (205b).

(205) a. ⟨hár só·le ʔulé·t⟩

har	so·-le	ʔule·t
go.2SG.HORT	ask-can	3PL.OBJ

You go ask them!

(Whistler, d:G8, JR) [RP]

b. ⟨yalulɛ mɪs ba·lɛʔ⟩

yalu-le	mis	ba·-le	ʔ
leave-1EXCL.HORT	2SG.OBJ	eat-can	‖

I'm going to let you be so that you can eat.

(Ultan, d:7.56, SG) [RP]

Previous descriptions and etymology: The suffixes /-les/ and /-len/ have been variously described as modals of ability, markers of volitional future, and imperatives. Whistler (1981:85) glosses /-les/ as 'can'. Whistler (1977a:174) notes the imperative function of /-les/, saying that it is "probably related to" the modal meaning of /-les/. In his grammar Radin describes the suffix ⟨-lɛn̓, -lɛn⟩ /-len/ as "volitional future" (Radin, b:36), but glosses it as 'might' in his only example: ⟨'a´L·lɛn⟩ /ʔaɬ-len/ 'he might absorb' (Radin, b:41). In her grammar Bright describes the suffix /-len/ as "qualificative," and glosses it 'able to' (Bright, b:5.7).

The suffixes /-les/, /-len/ and /-le/ may be related to what Pitkin describes as the Wintu "inevitable future" suffix {le} (1984:117 f.). Shepherd reconstructs Proto-Wintu */-le/ 'intentional future', giving rise to Wintu {le}, Patwin /-les/ and /-len/ 'can', and also the Patwin exclusive hortative suffix /-le/ (2005:33 f.). Both Pitkin and Shepherd point to a deeper historical relationship between this set of suffixes and the verb **lel-* 'to make' (> Patwin *leli* 'make', Wintu {lEl} 'make').

8.2.2.4. /-čin/ 'lest'

The suffix /-čin/ is a subordinating suffix with a meaning like 'lest' or 'in case'. It marks the verbs of subordinate clauses that express the consequences of failing to heed a warning or suggestion. The suffix /-čin/ is a final suffix, invariant in form, that selects the hortative stem of the verb to which it attaches.

In (206) the subordinate 'lest' clauses are bracketed. Example (206a) shows a 'lest' clause (*t'učučin mi* 'lest you drown') subordinate to a warning (*č'o·nan* 'watch out!'). Example (206b) shows a 'lest' clause (*mollawin mit holowčin* 'lest the ghost spook you') subordinate to a negative command (*harmuʔu ʔiwe pina* 'don't go there!'). Note that subordinate clauses marked with /-čin/ are not nominalizations. Their subjects are in the subjective case, not the possessive case.

(206) a. ⟨čǒ·nan, t'účučin mi⟩

č'o·-nan	[t'uču-čin	mi	]
watch-REFL	[drown-lest	2SG.SBJ	]

Watch out! [You might drown.]
(Whistler, d:G3, JR) [RP]

b. ⟨móllawin mit holówčin, hármuʔu ʔíwe pína⟩

[mollawin	mit	holow-čin	]
[ghost	2SG.OBJ	haunt-lest	]

har-muʔu	ʔiwe	pina
go-NEG	do.2SG.HORT	DIST.PROL

Don't go there, [the ghost might spook you.]
(Whistler, d:F70, HL) [HP$_R$]

The suffix /-čin/ 'lest' is not mentioned in the grammars of de Angulo, Radin, or Bright (de Angulo; Radin, b; Bright, b). In the analysis of Whistler (1977a), /-čin/ is a modal suffix meaning 'might', and is not associated with subordination. Whistler represents the one example of /-čin/ in this text as marking an independent clause: *mana·yučin*. 'You might miss.' (1977a:164). However, the context in Whistler (1977a) and in the source text (Bright, c:6.

NL84) suggests that this could be a subordinate 'lest' clause: *mana·yučin, ču ʔile bo*. 'Lest you miss, let me do it.' In the archival record, /-čin/ is attested only in situations where the gloss 'lest' would be appropriate: clauses that seem to be subordinate, and that express the consequences of failing to heed a warning or suggestion. In independent clauses glossed with the English modal 'might', verbs with inceptive /-t'o/ or tentative-inference /-mutʰere/ are typically used.

8.2.2.5. *Hill Patwin Tentative Inference /-mutʰere/ 'might'*

The suffix /-mutʰere/ indicates that the speaker thinks a statement is true, but is not sure. I follow Whistler (1986) in calling this a "tentative inference" suffix, and de Angulo in identifying it as a nonpast suffix. The suffix is attested in Cortina, Tebti, and Rumsey Hill Patwin. The suffix /-mutʰere/ is a first-conjugation suffix, taking the forms /-mutʰere/ and /-mutʰer/. It is a prefinal suffix, and selects the hortative stem of the verb to which it attaches.

Formal variation: The appearance of the final vowel in /-mutʰere/ is conditioned by the morphological class of the following suffix, as described in section 8.1. In addition to this regular variation, /-mutʰere/ appears in a variety of forms, conditioned by dialect, phonological environment, and syntactic environment.

In the Tebti, Cortina, and Rumsey dialects of Hill Patwin, the suffix /-mutʰere/ takes the form /-mutʰere/ after consonants (Whistler 1978) and /-mtʰere/ after vowels (207). This variation is parallel to that found for the subjunctive suffix /-mu/, to which /-mutʰere/ is related analogically if not etymologically (Whistler 1986:72).

(207) ⟨"he·i", 'ʋm pɔbɔ·´mterɛs pi·La·´" 'ʋm [. . .]⟩

"he·,"	ʔu-m	"po	bo·-mtʰere-s
well	say-SBJV	who	be.AN-might-FIN

piła,"	ʔu-m	[. . .]
there	say-SBJV	

"Well," he said, "somebody is staying there," he said [. . .]

(Radin, c:34/164, AL) [HP_T]

A cognate form *mut^{h}ere* in Lodoga Hill Patwin is a verb, not a suffix. Like the suffix in other dialects of Hill Patwin, this form is a stem of the first conjugation. But unlike the suffix, the Lodoga verb is not bound. It may be separated from the expected host verb (208a), and it does not change to */mt^{h}ere/—even when it appears directly after a vowel-final verb stem (208b).

(208) a. ⟨ču mut^{h}éribʊṣ hɑ·mbat̓i⟩

ču	mut^{h}ere-bus	ho·mba-t'i
1SG.SBJ	might-FIN	crazy-FUT

I think I'm gonna be crazy.
(Ultan, d:2.84, OM) [HP$_{L}$]

b. ⟨pi kó·ltu bó·mutherebus⟩

pi	ko·l-tu	bo·	mut^{h}ere-bus
3SG.SBJ	mouth-NMLZ$_{AG}$	be.AN	might-FIN

I think he's a singer.
(Whistler, d:A102, OM) [HP$_{L}$]

8.2.2.6. *Hill Patwin Past Tentative Inference /-mute·/ 'might.PAST'*

Cortina, Tebti, and Rumsey Hill Patwin have an additional tentative inference suffix /-mute·/. It is a final suffix, and selects the hortative stem of the verb to which it attaches. The allomorph /-mte/ occurs after vowels, and /-mute·/ occurs after consonants.

Whistler (1986:71 ff.) identifies the difference between /-mut^{h}ere/ and /-mute·/ as one of modality, saying that /-mute·/ occurs only in the irrealis mode. De Angulo identifies the difference as one of tense (de Angulo:15). Although /-mute·/ is most often attested in clauses with the irrealis particle *ka* (as in 209a), it is not always (209b). On the other hand the tense distinction is robust. Therefore I follow de Angulo in identifying /-mute·/ as a past-tense inferential suffix, rather than an irrealis mode inferential suffix.

(209) a. ⟨pika ʔɪmte⟩

pi ka ʔi-mte
3SG.SBJ IRR do-might.PAST
He did it (we think).
(Ultan, d:6.92, DL) [HP$_T$]

b. ⟨a´i, k'ɛdʊ´mtɛ tcu'ʊm.⟩

"ʔay, k'edu-mte ču," ʔu-m
Excl. forget-might.PAST 1SG.SBJ say-SBJV
"Why, I must have forgotten it!" she said.
(Radin, c:28/160, AL) [HP$_T$]

8.2.2.7. Hill Patwin Confident Inference /-ma, -muʔa/ 'must'

The confident inference suffix is attested in all dialects of Hill Patwin. In Lodoga Hill Patwin it takes the invariant form /-ma/. In other dialects it takes the form /-muʔa/ after consonants and /-mʔa/ after vowels. It is a final suffix, and selects the hortative stem of the verb to which it attaches.

The confident inference suffix may indicate a confident inference ("must have," as in 210a). It may also be used to mark a speculative question ("I wonder," as in 210b and 210c). Whistler (1986) analyzes this speculative usage as a metaphorical extension of the confident inference function. Though the confident inference suffix often co-occurs with the irrealis particle *ka~kam*, it may also be attested in clauses without this particle (210c).

(210) a. ⟨čučuka ʔe·ma ut husma⟩

čuču ka ʔey-ma ʔut hus-ma
dog IRR bite-must 3SG.OBJ vulture-OBJ
The dog must have bitten the buzzard (but nobody saw him).
(Ultan, d:2.60, OM) [HP$_L$]

b. ⟨he·-tuka har-mu-ʔa ka thay-ču?⟩

he·tuka har-muʔa ka tʰay-ču
where.ALL go-must IRR grandchild-RL
I wonder where my grandson could be.
(Whistler 1978:51/55, NL/HL) [HP$_R$]

c. ⟨hé·t'ŏkà harmuʔaʔ thâycùʔ⟩
he·t'uka   har-muʔa   ʔ   t^{h}ay-ču   ʔ
where.ALL   go-must || grandchild-RL ||
Where did my grandchild go?
(Bright, c:7.NL184, NL)   [HP$_C$]

8.2.2.8. *Hill Patwin and South Patwin Certainty /-boti, -beti/ 'CERT'*

The suffix /-boti, -beti/ is a final suffix, selecting the nominal stem of the verb to which it attaches. It is not attested in River Patwin. The suffix expresses certainty on the part of the speaker, whether from direct sensory experience (211a), from confident inference (211b), or because the information is from a credible source (211c).

(211) a. ⟨Eráboti chu⟩
ʔera*-boti   ču
cold-CERT   1SG.SBJ
I am cold.
(P. Vallejo, c:21.12)   [SP]

b. ⟨lábekê sóltitoʔ pépelet ʔébŏtì⟩ 'Oh brother He tried to killed us two?'
la·be-k^{h}e·   sult^{h}i-t'o   ʔ   p'epelet   ʔi-boti
elder.brother-VOC   kill-INCEP || 1INCL.DU.OBJ   COP-CERT
Brother, he will kill us!
(Bright, c:6.NL91, NL)   [HP$_C$]

c. ⟨yírma haybaʔaboti pi⟩
yir-ma   haybaʔa-boti   pi
leg-OBJ   hurt-CERT   3SG.SBJ
(he told me) his leg hurts.
(Whistler, d:F46, HL)   [HP$_R$]

The suffix varies in form. It takes the form /-boti/ when the subject is animate, and /-beti/ when the subject is inanimate. This variation of /o~e/ conditioned by animacy is analogous to the variation in the auxiliary verb *bo·/be·*, to which the suffix /-boti, -beti/ is etymologically related. See section 9.1.2 and Whistler (1986). In South Patwin the form /-woti/ is also attested, in Arroyo de la Cuesta and Curtin (Arroyo de la Cuesta; Curtin, b:228), alongside the form /-boti/ and apparently in free variation. This suggests a historical process of lenition whereby /b/ is becoming /w/ for certain lexemes in South Patwin, though this is the only known instance of this process.

8.2.3. Participial Forms

Patwin verbs may occur in one of three participial forms: the participle with the suffix /-ro, -ta, -taro/ 'PART'; the adverbial participle with the suffix /-ni, -n/ 'ADV'; and the bare nominal form of the verb stem. These three participial forms will be discussed individually below.

8.2.3.1. Participle /-taro/ 'PART'

The most common and semantically general participial form in Patwin is the participle, marked with a suffix /-taro/, here glossed 'PART'. It has three allomorphs: /-taro, -ta, -ro/. The variation between the three allomorphs is a mixture of phonological conditioning and dialect variation, discussed below. The participle suffix is a final suffix, selecting the participial stem of the verb.

Functionally /-taro/ is quite versatile, being used in clause chaining constructions, and for stative and perfective predication with the stative auxiliary *bo·/be·/boh/beh* 'be', or with the River Patwin active auxiliary *čeh* 'AUX'. For further discussion of the participle in these constructions, see sections 9.1.2 (for its use with the stative auxiliary), 9.1.3 (for its use with the RP auxiliary *čeh*), and 9.3.3 (clause chaining).

The participle is also one of the common citation forms for verbs. Table 8.6 shows six verbs elicited in isolation in various dialects, with the original glosses as they appear in the source documents.

Sometimes the participle is the main verb in an independent clause without an auxiliary verb. Generally these clauses have a stative meaning (212) or a perfective meaning (213). In another context River Patwin speaker Sarah Gonzales uses exclusively participles for the narrative voice in her rendition of the creation story (Bright, c:8.G43 ff.).[17]

Table 8.6. Participle as citation form (shown with original glosses)

t'etʰu·-ro	'swallow'	HP_L	(Ultan, d:5.24, OM)
tew-ta	'jumping'	HP_L	(Ultan AU[b]:5.13:45, OM)
p'orma-ro	'bad'	HP_C	(Ultan, d:6.78, NL)
t'ew-taro	'talking'	HP_R	(Whistler, d:G14, HL)
p'akupa-ro	'hammer sth. down'	RP	(Ultan, d:6.129, SG)
tʰep-ta	'to hit'	RP	(Haas:22, IM)

(212) a. ⟨pípɛl ṫɛwṫɛw ṗítaʔ⟩

pipel	t'ewt'ewp'ita	ʔ
pipel	t'ewt'ewp'ir-ta	ʔ
3DU.SBJ	converse-PART	‖

They two are talking.
(Whistler, d:A11, OM) [HP_L]

b. ⟨we·ł čheru·-ro.⟩

we·ł	čeru·-ro
salt	finish-PART

The salt is all gone.
(Whistler 1977a:162, NL/HL) [HP_R]

(213) a. ⟨sun lu·m-taro.⟩

sun	lu·m-taro
here	die-PART

She died here.
(Whistler 1977a:167, NL/HL) [HP_R]

b. ⟨wí:ta hàyú mʌt'ɛ́ptʌ̀⟩

wi·ta	hayu-ma	tʰep-ta
man	dog-OBJ	hit-PART

The man hit the dog.
(Haas:22, IM/WM) [RP]

Forms of the participle

-ro	after vowels
-ta	after consonants in HP_L, HP_T, HP_R?, RP
-taro	after consonants in HP_T, HP_C, HP_R?, SP

Formal variation: The participle suffix has three allomorphs: /-taro, -ta, -ro/. The variation among these allomorphs is partly phonologically conditioned and partly due to dialect variation.

In all dialects, /-ro/ is the allomorph that occurs after vowels. The suffixes /-ta/ and /-taro/ occur only after consonants. The pattern of variation between /-ta/ and /-taro/ is not conditioned by phonetic environment, but varies by dialect and to some extent by individual speaker. River Patwin and Lodoga Hill Patwin use /-ta/ exclusively, never /-taro/ (214a, 214b).[18] Cortina Hill Patwin uses /-taro/ exclusively, never /-ta/ (214c). The South Patwin materials from Vallejo all use /-taro/, never /-ta/ (214d). Neither form appears in Merriam's South Patwin material.

(214) a. ⟨hamta cu bo·⟩
hamta ču bo·
ham-ta ču boh-s
sit-PART 1SG.SBJ be.AN-FIN
I'm sitting.
(Ultan, d:7.54, SG) [RP]

b. ⟨čɛló lúmta bɔṣ⟩
č'elo· lu·m-ta bo-s
jackrabbit dead-PART be.AN-FIN
The jackrabbit is dead.
(Ultan, d:4.16, AN) [HP_L]

c. ⟨Loom tar´-rah bo´-si⟩
lum-taro bo·-say
die-PART be.AN-Q
Is he dead?
(Merriam:V72.71) [HP_C]

d. ⟨Hamtaro-bot Tan Is Wolema⟩

ham-taro	bo-t	tan	ʔi-s	wole-ma
sit-PART	be.AN-FIN	father	COP-FIN	right?-OBJ

He is seated at the right side of the Father.

(P. Vallejo, c:19.9.2) [SP]

The situation is less clear for Tebti and Rumsey Hill Patwin. In Rumsey Hill Patwin, Harry Lorenzo uses /-taro/ exclusively, never /-ta/ (215a). However, Merriam's vocabulary for Rumsey Hill Patwin has a few instances of /-ta/, none of /-taro/ (215b).

(215) a. ⟨hámtaro chu bo·s⟩

ham-taro	ču	bo·-s
sit-PART	1SG.SBJ	be.AN-FIN

I'm sitting (already down).

(Whistler, d:E61, HL) [HP_R]

b. ⟨Loom-tah bo-si⟩

lum-ta	bo·-say
die-PART	be.AN-Q

Is he dead?

(Merriam:V73.71) [HP_R]

In Tebti Hill Patwin, speaker Nelson Lowell uses /-taro/ exclusively (216a). But Tebti speaker Anderson Lowell uses both /-ta/ and /-taro/ with about equal frequency (216b, 216c). One notable constraint on this variation is that /-ta/ is the only form that Anderson Lowell uses when the participle appears with the stative auxiliary *bo·/be·* (see example 216b and section 9.1.2.2). However, there seem to be no other constraints conditioning the /-ta/~/-taro/ variation for Anderson Lowell: both /-ta/ and /-taro/ are used in clause-chaining constructions (example 216c, section 9.3.3), and both are attested on the same verb stems with no apparent difference in meaning.

(216) a. ⟨hamtaro cu bɒs⟩

ham-taro ču bo-s

sit-PART 1SG.SBJ be.AN-FIN

I'm sitting down (stative).

(Ultan, d:6.23, NeL) $[HP_T]$

b. ⟨[. . .] u-it·a´i lɪluna´ntabɔm.⟩

ʔuy-t^hay lelu-nan-ta bo-m

3SG.$POSS_K$-nephew make-REFL-PART be.AN-SBJV

[. . .] his nephew had recovered consciousness.

(Radin, c:60/187, AL) $[HP_T]$

c. ⟨katɛtcɛ·´ktu m·a·´iti pɛ·m·tarɔ t·u·´k'ʊm.⟩ 'He took a hold of old man coyote's foot and he pulled it out.'

kat^{h}it-sektu ma·y-ti p^{h}e·m-taro t°u·k°u-m

falcon-chief foot-ABL grasp-PART pull.out?-SBJV

Falcon Chief grasped him by the foot and pulled him out.

(Radin, c:12/148, AL) $[HP_T]$

In addition to the allophonic and dialectal variation among /-ro, -ta, -taro/ described above, the final vowel of the participle suffix, which is never stressed, sometimes assimilates to the preceding vowel's quality in fast speech.

8.2.3.2. *Adverbial Participle /-ni/ '*ADV*'*

The adverbial participle /-ni/ is a final suffix, and selects the participial stem of the verb to which it attaches. It takes the form /-ni/ after consonants, and usually /-n/ after vowels. The form /-ni/ is also sporadically attested after vowels.

Verbs marked with /-ni/ may function adverbially, as adjuncts of verbs. These may be either single-word manner adverbs (217a, 217b) or multiword adverbial clauses (217c).

(217) a. ⟨ʔuy ʔonok lomu·n henesa⟩

ʔuy-ʔonok	lomu·-n	hene-sa
3SG.POSS$_K$-wife	happy-ADV	arrive-PAST

His wife was happy when she came (came happily).
(Whistler, d:G101, HL) [HP$_R$]

b. ⟨láyuk̓an mi k̓aná·m⟩

layukʔa-n	mi	k'ana·-m
good-ADV	2SG.SBJ	sleep-SBJV

Did you sleep well?
(Whistler, d:F111, JR) [RP]

c. ⟨č̓opol połpoło-n čele·-bo te·-ču-pel⟩

[č'opol	połpoło-n	]	čele·	bo	te·-ču-pel
[tray	tap-ADV	]	travel	be.AN	child-RL-DU

My children must be going around [tapping on their trays].
(Whistler 1977a:165/171, NL/HL) [HP$_R$]

Verbs marked with /-ni, -n/ may also function as main verbs in a clause, used in constructions with the copula *ʔi/ʔih* 'COP' (see section 9.1.1.2) or the River Patwin active auxiliary *čeh* 'AUX' (section 9.1.3).

The adverbial participle/-ni/ is not mentioned in Bright's grammar (Bright, b) or Morgan's thesis (1971), and it is described only vaguely in the grammars of de Angulo and Radin (de Angulo; Radin, b). Whistler (1977a) distinguishes a "participle" from an "adverb-deriving" function for /-ni/, but in later publications Whistler treats both as functions of a single suffix (called "participle B" in 1978 and "adverbializer" in 1981).

Shepherd (2005) does not comment on the etymology of /-ni/. It is likely to be cognate with Wintu {n}, which Pitkin calls a subordinating suffix of potential temporal simultaneity (1984:118).

8.2.4. Voice

There are six voice suffixes: passive /-here/ 'PASS', causative /-ma/ 'CAUS', applicative /-pa/ 'APPL', comitative /-me/ 'COM', reciprocal /-p'iri/ 'RECIP', and reflexive /-nana/ 'REFL'. All of the voice suffixes select the hortative stem of the verb to which they attach. The passive, reciprocal, and reflexive suffixes are stems of the first conjugation (consonant stems). The causative, applicative, and comitative suffixes are of the second conjugation (unchanging stems). All of the voice suffixes are medial suffixes, and may be followed by inflectional suffixes or additional medial suffixes, including other voice suffixes.

Crosslinguistically, voice affixes are often defined by the changes they effect in the predicate's valency, but this analysis is not felicitous for Patwin voice suffixes. The passive, for example, is generally defined structurally, as an operation whereby the predicate's underlying object becomes the subject and the underlying subject becomes a peripheral element in the clause, reducing the clause's transitivity (e.g., Perlmutter and Postal 1983; Dixon and Aikhenvald 2000:1–29). The causative is also often defined structurally, as an operation where a new agent (the causer) is added as the clause's subject, causing the underlying subject (causee) to be demoted (usually to object), and increasing the clause's transitivity (e.g., Dixon and Aikhenvald 2000:1–29). However, in Patwin the passive suffix /-here/ is not always associated with a decrease in transitivity, and the causative suffix /-ma/ is not always associated with an increase in transitivity. This divergence of voice and valency in Patwin means that Patwin voice suffixes cannot be described in terms of their effect on argument structure or transitivity. Although they are typically associated with changes in valency, this is not their primary function.

Patwin voice suffixes will be described here in terms of their effect on focus of attention, following Croft (1994) and Martin (2000): the passive /-here/ turns the focus of attention away from the agent. The causative /-ma/ focuses attention on the cause of the activity, making the cause the subject. The applicative /-pa/ brings an oblique argument into the focus of attention, making this argument the object.[19] The comitative /-me/ specifically brings a comitative oblique argument into the focus of attention. The reciprocal /-p'iri/ highlights the reciprocity of the event. The reflexive /-nana/ highlights the reflexivity of the event. These functions are described in more detail for each affix below. Departures from expected patterns of valency change are also discussed for each affix. Verbs with multiple voice suffixes are discussed in section 8.2.4.7.

8.2.4.1. Passive /-here/ ‘PASS’

The passive suffix /-here/ is a first-conjugation suffix (consonant stem), varying in form between /-here/ and /-her/. It is a medial suffix, and selects the hortative stem of the verb to which it attaches. The passive turns the focus of attention away from the agent, removing the agent from the role of grammatical subject.

Hill Patwin and River Patwin examples are shown in (218). These examples are all prototypical passives from a crosslinguistic structural perspective: The patient (underlying object) of a verb with /-here/ appears in the subjective case, while the agent (underlying subject) is demoted to an oblique position, appearing in the agentive form of the possessive case (see section 4.6.1.3).[20] In (218a) the patient *t^{h}ir* ‘fish’ is the subject, while the agent *wi·tano* ‘by the man’ is in the agentive form of the possessive case. In (218b) the patient *ču* ‘I’ is the subject, while the agent *hayuno* ‘by the dog’ is in the agentive form of the possessive case. The agent is optional and is usually not expressed, as in (218c).

(218) a. ⟨t^{h}íɾ̱̃ wí·tanɔ ba·hɛ́rɪbʊṣ⟩

t^{h}ir	wi·ta-no	ba·-here-bus
fish	man-POSS_{V}	eat-PASS-FIN

The fish got eaten by the man.
(Ultan, d:2.76, OM) [HP_{L}]

b. ⟨hayunɷ cu ƛ̓abuhɛta boh⟩

hayuno	ču	ƛ̓abuheta	boh
hayu-no	ču	ƛ̓abu-her-ta	boh-s
dog-POSS_{V}	1SG.SBJ	bite-PASS-PART	be.AN-FIN

I was bitten by the dog.
(Ultan, d:7.46, SG) [RP]

c. ⟨pi bá·hérețibus⟩

pi	ba·-here-t’i-bus
3SG.SBJ	eat-PASS-FUT-FIN

It looks like he’s going to get eaten.
(Whistler, d:C65, OM) [HP_{L}]

The Patwin passive is not always associated with detransitivization, nor is the patient always realized as the subject. Consider the interesting use of the passive in (219). The subject *pi* 'he' in this example is not the patient undergoing the action, but the enabler of the action—a participant that a typologist might identify as the "causer" in a causative construction. The patient *nat* 'me', which in a prototypical passive construction would be in the subjective case, is here expressed in the objective case. The agent/causee 'them' is not overtly stated.

(219) ⟨thép-heres pi nat⟩
t^hep-here-s pi nat
hit-PASS-FIN 3SG.SBJ 1SG.OBJ
He let (them) hit me.
(Whistler, d:E52, HL) [HP_R]

An attempt at a literal translation of (219) might be, 'He was hit me (by them).' Structurally this is a passive that looks exactly like a prototypical causative: the subject is the causer and the patient remains in the objective case. Example (219) is a consistent use of the Patwin passive /-here/ however, in its function of turning the focus of attention away from the agent (i.e., the unexpressed causee "them" in 219).

Along with the passive suffix /-here/, there are other ways of expressing a passive or mediopassive meaning in Patwin (i.e., a clause in which the role or identity of the agent is downplayed or suppressed). A passive-like construction with a participle and the auxiliary *bo·/be·* 'be' is discussed in section 9.1.2.2. A passive-like use of the causative suffix /-ma/ is discussed in section 8.2.4.2.

Patwin passive /-here/ is related to Wintu passive {here}. Shepherd reconstructs Proto-Wintuan passive */-her/ (2005:28).

8.2.4.2. *Causative /-ma/ 'CAUS'*

The causative suffix /-ma/ 'CAUS' is an unchanging suffix, always realized as /-ma/. The causative functions to shift the focus of attention to the cause of the event, which is realized in the subjective case. It is a medial suffix, and selects the hortative stem of the verb to which it attaches. It can be used in a prototypically causative sense 'to make something happen', or a more permissive sense 'to enable something to happen'. Example (220a) shows the former sense: the verb root /t^{h}ep-/ 'hit' is suffixed with /-ma/ to make the stem /t^{h}ep-ma-/ 'to make someone hit'. Example (220b) shows a permissive sense of the causative: the verb root /win-/ 'see' is suffixed with /-ma/ to make the stem /win-ma-/ 'enable to see' (which Ida Mitchum offers as a translation for English 'show'). The pattern of case assignment is what one would expect for a causative construction: the causer is expressed in the subjective case (*ču* 'I' in both 220a and 220b) and the causee is expressed in the objective case (*ʔut* 'him' in both 220a and 220b).

(220) a. ⟨čú ʔút t^{h}épmaťibʊs ʔɛ·⟩

ču ʔut t^{h}ep-ma-t'i-bus ʔe·

1SG.SBJ 3SG.OBJ hit-CAUS-FUT-FIN PROX.SG.OBJ.IN

I am going to make him hit this.

(Ultan, d:4.68, AN) [HP$_{L}$]

b. win-ma-sa ču ʔut

see-CAUS-PAST 1SG.SBJ 3SG.OBJ

I showed (it) to him.

(Swadesh and Melton:36:15, IM) [RP]

A common function for causative /-ma/ is to convert predicates describing sensory experiences into predicates describing experienced properties. For example in (221a) the verb stem /ʔera*-/ means 'to experience cold' (note that the experiencer, *ču* 'I', is in the subjective case). In (221b) the same stem has been suffixed with /-ma/, creating the verb stem /ʔera*-ma-/ 'to be cold' (of an object, i.e., 'to cause to experience cold').

(221) a. ⟨Eráboti chu⟩

ʔera*-boti ču

cold-CERT 1SG.SBJ

I am cold.

(P. Vallejo, c:21.12) [SP]

b. ⟨Erámati⟩
ʔera⁎-ma-t°i
cold-CAUS-FIN
It is cold.
(P. Vallejo, c:21.12) [SP]

An interesting consequence of this function of the causative is that it doesn't always increase the transitivity of a predicate, and can in some cases reduce the transitivity of a predicate. This runs contrary to the cross-linguistic expectation of causative constructions increasing valency.[21] In the intransitive example (221b), the experiencer is suppressed, such that the causative verb stem /ʔera⁎-ma-/ 'to be cold' does not have a greater transitivity than its root /ʔera⁎-/ 'to experience cold'. Example (222) shows an even more extreme example, where the valency of the predicate actually decreases in the causative. In (222a) the predicate is transitive: /tʰu·bi-/ 'to smell something'. In (222b) this predicate has been suffixed with causative /-ma/, creating the intransitive predicate /tʰu·bu-ma-/ 'to smell' (i.e., 'to cause to experience smelling').

(222) a. ču no·p-ma tʰu·bi-bus
1SG.SBJ deer-OBJ smell-FIN
I am smelling the deer.
(Ultan, b:14:31, OM) [HP_L]

b. no·p tʰu·bu-ma-ro be-s
meat smell-CAUS-PART be.IN-FIN
The meat smells (bad).
(Ultan, b:14:19, OM) [HP_L]

Structurally the causative construction in (222b) is what a typologist would recognize as a passive: a detransitivized clause in which the underlying object is the surface subject, and the underlying subject is not a core argument. Semantically, however, the construction is an ordinary causative: the subject *no·p* 'meat' is the (nonagentive) causer of the activity described in the predicate and the focus of attention is thereby shifted to this causer.

Patwin causative /-ma/ is related to Wintu causative {m}, and Shepherd reconstructs Proto-Wintuan causative */-ma/ from these (2005:32).

8.2.4.3. *Applicative /-pa/* 'APPL'

The applicative suffix /-pa/ is an unchanging suffix, always realized as /-pa/. It selects the hortative stem of the verb to which it attaches. It is a general applicative suffix, in the sense that it increases the transitivity of a verb by adding an object argument.[22] Semantically it functions to widen the focus of attention to include an oblique participant, which is expressed in the objective case.

The suffix /-pa/ is sometimes described as a benefactive (de Angulo:30; Whistler 1981:85), but the object associated with this applicative construction is not always a beneficiary. In (223a) the applicative verb *ʔipa* 'do (APPL)' describes an activity that is happening for the benefit of the grammatical object *nat* 'me (OBJ)'. In (223b), on the other hand, the applicative verb *łe·ypa* 'throw (APPL)' describes an activity happening to the detriment of its grammatical object *kawa·yuma* 'horse (OBJ)'. In (223c) the grammatical object of *pʰo·hoparo* 'making a fire (APPL)' is *pima saw* 'that bread (OBJ)', the location where the activity is happening. And in (223d) the grammatical object of the verb *harpale* 'I'm gonna go (APPL)' is *sek-t'ok* 'green wood', the objective of the activity.

(223) a. ⟨nat ʔipaʔ⟩

nat	ʔi-pa	ʔ
1SG.OBJ	do-APPL	||

Do it for me!

(Ultan, d:7.87, SG) [RP]

b. ⟨pi wi·ta kawa·juma łe·jparo sa·ma čoka·bus⟩

pi	wi·ta	kawa·yu-ma	łe·y-pa-ro
DIST.SBJ	man	horse-OBJ	throw-APPL-PART

sa·-ma	č'oka·-bus
eye-OBJ	knock.out-FIN

That man threw a rock at the horse and knocked his eye out.

(Whistler, d:D99, OM) [HP_L]

c. ⟨píma sáw p^hó·hoparo⟩

pima saw p^ho·ho-pa-ro

DIST.OBJ.IN bread make.fire-APPL-PART

(He) is building a fire on top of that bread (buried in the ground).

(Whistler, d:A108, OM) [HP_L]

d. ⟨ču har-pa-le sek-ṫok⟩

ču har-pa-le sek-t'ok

1SG.SBJ go-APPL-1EXCL.HORT greenery-wood

I'll go for some green wood.

(Whistler 1977a:160/170, NL/HL) [HP_R]

Comitative applicatives are not marked with /-pa/, but have specific comitative marking. See section 8.2.4.4.

Because Patwin clauses may have more than one object argument, a Patwin verb may have more than one applicative suffix. An example is shown in (224), where the verb *harpapa* has two applicative suffixes. The root /har-/ means 'go'. With one applicative suffix, /har-pa-/ can mean 'go to get something', as in (223d), where the grammatical object is the objective of the activity. With two applicative suffixes, /har-pa-pa-/ in (224) means 'go get something for someone', where both the objective of the activity and the beneficiary of the activity are grammatical objects of the verb: *pima yiłma k'odoy* 'that heavy rock (OBJ)' and *nat* 'me', respectively. The whole sentence is glossed, 'Give me that heavy rock' in the source, and literally means 'Go for that heavy rock for me'.

(224) ⟨hárpapa nat píma yíłma k'odóy⟩

har-pa-pa nat pima yiłma k'odoy

go-APPL-APPL 1SG.OBJ DIST.SG.OBJ.IN heavy rock

Give me that heavy rock.

(Whistler, d:F84, HL) [HP_R]

Patwin applicative /-pa/ is related to Wintu benefactive {paq} and Nomlaki /-pa, -paq/. Shepherd reconstructs either */-pa/ or */-paq/ as the Proto-Wintuan benefactive (2005:32).

8.2.4.4. *Comitative 'COM'*

Comitative marking on the verb is a specific kind of applicative construction. It widens the scope of attention to include a comitative participant: something or someone that the agent has with her as she carries out the activity described by the verb. This participant may be expressed in the objective or comitative case. Comitative marking is most commonly attested on verbs of motion, including generic motion stems such as /har-/ 'go' and stems with more specific meanings like /tepu-/ 'emerge' and /witi·lu-/ 'run'. Examples of each of these stems with comitative /-me/ are shown in (225). Additionally (225d) shows a stative verb stem /bo-/ 'to be (locational)' in a comitative form, translated 'keep' (i.e., 'be there with').

(225) a. ⟨pi pé· hár̲mebus⟩

pi	pe·	har-me-bus
3SG.SBJ	what.OBJ	go-COM-FIN

He's taking something.
(Whistler, d:A84, OM) [HP_L]

b. ⟨ɛt·e·´ma kɔ·´ltcɪs· tɪp'umɛm.⟩

ʔete·-ma	kʰolčis	tepu-me-m
one-OBJ	sack	emerge-COM-SBJV

(He) went out with one sack.
(Radin, c:2/139, AL) [HP_T]

c. ⟨'ɛt·e·´ma c·ʊt·a, 'ʊlki·´taro wɪti·´lumɛm [. . .]⟩

ʔete·ma	sut°a	ʔolkitaro
ʔete·-ma	sut°a	ʔol-kir-taro
one-OBJ	brand(?)	up-move.with.hand-PART

witi·lumem	[. . .]
witi·lu-me-m	
run-COM-SBJV	

He seized a burning brand and ran with (it) [. . .]
(Radin, c:24/158, AL) [HP_T]

d. ⟨pi píma čáketma bómes⟩

pi	pima	čaket-ma	bo-me-s
3SG.SBJ	DIST.SG.IN.OBJ	all-OBJ	be.AN-COM-FIN

He's keeping it all (now).

(Whistler, d:F68, HL) [HP_R]

Comitative marking on the verb is used when something or someone is being taken along or carried during an activity. Comitative verbs of motion are often glossed 'bring', 'take along', 'carry', and so on. To express a more equal partnership in an activity (doing something along with someone), the comitative case is used. See section 4.6.2.2.

Comitative stems versus comitative suffix: When the comitative participant is grammatically inanimate, comitative marking on the verb sometimes takes the form of a suffix /-me/. This suffix selects the hortative stem of the verb to which it attaches. When the comitative participant grammatically animate, comitative marking on the verb sometimes takes the form of a stem change: the verb stem is a second-conjugation stem (unchanging) whose characteristic final vowel is /i·/.[23] Compare (226) with (225a) above. In (225a) the comitative participant *pe·* 'something' is inanimate, so the comitative verb stem takes the form /har-me-/. In (226) the comitative participant *mit* 'you' is animate, so the comitative verb stem takes the form /hari·-/. Both stems are comitative forms of the verb /hara·-/ 'go'. Other comitative stem changes are also attested for inanimate and animate comitative verbs.

(226) ⟨pi mit harí·te⟩

pi	mit	hari·-te
3SG.SBJ	2SG.OBJ	go.COM-Q.PAST

He guided you?

(Whistler, d:B4, OM) [HP_L]

Table 8.7 shows the four basic verbs of motion and the static verb *bo·* 'be.AN', with their inanimate and animate comitative counterparts. All of these forms are frequently attested, so citations of specific sources are omitted.

Table 8.7. Comitative verbs

Gloss	Stem	COM.IN	COM.AN
'go'	hara·-	har-me-	hari·-
'arrive'	hene·-	hen-me-	heni·-
'come'	were·-	were·-	weri·-
'travel'	čele·-	čeme·-	čeli·-
'be'	bo·	bo-me	bohil-

Three of the inanimate comitatives are clearly marked with the suffix /-me/: /har-me-/ 'bring (go with)', /hen-me-/ 'bring (arrive with)', and /bo-me-/ 'keep (be with)'. Two of the stems have undergone additional phonological and morphological changes in their inanimate causative. In /were·-/ the medial cluster /rm/ has been simplified to /r/; in /čeme·-/ the medial cluster /lm/ has been simplified to /m/. Additionally both of these verbs have been reanalyzed as second-conjugation (unchanging) verbs of the canon CVCV· (i.e., with a stem-final long /e·/ rather than the short /e/ of the comitative suffix).

The animate comitative is indicated by a stem change to a second-conjugation stem with the characteristic vowel /i·/, in all four of the verbs of motion. For /bo·/ the animate comitative is expressed with the suffix /-hil/, which is etymologically related to the /i·/ of the other verbs (see discussion in Shepherd 2005:32, 195).

The forms /čeme·-/ 'travel.COM.IN' and /čeli·-/ 'travel.COM.AN' are often translated simply as verbs of possession "keep," "have," or "own," with no overt indication of movement in the gloss (e.g., Whistler 1981:61). Nevertheless I include them in table 8.7 as comitative counterparts of /čele·-/ 'travel', which itself is always translated as a verb of motion: "travel," "go around," "go about," and so on. This is partially for formal reasons: /čeme·-/ and /čeli·-/ are probable forms for comitatives derived from /čele·-/, by analogy with the patterns described above for the other verbs of motion. The semantic shift is also plausible: though they may be used as generic verbs of possession, they are evidently historically derived from verbs meaning 'go about with'.

The inanimate comitative suffix /-me/ is related to the Wintu generic comitative {m}, and Shepherd reconstructs Proto-Wintuan */-m/ 'inanimate comitative' from these (2005:31). The characteristic vowel /i·/ on animate comitative stems may be related to the Wintu particular comitative {i·l}—see Shepherd (2005:32, 195).

Comitative case with comitative verbs: Comitative case marking on nominals is optional when the comitative nominal is an argument of the verb (i.e., when the verb stem has a comitative suffix or an inherent comitative meaning). Compare the parallel examples in (227). Both have the same comitative predicate (*hari·* 'take'), both have the same comitative argument ('gopher'), and both are spoken by the same speaker. Yet in (227a) the comitative argument is in objective case, and in (227b) the comitative argument is in the comitative case. Structurally (227a) is a canonical comitative applicative construction, where the normally oblique comitative participant is realized as the grammatical object; whereas in (227b) it is realized in a semantically transparent way, in the comitative case. The comitative predicate /hari·/ 'take' in (227a) thus has the same valency as its noncomitative counterpart /hara·/ 'go'. This is a clear demonstration that the Patwin comitative is not a canonical structural applicative: the oblique argument is not always realized as the grammatical object (see Dixon and Aikhenvald 2000).

(227) a. ⟨k'a´ima hari' ba·´lɛs·⟩

k'ay-ma	hari	ʔ	ba·-les
gopher-OBJ	go.COM.AN	||	eat-can

Take a gopher so that you can eat.
(Radin, c:5/142, AL) [HP_T]

b. ⟨k'a·´imada ha·´ri ba·´lɪc·.⟩

k'a·y-ma-da	ha·ri	ba·-les
gopher-OBJ-COM	go.COM.AN	eat-can

Take some gopher that you might eat it.
(Radin, c:13/149, AL) [HP_T]

If the choice between comitative and objective case conveys a specific meaning here, it is not clear what that meaning might be.[24]

8.2.4.5. Reciprocal /-p'iri/ 'RECIP'

The reciprocal suffix /-p'iri/ is a first-conjugation suffix (consonant stem), varying in form between /-p'iri/ and /-p'ir/. It is a medial suffix that selects the hortative stem of the verb to which it attaches.

(228) a. ⟨pípel ṫéwṫewṗita⟩
pipel t'ewt'ewp'ita
pipel t'ew-t'ew-p'ir-ta
3DU.SBJ REDUP-speak-recip-PART
them two talking together
(Whistler, d:A100, OM) [HP_L]

b. ⟨ʔupɛle·y limo·ṗiriła⟩
ʔupele·y limo·-p'iri-ła
3DU.POSS$_V$ kill-recip-LOC
when they killed each other
(Ultan, d:7.86, SG) [RP]

The presence of /-p'iri/ consistently indicates that the described event is semantically reciprocal—characterized by multiple agents are acting upon one another (as in 228b), or acting in a way that is oriented toward one another (as in 230). However, /-p'iri/ is not a structurally prototypical reciprocal marker. Notably it is not always associated with a reduction in transitivity. Compare the prototypical detransitivized structure in (228a) to the structure in (229), both spoken by Oscar McDaniel (HP_L). Both examples have the same verb—*t'ewt'ewp'ita* 'to talk together, converse'—but in (228a) it is intransitive (the two people denoted by the subject *pipel* 'they [DU]' are speaking to one another) and in (229) it is transitive (the people denoted by the subject *mile* 'you [PL]' are speaking to the person denoted by the object *nat* 'me').

(229) ⟨míle nát ṫéwṫéw ṗíta⟩

mile	nat	t'ewt'ewp'ita
mile	nat	t'ew-t'ew-p'ir-ta
2PL.SBJ	1SG.OBJ	REDUP-speak-recip-PART

You're talking to me.

(Whistler, d:A12, OM) [HP_L]

Another way that /-p'iri/ is not structurally prototypical is that it can occur on intransitive verb stems. Example (230) shows /-p'iri/ appearing on the intransitive stem /hene·-/ 'arrive' to create the stem /hen-p'iri-/ 'gather'.

(230) ⟨pi·´La hawe´r·pɛ p·a´n·tibɛ k'i·r hɛnp'i·´rmo [. . .]⟩ 'Then quickly did the clouds in the sky get together [. . .]'

pi·ła	hawerpe	panti	be	k'i·r	hen-p'ir-mu [. . .]
then	quickly	above	be.IN	cloud	arrive-recip-SBJV

Then the clouds above quickly gathered [. . .]

(Radin, c:8/144, AL) [HP_T]

Patwin reciprocal /-p'iri/ is related to Wintu reciprocal {p'ur}; Shepherd reconstructs Proto-Wintuan reciprocal */-p'ur/ from these (2005:32).

8.2.4.6. *Reflexive /-nana/* 'REFL'

The reflexive suffix /-nana/ is a first-conjugation suffix (consonant stem), varying in form between /-nana/ and /-nan/. It is a medial suffix, and selects the hortative stem of the verb to which it attaches. Semantically /-nana/ is a prototypical reflexive marker, signifying that the activity described in the verb is being performed by the subject and directed at the subject, as in (231).

(231) ⟨pi thépnanta⟩

pi	t^hep-nan-ta
3SG.SBJ	hit-REFL-PART

He hit himself.

(Whistler, d:A101, OM) [HP_L]

The reflexive argument need not always be the patient or even underlyingly in the objective case. Example (232) shows two examples of the verb /łe·ye-/ 'put, drop' marked with reflexive /-nana/. In (232a) the reflexive stem /łe*y-nana-/ means 'put oneself (somewhere)', and the reflexive argument is the patient (that which is put somewhere). In (232b) the same reflexive stem /łe·y-nana-/ means 'put (something) on oneself', and the reflexive argument is the spatial goal (the place where something is put).

(232) a. ⟨Thleynantarobot⟩ 'Abed'
łe*y-nan-taro bo-t
put-REFL-PART be.AN-FIN
one has lain oneself down
(P. Vallejo, c:26.9) [SP]

b. ⟨łè·nʌ́tàròbô⟩ 'to put on self. carry on self (to put on a hat)'
łe·y-nan-taro bo
put-REFL-PART be.AN
put (something) on oneself
(Bright, c:10.DL130, DL) [HP_T]

The reflexive /-nana/ is related to Wintu reflexive {n}, for which Shepherd reconstructs Proto-Wintuan reflexive */-na/ (2005:32).

Reflexive raising construction: Verbs of speaking can be marked with reflexive /-nana/ in a sort of "raising" construction. In these constructions the complement of the verb of speaking is a clause (reporting what is said) and the speaker is the same as the subject of this clause. The schematic in (233) shows how this structure is related to raising constructions in a derivation-like presentation. In the underlying structure (labeled UR), coreferential referring expressions (NP_i) are the subjects of both the matrix clause and the subordinate clause. In the raising step, the subject of the subordinate clause is raised into the matrix clause. Finally, in the reflexive step, the verb 'say' is marked reflexive, creating a meaning like 'say of oneself that ...'.

(233)	**UR:**	NP_i	say		[NP_i	V . . .]
	Raising:	NP_i	say	NP_i	[$\_\_\_i$	V . . .]
	Reflexive:	NP_i	say-REFL		[$\_\_\_i$	V . . .]

Examples of this reflexive raising construction are shown in (234). In (234a) the verb *momhunanta* 'telling of oneself' is the head of the construction; the matrix subject *pi* 'he' is understood to be the subject of the subordinate clause *piła bo·t'ibus* 'will be there'. In (234b) the verb *ʔunanas* 'say of oneself' is the head of the construction; the matrix subject *pi* 'he' is understood to be the subject of the discontinuous subordinate clause *wini . . . mit* 'see you'. Note that the subordinate verb in (234a) is tensed, contrary to typological expectations for a typical raising construction (see analyses in Davies and Dubinsky 2004).

(234) a. ⟨pínat mɓ́mhunánta píła bɓ́·ṫibuṣ⟩

pi	nat	<u>momhu-nan-ta</u>	[piła	bo·-t'i-bus
3SG.SBJ	1SG.OBJ	<u>tell-REFL-PART</u>	[DIST.LOC	be.AN-FUT-FIN

He <u>told</u> me he [will be there].

(Ultan, d:2.112, OM) [HP_L]

b. ⟨wini-ʔunana-s mit pi.⟩ 'He himself said he saw you.'

[wini	]	<u>ʔu-nana-s</u>	[mit	]	pi
[see	]	<u>say-REFL-FIN</u>	[2SG.OBJ	]	3SG.SBJ

He <u>said</u> he [saw you].

(Whistler 1978:53/55, NL/HL) [HP_R]

The verb *ʔi·* 'do' is used in the same kind of reflexive raising construction, as in (235), presumably functioning as an intensifier.

(235) ⟨wɪ´n·i 'i·´nanacamɪt·.⟩ 'He saw you actually.'

[wini	]	<u>ʔi·-nana-sa</u>	[mit	]
[see	]	<u>do-REFL-PAST</u>	[2SG.OBJ	]

(He) <u>did</u> (himself) [see you].

(Radin, c:5/141, AL) [HP_T]

Whistler analyzes /ʔunana-/ and /ʔi(·)nana-/ as validationals, marking statements as "someone else's definite assertions" (1986:66), but without commenting on their similarity to raising constructions.

8.2.4.7. *Interactions*

More than one voice suffix may occur together in one verb. In this situation each suffix contributes in a predictable way to the meaning of the derived stem. The meaning of the suffix closer to the root is parsed first.

For example in (236a) the verb root /limo·-/ 'kill, fight' is marked with /-p'iri/ 'RECIP', creating the stem /limo-p'iri-/ 'fight each other'. The causative /-ma/ is added to this stem, creating the stem /limo-p'iri-ma-/ 'cause to fight each other'. In (236b) the root /limo·-/ 'kill, fight' is marked with /-ma/ 'CAUS', creating the stem /limo·-ma-/ 'cause to kill'. The applicative /-pa/ is added to this stem with a beneficiary interpretation, creating the stem /limo·-ma-pa-/ 'cause to kill for someone'.

(236) a. ⟨chu ʔúpelet límoṗırmaro⟩

ču	ʔupelet	limo-p'ir-ma-ro
1SG.SBJ	3DU.OBJ	kill-RECIP-CAUS-PART

I made them two fight each other.
(Whistler, d:C6, OM) [HP_L]

b. ⟨limo·mapa nat⟩

limo·-ma-pa	nat
kill-CAUS-APPL	1SG.OBJ

Have him kill (him) for me.
(Ultan, d:7.87, SG) [RP]

The applicative voice suffix may also appear multiple times on one verb, as in (224) above.

8.2.5. Negative Suffixes /-mele·, -mu u, -mur/ 'NEG'

The negative suffixes all select the hortative stem of the verb to which they attach. The suffix /-mele·/ is a prefinal suffix; /-muʔu/ and /-mur/ are final suffixes. Etymologically they are related to the subjunctive suffix /-mu/.

The negative suffix /-mele·/ is attested in all dialects, /-muʔu/ is attested only in Hill Patwin, and /-mur/ only in River Patwin. For discussion of the negative suffixes, see section 9.4.

8.2.6. Concessive /-ka, -kam/ 'CONC'

The concessive suffix is a final suffix that selects the hortative stem of the verb to which it attaches. It takes two forms /-ka, -kam/, varying by dialect: in River Patwin and Lodoga Hill Patwin the concessive suffix is /-kam/, while in other dialects of Hill Patwin the concessive suffix is /-ka/. The concessive is not attested in South Patwin.

The concessive appears on subordinate concessive clauses, contributing a meaning like "although," or "in spite of the fact that." The matrix clause then expresses a proposition that occurs contrary to the expectation set up in the concessive clause. For example in (237a) the concessive clause *lenčul ču harat'o ʔika ʔ* 'I was going to go yesterday' refers to an expected action of going. The matrix clause runs contrary to this expectation: *harmuʔu ʔelesa* 'didn't go'. Similarly in (237b) the concessive clause *hara⁎t'ika* 'was going to go' refers to an expected action of going. The matrix clause runs contrary to this expectation: *ču harmu ʔele·sa ʔ* 'I didn't go'. In (237c) the concessive clause *henkam* 'arrived' sets up an expectation that the person who arrived is present. The matrix clause runs contrary to this expectation: *pi k'elt^{h}uro hani* 'he went back'.

(237) a. ⟨lɛncul cu haratɔ ʔi kaʔ harmoʔo ʔelɛsa⟩

[lenčul	ču	hara-t'o	ʔi-ka	]	ʔ
[yesterday	1SG.SBJ	go-INCEP	COP-CONC	]	||
har-muʔu	ʔele-sa				
go-NEG	NEG-PAST				

[I was going to go yesterday] but I didn't go.

(Ultan, d:6.28, DL) [HP$_T$]

b. ⟨hàráttì k'ʌcu hármʊ̀ ʔɛ̀lɛ́·sàʔ⟩

[hara⁎-t'i-ka	]	ču	har-mu	ʔele·-sa	ʔ	
[go-FUT-CONC	]	1SG.SBJ	go-SBJV	NEG-PAST	‖	

[(I) was going to go] but I didn't.

(Bright, c:6.NL117, NL) [HP$_{C}$]

c. ⟨hɛkam pi k̓ɛ̀lt^{h}ʊro hani⟩

[henkam	]	pi	k'elt^{h}uro	hani
[hen-kam	]	pi	k'elt^{h}u-ro	har-ni
[arrive-CONC	]	3SG.SBJ	go.back-PART	go-RPAST

[(He) came] but he went back.

(Ultan, d:7.50, SG) [RP]

Note that the tense in the concessive clause is relative to the tense of the matrix clause. For example the future tense marking in (237b) does not indicate an absolute future tense 'will go'. Rather the concessive clause is in the future compared to the past time referenced in the matrix clause 'I didn't go'. Thus the future tense marking in (237b) has a future-of-the-past meaning: 'was going to go'.

The concessive suffix /-ka, -kam/ is related to the irrealis particle *ka, kam* 'IRR'. The two are formally similar, and have similar functions. However, their forms and functions are not identical, so the two must be analyzed as separate entities in synchronic Patwin grammar. The concessive suffix always occurs on the verb and conditions the hortative stem of the verb to which it attaches, whereas the irrealis particle is not restricted to occurring after the verb and does not condition the hortative stem. In Lodoga Hill Patwin the two forms are even distinct on a segmental level, with /-kam/ used for the concessive suffix and *ka* used for the irrealis particle. See section 9.2.3 for a discussion of the irrealis particle.

8.2.7. River Patwin Conditional Suffix /-nini/ 'COND'

The conditional suffix /-nini/ 'COND' is a final suffix that selects the hortative stem of the verb to which it attaches. It is invariant in form. It is attested only in the River Patwin of speaker Sarah Gonzales. It signifies that the verb to which it attaches is a subordinate verb in an "if" clause. See examples in (238).

(238) a. ⟨me·m k̓ayunini me·mʊl?⟩

[me·m	k'ayu-nini	]	me·mul	?
[water	want-COND	]	drink.2SG.HORT	‖

[If you're thirsty], drink!

(Ultan, d:7.82, SG) [RP]

b. ⟨pi me·mʊl nenni coyyiʔati⟩ 'If he drinks he gets sick'

[pi	me·mul-nini	]	čoyi-ʔa-t'i
[3SG.SBJ	drink-COND	]	sick-VBLZ$_S$-FUT

[If he drinks], he will get sick.

(Bright, c:8.G82, SG) [RP]

The form of the conditional suffix is not definitely known, due to sparse attestation and variation by researcher. Interviewing River Patwin speaker Sarah Gonzales, Ultan transcribes the conditional as the suffix ⟨-nini⟩ (several instances in Ultan, d:7.82). With the same speaker, Bright transcribes ⟨nénni, nenni, nènni⟩ (Bright, c:8.G78, G79, G82, G83). Other River Patwin sources have no attestation of the conditional suffix. The form then may be either /-nini/ or /-neni/. Since Ultan's transcription is generally more accurate than Bright's, I tentatively analyze the form as /-nini/.

The suffix /-nini/ forms subordinate clauses, but it is not a nominalizing suffix. The subject of a verb marked with /-nini/ is in the subjective case, not the possessive case (e.g., 184b, 238b).

8.2.8. Suffix /-wa/ in de Angulo

The suffix /-wa/ is attested only in the speech of Cortina Hill Patwin speaker Fred Gonzales, and its semantic and grammatical functions are not clear. It selects the hortative or participial stem of the verb to which it attaches. It is described in de Angulo's grammar as a conditional suffix (de Angulo:28), but its use in texts suggests a more general irrealis function. Only two examples, shown in (239), appear in the texts at the end of the grammar. In (239a) the clause marked with /-wa/ is a kind of concessive clause, expressing a desire that will remain unrealized. In (239b) /-wa/ seems to express uncertainty.

(239) a. ⟨oo mit-da har-wa tcu di-ła tcupi ele-ti har-mu⟩

[ʔo·	mitda	har-wa	ču	diła	]
[yes	2SG.COM	go-*wa*	1SG.SBJ	home.LOC	]

ču	pi	ʔele-t'i	har-mu
1SG.SBJ	DECL	NEG-FUT	go-SBJV

[Yes, I would like to go with you], but I can't leave.
(de Angulo:99, FG) [HP$_C$]

b. ⟨pe i-bo-wa łila-bo-wa pi behna łiłila hara-sa pi⟩

[pe	ʔi-bo-wa	łila-bo-wa	pi	]
[what	COP?-?-*wa*	shoot-?-*wa*	3SG.SBJ	]

behna	łiłila	hara-sa	pi
morning	hunt	go-PAST	3SG.SBJ

[I wonder if he killed anything.] He went out hunting this morning.
(de Angulo:115, FG) [HP$_C$]

The translations of the sentences in (239) are given exactly as they appear in de Angulo's grammar. The translation of (239a) suggests that the clause marked with /-wa/ is a subordinate clause, while the translation of (239b) suggests that the clauses marked with /-wa/ may not be subordinate clauses. Note that the subjects of clauses marked with /-wa/ appear in the subjective case, so these clauses are not nominalizations.

8.2.9. South Patwin Suffix /-tk°a/

A suffix ⟨-tca⟩ /-tk°a/ is attested about a dozen times in the South Patwin materials of Vallejo. It selects the /u/-final stem of verbs in the third conjugation, so it may select the hortative or participial stem of the verb to which it attaches.[25] It is invariant in form and is always attested as the final suffix on the verb.

The function of /-tk°a/ is not known. It tends to be associated with stative contexts, as in (240a) and (240b), but is occasionally attested for activities (240c). It is attested in expressions referring to both the present (240a) and the past (240b, 240c).

(240) a. ⟨Thlotutca Eubo wita!⟩

ɬotu-tk°a ʔew bo wita

bad-*tk°a* PROX.SG.SBJ be.AN man

That is a bad fellow!

(P. Vallejo, c:21.7) [SP]

b. ⟨Pal lal pissú botca⟩

pal lal pisu* bo-tk°a

now light create be.AN-*tk°a*

Then light was made. (P. Vallejo, c:19.7.5) [SP]

c. ⟨Uputca OlelboSalti: Tepí Sanda!⟩

ʔupu-tk°a ʔolel bo salti, "tepi* san-da"

say-*tk°a* up be.AN spirit emerge sun-COM?

God said, "Let there be light!"

(P. Vallejo, c:19.9.1) [SP]

8.3. EVENT AND PARTICIPANT PLURALITY

Event and participant plurality are expressed with a variety of markers, all closely associated with the verb root: reduplication, conjugational class alternation, vowel length alternation, and root-bound suffixation. The choice of marking is not predictable and must therefore be lexically specified. However, certain patterns of marking emerge that are discussed in this section.

8.3.1. Reduplication

Reduplication of the stem can indicate event plurality (as in examples 241a and 241b) or plurality of the most affected argument (241c, 241d). The plurality of the event may refer to multiple instances of one event, as in (241a), where /win-wini-/ 'see intermittently' (< /wini-/ 'see') describes multiple, separate events of seeing. It may also refer to a single event involving repetitive action, as in (241b), where /ƛ̓eb-ƛ̓e·bi-/ 'nibble' (< /ƛ̓ebi/ 'to chip') describes a continuous activity. Reduplication used to mark the plurality of the most affected object may indicate a plurality of the grammatical object for transitive verbs, as in (241c), or a plurality of the grammatical subject for intransitive verbs, as in (241d).

(241) a. ⟨lɛni cu wɪnwɪnta ʔałpas⟩

leni ču win-win-ta ʔałpa-s

yesterday 1SG.SBJ REDUP-see-PART do.all.day-FIN

Yesterday I was seeing (it) off and on.

(Ultan, d:6.133, SG) [RP]

b. ⟨ƛ̓ebƛ̓é·bum ʔíwe píma⟩

ƛ̓eb-ƛ̓e·bu-m ʔiwe pima

REDUP-chip-SBJV do.2SG.HORT DIST.SG.OBJ.IN

Don't nibble on that.

(Whistler, d:F97, HL) [HP$_R$]

c. ⟨le·ni pi p^{h}ʊmp^{h}ume·sa⟩

le·ni pi p^{h}um-p^{h}ume·-sa

yesterday 3SG.SBJ REDUP-roast-PAST

She roasted the meat yesterday (lot of meat).

(Ultan, d:7.59, SG) [RP]

d. ⟨čaket pile hamhamtaro bo·s sú·ɬła⟩

čaket pile ham-ham-taro bo·-s su·ɬ-ła

all 3PL.SBJ REDUP-sit-PART be.AN-FIN floor-LOC

They're all sitting on the floor.

(Whistler, d:F95, HL) [HP$_R$]

Formally, reduplication consists of part of the stem that is copied (the reduplicant) and prepended to the verb as a prefix. Reduplication of the verb stem is usually a reduplication of the first CVC sequence, as in the examples in (241).[26] CV reduplication is also attested, as in the examples in (242).[27]

(242) a. ⟨huhʊpta⟩ /hu-hup-ta/ 'keep on diving'
(< /hupu·-/ 'dive'; Ultan, d:7.66, SG) [RP]

b. ⟨t'at'alltʌ⟩ /t'a-t'al-ta/ 'falls many times'
(< /t'ala·-/ 'fall'; Bright, c:8.G83, SG) [RP]

c. ⟨ṫeṫe·u̯ta⟩ /t'e-t'e·w-ta/ 'talking'
(< /t'e·we-/ 'speak'; Ultan, d:7.71, SG) [RP]

More rarely, CVCV reduplication is attested, as in the examples in (243). CVCV reduplication is sometimes associated with a meaning of *result* plurality, as Whistler suggests (1981:77). In (243a) a CVCV reduplication of the verb /t'eba·/ 'to make a nick' refers to a plurality of the result of this activity: multiple chips coming off of something. Similarly in (243b) a CVCV reduplication of the verb /k'opa·/ 'to cut down' refers to a plurality of the result of this activity: multiple objects having been broken off. However, CVCV reduplication may also have an ordinary interpretation of event plurality, as in (243c). Here the reduplicated stem /p'etʰu-p'etʰu-/ refers to multiple events of hunting, not to a plurality of the results of hunting.

(243) a. ⟨ṫebaṫebas⟩ /t'eba-t'eba-s/ 'chips coming off'
(< /t'eba·/ 'to make a nick'; Whistler, d:G18, HL) [HP_R]

b. ⟨k̓ópak̓óparo⟩ /k'opa-k'opa-ro/ 'all broke off'
(< /k'opa·/ 'to cut down'; Whistler, d:G19, HL) [HP_R]

c. ⟨ṗɛtʰuṗɛtʰuro⟩ /p'etʰu-p'etʰu-ro/ 'hunting all the time'
(< /p'etʰi/ 'hunt'; Ultan, d:7.87, SG) [RP]

Interestingly, CVCV reduplication is sensitive to verb stem ablaut. For example, in (243c), the participle suffix /-ro/ 'PART' selects the participial stem of the verb. Not only is the root in its participial stem form /p'etʰu-/, but the reduplicant is as well. Compare this to (244), where the interrogative suffix /-bo/ selects the agentive stem. Both the root and the reduplicant take the agentive stem form of the same verb /p'et^{h}i-/.

(244) ⟨p'etip'etibo⟩ /p'et^{h}i-p'et^{h}i-bo/ 'hunt (habitual, interrogative)' (Bright, c:8.G88, SG) [RP]

Verbs generally retain their conjugational class when reduplicated. However, some verbs change conjugational class in their reduplicated forms. For example the third-conjugation verb /bali-/ 'tell' (RP) becomes a first-conjugation verb in its reduplicated form /bal-bal-/ 'tell lots' (Ultan, d:7.71, SG). On the other hand the first-conjugation verb /p^{h}u·łu-/ 'whistle' (HP) becomes a third-conjugation verb in its reduplicated form /p^{h}uł-p^{h}u·łi-/ 'whistle habitually' (Whistler, d:F100, G99, HL). Further lexicographical work is needed to determine the extent of these conjugation changes in the lexicon.

For verbs whose first vowel is short, the reduplicant always has a short vowel. For verbs whose first vowel is long, the reduplicant is sometimes attested with a long vowel and sometimes with a short vowel. Vowel length is generally preserved in the stem following the reduplicant, though shortening of the characteristic vowel is common in these stems (and in stems with more than two syllables generally). Reduplication may derive a stem with multiple long vowels, in an exception to the general constraint of one long vowel per word. For example the verb stem /č'a·k-/ 'split into little pieces' reduplicates to /č'a·k-č'a·k-/ 'split lots of things into little pieces' (Ultan, d:7.72, SG).

CVC reduplication may result in neutralization of aspiration, as in (245a), where the reduplicant-final /t^h/ is deaspirated. Voicing, however, is retained in this position, as in (245b).

(245) a. ⟨yɛtyɛt^{h}e·wta⟩ /yet-yet^{h}e·w-ta/ 'dream all the time' (< /yet^{h}e·we-/ 'dream'; Ultan, d:7.64, SG) [RP]

b. ⟨k̓obk̓obo·luro⟩ /k'ob-k'bo·lu-ro/ 'buying lots of things' (< /k'obo·li/ 'buy'; Ultan, d:7.99, SG) [RP]

Derived verbs are subject to reduplication following the general CVC reduplication pattern. For example the verb ⟨mu·łmu·łenʔa-⟩ /mu·ł-mu·łen-ʔa-/ 'to have kids' is derived from the kinship term /mu·łe/ 'male's child' verbalized with /-ʔa/ and reduplicated (Whistler, d:G107, HL). The verb ⟨ʔolʔolpʰuta⟩ /ʔol-ʔol-pʰur-ta/ 'breathe (iterative)' is a reduplicated form of /ʔol-pʰur-/ 'inhale', a compound form beginning with the directional /ʔol/ 'up'.

8.3.2. Inflectional Class Alternation

Some verbs change their inflectional class to express plurality of the event or plurality of the affected object. For example the River Patwin verb /kʰayłeye-/ 'throw away' is a verb of the first conjugation (consonant stem). When the affected argument is plural, the stem changes to a second-conjugation verb (unchanging stem) with the characteristic vowel /a/: /kʰayłeya-/ (Ultan, d:7.72, SG). Similarly the Lodoga Hill Patwin verb /kʰesa·-/ 'to make one hole' is a verb of the second conjugation (unchanging stem). When referring to a plurality of hole-making events, the stem changes to a third-conjugation verb (*i*-stem): /kʰesi-/ 'to make lots of holes' (Whistler, d:C16, OM). Further lexicographical work is needed to obtain a full inventory of inflectional class changes associated with verbal plurality in each dialect.

8.3.3. Vowel Length Alternations

Verbal plurality is sometimes associated with a change in the length of a root-internal vowel (i.e., a stem vowel other than the stem-final characteristic vowel). For example, in both Hill Patwin and River Patwin, the verb /tʰep/ 'hit' refers to a single act of hitting. To refer to a plurality of hitting events or to a plurality of affected objects, the root-internal vowel is lengthened: /tʰe·p-/ 'hit many times, hit many things' (Ultan, d:7.73, SG; Whistler, d:F63, HL, and B67, OM).

Vowel length alternations indicating verbal plurality may be accompanied by changes in inflectional class. For example the verb /č'ura·/ 'tear one thing' is a verb of the second conjugation (unchanging) with a short root-internal vowel /u/. To indicate tearing a plurality of objects or events, the root vowel is lengthened, and the verb changes to the first conjugation (consonant stem): /č'u·ru-/ 'tear multiple objects, tear multiple times' (Whistler, d:G21, HL; Ultan, d:3.12, OM). Similarly the Rumsey Hill Patwin verb /limba·ki-/ 'blink once' is a verb of the third conjugation (*i*-stem) with a long root-internal vowel /a·/. To indicate a plurality of blinking events, the vowel is shortened, and the verb changes to the first conjugation (consonant stem): /limbaka-/ 'blink at intervals, occasional flashes' (Whistler, d:G98, HL).

8.3.4. Root-Bound Suffixes

This section describes the root-bound suffixes associated with event plurality and event singularity. Dialect-specific arrays of suffixes will be discussed for Hill Patwin and River Patwin separately. The semelfactive suffix /-tʰi/, attested in all dialect groups, is discussed in its own section. Outside of this section these root-bound suffixes are not glossed separately, but are considered to be part of the verb stem.

8.3.4.1. River Patwin Suffixes /-oho, -to, -kʰo/

The River Patwin root-bound suffixes /-oho/ 'contiguous', /-to/ 'delimitative', and /-kʰo/ 'iterative' indicate the nature of the event's temporal structure.

Verbs marked with /-oho/ 'contiguous' stand in opposition to verb forms expressing iterative (noncontinuous) events. For example the verb /č'ak-oho-/ 'split once' expresses one contiguous event of splitting, as opposed to /č'a·ka-/ 'split into many pieces', which expresses an iterated action of splitting (Ultan, d:7.94, SG). Similarly the verb /pʰuł-oho-/ 'blow on once' expresses one contiguous event of blowing, as opposed to /pʰułu-/ 'blow on', which expresses an iterated activity of blowing on something (as while winnowing seeds in a basket; Whistler, d:E84).

Verbs marked with /-oho/ also stand in opposition to verb forms marked with /-to/ 'delimitative', which express single, circumscribed instances of events that otherwise have no inherent endpoint. Thus the contiguous verb /sopir-oho-/ 'spin' describes a continuous event of turning, whereas the delimitative verb /sopir-to/ 'turn around once' describes a circumscribed event of turning (Snyder, b:SG; Whistler, d:F17, JR). Similarly the contiguous verb /hoyel-oho-/ 'roll' describes a continuous event of rolling, whereas the delimitative verb /hoyeł-to-/ 'move a little sideways' describes a circumscribed event of a similar motion (Whistler, d:F17, JR). The delimitative suffix /-to/ is not attested in River Patwin outside of this opposition to /-oho/.

The suffix /-kʰo/ 'iterative' is attested on only two verbs in River Patwin, and is associated with repeated, short events. In both verbs /-kʰo/ stands in semantic opposition to the contiguous suffix /-oho/. The iterative verb /k'e·p-kʰo-/ 'keep on dripping' stands in opposition to the contiguous verb /k'ep-oho-/ 'dripping water out (seeping?)' (Ultan, d:7.66, SG). Similarly the iterative verb /pʰu·ł-kʰo-/ 'lots of short blows' stands in opposition to the contiguous verb /pʰuł-oho-/ 'blow on once' (Ultan, d:7.94, SG).[28] In both examples /-kʰo/ is associated with lengthening of the root vowel, which may itself be a separate expression of pluractionality (see section 8.3.3).

All three suffixes /-oho, -to, -kʰo/ attach directly to the root, directly following the final consonant in the root.[29]

Table 8.8 shows attested River Patwin verbs marked with the suffixes described in this section.

8.3.4.2. *Rumsey Hill Patwin Suffixes /-to, -ko/*

The suffixes /-to/ and /-ko/ are attested in the speech of Rumsey Hill Patwin speaker Harry Lorenzo. They are formally similar to River Patwin /-to/ and /-kʰo/, but functionally distinct.

Rumsey Hill Patwin /-to/ is associated with single, circumscribed events, as in /dibil-to-/ 'roll over once' and /ƛ'ere·-to-/ 'cry out once, make a noise once' (Whistler, d:C21, F98, HL). Semantically, then, Rumsey /-to/ is similar to River Patwin delimitative /-to/. However, rather than occurring directly on the consonant-final root, Rumsey /-to/ always occurs after a vowel in biconsonantal roots. Moreover Rumsey /-to/ does not stand in opposition to /-oho/, as in River Patwin. Instead stems with /-to/ stand in opposition to verb stems that are marked with /-ko/ (for biconsonantal roots) or without /-ko/ (for triconsonantal roots), and that are generally subject to vowel lengthening. This complex pattern is described in Whistler (1981)

Table 8.8. Attested delimitative, contiguous, and iterative verbs in River Patwin

Unmarked	**Delimitative**	**Contiguous**	**Iterative**
	sopir-to- 'turn around once'	sopi·r-oho- 'spin'	
	hoyeł-to 'move a little sideways'	hoyel-oho- 'roll'	
		k'ep-oho- 'seep?'	k'e·p-kʰo- 'keep on dripping'
pʰułu- 'blow on'		pʰuł-oho- 'blow on once'	pʰu·ł-kʰo- 'lots of short blows'
č'a·ka- 'split into pieces'		č'ak-oho- 'split once'	
nala- 'lick'		nal-oho- 'lick once'	

Sources: Bright, c:1.G171; Ultan, d:7.65, 7.66, 7.72, 7.78, 7.94, 7.95; Whistler, d:E84, F17, F114; and Snyder, b.

and summarized in table 8.9. Also shown in table 8.9 is the generalized role of /-ko/, which may mark both delimitative and iterative stems. The choice of /-ko/ versus /-to/ for delimitative verbs is lexically specified in Rumsey Hill Patwin.

No cognate of River Patwin /-oho/ 'contiguous' is clearly attested in Hill Patwin with an analogous function. The verbalizer /-ho/ is present in both Hill Patwin and River Patwin, but is functionally distinct from River Patwin /-oho/. (See section 4.10.1.)

8.3.4.3. *Semelfactive /-tʰi/*

An additional suffix associated with verbal number is semelfactive /-tʰi/, attested in Hill Patwin, River Patwin, and South Patwin. The suffix /-tʰi/ is of the third conjugation (*i*-stem) and therefore has two allomorphs: /-tʰi/ and /-tʰu/. This suffix can be associated with event and participant singularity. These may be true semelfactives (instantaneous and not involving a change of state, like /pʰo·k-tʰi-/ 'sound of one clap'; Whistler, d:G84), or they may involve a change of state (like /sul-tʰi-/ 'kill'; frequently attested), or they may be circumscribed, durative events (like /pʰuł-tʰi-/ 'blow on'; Whistler, d:G106, HL). However, verbs marked with /-tʰi/ may also refer to continu-

Table 8.9. Delimitative and iterative verbs in Rumsey Hill Patwin with /-to/ and /-ko/

Delimitative	**Iterative**	**Source**
CVCV·-to-	CV·C-ko-	
hele·-to- 'slice off once'	he·l-ko- 'slice off many times'	F98
pʰele·-to- 'spread on once'	pʰe·l-ko- 'spread on many times'	G110
CVCV·-ko-	CV(·)C-ko-	
liwi·-ko- 'gesture once with hand'		
ƛ'utu·-ko- 'scratch once'	ƛ'u·t-ko- 'scratch repeatedly'	F95
ƛ'iti·-ko- 'press lightly'	ƛ'i·t-ko- 'press lightly, repeatedly'	F95
sutu·-ko- 'inhale once'	su·t-ko- 'inhale repeatedly'	F81
CVCVC-to-	CVCV·Co-	
dap'ir-to- 'twist once'	dap'i·ro- 'keep twisting'	G35
sibir-to- 'turn around once'	sibi·ro- 'twirl, go around'	F64, G35

All words spoken by Rumsey Hill Patwin speaker Harry Lorenzo. Third column is page numbers for sample attestations in Whistler's notebooks.

ous states, like /łop-tʰi-/ 'to be crossed' (Whistler, d:A59, OM) or /lek-tʰi-/ 'to be tired' (Radin, c:70/196, AL). I follow Whistler (1981) in calling /-tʰi/ "semelfactive," though it is associated with other meanings as well.

A selection of semelfactive forms and attested stems is shown in table 8.10. Note that regardless of the inflectional class of the stem, /-tʰi/ attaches directly to the final consonant of the root. Of the stems in table 8.10, /k'e·le-/ 'folded all up' is in the first conjugation, /puta·-/ 'jump up and down' is in the second conjugation, and /leki-/ 'hurry' is in the third conjugation. The conjugation class and exact meaning of /sulu-/ 'kill' is unknown, as the verb is rarely attested in its nonsemelfactive form. The stem of /ʔok-tʰi-/ 'vomit', a verb attested in all three of the major dialect groups, is apparently onomatopoeic.

Shepherd identifies the Wintu transitive suffix /-č/ as a cognate of Patwin /-tʰi/, reconstructing a Proto-Wintuan mediopassive */-čʰ/ (2005: 71–72). Some of the semelfactive verbs in Patwin are old in Wintuan and can be reconstructed in the protolanguage. Of the verbs in table 8.10, Shepherd reconstructs Proto-Wintuan forms for two: */leq-čʰu-/ 'to be tired'

Table 8.10. Semelfactive verbs and their stems

Stem	Semelfactive	Source
k'e·le- 'folded all up'	k'e·l-tʰi- 'folded once'	(Whistler, d:G47, HL)
puta·- 'jump up and down'	put-tʰi- 'jump down'	(Whistler, d:G61, HL)
ƛ'o·p- 'put inside (a lot)'	ƛ'op-tʰi- 'put inside (one)'	(Whistler, d:G74, HL)
leki- 'hurry'	lek-tʰi- 'tired'	(Bright, c:10.DL87, 9.DL18)
sulu- 'kill (?)'	sul-tʰi- 'kill'	(Radin, c:59/186, AL)
[onom.]	ʔok-tʰi- 'vomit'	(Whistler, d:E77, JR)

and */ʔok-čʰi-/ 'vomit' (2005:72). The antiquity of the suffix may account for its diffused meaning synchronically in Patwin.

8.4. NOMINALIZATION

The verb may appear in a nominalized form, functioning as the head of a subordinate clause or as a noun. Nominalizing suffixes are final suffixes, in the sense that they cannot be followed by any further verbal suffixes, but they may be followed by nominal morphology such as case-marking suffixes.

8.4.1. Bare Stem Nominalization

Verbs may appear in their nominal stem form with no verbal inflectional suffixes, in which case they are functionally nominalized verbs. In this form verbs may be used as nouns or as heads of nominalized clauses. In spite of their formal similarity, bare nominal stem verbs in these two functions are in morphologically distinct categories. Used as nouns they are morphologically inanimate nouns; their possessors take the inanimate possessive form of the possessive case. Used as heads of nominalized clauses, they are morphologically nominalized verbs; their subjects take the agentive form of the possessive case.

8.4.1.1. Bare Nominal Stem Verbs as Heads of Clauses

Bare nominal stem verbs may appear as heads of subordinate clauses. In (246) the nominal stems of the verbs *hene·* 'arrive' and *poroho* 'break (once)' are used as heads of subordinate clauses functioning as arguments of a matrix verb. In (246a) the phrase *nay na·me hene·* 'my arriving for the last time', headed by the bare-stem nominalized verb *hene·* 'arriving', is the complement of the copular verb *ʔis*. In (246b) the bare-stem nominalized verb *porohoma* 'breaking' is the object of the matrix verb *winis* 'to see', and is accordingly marked with the objective case suffix /-ma/.

(246) a. ⟨nay na·me hene· ʔis⟩

[nay	na·me	hene·	]	ʔi-s
[1SG.POSS$_V$	last.time	arrive$_{NMNL}$	]	COP-FIN

This is [the last time I come].
(Whistler, d:F55, HL) [HP$_R$]

b. ⟨č⁼u winis pʰɔřɔhɔmaʔ⟩

ču	wini-s	[poroho-ma	]	ʔ
1SG.SBJ	see-FIN	[break$_{NMNL}$-OBJ	]	‖

I saw (him) [break (it)].
(Snyder, b:SG) [RP]

Subordinate clauses headed by bare nominal stem verbs may also function as purposive clauses, as in (247).

(247) a. ⟨hara·t̓is cuʔ namın k̓a·yma č̓o·wiʔ⟩

hara·-t'i-s	ču	ʔ	[namin
go-FUT-FIN	1SG.SBJ	‖	[1SG.POSS$_{AN}$

k'a·y-ma	č'o·wi	]	ʔ
old.lady-OBJ	look.at$_{NMNL}$	]	‖

I'm going [to see my old lady].
(Ultan, d:6.104, DL) [HP$_T$]

b. ⟨neʔpelʔ t'ákahoʔ háttàcèy⟩

nepel	[t'akaho	]	hatta	če·
nepel	[t'akaho	]	har-ta	čeh-s
1DU.EXCL.SBJ	[gather.acorns$_{NMNL}$	]	go-PART	AUX-FIN

We are going [to gather acorns].

(Bright, c:8.G97, SG) [RP]

Bare nominal stem verbs are also occasionally attested as heads of independent clauses. These may be structurally active clauses like (248a), where the patient is in the objective case (*nat* 'me'). They may also be structurally passive clauses like (248b), where the patient is in the subjective case (*pi* 'it'). In both structures the agent is realized in the agentive form of the possessive case (*hayuno* 'dog' in 248a; *ʔuy* 'he' in 248b), consistent with the nominalized status of the verb.

(248) a. ⟨hayunɒ nat wɪnɪ·⟩

hayu-no	nat	wini·
dog-POSS$_V$	1SG.OBJ	see$_{NMNL}$

The dog saw me.

(Ultan, d:6.77, DL) [HP$_T$]

b. ⟨ʔuy poroho pa pi⟩

ʔuy	poroho	pa	pi
3SG.POSS$_V$	break$_{NMNL}$	Q	DIST.SG.SBJ

Did he break it?

(Ultan, d:7.96, SG) [RP]

8.4.1.2. *Bare Nominal Stem Verbs as Nouns*

Bare nominal stem verbs may also function as ordinary referring expressions, in which function they are inanimate nouns. Example (249a) shows the Hill Patwin noun *ba·* 'food', the nominal stem of the verb *ba·* 'eat'.[30] Example (249b) shows the noun *hiłi·* 'beads', the nominal stem of the verb *hiłi·* 'to wear around the neck'. Both are shown with pronoun possessors, taking the inanimate form of the possessive case (marked with the suffix /-no, -nu/). This shows that they are grammatically inanimate nouns.

(249) a. ⟨ɔle·´nu ba·⟩ /ʔule·nu ba·/ ‘their food’
(Radin, c:42/172, AL) [HP$_T$]

b. ⟨náno hɪłi⟩ /na∗no hiłi∗/ ‘my beads’
(Bright, c:1.G126, SG) [RP]

8.4.2. Finite Suffix as Nominalizer

The finite suffix /-s/ (HP and RP) and /-t°i/ (SP) sometimes functions as a nominalizer—that is to say, verbs inflected with this suffix may function as referring expressions.[31] For example the noun *ʔečes* ‘thief’ is attested in Hill Patwin and River Patwin, derived from the verb *ʔe·če* ‘steal’ with /-s/ functioning as a nominalizer (e.g., Whistler, d:E2; Bright, c:8.G47, 9.DL21). The noun *ba·s* ‘food’ is also attested in Rumsey Hill Patwin and River Patwin, derived from the verb *ba·* ‘eat’ (e.g., Whistler, d:E60; Ultan, d:7.52). Similarly the noun *č’odit°i* ‘horse’ is attested in South Patwin, derived from the verb *č’odi* ‘crawl, go on four legs’, with /-t°i/ functioning as a nominalizer (P. Vallejo, c:23.10). Note that in *ʔečes* ‘thief’ and *č’odit°i* ‘horse’, the agent is the referent, whereas in *ba·s* ‘food’, the patient is the referent. Nouns derived with the finite suffix are inanimate, as shown by the absence of animate object marking in both examples (250) and the inanimate possessive agreement in (250a).

(250) a. ⟨pi na·no ba·s ʔetta⟩

pi	na·no	ba·s	ʔetta
pi	na·no	ba·-s	ʔeč-ta
DIST.SG.SBJ	1SG.POSS$_{IN}$	eat-FIN	steal-PART

He stole my food.
(Whistler, d:E3, JR) [RP]

b. ⟨Tchoditi mi hempam⟩

č’odi-t°i	mi	henpa-m
crawl-FIN	2SG.SBJ	find-SBJV

Did you find your horse?
(P. Vallejo, c:25.11) [SP]

The use of the finite suffix as a nominalizer is unpredictable and therefore must be lexically specified. It also varies by dialect: though nominalizing /-s/ is attested in *ba·s* in River Patwin and Rumsey Hill Patwin, the bare stem *ba·* is used for 'food' in South Patwin and most dialects of Hill Patwin.

Shepherd reconstructs nominalization as the original function of Proto-Wintuan */-s/, which gave rise to Patwin /-s/ 'FIN' and Wintu /-s/ 'generic aspect (and nominalizer)'. Some derived nominals with */-s/ can be reconstructed for Proto-Wintuan, including **ba·s* 'food, eating' (2005: 32). Thus the nominalizing function of /-s/ is older than its tense-marking function. The use of the finite suffix for nominalization in South Patwin *č'odit°i* 'horse' shows that the construction is still productive in recent time. The use of South Patwin's innovative finite suffix form /-t°i/ for nominalizations shows that it is the finite suffix that is used for nominalizations (/-s/ in HP and RP, /-t°i/ in SP), and not some historically related nominalizing suffix /-s/ inherited from Proto-Wintuan.

8.4.3. Agentive Nominalizer /-tu/ 'NMLZAG'

The agentive nominalizer /-tu/ 'NMLZ_{AG}' can attach to either verbal or nominal stems. See table 8.11. It can also derive multiword noun phrases from clauses, as in the examples in (251).

(251) a. *no·pma lelitu* 'Deer Maker'
< *no·p* 'deer' + /-ma/ 'OBJ' + *leli* 'make'
(Radin, c:100–109, AL) [HP_{T}]

b. ⟨herak taltu⟩ *łarak t'altu* 'aurora'
< *łarak* 'star' + *t'ali* 'lie down'
(Curtin, b:132) [SP]

The agentive nominalizer is unusually eccentric in the form of verb stem it selects. Generally it selects the agentive stem of the verb—that is, first-conjugation verbs ending in a vowel and third-conjugation verbs ending in /i/. But in some cases the agentive nominalizer attaches to what appears to be the consonant-final morph of first-conjugation verbs. In at least two cases /-tu/ selects a unique consonant-final morph of a third-

Table 8.11. Agentive nominalizer /-tu/ on verbal and nominal stems

Stem		Nominalized		Source
witi·li	'run'	witi·l-tu	'foot-racer'	(Whistler, d:A40, 1981:66)
łala	'rot' (v.)	łala-htu	'wet'	(Swadesh and Melton AU:23:52)
huračaʔa	'drunk' (adj.)	huračaʔa-htu	'drunkard'	(Ultan, d:7.104, SG)
ko·l	'mouth'	ko(·)l-tu	'singer'	(McKern 1922:251)
mat	'ear'	mat-tu	'someone with big ears'	(Whistler, d:B35, OM)
łube	'property'	łube-tu	'someone who has a lot of property'	(Whistler, d:F77, HL)

conjugation (*i*-stem) verb: *witi·ltu* 'foot-racer' (< /witi·li-/ 'run' + /-tu/, attested frequently in HP and RP, e.g., Whistler, d:A40; Ultan, d:7.51) and *t'altu* 'faller' (< /t'ali-/ 'fall' + /-tu/, in SP ⟨herak taltu⟩ /łerak t'altu/ 'aurora'; Curtin, b:132). See table 8.12 for a summary of stems selected by /-tu/.

Allomorphs of NMLZ$_{AG}$

-tu	regular
-htu	after vowels in RP
-stu	after vowels in HP$_R$

Formal variation across dialects: In River Patwin the agentive nominalizer is /-htu/ after vowels. Example (252) shows instances of River Patwin /-htu/ from the written archive. This form can also be heard on the audio recording of Ida Mitchum (Swadesh and Melton). In Rumsey Hill Patwin the agentive nominalizer is /-stu/ after vowels (253). In all other dialects the agentive nominalizer is always /-tu/, whether after vowels or consonants.

(252) a. ⟨k̓erek̓ahtu⟩ /k'erek'a-htu/ 'smaller'
(Whistler, d:C74, JR) [RP]

b. ⟨chu k̓úhumelé·htu⟩

ču	k'uhu-mele·-htu
1SG.SBJ	cough-NEG-$NMLZ_{AG}$

I never did cough, seldom cough, I don't cough.

(Whistler, d:F30, JR) [RP]

(253) ⟨k̓acastu⟩ /k'ača-stu/ 'one who cuts all the time'
(Whistler, d:E55, HL) [HP_R]

Agentive nominalized verbs as predicates: Agentive nominalized verbs may occur as nonverbal predicates without auxiliary verbs, in which case they express a habitual state or activity. These clauses are often glossed in English with words like "always" or in a negative context "never." See examples in (254).

(254) a. ⟨pi ʔá·na ṗéthimelé·tu⟩

pi	ʔa·na	p'etʰi-mele·-tu
3SG.SBJ	very	hunt-NEG-$NMLZ_{AG}$

He is not really a hunter.

(Whistler, d:C40, OM) [HP_L]

b. ⟨pi thanó·melé·htu⟩

pi	tʰano·-mele·-htu
3SG.SBJ	win-NEG-$NMLZ_{AG}$

He never wins.

(Whistler, d:F122, JR) [RP]

c. ⟨cu ʔu·t layukam ʔelɛhtu⟩

ču	ʔu·t	layukʔa-m	ʔele-htu
1SG.SBJ	3SG.OBJ	good-SBJV	NEG-$NMLZ_{AG}$

I never did like him.

(Ultan, d:7.73, SG) [RP]

d. ⟨cu hoya piła harahtu⟩

ču	hoya	piła	hara-htu
1SG.SBJ	previously	there	go-NMLZ_{AG}

I used to go there.

(Ultan, d:7.81, SG) [RP]

Agentive nominalized adjectives: The agentive nominalizer may also appear on adjective stems. The semantic contribution of the nominalizer in this context is sometimes not clear, as in *bentu* 'big' < *ben* 'big'. In some cases adjectives with the agentive nominalizer may function as adverbs, as in (255).

(255) ⟨chu béntu wití·libus⟩

ču	ben-tu	witi·li-bus
1SG.SBJ	big-NMLZ_{AG}	run-FIN

I'm running pretty fast.

(Whistler, d:B45, OM) [HP_L]

8.4.4. Relativizers /-hVm, -sem, -sok/

Relative clauses in Patwin are nominalizations. The verb of the relative clause may appear either in its bare nominal stem form or with an overt relativizing suffix /-hVm/ ('REL', HP & SP), /-sem/ ('REL', RP), or /-sok/ ('REL_{OBL}', HP). All of the relativizing suffixes select the nominal stem of the verb to which they attach. For more on the morphological, syntactic, and semantic structure of relative constructions, including examples, see section 6.5.

8.4.5. Diminutive /=men/ 'DIM'

The diminutive nominalizing element /=men/ 'DIM' is used to derive nouns. Prototypically the derived diminutives refer to small creatures such as insects, birds, and snakes, but other referents are also attested (stars, tears, mythically large snakes). It is attested in Hill Patwin and River Patwin. When it appears with verb stems, the verb takes the agentive stem form (256a). However, /=men/ is highly eccentric in its occurrence. It may occur with a verb suffixed with /-s/—probably the finite suffix in its nomi-

Table 8.12. Eccentric stem selection of the agentive nominalizer

/i/-final morph of third-conjugation verb stems				
leli	'make'	leli-tu	'maker'	(Radin, c:100-109, AL)
di·hi	'dwell'	di·hi-tu	[as predicate]	(Swadesh and Melton AU:42:55, IM)
noki	'ripe'	noki-htu	'ripe'	(Swadesh and Melton AU:55:26, IM)
muhi	'sing'	muhi-htu	'singer'	(Ultan, d:7.61, SG)
Consonant-final morph of third-conjugation verb stems				
witi·li	'run'	witi·l-tu	'foot-racer'	(Whistler, d:A40, OM)
łerak t'ali	'stars lie down'	łerak t'al-tu	'aurora'	(Curtin, b:132)
Vowel-final morph of first-conjugation verb stems				
łala·	'rotten, rot' (v.)	łala-htu	'wet'	(Swadesh and Melton AU:23:52, IM)
łupuku	'soft'	łupuku-htu	'soft'	(Swadesh and Melton AU:55:41, IM)
t^hekala	'bright'	t^hekala-htu	'bright'	(Swadesh and Melton AU:56:39, IM)
ʔele·	'NEG'	ʔele-htu		(Swadesh and Melton AU:55:13, IM)
hupu·	'dive'	hupu-htu	'diver'	(Ultan, d:7.66, SG)
-p'iri	'REFL'	-p'iri-htu		(McKern 1922:244)
Consonant-final morph of first-conjugation verb stems				
łakala	'play'	łakal-tu	'gambler'	(Radin, c:51, AL)
bene·	'big'	ben-tu	'big	(Whistler, d:A50, OM)
t°ewe·	'fly/speak'	t°ew-tu	'one who dances'	(McKern 1922:247)

nalizing function (256b). It may occur with a noun (256c) or with a fully reduplicated noun (256d). It may occur with an onomatopoeic expression (256e). It may even occur with a multiword clause (256f) or a multiword clause inflected with /-s/ (256g). Nominals derived with /=men/ are formally and semantically idiosyncratic, and must be lexically specified.[32] In the following list of examples the source is appendix A of Whistler's (1976) MA thesis, unless otherwise specified.

(256) a. /č'esi=men/ 'click beetle' (< /č'esi-/ 'sneeze') [HP]

b. /hupu-s=men/ 'grebe' (< /hupu-/ 'dive') [HP]

c. /tus=men/ 'tears' (< /tu·s/ 'face'; Swadesh and Melton:36:02) [RP]

d. /yomta-yomta=men/ 'black widow spider' (< /yomta/ 'doctor') [HP_L]

e. /surutsurut=men/ 'centipede' [HP_L]

f. / tʰo·ɬ pili=men/ 'legendary snake' ("mountain wrapper") [HP_T]

g. /pʰo· ʔeče-s=men/ 'shrew' ("fire stealer") [HP_L]

Etymologically /=men/ is related to the Wintu compounding noun /-men, -met/ 'type, kind, variety'. A compounding noun, described by Pitkin as a "compounded dependent noun," is an element that was historically a noun but can no longer occur independently and is found only in compounds. Shepherd reconstructs Proto-Wintuan compounding noun */-men/ 'thing' (2005:36).[33]

Because it may occur with verbs and phrases inflected with finite /-s/, diminutive /=men/ cannot be analyzed as a noun or a compounding noun in Patwin. Combinations of finite verbs with nouns are not otherwise attested in Patwin, whether as relative constructions (for which a case-marked nominal stem verb is used) or as compounds (in which initial verbs are never inflected for tense).

8.5. VERB COMPOUNDING

As with other parts of speech, verbs may appear in compound constructions, where two free roots combine together to form a single derived stem. In a compound construction, the second root is the head and the first root modifies the head. The second root bears any inflectional morphology that appears on the word and undergoes stem ablaut (see section 8.1). The first element, if it is a verb, appears in its nominal stem form.

Verb-verb compounds are frequently attested where the second member of the compound is an experiential verb: *k'ayi* 'want, like' (HP); *k'aya* 'want, like' (HP$_{L}$); *ʔoyaʔa* 'want, like' (RP); *suka* 'want, like' (RP); *čoyi* 'suffer'; or, occasionally, *mutu* 'hear, feel'. See examples in (257).

(257) a. ⟨chu múhik̓ájabus⟩
ču muhi-k'aya-bus
1SG.SBJ sing-want-FIN
I want to sing.
(Whistler, d:A101, OM) [HP$_{L}$]

b. ču hara-ʔoyaʔa-ro
1SG.SBJ go-want-PART
I wanted to go.
(Swadesh and Melton:57:25, IM) [RP]

c. ⟨mula yeLte har̲asű̃kar̲o⟩
mula yelti hara-suka-ro
mule behind go-want-PART
The mule wanted to go on behind.
(Waterman:11, TO) [RP]

d. ⟨k'ʌ̀náčoibʊṣ cʊʔ⟩
k'ana·-čoyi-bus ču ʔ
sleep-suffer-FIN 1SG.SBJ ||
I am sleepy (lit. 'sleep-suffering').
(Bright, c:2.MB18, MB) [HP$_{L}$]

e. ⟨'a·´na tcu´yimʋ·`tabɔnisa.⟩
ʔa·na čoyi-mut-ta bo-ni-sa
much suffer-feel-PART be.AN-RPAST-PAST
He was badly hurt (lit. 'suffering-felt').
(Radin, c:96/220, AL) [HP$_{T}$]

These compound constructions are frequent enough that Whistler analyzes *k'ayi* and *mutu* as affixes in this context (1981:84). However, since the second element in these constructions can also occur on its own as a free verb, it is more felicitous to analyze the constructions as compounds.

Compounds where the first root is a directional and the second root is a verb are also common. See section 7.1. Noun-verb compounds are not attested.

8.6. VERB CITATION FORMS

There is no single preferred citation form for verbs. Verbs elicited in isolation may take the form of bare stems of the nominal stem class or the hortative stem class. Verbs elicited in isolation also sometimes take the participle form (with the suffix /-ta, -ro, -taro/). Sometimes when asked for a verb, speakers respond with an inflected form—usually the participle accompanied by the auxiliary *bo·/be·* inflected with the finite suffix. Citation forms are also sometimes accompanied by the first-person singular subject pronoun *ču·* 'I'.

NINE

The Clause

The clause consists of a predicate and its arguments and adjuncts. When an auxiliary verb is present in the clause, inflectional suffixes appear on the auxiliary, and the predicate appears in a nominal or nonfinite form. Otherwise, inflectional suffixes appear on the verb. Section 9.1 discusses auxiliary verbs. Section 9.2 describes optional sentence particles, which provide information on the mode of the sentence: declarative, interrogative, irrealis, or reportative. Subordinate clauses are discussed in section 9.3, clausal negation in section 9.4, and comparative clauses in section 9.5.

Nominals are optional in the Patwin clause: the predicate's arguments do not need to be overtly expressed. When a nominal is expressed, its grammatical role (subject, object, locative, etc.) is indicated by case marking on the nominal and its modifiers (see chapters 4–6).

Elements of the clause are freely ordered, with some exceptions. The subject, object(s), and oblique nominals are freely ordered with respect to one another and with respect to the verb. Arguments may even be distributed across the clause in discontinuous noun phrases (see section 6.7). Adverbs and subordinate clauses tend to be clause-initial. Within subordinate clauses the verb or auxiliary verb has a strong tendency to be clause-final. Sentence particles have a strong tendency to appear in second position (after the first word or phrase), though they are also attested clause-finally.

9.1. AUXILIARY VERBS

Auxiliary verbs are semantically bleached verbs that bear the inflectional information of a clause but are not the predicate. They may occur with nonfinite verbal predicates ("main verbs") or with nonverbal predicates (nominals, adjectives, or directionals). Though previous descriptions of Patwin have labeled some bound morphemes as auxiliaries, here only syntactically free elements are considered to be auxiliaries.

9.1.1. Copula *i*/ *ih* 'COP'

The copula *ʔi*/*ʔih* is most frequently attested with nominal predicates: nouns, pronouns, kinship terms, and nominalized verbs. It also frequently occurs as the auxiliary accompanying verbs marked with inceptive /-t'o/. In Tebti and Rumsey Hill Patwin, it is infrequently attested as an auxiliary verb with participial verb predicates. These functions are discussed in sections 9.1.1.1 and 9.1.1.2.

In Hill Patwin and South Patwin the copula always takes the form /ʔi/. In River Patwin the copula always takes the form /ʔih/ underlyingly, though the /h/ may not be realized in the surface form due to optional /h/ vocalization (see section 3.5.3). Compare the Hill Patwin and River Patwin forms in (258), both being examples of the copula taking the participle suffix. In Hill Patwin the copula *ʔi* conditions the allomorph /-ro/ of the participle suffix, which occurs only after vowels. In River Patwin the copula *ʔih* conditions the allomorph /-ta/ of the participle suffix, which occurs only after consonants.

(258) a. ⟨i·´ro⟩ /ʔi-ro/ → [ʔiro] (Radin, c:51, AL) [HP_T]

b. ⟨ʔita⟩ /ʔih-ta/ → [ʔita] (Ultan, d:7.82, SG) [RP]

The copula is related to the verb 'to do, to use': *ʔi·* in Hill Patwin and *ʔih* in River Patwin. Unlike the verb, the copula *ʔi* never has a long vowel in Hill Patwin.

9.1.1.1. Copula with Nonverbal Predicates

The copula is most frequently attested as an auxiliary verb with nominal predicates. Example (259a) shows *ʔi* with a noun predicate *bi·t* 'meadowlark'. Example (259b) shows *ʔi* with a pronoun predicate *pi* 'that'. Example (259c) shows *ʔi* with a kinship term predicate *te·ču* 'my child'. Example (259d) shows *ʔi* with a possessive case pronoun *mato* 'yours'.

(259) a. ⟨ʔew ʔis bi·t⟩

ʔew ʔi-s bi·t

PROX.SG.SBJ COP-FIN meadowlark

That is a meadowlark.

(Whistler, d:D27, HL) [HP_R]

b. ⟨pe· ʔɪsaj pi⟩

pe· ʔi-say pi

what COP-Q DIST.SG.SBJ

What is that?

(Whistler, d:D28, HL) [HP_R]

c. ⟨tÉ·čuʔɪbuṣ⟩

te·-ču ʔi-bus

woman's.child-RL COP-FIN

That's my child.

(Ultan, d:4.4, AN) [HP_L]

d. ⟨ʔelé·s máto ʔim pi⟩

ʔele·-s mato ʔi-m pi

NEG-FIN $\text{2SG.POSS}_\text{IN}$ COP-SBJV DIST.SG.SBJ

It's not yours.

(Whistler, d:G51, HL) [HP_R]

The copula is also attested with nominalized clausal predicates. In (260a) the nominalized clause *na·min k'a·y-no leli* 'made by my lady' is the complement of the copula *ʔis*. In (260b) the nominalized clause *sun haka-lay ʔele·* 'ants being absent here' is the only overt argument of the copula *ʔis*.

(260) a. ⟨ʔew ʔo·k ʔis na·min k̓a·yno leli⟩

ʔew ʔo·k ʔi-s [na·min

PROX.SG.SBJ basket COP-FIN [$\text{1SG.POSS}_\text{K-F}$

k'a·y-no leli]
old.woman-POSS$_V$ make$_{NMNL}$]

That basket is/was [made by my lady].
(Whistler, d:D29, HL) [HP$_R$]

b. ⟨sun hakalaj ʔele· ʔis⟩
[sun hakalay ʔele·] ʔi-s
[here ants be.absent$_{NMNL}$] COP-FIN
There are [no ants here].
(Whistler, d:D33, HL) [HP$_R$]

9.1.1.2. *Copula with Verbs*

In addition to functioning as a copula in clauses with nonverbal predicates, *ʔi/ʔih* may function as an auxiliary verb in a clause with a verbal predicate. The main verb may be a participle (261) or an adverbial participle (262). It is not clear what the semantic contribution of the copula is in these constructions. Neither construction occurs frequently.

(261) a. ⟨čupa·rɑ ʔɪs pi⟩
č'upa·-ro ʔi-s pi
finished-PART COP-FIN 3SG.SBJ
He's finished.
(Ultan, d:6.85, DL) [HP$_T$]

b. ⟨čoro ʔih ʔu·t k̓akmacin⟩
č'o-ro ʔih ʔu·t k'ak-ma-čin
watch-PART COP.2SG.HORT 3SG.OBJ hot-CAUS-lest
Watch out, you might burn him.
(Ultan, d:7.97, SG) [RP]

(262) ⟨muhú·n hán ʔínisa⟩

muhu·n han ʔinisa
muhu·-n har-n ʔi-ni-sa
sing-ADV go-ADV COP-RPAST-PAST
used to go singing
(Whistler, d:F102, HL) [HP_R]

Verbs marked with the inceptive suffix /-t'o/ are also frequently accompanied by the copula *ʔi/ʔih*. See section 8.2.1.8 for a discussion of this construction.

9.1.2. Stative Auxiliary *bo·/be·/boh/beh* 'be'

The stative auxiliary occurs frequently in all dialects. The stem agrees with the subject in animacy: if the subject is an animate noun, a kinship term, or a pronoun with an animate referent, the stative auxiliary takes the form /bo·/ (HP) or /boh/ (RP), glossed here 'be.AN'. If the subject is not animate, the stative auxiliary takes the form /be·/ (HP) or /beh/ (RP), glossed 'be.IN'.

The auxiliary *boh/beh* is always underlyingly consonant-final in River Patwin. Thus, due to optional /h/ vocalization (see section 3.5.3), the River Patwin stative auxiliary varies between its consonant-final form /boh, beh/ and a vowel-final form /bo·, be·/. (Optional vowel shortening yields the additional surface forms /bo, be/.) Three examples of the form /beh/ are shown in (263). Note that in (263a) the stem conditions the /-ni/ allomorph of the remote past suffix, which tends to occur after consonants (see section 8.2.1.5). In (263b) the future tense suffix /-t'i/ occurs directly after the stem-final /h/, showing that the auxiliary is in the fourth conjugation (see section 8.1). In (263c) the finite suffix /-s/ is elided in the surface form, preventing the word-final cluster */hs/ (see section 3.2.1).

(263) a. ⟨botɔk ʔewła bɛhni⟩

botok ʔewła beh-ni
tree PROX.LOC be.IN-RPAST
There was a tree there (not any more).
(Ultan, d:7.44, SG) [RP]

b. ⟨bɛhna pi piʔuro bɛhṫi⟩

behna	pi	piʔu-ro	beh-t'i
morning	DIST.SG.SBJ	do.that.way-PART	be.IN-FUT

It will be that way tomorrow.

(Ultan, d:7.97, SG) [RP]

c. ⟨pa· pi piʔuro bɛh⟩

pa·	pi	piʔuro	beh
pa·	pi	piʔu-ro	beh-s
now	DIST.SG.SBJ	do.thus-PART	be.IN-FIN

It's that way now.

(Ultan, d:7.97, SG) [RP]

The forms /boh, beh/ are also possibly attested in South Patwin. On one page of Vallejo's word lists the form ⟨bo'thla⟩ is repeatedly attested—the animate stative auxiliary, nominalized and followed by the locative case suffix /-ɬa/ (P. Vallejo, c:26.2). The symbol ⟨'⟩ commonly indicates glottalization in other sources, but Vallejo does not use it this way, and the symbol is only very rarely attested in his manuscripts. It is therefore probable that in this case he meant to indicate some sound that he found notable, which may be the syllable-final /h/ found in the River Patwin cognate *boh*. In Merriam's South Patwin vocabulary the form ⟨bĕh⟩ is attested once (Merriam:V76.69). Merriam generally uses either ⟨eh⟩ with a final ⟨h⟩ or ⟨ĕ⟩ with a breve ⟨˘⟩ to indicate a vowel quality like [ɛ]. The combined presence of the final ⟨h⟩ and the breve may indicate a phonetic sequence like [ɛh], that is, the /h/-final form /beh/. Given this evidence we may tentatively conclude that the /h/-final stems /boh-, beh-/ are present in South Patwin. We can also guess that these stems would be subject to the same process of /h/ vocalization as in River Patwin, thus yielding the surface forms /boh, beh, bo·, be·/ for the South Patwin stative auxiliary.

In Hill Patwin the stative auxiliary is always /bo·, be·/, with no /h/ in the stem. The stative auxiliary triggers the /-m/ allomorph of the subjunctive suffix in Hill Patwin, which is the form found after vowels (as in ⟨bɔ·`m⟩ /bo·-m/; Radin, c:51, AL). Similarly the /-mʔu/ allomorph of the negative suffix is attested after the stative auxiliary, which again is the form found after vowels (as in ⟨bo·-mʔu⟩, Whistler 1977a:169, NL/HL).

9.1.2.1. *Stative Auxiliary with Nonverbal Predicates*

Where the copula is used with nominal predicates, the stative auxiliary is used with adjectival predicates (264) and directional predicates (265).

(264) a. ⟨ʔɛ́u̯ṫɪpa ʔá·na láɪ̯kʔabɛ́ṣ⟩
ʔew   t'ipa   ʔa·na   laykʔa   be-s
PROX.SG.SBJ   bread   much   good   be.IN-FIN
This bread is good.
(Ultan, d:2.100, OM)   [HP$_{L}$]

b. ⟨ʔew k̓ucij bo·s⟩
ʔew   k'učuy   bo·-s
PROX.SG.SBJ   small   be.AN-FIN
This one is small.
(Whistler, d:D38, HL)   [HP$_{R}$]

(265) a. ⟨pi thók pát bɛ·s⟩
pi   t^{h}ok   pat   be·-s
DIST.SG.SBJ   tree   outside   be.IN-FIN
That tree is outside.
(Whistler, d:A58, OM)   [HP$_{L}$]

b. ⟨t'ʌsʌlay k̓òdôy cíntȉbô·s⟩
t'asalay   k'odoy   čenti   bo·-s
lizard   rock   under   be.AN-FIN
The lizard was underneath the rock.
(Bright, c:6.NL134, NL)   [HP$_{C}$]

9.1.2.2. *Stative Auxiliary with Verbal Predicates*

The stative auxiliary is also frequently attested with participle verb predicates. This construction is used in reference to static situations (stative predication) or to events that have been completed (perfective aspect). It can also be used as a passive or mediopassive construction.

Sentences with participle verbs and the stative auxiliary may have a stative meaning. In such a construction the verb stem may be inherently stative, like /sik'i·to-/ 'to be skinny', /nari-/ 'to hate', or /mana-/ 'to be like' (266). Such constructions also may be used to convey a stative meaning with verb stems whose nonparticipial forms would be interpreted as active, like /hama·-/ 'to sit' and /łeynana-/ 'to lay oneself down' (267).

(266) a. ⟨ʔew wí·ta sik̓í·toro bo·s⟩
ʔew wi·ta sik'i·to-ro bo·-s
PROX.SG.SBJ man be.skinny-PART be.AN-FIN
That man is skinny.
(Whistler, d:G47, HL) [HP$_R$]

b. ⟨pi nat náruro bo·s⟩
pi nat naru-ro bo·-s
3SG.SBJ 1SG.OBJ hate-PART be.AN-FIN
He hates me.
(Whistler, d:A76, OM) [HP$_L$]

c. pi· [nay ʔi·]
pi· [nay ʔih]
3SG.SBJ [1SG.POSS$_V$ COP.NMNL]

manara bo·
mana-ro boh-s
be.like-PART be.AN-FIN

He looks like me. (lit. 'He is like [I am].')
(Swadesh and Melton:9:56, IM) [RP]

(267) a. ⟨hamtaro cu bɒs⟩
ham-taro ču bo-s
sit-PART 1SG.SBJ be.AN-FIN
I'm sitting down (stative).
(Ultan, d:6.23, NeL) [HP$_T$]

b. ⟨Thleynantarobot⟩
ɬey-nan-taro bo-t
put-REFL-PART be.AN-FIN
abed, lying down
(P. Vallejo, c:26.9) [SP]

The stative auxiliary can also be used with a participle predicate to express a perfective meaning, referring to past events that have been completed (268).

(268) a. ⟨nát˺ ɬla·ṛa bɔṣ⟩
nat ɬila·ra bos
nat ɬila·-ro bo-s
1SG.OBJ shoot-PART be.AN-FIN
I'm wounded (shot).
(Ultan, d:5.8, OM) [HP_L]

b. ⟨ču k̓odoyma yó·wuro bo·s⟩
ču k'odoy-ma yo·wu-ro bo·-s
1SG.SBJ money-OBJ lose-PART be.AN-FIN
I lost my money.
(Whistler, d:G103, HL) [HP_R]

c. ⟨pi t̓akaho hatabE·⟩
pi t'akaho hata be·
pi t'aka-ho har-ta beh-s
3SG.SBJ acorn-VBLZ go-PART be.IN-FIN
He went to gather acorns (already gone).
(Ultan, d:7.58, SG) [RP]

Finally, the stative auxiliary with participles can express a passive meaning, as in the examples in (269). The construction can be a fully functional passive, with the agent specified in the agentive form of the possessive case, as in (269a). Here *ʔuy* '3SG.POSS$_V$' indicates the agent (i.e., "by him"). The other examples in (269) might be interpreted as mediopassives, that is, descriptions of activities that shift focus away from the agent.

(269) a. ⟨leluro bɛs ʔuy (layukʔarɒ bɛs)⟩
lelu-ro be-s ʔuy
make-PART be.IN-FIN 3SG.POSS$_V$

(layuk-ʔa-ro be-s)
good-VBLZ-PART be.IN-FIN

He fixed it. (lit. 'It was made by him, it is good.')
(Ultan, d:6.99, DL) [HP$_T$]

b. ⟨dɒ́kɒ·sɪn k̓acarɒ bɛ́nɪsà⟩
doko·-sin k'ača-ro be-ni-sa
knife-INS cut-PART be.IN-RPAST-PAST
It was cut by a knife.
(Ultan, d:6.104, DL) [HP$_T$]

c. ⟨ʔew wilak piro lelurobe ʔew⟩
ʔew wilak piro leluro
ʔew wilak pi-ro lelu-ro
PROX.SG.SBJ world do.thus-PART make-PART

be ʔew
beh-s ʔew
be.IN-FIN PROX.SG.SBJ

Thus the world was made.
(Ultan, d:7.30, SG) [RP]

d. ⟨Matto bohil pissurubot [. . .]⟩
mato bohil pisu-ro bo-t
2SG.POSS$_{IN}$ will? do-PART be.AN-FIN
Thy will be done [. . .]
(P. Vallejo, c:11.5) [SP]

9.1.3. River Patwin Active Auxiliary *čeh* 'AUX'

The active auxiliary verb *čeh* is found only in River Patwin. It is used for active clauses, whereas *boh/beh* is used for stative clauses. The pair of examples in (270) shows this contrast. Example (270a) is a grammatical sentence describing the activity of crying with the auxiliary *čeh*. Example (270b) shows the same sentence substituting the auxiliary *boh*, which was rejected as ungrammatical by River Patwin speaker Sarah Gonzales.

(270) a. ⟨pi wa·t^{h}uro CE·⟩

pi	wat^{h}uro	če·
pi	wat^{h}u-ro	čeh-s
3SG.SBJ	cry-PART	AUX-FIN

He is crying.
(Ultan, d:7.99, SG) [RP]

b. ⟨(no pi wa·t^{h}uro bo·)⟩

*pi	wat^{h}uro	bo·
pi	wat^{h}u-ro	boh-s
3SG.SBJ	cry-PART	be.AN-FIN

[ungrammatical]
(Ultan, d:7.99, SG) [RP]

Čeh is irregular, having the allomorphs /čeh-/ (nominal, agentive, and past stems, as defined in section 8.1) and /čel-/ (hortative and participial stems). Example (271a) shows an occurrence of the stem /čeh-/, with the finite suffix /-s/ elided in the surface form to prevent the word-final cluster */hs/ (see section 3.2.1). In (271b) the stem of the active auxiliary surfaces as [če·], the stem-final /h/ having undergone /h/ vocalization (see section 3.5.3). In (271c) the hortative stem form /čel-/ is conditioned by the remote past suffix /-ni/ 'RPAST'.

(271) a. ⟨yɪ·wɪtma cu léluro cɛh⟩
yiwitma   ču   leluro   čeh
yiwit-ma   ču   lelu-ro   čeh-s
acorn.soup-OBJ   1SG.SBJ   make-PART   AUX-FIN
I'm making acorn soup.
(Ultan, d:7.46, SG) [RP]

b. ⟨le·ni pi piyuro ce·sa⟩
le·ni   pi   piʔuro   če·sa
le·ni   pi   piʔu-ro   čeh-sa
yesterday   3SG.SBJ   do.thus-PART   AUX-PAST
He was doing that yesterday.
(Ultan, d:7.98, SG) [RP]

c. ⟨le·ni pi piyuro cɛlni⟩
le·ni   pi   piʔu-ro   čel-ni
yesterday   3SG.SBJ   do.thus-PART   AUX-RPAST
He was doing that yesterday.
(Ultan, d:7.98, SG) [RP]

Čeh is not attested with nonverbal predicates. When *čeh* is present as an auxiliary verb, the predicate is always a participial verb. The predicate may be marked with the participle suffix /-ta/ (272) or, less frequently, the adverbial participle suffix /-ni/ 'ADV' (273).

(272) a. ⟨háta cu cé núhɪn⟩
hata   ču   če   nuhin
har-ta   ču   čeh-s   nuh-in
go-PART   1SG.SBJ   AUX-FIN   boat-INS
I'm going by boat.
(Ultan, d:7.20, SG&HG) [RP]

b. ⟨pípel ṫeṫéwta ché⟩
pipel t'et'ewta če
pipel t'et'ew-ta čeh-s
3DU.SBJ talk-PART AUX-FIN
Them two are talking.
(Whistler, d:C83, JR) [RP]

(273) a. layukʔan mi če·bo
layukʔa-n mi čeh-bo
good-ADV 2SG.SBJ AUX-Q
Are you well?
(Swadesh and Melton: 1:53, IM) [RP]

b. ⟨sórsorun ču che⟩
sorsorun ču če
sorsoru-n ču čeh-s
grope-ADV 1SG.SBJ AUX-FIN
I'm groping around.
(Whistler, d:F120, JR) [RP]

Čeh can also be used as a main verb, meaning something like 'to be around, to be moving around'. Because of this meaning, and because of the existence of the allomorph /čel/, it is likely that the auxiliary *čeh* 'AUX' is etymologically related to the verb *čele·* 'travel'.

(274) a. ⟨pi CE·sa⟩
pi če·sa
pi čeh-sa
3SG.SBJ be.around-PAST
He was around.
(Ultan, d:7.104, SG) [RP]

b. ⟨sʊn cu cɛh (cɛ·)⟩

sun	ču	čeh	(če·)
sun	ču	čeh-s	(čeh-s)
here	1SG.SBJ	be.around-FIN	be.around-FIN

I'm here (moving around).

(Ultan, d:7.54, SG) [RP]

9.1.4. Negative Auxiliary *ele·* 'NEG'

As a lexical verb, *ʔele·* means 'to be absent (INTR)' or 'to lack (TRANS)'. It is also frequently used as a negative auxiliary verb—that is, an auxiliary that functions to express clausal negation. Negative auxiliary verbs are typologically unusual, but attested in Uralic languages such as Finnish (see Karlsson 1999:108 ff.). See section 9.4 for a discussion of negation, including the use of *ʔele·*.

9.1.5. Nonverbal Predication with No Auxiliary

Independent clauses are sometimes attested that have nonverbal predicates and no auxiliary verb. These clauses lack an overt verb of any kind. They are equative copular clauses, stating identities between two noun phrases. For example (275a) states that *nano yet* 'my name' is *dana* 'Donald'. Similarly (275b) states that *ʔew* 'those' are *leytaba na·min* 'my relatives'.

(275) a. ⟨nanɒ yɛt dána⟩

nano	yet	dana
1SG.POSS$_{IN}$	name	Donald

My name is Donald.

(Ultan, d:6.100, DL) [HP$_T$]

b. ⟨léytaba na·mɪn ʔew⟩

leyta-ba	na·min	ʔew
relative-PL	1SG.POSS$_{K\text{-}F}$	PROX.SG.SBJ

Those are my relatives.

(Whistler, d:G55, HL) [HP$_R$]

9.2. PARTICLES

Particles are noninflecting function words that indicate the grammatical mood of the clause: declarative *pi* 'DECL', interrogative *pa* 'Q', or irrealis *ka/kam* 'IRR'. Hill Patwin has an additional particle, reportative *ʔupu/ʔupum* 'REPRT', which is etymologically related to the verb *ʔupu* 'to say' found in River Patwin and South Patwin. Particles are usually the second element in a clause, after the first word or constituent. Only one particle may be present in a clause. Particles are optional, and they appear in a minority of clauses. The functions they serve can also be indicated by bound morphology on the verb. The declarative and interrogative particles rarely co-occur with functionally equivalent morphology on the verb, though they may. In Hill Patwin the irrealis and quotative particles rarely occur *without* irrealis morphology on the verb, though they may. In River Patwin the irrealis particle does not co-occur with irrealis verbal morphology. Each particle is discussed individually below.

9.2.1. Declarative Particle *pi* 'DECL'

The declarative particle *pi* signifies that the clause is declarative and finite. It does not occur in interrogative, hortative, or subjunctive clauses. Thus it has a similar function to the finite suffix /-s, -t°i/, with which it rarely co-occurs. The declarative particle is optional.

Example (276a) shows the declarative particle in a clause that has a verb, but without the finite tense marker /-s/ (*hene·t'i* 'will arrive'). Example (276b) shows the declarative particle in a clause that has neither a verb nor an auxiliary verb.

(276) a. ⟨wi-no nat sul-thu-m ʔele·-ła, pi-ču hene·-ṫi.⟩

[wino	nat	sult^h^u-m	ʔele·-ła	]
[person.POSS$_V$	1SG.OBJ	kill-SBJV	NEG-LOC	]

pi	ču	hene·-t'i
DECL	1SG.SBJ	arrive-FUT

[If nobody kills me] I'm coming back.
(Whistler 1977a:159/170, NL/HL) [HP$_R$]

b. ⟨małá·n pípi⟩
ma-ła·n pi pi
2SG-brother DECL 3SG.SBJ
He is your brother.
(Ultan, d:7.53, SG) [RP]

Though the declarative particle rarely co-occurs with the finite tense marker, they are sometimes attested in the same clause, as in (277).[1]

(277) ⟨piʔuro pi pi lójta lú·bus⟩ 'died.'
piʔuro pi pi loyta lu·bus
piʔu-ro pi pi loyta lu·mu-bus
do.thus-PART DECL DIST.SG.SBJ girl die-FIN
Then that girl died.
(Whistler, d:A55, OM) [HP_L]

9.2.2. Interrogative Particle *pa* 'Q'

The interrogative particle *pa* 'Q' signifies that the clause is a question. It is optional, and tends to occur only in the absence of interrogative suffixes on the verb.

The interrogative particle may occur in clauses entirely lacking either a verb or an auxiliary verb, as in the examples in (278).

(278) a. ⟨hétipa hetipa⟩
heti pa heti pa
where.ABL Q where.ABL Q
Where are you? Where are you?
(Whistler, d:C22, OM) [HP_L]

b. ⟨małá·n papi⟩
ma-ła·n pa pi
2SG-brother Q 3SG.SBJ
Is he your brother?
(Ultan, d:7.53, SG) [RP]

The interrogative particle may also occur in clauses where a verb is present but lacks interrogative morphology. Example (279) shows two examples where the verb lacks an interrogative suffix: the only indications of interrogativity are the particle *pa* and the indefinite pronouns *peyła* 'when' and *po* 'who'.

(279) a. ⟨pełа pami wɛre·tɪ⟩
peyła pa mi were·-t'i
when Q 2SG.SBJ come-FUT
When are you coming back?
(Ultan, d:2.28, OM) [HP$_{L}$]

b. ⟨popa pʰumɛt̓i⟩
po pa pʰume-t'i
who.SBJ Q roast-FUT
Who will roast the meat?
(Ultan, d:6.76, DL) [HP$_{T}$]

Even in the absence of verbal interrogative morphology, *pa* is optional: in (280) the only indication of interrogativity is the presence of the indefinite pronoun *pe*yła* 'when'. There is no interrogative morphology on the verb, and the interrogative particle *pa* is not present.

(280) ⟨Pā´hlă me hen-net-te⟩
pe*yła mi hene-t'i
when 2SG.SBJ arrive-FUT
When are you coming back?
(Merriam:V72.71) [HP$_{C}$]

Rarely, the interrogative particle occurs in clauses with verbs also inflected for interrogativity. Example (281) shows a clause with *pa* where the verb is also marked with an interrogative suffix.

(281) ⟨matɑ nɔ́npa ʔɪṣɛ́⟩

mato nun pa ʔi-sey

2SG.POSS_{IN} gun Q COP-Q

Is that your gun?

(Ultan, d:4.38, AN) [HP_L]

9.2.3. Irrealis Particle *ka/kam* 'IRR'

The irrealis particle signifies that the clause is in an inferential irrealis mode: the speaker is stating something inferred from available evidence but not known with certainty. This mode is often translated into English as "must have" or "might".

In Hill Patwin the irrealis particle takes the form /ka/, and is generally accompanied by verbal morphology signifying epistemic modality: the confident inference suffixes /-ma/ (HP_L, as in 282a) and /-m(u)ʔa/ (other HP dialects, as in 282b), or a tentative inference suffix like /m(u)te·/ (282c).[2]

(282) a. ⟨pílɛka k̓ayúma⟩

pile ka k'ayu-ma

3PL.SBJ IRR walk-must

They must have been walking.

(Ultan, d:2.92, OM) [HP_L]

b. ⟨po-ka na·no hiłi· har-me-m-ʔa.⟩

po ka na·no hiłi· har-me-mʔa

who.SBJ IRR 1SG.POSS_{IN} beads go-COM-must

Someone must have taken my beads!

(Whistler 1978:52/55, NL/HL) [HP_R]

c. ⟨bakohomte ka pi⟩

bakoho-mte ka pi

count-might.PAST IRR 3SG.SBJ

He must have been counting.

(Ultan, d:6.95, DL) [HP_T]

In River Patwin the irrealis particle takes the form /kam/, and is not accompanied by modal verb morphology.

(283) a. ⟨pikam hɛnta⟩

pi	kam	hen-ta
3SG.SBJ	IRR	arrive-PART

He must have come.
(Ultan, d:7.98, SG) [RP]

b. ⟨bɛhna cu ba·ṫikam⟩

behna	ču	ba·-t'i	kam
morning	1SG.SBJ	eat-FUT	IRR

I might eat tomorrow.
(Ultan, d:7.81, SG) [RP]

The irrealis particle is usually a second-position element, occurring after the first word or constituent of the clause. It is sometimes attested in clause-final position, as in (283b).

9.2.4. Hill Patwin Reportative Particle *upu/ upum* 'REPRT'

The reportative particle marks a statement as hearsay, and is sometimes translated 'it is said' or 'I hear'. In Tebti and Rumsey Hill Patwin the reportative takes the form *ʔupu* (284a); in Lodoga Hill Patwin the reportative takes the form *ʔupum* (284b). When the reportative particle is present in a clause, the verb usually appears in the subjunctive.

(284) a. ⟨mi ʔupu were·-m⟩

mi	ʔupu	were·-m
2SG.SBJ	REPRT	come.COM-SBJV

I hear you took them.
(Whistler 1978:53/55, NL/HL) [HP_R]

b. ⟨pí ʔúpʰum nɒ́pma łilá·bɒ<m⟩

pi	ʔupum	nop-ma	łila·	bo-m
3SG.SBJ	REPRT	deer-OBJ	shoot	be.AN-SBJV

I heard he shot a deer.

(Ultan, d:2.98, OM) [HP_L]

The reportative particle is attested only in Hill Patwin, and is etymologically related to the verb *ʔupu* 'to say' in River Patwin and South Patwin. Whistler (1986) describes the reportative particle as a "quotative," but it is not used to directly report speech like a canonical quotative.

9.3. SUBORDINATE CLAUSES

There are a number of markings a verb may take to indicate that it is functioning as the head of a subordinate clause. Some of these markings occur only on verbs when they are the heads of subordinate clauses: case suffixes, the suffix /-čin/ 'lest', the River Patwin conditional suffix /-nini/ 'COND', and the relativizing suffixes /-hVm, -sem, -sok/. Other markings used for subordinate clauses are also attested on independent clauses: the inceptive suffix /-t'o/ 'INCEP', hortative suffixes, the subjunctive mood suffix /-mu/ 'SBJV', the participle suffix /-taro/ 'PART', and the verb in its bare nominal stem form. Some subordinate clauses are nominalizations: those whose verbs are marked with case suffixes, relativizing suffixes, and those whose verbs appear in their bare nominal stem form. In these nominalized subordinate clauses, the subject appears in the agentive form of the possessive case. Other subordinate clauses are not nominalizations: those marked with /-čin/ 'lest', /-nini/ 'COND', /-t'o/ 'INCEP', hortative suffixes, subjunctive /-mu/, and the participle /-taro/. In these subordinate clauses the subject appears in the subjective case. Thus the subordinate clause in Patwin is not a well defined type of clause from a morphosyntactic perspective: no morphosyntactic property unites subordinate clauses, except that they are structurally subordinate to another clause. The types of markings attested for subordinate clauses are summarized in table 9.1.

The verbal suffixes mentioned in table 9.1 are discussed in chapter 8. Re-

Table 9.1. Markings for subordinate clauses

	Nominalizations	**Not nominalizations**
Attested only in subordinate clauses	cases relativizers	-čin 'lest' -nini 'COND'
Attested also in independent clauses	bare nominal stem	-t'o 'INCEP' hortatives -mu 'SBJV' -taro 'PART'

lativizers and relative clauses are discussed in section 6.5. In this section the following types of subordinate clauses will be addressed: complement clauses (9.3.1), clauses with oblique case marking (9.3.2), clause chaining with participles (9.3.3), and quotative constructions (9.3.4).

9.3.1. Complement Clauses

Complement clauses are subordinate clauses that are arguments of the matrix predicate. There are two marking strategies for Patwin complement clauses: the verb may appear in its bare nominal stem form or the verb may take a hortative suffix.

In the first type of complement clause the verb of the complement clause appears in its bare nominal stem form. It is unmarked for case, although it functions as the object of the matrix verb. The subject of the complement clause appears in the agentive form of the possessive case. See examples in (285).

(285) a. ⟨chu mutú·bus ʔúj mó·mhuro bé·⟩

ču	mutu·-bus	[ʔuy	momhu-ro
1SG.SBJ	hear-FIN	[3SG.POSS$_{V}$	tell-PART

be·	]
be.IN$_{NMNL}$	]

I heard [him telling].

(Whistler, d:C69, OM) [HP$_{L}$]

b. ⟨mómhu nat hékun ʔi· ʔe·⟩

momhu	nat	[hekun	ʔi·
Tell	1SG.OBJ	[how	do_{NMNL}

ʔe·	]
PROX.OBJ.IN	]

Tell me [how to do this].
(Whistler, d:F41, HL) [HP_R]

c. ⟨chu thícharobo nay hékeła hára⟩

ču	t^hiča-ro	bo	[nay
ču	t^hiča-ro	boh-s	[nay
1SG.SBJ	know-PART	be.AN-FIN	[1SG.$POSS_V$

hekeła	hara	]
hekeła	hara	]
where	go_{NMNL}	]

I know [where I'm going].
(Whistler, d:F22, JR) [RP]

In the second type of complement clause the verb takes a hortative suffix. In this type of clause the subject is in the subjective case, like *pi* 'he' in (286a).

(286) a. ⟨mi momhu ʔut pi jorʔadi⟩ 'You tell him to (go over there +) let him work that.'

mi	momhu	ʔut	[pi
2SG.SBJ	tell	3SG.OBJ	[3SG.SBJ

yorʔa-di	]
work-3HORT	]

You tell him [he should work].
(Whistler, d:D106, OM) [HP_L]

b. ⟨mo·mhu ʔut ṫok depi łeydi pho·ła⟩

momhu	ʔut	[t'ok	depi	łey-di
tell	3SG.OBJ	[wood	again	put-3HORT

p^ho·-ła	]
fire-LOC	]

Tell him [to put more wood on the fire].

(Whistler, d:F40, HL) [HP_R]

9.3.2. Clauses with Oblique Case Marking

The locative case suffix /-ła/ may appear on the verb heading a subordinate clause. Such a subordinate clause is a nominalization, its subject taking the agentive form of the possessive case. The locative case suffix, like all case suffixes, selects the nominal stem of the verb to which it attaches. The inanimate allomorph of the locative case /-ła/ is always used in this function, never the animate form /-tin/.

Subordinate clauses with locative case marking may function as temporal adjuncts, describing background events that are temporally simultaneous with the event in the matrix clause. Such clauses may be translated into English with subordinating complementizers like "while ..." and "when ...," as in the examples in (287).

(287) a. ⟨san·u aLa·´La mɩ´n·tʊm.⟩ 'The sun went down and it became dark.'

[san-no	ʔała·-ła	]	mint^{h}u-m
[sun-$POSS_V$	set-LOC	]	darken-SBJV

[When the sun set] it became dark.

(Radin, c:39/169, AL) [HP_T]

b. ⟨nay ba·ro ce·ła hénɛsaʔ⟩

[nay	ba·ro	če·ła	]	henesa	ʔ
[nay	ba·-ro	čeh-ła	]	hene-sa	ʔ
[1SG.$POSS_V$	eat-PART	AUX-LOC	]	arrive-PAST	||

He came [while I was eating].

(Ultan, d:6.132, SG) [RP]

c. ⟨Sannó héthla bothla mi thleinanmita⟩ 'Where was the Sun when you lay down.'

[san-no heła bo-ła] mi
[sun-POSS$_V$ where be.AN-LOC] 2SG.SBJ

łey-nan-mitºa
put-REFL-PAST.Q

You lay down [when the sun was where]?
(P. Vallejo, c:23.3) [SP]

In Hill Patwin and River Patwin, subordinate clauses with locative case marking may also function as conditional clauses ("if…"). (No conditional clauses are attested in South Patwin.) Example (288a) shows such a construction from Cortina Hill Patwin with the subordinate verb *pisiła* 'at bothering'. Example (288b) is from River Patwin with the subordinate verb *bomeła* 'at being with (having)'.

(288) a. ⟨wínònát písìłàʔ bálèdàʔ⟩

[wino nat pisi-ła] ʔ
[person.POSS$_V$ 1SG.OBJ bother-LOC] ||

ba-leda ʔ
eat-EXCL.HORT ||

[If people bother me], I will eat (them).
(Bright, c:6.NL76, NL) [HP$_C$]

b. ⟨mat kanó·wa boméhła pọlti halén·ta⟩

[mat kano·wa bomeła]
[mat kano·wa bome-ła]
[2SG.POSS$_V$ boat be.AN.COM-LOC]

polt'i halenta
polt'i har-len-ta
across go-can-PART

[If you had a boat], you could go across.
(Ultan, d:7.52, SG) [RP]

The allative case suffix /-tuka, -t'uka/ 'toward' can mark subordinate clauses with the meaning "until . . . ," as in (289).

(289) ⟨[. . .] ga·´turobɔ·`ti na·´it'ɛ·`wɛt'uka.⟩
[. . .] ka·t^hu-ro bo·-t^hi
hide.INTR-PART be.AN-2nSG.HORT

[na·y t'e·we-t'uka]
[1SG.POSS$_V$ speak-ALL]

[. . .] be hidden [until I speak].
(Radin, c:102/225, AL) [HP$_T$]

9.3.3. Clause Chaining

A clause chain is a series of clauses headed by participles (medial clauses) followed by one finite clause (the final clause).[3,4] The medial clauses are subordinate to the final clause from a syntactic perspective, since they inherit their tense from the final clause. However, the medial clauses do not present background information as with a typical subordinate clause. Rather, they present foreground information, at the same level of prominence as the information in the final clause. There is no upper limit to the number of clauses that can make up a clause chain.

Example (290) shows a clause chain with two medial clauses, describing a sequence of events in a narrative: Coyote first gathers his good beads, then puts them in a sack, and then takes them to Mink. The verb in the final clause is inflected with subjunctive /-mu/, the inflection used by speaker Anderson Lowell for the narrative voice in traditional stories.

(290) ⟨sɛdɛ´utc'iak 'u·´no la´iyɔk hɪLi·´ p'ɪL·taro ɛte·´ma kɔ´ltcɪs 'ʋlkitaro ha´rmem tasi·´tuka.⟩

[sedew-č'iyak ʔu·no layuk hiɬi·
[coyote-old.man 3SG.POSS$_{IN}$ good beads

p'iɬ-taro] [ʔete·-ma k^holčis
gather-PART] [one-OBJ sack

ʔol-kir-taro] har-me-m t^hasi·-tuka.
up-move-PART] go-COM-SBJV mink-ALL

[Old Man Coyote gathered his good beads], [put them in a sack], and took them to Mink.
(Radin, c:5/142, AL) [HP$_T$]

All clauses in a clause chain must have the same subject, but they do not need to share other arguments or adjuncts. For example in (291) the grammatical object of the medial verb *patɬeytaro* 'take out' is *doko·* 'knife'. In the final clause that follows, this knife is referenced with an oblique pronoun *pisin* 'with it'. The grammatical object of this final clause is *ʔu·no k'olay* 'his hide', which is not the object of any of the medial clauses in the chain. The subject remains constant in all three clauses.

(291) ⟨pi·´ropal 'u·´nɔdɔko·` paLita·´ro 'u·´nokɔla`i picɪn p'i·´rt·ʋm.⟩ 'Then he took out his knife and skinned a hide with it.'

[pi·-ro pal] [ʔu·no doko·
[do.thus-PART then] [3SG.POSS$_{IN}$ knife

pat-ɬey-taro] ʔu·no k'olay pisin
out-put-PART] 3SG.POSS$_{IN}$ hide DIST.INS

p'irt^{h}u-m
skin-SBJV

[Then (he) did that], [took out his knife], and skinned a hide with it.
(Radin, c:105/228, AL) [HP$_T$]

Clause chains may represent sequences of events, as in examples (290) and (291). However, the relationship between the clauses in a clause chain is not restricted to one of temporal sequence. For example a clause chain may describe the motion associated with an event, as in (292). In (292a) the medial verb *tewtaro* 'flying' expresses the type of motion, while the final verb *haras* 'go' describes the direction of the motion. In (292b) the medial verb *duhta* 'carrying on the back' expresses a specific activity, while the final verb *were·sa* 'brought' describes the direction of the motion.

(292) a. ⟨Beet ă o-tar´-rah har´-ras⟩
[bit tew-taro] hara-s
[meadowlark fly-PART] go-FIN
The meadowlark is flying.
(Merriam:V72.72) [HP_C]

b. [duh-ta] were·-sa
[carry.on.back-PART] come.COM-PAST
I packed it on my back.
(Swadesh and Melton:1:02:08, IM) [RP]

Clause chains may also describe the progress of an event in time, as in (293). In (293a) the completion of the event is expressed with the verb *č'upa·ro* 'finishing'. In (293b) the inception of the event is expressed with the verb *yayo·s* 'start'.

(293) Clause chains expressing aspect
a. ⟨hɔlu·´ro tc'upa·´ro [. . .]⟩
[holu·-ro] [č'upa·-ro] [. . .]
[make.hole-PART] [finish-PART]
(Old Man Coyote) finished making a hole [. . .]
(Radin, c:7/144, AL) [HP_T]

b. [muhu-ro] ču yayo·-s
[sing-PART] 1SG.SBJ start-FIN
I started to sing.
(Swadesh and Melton:57:39, IM) [RP]

Clause chains may also express the cause of an event, as in (294).

(294) a. ⟨móllawin ču wíntaro dúk̓as⟩
[mollawin ču win-taro] duk'a-s
[ghost 1SG.SBJ see-PART] feel.bad-FIN
[I saw a ghost] and I feel no good.
(Whistler, d:F70, HL) [HP_R]

b. ⟨pi k̓asʔabohta k̓anaro bo·⟩
[pi k'asʔa bohta]
[pi k'asʔa boh-ta]
[3SG.SBJ be.old.lady be.AN-PART]

k'anaro bo·
k'ana-ro boh-s
sleep-PART be.AN-FIN

She sleeps [because she's old].
(Ultan, d:7.93, SG) [RP]

In Hill Patwin, clause chaining may also be used for conditional clauses. An example is shown in (295), where the participle *ba·ro* 'eating' is the head of the conditional clause *pima ču ba·ro* 'if I eat that'.

(295) ⟨píma chu bá·ro chóji?amutherebus⟩
[pima ču ba·-ro]
[3SG.SBJ.IN 1SG.SBJ eat-PART]

čoyi-ʔa mut^{h}ere-bus
suffering-$VBLZ_S$ might-FIN

[If I eat that] I'll get sick.
(Whistler, d:B115, OM) [HP_L]

9.3.4. Quotative Constructions

The verb “to do, say” is used to mark direct quotes: *ʔu* in Hill Patwin and *ʔuh* in River Patwin. In Hill Patwin this verb invariably occurs directly after the quote (as in 296a and 296b), but in River Patwin it is attested both before and after the quote (296c, 296d).

(296) a. ⟨sɛ́dᴇᴡ píła nɔ́p bɔ́s ʔúbʊṣ⟩ ‘Coyote said there’s a deer there (it must have been there, he said.’

sedew,	“piła	nop	bo-s,”	ʔu-bus.
coyote	DIST.LOC	deer	be.AN-FIN	say-FIN

Coyote said, “There’s a deer there.”
(Ultan, d:3.34, OM) [HP$_L$]

b. ⟨“hace·´ hoyuna·´n,” ’ʊm ’u·´ite’at katɛtts’ɛ·´ktuma.⟩

“hase·	ʔ	hoyunan,”	ʔum
har-se	ʔ	hoyunan	ʔu-m
go-1DU.INCL.HORT	‖	get.ready	say-SBJV

ʔu·yt^{h}ayat	kat^{h}it-sektuma.
ʔu·y-t^{h}ay-t	kat^{h}it-sektu-ma
3SG.POSS$_K$-nephew-OBJ	falcon-chief-OBJ

“Let us get ready to go,” (he) said to his nephew Falcon Chief.
(Radin, c:56/183, AL) [HP$_T$]

c. ⟨ʔusa pi bɛnta kewe piła be·⟩ ‘he said there’s a big house there’

ʔusa	pi,	“benta	kewe
ʔuh-sa	pi	benta	kewe
say-PAST	3SG.SBJ	big	house

piła	be·.”
piła	beh-s
DIST.LOC	be.IN-FIN

He said, “There’s a big house there.”
(Ultan, d:7.83, SG) [RP]

d. ⟨mé·mła mis cé·n yí·lale ʔuta⟩

"me·mła mis če·n yi·lale,"
me·m-ła mis če·n yi·la-le
water-LOC 2SG.OBJ down send-1EXCL.HORT

ʔuta.
ʔuh-ta
say-PART

"I'll send you down in the water," (he) said.
(Ultan, d:7.23, SG) [RP]

In connected narratives, direct quotes may also appear without a verb of saying, as in the examples in (297).

(297) a. ⟨no·p-ʔilay silay-ʔilay-pel-ma: "ha-bu łakal-mu!"⟩

no·p-ʔilay silay-ʔilaypelma, "habu łakalmu!"
no·p-ʔilay silay-ʔilay-pel-ma har-bu łakal-mu
deer-child bear-child-DU-OBJ go-1PL.INCL.HORT play-SBJV
The deer children (said) to the bear children, "Let's go play!"
(Whistler 1977a:162/170, NL/HL) [HP$_{R}$]

b. ⟨no·p-č̓iyak: "win-ma sul-thu-nol ʔi-bosa pi silay-k̓ay."⟩

no·p-č'iyak, "win-ma sult^{h}u-nol
deer-old.man person-OBJ kill-always

ʔi-bosa pi silay-k'ay."
COP-HAB DIST.SG.SBJ bear-old.lady

Old Man Deer (said), "That Bear Old Lady is always killing people."
(Whistler 1977a:161/170, NL/HL) [HP$_{R}$]

c. ⟨no·p-k̓ay-ma: "ma·t-ma čhen-tuka wičiso-nan!⟩

no·p-k'ay-ma, "ma·t-ma čen-tuka wičiso-nan!"
deer-old.lady-OBJ ear-OBJ down-ALL pull-REFL
(She said) to Old Lady Deer, "Pull down your ear!"
(Whistler 1977a:161/170, NL/HL) [HP$_{R}$]

Note that in quotative constructions, the speaker appears in the subjective case (like *sedew* 'coyote' in 296a and *no·p-ʔilay* 'deer children' in 297a) and the person to whom the speech is directed appears in the objective case (like *ʔu·ytʰayat katʰit-sektuma* 'to his nephew Falcon Chief' in 296b and *no·p-k'ayma* 'to Old Lady Deer' in 297c).

9.4. NEGATION

Negation in Patwin is expressed with a combination of bound morphology on the verb (the subjunctive suffix /-mu/ or one of the negative suffixes /-mele·, -muʔu, -mur/) and free auxiliaries (the negative auxiliary *ʔele·* or in River Patwin the stative auxiliary *boh/beh* 'be'). The noun *ʔur* 'nothing' may also be used to mark negative constructions. The expression of negation varies among and within dialects.

Negation with the subjunctive: In one common construction in Hill Patwin and River Patwin, a verb marked with the subjunctive suffix /-mu/ is accompanied by the negative auxiliary *ʔele·*, as in the examples in (298).

(298) a. ⟨ʔɛlɛs cu balʔam⟩

ʔele-s ču balʔa-m

NEG-FIN 1SG.SBJ lie-SBJV

I'm not lying.

(Ultan, d:6.100, DL) [HP$_T$]

b. ⟨[. . .] pi k̓obó·lum ʔele·t'i⟩

[. . .] pi k'obo·lu-m ʔele·-t'i

3SG.SBJ pay-SBJV NEG-FUT

[. . .] he won't pay me back.

(Whistler, d:G71, HL) [HP$_R$]

c. ⟨limo·m ʔelesa ʔut⟩

limo·-m ʔele-sa ʔut

kill-SBJV NEG-PAST 3SG.OBJ

He didn't kill him (yesterday).

(Ultan, d:7.86, SG) [RP]

In River Patwin a verb marked with subjunctive /-mu/ may be accompanied by the stative auxiliary *boh/beh* 'be' to form a negative statement (299).

(299) a. ču pe·ʔum bo·
ču pe·ʔu-m boh-s
1SG.SBJ do.what-SBJV be.AN-FIN
I did not do anything. (orig. 'I did not say.')
(Swadesh and Melton:9:13, IM) [RP]

b. ⟨čú· háȓʌʔoya ʔam boʔ⟩
ču· hara-ʔoyaʔam bo ʔ
ču· hara-ʔoyaʔa-m boh-s ʔ
1SG.SBJ go-want-SBJV be.AN-FIN ||
I don't want to go.
(Bright, c:8.G37, SG) [RP]

In Hill Patwin and River Patwin the noun *ʔur* 'nothing' may mark negative constructions. In (300a) negation is indicated only with the subjunctive /-mu/ and the noun *ʔur*. In (300b–300d) an auxiliary is also present: *ʔele·* 'NEG' in (300b), *boh* 'be.AN' in (300c), and *beh* 'be.IN' in (300d).

(300) a. ⟨pêycù hé·łáʔ ʔònók'amʔurʔ⟩
pe· ču he·ła ʔ
what.OBJ 1SG.SBJ where ||

ʔonokʔa-m ʔur ʔ
marry.woman-SBJV nothing ||

I didn't get married anyplace. (lit. 'I didn't marry anything anywhere.')
(Bright, c:7.NL153, NL) [HP_C]

b. ⟨pi ʔelé·ti pi ʔúmʔùrʔ⟩
pi ʔele·-t'i piʔu-m ʔur ʔ
3SG.SBJ NEG-FUT do.that-SBJV nothing ||
He can't do it.
(Bright, c:1.G114, SG) [RP]

c. ⟨limo·m ʔurbo⟩

limo·m ʔur bo

limo·-m ʔur boh-s

kill-SBJV nothing be.AN-FIN

He didn't kill him (just now).

(Ultan, d:7.86, SG) [RP]

d. ⟨ʔúr be p̓ırá·mam⟩

ʔur be p'era·mam

ʔur beh-s p'era·-ma-m

nothing be.IN-FIN cold-CAUS-SBJV

It's not cold. (Whistler, d:E81, JR) [RP]

Negation with negative suffixes: A family of negative suffixes /-mele·, -muʔu, -mur/ 'NEG' are elaborations of the subjunctive suffix /-mu/. All of these suffixes select the hortative stem of the verb to which they attach. The suffix /-mele·/ is a prefinal suffix; /-muʔu/ and /-mur/ are final suffixes.

The negative suffix /-mele·/ is historically a blend of subjunctive /-mu/ and the negative auxiliary *ʔele·*. This suffix is attested in all three of the major dialect groups, and is the only negative marking definitely attested in South Patwin.[5] Examples are shown in (301). Note that there is no /u/ present in the suffix, regardless of whether it follows a consonant or a vowel.

(301) a. ⟨pi t̓álmelé·s⟩ 'he not fall down'

pi t'al-mele·-s

3SG.SBJ fall-NEG-FIN

He is not falling down.

(Whistler, d:A114, OM) [HP_L]

b. wičik-mele·-ro

strong-NEG-PART

weak

(Swadesh and Melton:50:53, IM) [RP]

c. ⟨winmeleti⟩
win-mele*-t°i
see-NEG-FIN
blind
(P. Vallejo, c:22.2) [SP]

Another elaboration of the subjunctive suffix is the negative suffix /-muʔu/, derived historically from the subjunctive suffix /-mu/ and the verb *ʔu* 'say' (Whistler 1977a, 1978). This suffix varies in form between /-muʔu/ after consonants (as in 302b) and /-mʔu/ after vowels (302a, 302c). It is attested only in Hill Patwin. It may be the only marker of negation in the clause (302a), or it may be accompanied by the negative auxiliary *ʔele·* (302b) or the noun *ʔur* 'nothing' (302c).

(302) a. ⟨tcu hari·´m·'u⟩

ču	hari·-mʔu
1SG.SBJ	take-NEG

I didn't take it.
(Radin, c:49/177, AL) [HP_T]

b. ⟨he·-ła mi win-muʔu ʔele·-ṫi ʔut.⟩

he·ła	mi	win-muʔu	ʔele·-t'i	ʔut
where	2SG.SBJ	see-NEG	NEG-FUT	3SG.OBJ

You won't ever see her again.
(Whistler 1977a:167/172, NL/HL) [HP_R]

c. ⟨ḱáčumʔu ʔúr ʔuy bé·s⟩

k'aču-mʔu	ʔur	ʔuy	be·-s
cut-NEG	nothing	$3SG.POSS_V$	be.IN-FIN

She didn't cut it off. (lit. 'by her')
(Whistler, d:F78, HL) [HP_R]

The negative suffix /-mur/ is derived historically from subjunctive /-mu/ and the noun *ʔur* 'nothing'. These two elements have coalesced into a suffix with no glottal stop and with a short vowel /u/. The suffix /-mur/ is attested only in River Patwin. In (303a) the verb marked with /-mur/ is accompanied by the auxiliary *boh*. In (303b) the verb marked with /-mur/ is accompanied by the negative auxiliary *ʔele·*.[6]

(303) a. ču· sun bohmur bo·
ču· sun boh-mur boh-s
1SG.SBJ here be.AN-NEG be.AN-FIN
I am not here.
(Swadesh and Melton:9:29, IM) [RP]

b. ⟨pi mé·mòlmúr ʔèlé·roʔ⟩
pi me·mul-mur ʔele·-ro ʔ
3SG.SBJ drink-NEG NEG-PART ||
Can't he drink
(Bright, c:8.G87, SG) [RP]

Negation with no verbal suffix: Negation with no subjunctive or negative suffix is rare. In one rare River Patwin construction, negative statements may be marked only by the presence of the noun *ʔur* 'nothing' and the auxiliary *boh/beh* 'be'. Example (304) is an instance of such a clause. The verb is in its bare hortative form, though the clause is not a command. Negation here is expressed with a combination of the noun *ʔur* 'nothing' and the auxiliary *bo*.[7]

(304) ⟨pípel mé·mul ʔur bo⟩
pipel me·mul ʔur bo
pipel me·mul ʔur boh-s
3DU.SBJ drink nothing be.AN-FIN
Those two didn't drink.
(Whistler, d:E19, JR) [RP]

Negative commands: In a negative command the verb is marked with the subjunctive suffix or a negative suffix, and accompanied by the verb *ʔi·/ʔih* 'do' in a second-person hortative form, functioning as an auxiliary. The second-person singular hortative form of this verb is /ʔiwe/ in Hill Patwin

(305a, 305b) and /ʔih/ in River Patwin (305c, 305d). In (305b) and (305d) the noun *ʔur* 'nothing' is also present.

(305) a. ⟨píma bá·m ʔíwe⟩

pima ba·-m ʔiwe

DIST.SG.IN.OBJ eat-SBJV do.2sg.hort

Don't eat that!

(Whistler, d:D28, HL) [HP_R]

b. ⟨Kle´-lam oor-re-wĕh´⟩

łila-m ʔur ʔiwe

shoot-SBJV nothing do.2sg.hort

Don't shoot!

(Merriam:V73.69a) [HP_R]

c. ⟨bi·rmur ʔih⟩

bi·r-mur ʔih

wipe-NEG do.2sg.hort

Don't wipe it.

(Whistler, d:F11, JR) [RP]

d. ⟨ʔéwum ʔur ʔíh⟩

ʔewu-m ʔur ʔih

do.like.this-SBJV nothing do.2sg.hort

Don't do it that way!

(Whistler, d:F24, JR) [RP]

9.5. COMPARATIVE CONSTRUCTIONS

Comparative constructions use a verb of comparison (*čawi* 'beat, be better than' in HP; *tukt*^{h}*i* 'pass' in RP) and an adjective or verb to describe the parameter along which the comparison is made. The comparee (that which is being compared) appears in the subjective case; the standard (that which is being compared against) is in the objective case.[8] Comparative constructions are not well attested, so the information in this section may be regarded as tentative.

When an adjective describes the parameter of comparison it appears in its bare stem form, as in the examples in (306). In (306a) the parameter of comparison is indicated by the adjective *huyma* 'pretty'. The comparee is the subjective case *ʔew loyta* 'this girl', and the standard is the objective case *ʔut* 'her'. In (306b) the parameter of comparison is indicated by the adjective *k'učiy* 'small'. The standard is the objective case noun *wululukma* 'flicker', and the comparee is not overtly stated. Such constructions are monoclausal.

(306) a. ⟨ʔɛ́w lɔ́yta húyma čáwɪ ʔíbʊs ʔút⟩ 'this girl is prettier than the other one'

ʔew	loyta	huyma	čawi	ʔi-bus	ʔut
PROX.SG.SBJ	girl	pretty	beat	COP-FIN	3SG.OBJ

This girl is prettier than her.
(Ultan, d:4.72, AN) [HP_L]

b. ⟨wululukma chawi k̓ucij bo·s⟩

wululuk-ma	čawi	k'učuy	bo·-s
flicker-OBJ	beat	small	be.AN-FIN

(It) is smaller than a flicker.
(Whistler, d:D38, HL) [HP_R]

When a verb describes the parameter of comparison, the comparative construction is biclausal. For example in (307a) the parameter of comparison is indicated by the verb *huymaro* 'being pretty', which is the head of its own independent clause *Mary huymaro bos* 'Mary is pretty'. The standard of comparison is introduced in its own subordinate clause, *čawuro Sallyt* 'compared to Sally'. In a similar construction in (307b), *ʔa·na ču k'odoyma čeli·bus* 'I have a lot of money' is an independent clause. The standard of comparison is introduced in its own subordinate clause, *mit čawi* 'compared to you'. In the River Patwin comparative construction in (307c), the parameter of comparison is stated with a nominalized verb in the locative case with *yuyʔała* 'at being tall', which functions as a subordinate clause. The main clause *Virgil Pamet tuktʰuro* means 'Virgil passes Pam', where the comparee *Virgil* is the subject and the standard of comparison *Pamet* is the object.

(307) a. ⟨Máry húymarɷbɔṣ čáwʊṛɷ Sálɪt⟩
Mary huyma-ro bo-s čawu-ro Sally-t
Mary pretty-PART be.AN-FIN beat-PART Sally-OBJ
Mary is prettier than Sally.
(Ultan, d:4.72, AN) [HP_L]

b. ⟨ʔá·na chu k̓odójma chelí·bus mit cháwɪ⟩
ʔa·na ču k'odoy-ma čeli·-bus mit chawi
lots 1SG.SBJ money-OBJ have-FIN 2SG.OBJ beat
I have more money than you.
(Whistler, d:C23, OM) [HP_L]

c. ⟨Virgil Pa·mɛt tukt^h^uro yuyʔała⟩
Virgil Pæ·met tukt^h^uro yuyʔała
Virgil Pæ·m-t tukt^h^u-ro yuyʔa-ła
Virgil Pam-OBJ pass-PART tall-LOC
Virgil is taller than Pam (Virgil passed Pam in height).
(Ultan, d:7.93, SG) [RP]

9.6. CLAUSE COORDINATION WITH CONNECTOR /= u/ 'CONN'

Clauses may be coordinated with the connector enclitic /=ʔu/ 'CONN'. In two coordinated clauses the connector appears in the second clause. It appears immediately following the first word or constituent of the clause and cliticizes to it.

(308) a. ⟨tc'i·´yak pʊtcʊ·´m lʊmk'a´iyɪhɪm. katɛtts'ɛ·´ktu'u tc'ʊ·´bi l·e·´l·am.⟩ 'The old man got well for he was about dead. Then old man chicken-hawk made a storage bin.'
[č'i·yak puču·-m lum-k'ayi-hem]
[old.man be.well-SBJV die-want-REL]

[kat^{h}it-se·ktu=ʔu   č'u·bi   le·la-m   ]
[falcon-chief=CONN   storage.bin   make.PL-SBJV   ]

[The old man who had almost died got well,] [and Falcon Chief made storage bins.]

(Radin, c:45/174, AL) [HP$_{T}$]

b. ⟨yɛl bɛ·´hɛna'o nɔk·'omo tc'upa·´ro nu´nda'o ha·´rmu.⟩ 'The next day he got the arrow fixed and with his gun, too, he went out.'

[yel   behna=ʔu   nok'o-ma   č'upa·-ro   ]
[behind   morning-CONN   arrow-OBJ   fix-PART   ]

[nun-da=ʔu   ha·r-mu   ]
[bow-COM=CONN   go-SBJV   ]

... [and the next morning he finished the arrows,] [and went with his bow.]

(Radin, c:31/163, AL) [HP$_{T}$]

The connector /=ʔu/ has also been attested in nominal coordination, though infrequently. In (309a) the connector appears on each coordinand, *no·p* 'meat' and *p^{h}akp^{h}akma* 'egg', to create the phrase *no·pʔu p^{h}akp^{h}akmaʔu* 'meat and eggs'. Note that /=ʔu/ occurs after the object case suffix /-ma/ in *p^{h}akp^{h}akmaʔu* 'eggs'. The other coordinand has no object suffix, because the noun *no·p* 'meat' is grammatically inanimate. In (309b) the connector appears on the comitative noun *t'ipada* 'with acorn bread'. The comitative suffix is the most commonly used marker for nominal coordination (see section 6.6); the addition of the connector /=ʔu/ here is interesting. It may signify that *t'ipadaʔu* is part of a second, coordinated clause whose predicate is not overt, such that the translation of (309b) may be more properly stated thus: 'She fed him fish, and also (she fed him) acorn bread.'

(309) a. ⟨no·pʔu p^{h}akp^{h}akmaʔuˇ wɛrɛ nat⟩

no·p=ʔu   p^{h}akp^{h}ak-ma=ʔu   were   nat
meat=CONN   egg-OBJ=CONN   bring   1SG.OBJ

Bring me meat and eggs.

(Ultan, d:7.74, SG) [RP]

b. ⟨thi·r-ma ba·-ma-s, ṫipa-da-ʔu.⟩

tʰi·r-ma	ba·-ma-s,	t'ipa-da=ʔu
fish-OBJ	eat-CAUS-FIN	acorn.bread-COM-CONN

She fed him fish and acorn bread.

(Whistler 1978:54/56, NL/HL) [HP_R]

APPENDIX

Attested Pronouns by Dialect

Due to the complexity of the pronoun data in the archive, I have separately tabulated every attested form of a pronoun for each dialect; these tables are presented here in section A.1. This is a more "surfacy" presentation of dialect variation in pronouns, with the details of pronoun morphology being discussed in chapter 5. Following the tables, the attested pronoun data for each dialect is discussed in section A.2.

A.1. TABLES OF ATTESTED PRONOUNS BY DIALECT

These tables are the end result of a process that distilled away various uninteresting sources of variation in the archive, such as variation in orthographic representation and variation by researcher (see section 1.3.2). Where some feature of a pronoun is not reconstructable from the available evidence, this uncertainty is indicated in the table. For example the length of the vowel in the only attested form for first-person singular inanimate possessive pronoun in Cortina Hill Patwin is not clear. The source, Merriam's Klet´-win vocabulary, shows us ⟨Nan´-no⟩ (Merriam:V72.17). The stress is clearly indicated to be on the first syllable (Merriam wrote stress with an acute accent following the stressed syllable), and gives us enough information to identify the consonants (both /n/) and the vowel qualities (/a,o/), but Merriam does not record distinctions of vowel length. Instances of this same pronoun and the related form /na(·)nu/ recorded for other dialects show variation in the length of the first vowel, though the second one is always short. The table of Cortina Hill Patwin forms therefore records /ná*no/ in this cell, indicating that the length of the first vowel is not known (see table A.7).

I have only taken this precaution where there is a significant uncertainty. Consider the similar case of the second-person singular inanimate possessive in Cortina Hill Patwin: strictly speaking the vowel length is not known in this case either, since the only elicited form is from Merriam (as in the previous example). However, since the form /mato/ is widely attested in all other dialects and since there is only one definite instance of /ma·to/ (in Lodoga Hill Patwin), I assume that Merriam's ⟨mah-to⟩ represents the overwhelmingly more common /mato/. The forms shown here are therefore to be taken with a grain of salt, as with any project that partially relies on old written sources.

Forms that are particularly problematic are indicated by parentheses in the tables of attested forms and discussed further in the following section.

A.2. DISCUSSION OF PRONOUN DATA

In this section the data from the individual dialect paradigms shown in the tables of attested forms (tables A.1–A.16) will be discussed. Here the data itself is under discussion: unexpected forms, probable errors of elicitation or analysis, problems associated with individual sources, and so on. The systematic variation of meaningful elements is discussed in chapter 5).

A.2.1. Lodoga Hill Patwin

The attested pronoun forms for Lodoga Hill Patwin are shown in tables A.1–A.3.

The aberrant agentive pronoun *néč̓u* '1PL.EXCL.POSS$_V$' (which lacks the expected POSS$_V$ case suffix /-y/) is attested only once in any dialect, spoken by Oscar McDaniel in the phrase ⟨néċu cháket thonó·łe⟩ *neč̓u čaket tʰono·ła* 'when we all dance' (Whistler, d:B49). It is possible that this represents a false start, that is, 'we— when all dance . . .'.

The aberrant subjective case pronoun /ʔupele·/ '3DU.SBJ' is attested only once in any dialect, by speaker Oscar McDaniel, and may actually be an agentive pronoun (the subject of a subordinate clause). This form is unexpected for two reasons. First, in the (nonsubordinate) subjective case, the dual suffix invariably takes the form /-pel/ in the subjective except for this instance, where it appears to take the form /-pele·/. Second, the third-person personal pronoun root form /ʔu·-/ is only attested in nonsubject cases outside of this one form. It could be that this is actually the agentive

Table A.1. Attested Lodoga Hill Patwin personal pronouns in structural cases

	SBJ	OBJ	POSS$_{IN}$	POSS$_{AN}$	POSS$_{V}$	POSS$_{K}$
1SG	ču· ču	nat	ná·no náno	ná·min námin	nay	na·y- nay-
1DU.INCL	p’épel p’epél	p’epelet	p’épelno p’epélno	p’épelnomin p’epélnomin	p’épeley	p’epéley-
1DU.EXCL	népel nepél	népelet	népelno nepélno	népelnomin	népeley	
1PL.INCL	p’éle	p’elet	p’elé·no	p’elé·nomin p’élenomin	p’eléy	
1PL.EXCL	néč’u neč’ú·	néč’ut neč’út	neč’ú·no neč’úno neč’uno	neč’ú·nomin neč’ú·min	neč’úy (néč’u)	
2SG	mi· mi	mi·t mit	(má·to) máto mató	mátomin matómin		ma- mat-
2DU	mípel mipél	mípelet mipélet	mípelno mipélno	mípelnomin	mipeléy	
		(mápelet)	mápelno mapélno	mápelnomin		mapéley-
2PL	míle	milé·t mílet milét	milé·no mileno	mílenomin mílé·min		
			malé·no maleno	malé·nomin mále·min	maléy	maléy-
3SG	pi· pi	ʔu·t ʔut	ʔú·no ʔúno ʔú*nu	ʔú·nomin ʔúnomin	ʔuy	ʔu·y- ʔuy-
3DU	pípel (ʔupelé·)	ʔúpelet	ʔúpelno ʔupélno	ʔupé·lnomin ʔúpelnomin	ʔúpeley	
3PL	píle pilé	ʔulé·t ʔúlet ʔulét	ʔulé·no ʔúleno ʔulén	ʔulé·nomin ʔúlenomin	ʔúley ʔuléy	

Table A.2. Attested Lodoga Hill Patwin demonstratives in structural cases

	SBJ	OBJ	POSS$_{IN}$	POSS$_{AN}$	POSS$_{V}$	POSS$_{K}$
PROX.SG	ʔew	ʔe· (IN) ʔe (IN) ʔéwet (AN)	ʔewetno			
DIST.SG	pi· pi	pimá· (IN) píma (IN)				
PROX.DU	ʔéwpel					
DIST.DU	pípel	pípelet				
PROX.PL	ʔéwle		ʔéwletno			
DIST.PL	píle pilé	pilé·t				

Table A.3. Attested Lodoga Hill Patwin pronouns in semantic cases

	COM	LOC	ALL	ABL	PROL
1SG	ná·da		náttuka	nátti	
1DU.INCL					
1DU.EXCL					
1PL.INCL					
1PL.EXCL					
2SG	mí·da		míttuka		
2DU					
2PL					
3SG	ʔú·da		ʔútuka	ʔútti	
3DU	ʔúpelda				
3PL					
PROX.SG		ʔéwła (IN)	ʔéwtuka		ʔéwna
DIST.SG		píła (IN)	pítuka	píti	pína
PROX.DU					
DIST.DU	pípelda				
PROX.PL					
DIST.PL					

Table A.4. Attested Tebti Hill Patwin personal pronouns in structural cases

	SBJ	OBJ	POSS_{IN}	POSS_{AN}	POSS_{V}	POSS_{K}
1SG	ču· ču	na·t nat	ná·no náno ná·nu nánu	ná·min námin	nay (ču)	nay-
1DU.INCL	p’épel	p’epelet	p’epelno (p’epelé·no)	p’épelnomin (p’epelé·nomin)	p’epeley	p’épeley-
1DU.EXCL	népel nepél	népelet	népelno (nepelé·no)	népelnomin (nepelé·nomin)	nepelé·y népeley	népeley-
1PL.INCL	p’éle p’elé·		p’elé·no	p’elé·nomin p’élenomin p’elé·min	p’elé·y p’eléy	p’eley-
1PL.EXCL	néč’u	neč’ú·t neč’ut	neč’ú·no	neč’ú·nomin néč’unomin		neč’u- neč’úy-
2SG	mi· mi	mi·t mit	máto	má·tomin mató·min mátomin	ma ma·t mat	ma·- ma- mat-
2DU	mí·pel mipé·l mípel	mípelet	mipeleno mipelno	mípelnomin		mipeley-
			mapelé·no mapelno	(mapelé·nomin)	mapelé·y mápeley	mápeley-
2PL	mí·le milé· míle (mip)	milé·t milét	milé·no mileno	milé·nomin		míley-
			malé·no máleno	malé·nomin	malé·y	maley-
3SG	pi· pi	ʔu·t ʔut	ʔú·no ʔúno	ʔú·nomin ʔúnomin ʔú·numin	ʔuy ʔuy	ʔu·y- ʔuy-
3DU	pípel pipél (ʔupel)	ʔú·pelet ʔúpelet	ʔupelé·no ʔupeleno ʔupelno	ʔúpelnomin (ʔupelé·nomin)	ʔupelé·y ʔúpeley	ʔúpeley-
3PL	pí·le pilé· píle pilé	ʔú·let ʔulé·t ʔulét	ʔulé·no ʔuléno	ʔulé·nomin	ʔulé·y ʔuléy	ʔúley ʔuléy-

Table A.5. Attested Tebti Hill Patwin demonstratives in structural cases

	SBJ	OBJ	$POSS_{IN}$	$POSS_{AN}$	$POSS_{V}$	$POSS_{K}$
PROX.SG	ʔe·w ʔew	ʔe· (IN) ʔe (IN) ʔé·wet (AN) ʔewet (AN)				
DIST.SG	pi· pi	pí·ma (IN) píma (IN) pimá (IN) pi·t (AN) pit (AN)	pí·no	pinomin		pi-
PROX.DU	ʔéwpel	ʔéwpelet				
DIST.DU	pípel pipél		pipélno	pípelnomin		
PROX.PL	ʔéwle ʔewlé·	ʔéwlet				
DIST.PL	pí·le pilé· píle pilé		pilé·no	pilé·nomin		píley-

Table A.6. Attested Tebti Hill Patwin pronouns in semantic cases

	COM	INS	LOC	ALL	ABL	PROL
1SG	ná·da nada natda náyda			natt'uka		
1DU.INCL						
1DU.EXCL						
1PL.INCL						
1PL.EXCL						
2SG	midá					
2DU						
2PL						
3SG	ʔú·da		ʔú·tin	ʔú·tt'uka		
3DU			ʔupé*letin			
3PL	ʔulé·da					
PROX.SG		ʔéwsin	ʔéwła (IN)			ʔéwna

Table A.6. Continued

	COM	INS	LOC	ALL	ABL	PROL
DIST.SG		pisin	pí·ła (IN) piłá· (IN) píła (IN) piłá (IN)	pí·t'uka píttuka pít'uka pítuka	piná·k pinák	pí·na piná· pína piná
PROX.DU						
DIST.DU						
PROX.PL	ʔewlé·da					
DIST.PL						

Table A.7. Attested Cortina Hill Patwin personal pronouns

	SBJ	OBJ	POSS$_{IN}$	POSS$_{AN}$	POSS$_{V}$	POSS$_{K}$
1SG	ču	na·t nat	ná·no náno ná·nu nanu	ná·min námin	nay	nay-
1DU.INCL	p'épél	p'épelet p'epelét	p'epéleno ʔepeleno	p'epélenómin		p'epéley-
1DU.EXCL	népel nepél	népelet	nepélno		népeley	
1PL.INCL	p'éle	p'elét				p'eléy-
1PL.EXCL	néč'u neč'ú	néč'ut				
2SG	mi· mi	mi·t mit	máto	mátomin matómin	ma·t mat	ma- mat-
2DU	mípel mipél	mípelet	mípelno mipélno mapéleno			mipeley- mapéley-
2PL	míle milé	milét	miléno malé·no			miléy-
3SG	pi	ʔu·t ʔut	ʔú·no ʔúno ʔúnu	ʔú*numin ʔúnomin (ʔú*no ʔis nómin)	ʔuy	ʔuy-
3DU	pípel pipél	ʔúpelet ʔupelét	ʔupélno		ʔupeléy	ʔúpeley-
3PL	píle	ʔulet	ʔulé·no			ʔuléy-

Table A.8. Attested Cortina Hill Patwin demonstratives

	SBJ	OBJ	POSS$_{IN}$	POSS$_{AN}$	POSS$_{V}$	POSS$_{K}$	INS	LOC	PROL
PROX.SG	ʔew	ʔe· (IN) ʔe (IN) ʔewét (AN)	ʔéweno				ʔéwsin	ʔéwła (IN)	
DIST.SG	pi	pima (IN) pi·t (AN) pit (AN)						piła	pína
PROX.DU			(ʔéwpéleno)						
DIST.DU									
PROX.PL			(ʔéwléno)						
DIST.PL									

Table A.9. Attested forms in de Angulo's grammar—Cortina Hill Patwin?

	SBJ	OBJ	POSS$_{IN}$	POSS$_{AN}$	POSS$_{V}$	POSS$_{K}$	COM
1SG	ču	nat	nanu	nanumin		nay-	natda
1DU.INCL	p'epel	p'epet	p'epelnu	p'epelnumin		p'epeley-	
1DU.EXCL	nepel	nepet	nepelnu	nepelnumin		nepeley-	
1PL.INCL	p'ele	p'elet	p'elenu	p'elenumin		p'eleney-	
1PL.EXCL	nele	nelet	nelenu	nelenumin		neleney-	
2SG	mi	mit	matol	matomin		ma-	mitda
2DU	mipel	mipet	mipelnu	mipelnumin			
2PL	mile	milet	milenu	milenumin			
3SG	pi	ʔut	ʔunu	ʔunamin		ʔuy-	
3DU	pipel		ʔupelnu	ʔupelnumin			
3PL	pile						
DIST.SG							
DIST.DU	pipel	pipet					
DIST.PL	pile	pilet	pilenu	pilenumin			
PROX							

Table A.10. Attested Rumsey Hill Patwin personal pronouns

	SBJ	OBJ	POSS$_{\text{IN}}$	POSS$_{\text{AN}}$	POSS$_{\text{V}}$	POSS$_{\text{K}}$	COM	ALL
1SG	ču	na·t nat	ná·no ná·nu nanu	ná·min	nay	nay-	ná·da	náttuka ná·t'uka
1DU.INCL	p'épel	p'epelet	p'epéleno	p'épelemin ʔepelemin		p'epéley- ʔepéley-		
1DU.EXCL	nepel	nepelet			nepeley			
1PL.INCL	p'éle	p'elé·t						p'elet'uka
1PL.EXCL	neč'u					neč'úy-		
2SG	mi	mi·t mit	máto matok	mátomin	mat mi	ma- mat-	mí·da	
2DU	mipel	mipelet				mápeley-		
2PL	mile	milé·t	milé·no malé·no					
3SG	pi	ʔu·t ʔut (ʔú·tal)	ʔú·no	ʔú·nomin	ʔuy	ʔuy-		
3DU	pípel		ʔúpelno		ʔupeley	ʔúpeley-		
3PL	píle pilé	ʔulé·t	ʔulé·no	ʔule*min		ʔúley-		

Table A.11. Attested Rumsey Hill Patwin demonstratives

	SBJ	OBJ	POSS$_{\text{IN}}$	POSS$_{\text{AN}}$	POSS$_{\text{V}}$	POSS$_{\text{K}}$	INS	LOC	ABL	PROL
PROX.SG	ʔew	ʔe· (IN) ʔéwet (AN)				ʔéwey		ʔéwła (IN)		
DIST.SG	pi	píma (IN) pi·t (AN)					pisin	piła (IN)	pinak	pína
PROX.DU	ʔéwpel									
DIST.DU	pípel									
PROX.PL					ʔewley					
DIST.PL	píle, pilé									

Table A.12. Attested River Patwin first- and second-person pronouns in structural cases

	SBJ	OBJ	POSS$_{IN}$	POSS$_{AN}$	POSS$_{V}$	POSS$_{K}$
1SG	ču· ču	na·t nat	ná·no náno ná∗nu	ná·min námin (náymin) (ná·mil)	na·y nay	na·y- nay-
1DU.INCL	p'épel p'epél	p'epelet p'epé·t p'epet	p'épeleno	p'épelemin p'epélemin		p'epeley- ʔepeley-
1DU.EXCL	népel nepél	népelet nepé·t népet nepét	népeleno nepéleno nepeléno nepélno	népelemin nepélemin	népeley	népeley- nepéley-
1PL.INCL	p'éle p'elé	p'elé·t p'elet	p'elé·no	p'elé·min	p'eléy	p'éley- p'eléy-
1PL.EXCL	néč'u neč'ú	néč'ut	néč'uno neč'unó	néč'umin neč'úmin	né·č'uy	néč'uy- neč'úy-
2SG	mi· mi	mi·s mis	mató mátono matóno matok	mátomin matómin	mat	ma- mat-
2DU	mí·pel mípel mipél	mipelet mí·pet mípet		mipelemin		
			mápeleno mapéleno mapeléno mápelno mapélno	mápelemin mapélemin	mapeley	mápeley- mapéley-
2PL	mí·le míle milé· milé	milé·t milet				
			malé·no maléno	malé·min malémin	maléy	malé·y- maléy-

Table A.13. Attested River Patwin third-person pronouns in structural cases

	SBJ	OBJ	$POSS_{IN}$	$POSS_{AN}$	$POSS_{V}$	$POSS_{K}$
3SG	pi· pi	ʔu·t ʔut	ʔú·no ʔúno	ʔú·min ʔúmin, ʔumín	ʔuy	ʔú·y- ʔuy-
3DU	pí·pel pípel pipél	ʔúpelet ʔupelét ʔú·pet ʔúpet ʔupé·t ʔupét	ʔupéleno ʔupeléno ʔúpelno ʔupélno	ʔúpelemin ʔupélemin	ʔúpeley	ʔúpeley- ʔupéley-
3PL	pí·le píle pilé· pilé	ʔú·let ʔulé·t ʔúlet ʔulét	ʔulé·no ʔuléno	ʔulé·min ʔulémin	ʔúley ʔuléy	ʔulé·y- ʔuléy- ʔúley-
PROX.SG	ʔew	ʔe·s (IN) ʔes (IN) ʔéwet (AN)	ʔewéno (ʔewno) (ʔewe)	ʔewemin		
DIST.SG	pi· pi	píma (IN) pimá (IN) pi·t (AN)				
PROX.DU	ʔéwpel ʔewpél					
DIST.DU	pípel pipél			pipelemin		pípeley-
PROX.PL		ʔéwle				
DIST.PL	pí·le píle pilé		pilé·no			

Table A.14. Attested River Patwin pronouns in semantic cases

	COM	INS	LOC	ABL	PROL
1SG	ná·da				
1DU.INCL					
1DU.EXCL					
1PL.INCL					
1PL.EXCL					
2SG	mísda				
2DU					
2PL					
3SG	ʔú·tda ʔú·da ʔúda				
3DU	ʔupélda				
3PL	ʔú·leda ʔulé·da ʔuléda				
PROX.SG		ʔéwmatin (AN)	ʔéwła (IN)	ʔéwnak	
DIST.SG	pida		píła (IN) piłá (IN)	pínak pinák	pína piná
PROX.DU					
DIST.DU					
PROX.PL					
DIST.PL					

pronoun *ʔupele(·)y* '3DU.POSS$_V$', even though it appears to be attested as the subject of an independent clause. The clause in question is probably in fact a dependent clause, intended to be subordinate to the previously elicited clause. See (310).

(310) Sequence of elicited clauses
(Whistler, d:A11, OM) [HP$_L$]

pipel *t'ewt'ewp'ir-ta*
3DU.SBJ converse-PART
'Them two are talking.'

Table A.15. Attested South Patwin pronouns in Merriam, Arroyo de la Cuesta, Curtin, etc.: SP_M

	SBJ	OBJ	$POSS_{IN}$	$POSS_{AN}$	$POSS_V$	$POSS_K$	LOC
1SG	ču*	ču*t	čú*no čú*do			ču*y- ču*	
1DU.INCL						(ʔépeley-)	
1DU.EXCL							
1PL.INCL	p'ele			(p'elé*nomin)		(p'eley-)	
1PL.EXCL	neč'u						
2SG	mi	(mat)	máto			ma-	
2DU	mípel						
2PL	milé*						
PROX.SG	ʔew						ʔéwła (IN)
DIST.SG	pi						
SG /u·/		ʔu*t ʔit (?)				ʔu*y-	
PROX.DU							
DIST.DU	pipel						
DU /u·/	ʔupel						
PROX.PL	ʔéwle						
DIST.PL	píle						
PL /u·/							

⟨ʔópɛlé·⟩ *tʰi·ro* *hara·-ti*
3DU.?? fish(v).NMNL go-ABL?
'Them two are going down fishing.'

Probable combined gloss: 'Them two are talking about them going down fishing.' (in this case ⟨ʔópɛlé·⟩ would be *ʔupele(·)y* '3DU.$POSS_V$', as its form suggests)

The attested second-person dual objective form /mápelet/ is also unexpected. This is the only nonpossessive second-person pronoun attested with the root form /ma·-/ in any dialect, except for the even more unexpected form /mat/ '2SG.OBJ', attested once in South Patwin (see section 5.2.5).

Table A.16. Attested South Patwin pronouns in the Vallejo sources: SP_V

	SBJ	OBJ	$POSS_{IN}$	$POSS_{AN}$	$POSS_V$
1SG	ču*		čú*no ču*n		
1DU.INCL					
1DU.EXCL					
1PL.INCL					
1PL.EXCL	neč'u	neč'u*m	néč'unu téč'unu	neč'unomin	
1PL?	čuy	čuynam čuyam ču*m	čuyno		
2SG	mi ʔu*	mit	máto matom maton mátono	mátonomin mátomin	
2DU					
2PL	milé*		mile*no malé*no	milé·nomin	
PROX.SG	ʔew				
DIST.SG	pi*	pi·m			
SG / u·/		ʔu*t	ʔú*no	ʔú*nomin	
PROX.DU					
DIST.DU					
DU / u·/					
PROX.PL	ʔéwle (ʔéwma)				
DIST.PL	pilé	pilé*m	pilé·no	pilé·nomin	piley
PL / u·/					

The second-person singular inanimate possessive form /ma·to/ is not particularly unexpected, but it is the only attestation of this particular pronoun with a long vowel in any dialect. The root /ma·-/ does have a long vowel though (across the various pronouns in which it occurs), so an optional length here is to be expected.

A notable feature of Lodoga Hill Patwin is the double case marking on proximal demonstratives functioning as possessors of nouns. In these

$POSS_K$	COM	LOC	ABL
ču*y-	ču*da		
ma- mat			
		ʔéwła (IN)	ʔewnak
		piłá* (IN)	pinak
ʔu*y			
pilé*y			

forms the possessive case suffix is preceded by the objective case suffix /-t/. This double case marking is not attested for possessive pronouns in any other dialect or for any other possessive pronouns in the Lodoga dialect. Outside of the Lodoga proximal demonstratives, double case marking in possessives is only attested for kinship terms, where it is obligatory. (See section 4.6.1.3.)

A.2.2. Tebti Hill Patwin

The attested pronoun forms for Tebti Hill Patwin are shown in tables A.4–A.6. The attested long vowels here should be taken with a grain of salt, since Radin—a primary source for Tebti material—is very liberal in transcribing length (on both consonants and vowels!).

The agentive form /ču/ is attested only once (in any dialect) and may actually be a (nonsubordinate) subject pronoun. The attestation is shown in (311). In one analysis it is the subject of the nominalized verb *hene·-ła* 'when (I) arrive', in which case it would be an agentive pronoun (POSS$_V$). Other analyses would have it as the subject of the adverbial participle *t'ew-ni* 'speaking' or of the main verb *čele·-t'i* 'will travel'—in either of these cases it would be the ordinary subjective case pronoun *ču*.

(311) ⟨pirupi tcu´ pi·´La hɛne·´La bano·´n t·'e´uni; tcɛlɛ·´ti mat mut hɛ·´rika.⟩

pi-ro	pi	ču	pi·ła
DIST.VBL-PART	DECL	1SG??	DIST.LOC

hene·-ła	bano·-n	t'ew-ni,
arrive-LOC	loud-ADV	speak-ADV

čele·-t'i	mat	mut-here	ka.
travel-FUT	2SG.POSS$_V$	hear-PASS	IRR

Then when I arrive there speaking loudly, I will move so that I am heard by you. (Radin, c:57/184)

a) Then, when I arrive there speaking loudly, (I) will travel so that (I) am heard by you. (POSS$_V$)

b) Then I, when arriving there speaking loudly, will travel so that (I) am heard by you. (SBJ)

Because of this ambiguity and because the form *ču* is not recorded as an agentive pronoun in any other dialect or anywhere else in Tebti Hill Patwin, this possible use of *ču* as an agentive can be considered a very weak attestation.

The dual animate possessive forms /p'epelé·nomin, nepelé·nomin, mapelé·nomin, ʔupelé·nomin/ should also be considered dubious. They are taken from the paradigm of pronouns in Radin's grammar, but the two-syllable form of the dual suffix /-pele·/ is almost never attested before the complex animate possessive marker /-no-min/ outside of these forms.[1]

It is possible that Radin did not actually hear these forms, but extrapolated them from other pronouns that he had actually elicited. The first-person dual inanimate possessive forms with the two-syllable suffix /-pele·/ should also be considered dubious for the same reason, although they are somewhat less rare.

The form /mip/ '2PL.SBJ' is from Merriam (V71), and is probably some sort of transcription error. It may be the beginning of a dual second-person pronoun like *mipel* that was written on the wrong line at first and then forgotten.

A.2.3. Cortina Hill Patwin

The attested pronoun forms for Cortina Hill Patwin are shown in tables A.7 and A.8. The sources are Bright's field notes with speaker Nora Lowell (Bright, c:books 6 and 7) and Merriam's two vocabulary lists (Merriam: V72,V75) from unnamed speakers. Merriam's two lists are probably drawn from the same field notes and so are really not independent sources. Because of the scarcity of sources, the Cortina data is not very strong; any conclusions drawn from it are to be considered tentative. Another potential source, de Angulo's grammar, is discussed in the following section.

Merriam records one Cortina Hill Patwin form where an animate possessive suffix is separated from the stem by what appears to be a tensed copula: see (312). This is likely to be some kind of elicitation error or transcription error. Possessive suffixes are not otherwise attested separated from their stems, in pronouns or elsewhere.

(312) ⟨Oo´-no-is no´-min ah´-nah⟩

ʔu*-no	ʔi-s	no-min	ʔana
3SG-POSS	COP-FIN	POSS-$POSS_{AN}$	head

his head

(Merriam:V72.5) [HP_C]

A.2.4. De Angulo's Patwin Paradigm

The pronoun forms attested in Jaime de Angulo's grammar are shown in table A.9. The paradigm of pronouns presented in this grammar (de Angulo:13) is unusually regular, displaying little allomorphy. A suppletive form that is otherwise universally attested, the first-person plural exclusive stem /neč'u·-/ is missing, replaced by the regular /nele·-/, which is not found in any other source. De Angulo also gives ⟨nanumin⟩ as the form for 1SG.POSS$_{AN}$, using the /-numin/ suffix that he gives for every other animate possessive form. But /nanumin, nanomin/ are not attested in any other document consulted for this study. Instead River Patwin and Hill Patwin always have some variant of a two-syllable pronoun *na(·)min*, which de Angulo does not show.

The de Angulo paradigm thus has the appearance of a paradigm that was extrapolated from only a few forms that were actually elicited. Forms like /nele-/ and /nanumin/ were likely constructed by the regular application of morphology that de Angulo observed in other pronouns, then reported alongside those forms that he actually elicited. Until his field notes are located, we cannot tell what forms de Angulo actually elicited from Mr. Gonzales. Unfortunately this promising source for a poorly attested dialect must be ignored.

A.2.5. Rumsey Hill Patwin

The attested pronoun forms for Rumsey Hill Patwin are shown in tables A.10 and A.11. The Rumsey dialect is well attested. It is the only dialect to have published stories: Whistler (1977a, 1978).[2]

It is also attested in Whistler's field notebooks with speaker Harry Lorenzo (Whistler, d), Bright's field notebooks with speaker Daisy Lorenzo (who also gave Ultan Tebti forms), Merriam's vocabulary list with unnamed speakers (Merriam:V73), and a short list from Gibbs (1853). Because of this relatively large number of resources, the Rumsey forms may be considered fairly solid.

Harry Lorenzo gives Whistler an objective third-person form *ʔu·tal*, glossing it 'her' and saying it is "used for a girl":

(313) ⟨híma?aro ču ?ú·tal hális⟩

hima?aro	ču	<u>?u·tal</u>	hali-s
always	1SG.SBJ	<u>her?</u>	think-FIN

I'm thinking about her.

(Whistler, d:G30, HL) [HP$_R$]

This is the only attested instance of *?u·tal*; the suffix /-al/ or /-tal/ is not familiar from any other word—nor is biological gender generally indexed morphologically in Patwin. The regular third-person objective pronoun *?u·t* is regularly used for both 'her' and 'him', even by Chairman Lorenzo, as in (314).

(314) a. ⟨łahu-bu ?ut.⟩

łahu-bu	<u>?ut</u>
seek-1PL.HORT	<u>3SG.OBJ</u>

Let's look for <u>her</u>.

(Whistler 1977a:167/172, NL/HL) [HP$_R$]

b. ⟨wini-sa ču ?ut.⟩

wini-sa	ču	<u>?ut</u>
see-PAST	1SG.SBJ	<u>3SG.OBJ</u>

I saw him.

(Whistler 1978:53/55, NL/HL) [HP$_R$]

A.2.6. River Patwin

The attested pronoun forms for River Patwin are shown in tables A.12–A.14.

The first-person animate possessive form ⟨ni´-min⟩ is attested once in Merriam (V75). I tentatively render this /ná∗ymin/, according to Merriam's usual orthography. This form can be considered very dubious, since it is not attested in any other source or dialect, and since the expected /na(·)min/ is strongly attested, even in Merriam's lists.

The three-syllable dual inanimate possessive pronouns are apparently in free variation with their two-syllable counterparts for Sarah Gonzales. Both three-syllable and two-syllable dual inanimate possessive pronouns are attested in Snyder's slip file (Snyder, b), all spoken by Sarah

Gonzales: ⟨ubɛlno⟩ /ʔupelno/ 'their (DU.POSS$_{IN}$)', ⟨nɛbɛlno⟩ /nepelno/ 'our (DU.EXCL.POSS$_{IN}$)', ⟨mabɛlɛno⟩ /mapeleno/ 'your (DU.POSS$_{IN}$)', ⟨p⁼ɛbɛlɛno⟩ /p'epeleno/ 'our (DU.INCL.POSS$_{IN}$)'. The two-syllable variants are also attested in Bright's field notebooks with Sarah Gonzales (Bright, c:books 1, 2, 3 and 8). Outside of this, only the three-syllable variants are attested for dual inanimate possessives in River Patwin.

The proximal singular inanimate possessive form *ʔewe* is attested only in Merriam's lists, where it is accompanied in one of the lists by a question mark: ⟨ĕ-we?, Eh-we, Ĕ-wĕ⟩ (Merriam:V74.56, V75.56). This form is unexpected, as it does not bear the regular inanimate possessive suffix /-no/, and it can be considered dubious.

A.2.7. South Patwin

South Patwin is a poorly attested dialect, and also the most divergent dialect of Patwin. These two factors make the South Patwin data questionable at best. The data in tables A.15 and A.16 should be taken with several grains of salt.

To compound the data scarcity problem, the two major sources for South Patwin—Vallejo's set of Suisun manuscripts and Merriam's "Poo´-e-win" word-list (V76)—have significantly different patterns of morphology for pronouns. I have therefore separated them into two tables, with the few forms attested outside of these two authors' work included in the Merriam table (table A.15). Vallejo's materials (see table A.16) give the most idiosyncratic picture of South Patwin pronouns. In Merriam's South Patwin (SP$_{M}$) only the regular /-t/ occurs as an objective case suffix. Vallejo's South Patwin (SP$_{V}$) is unique among the dialects in this study in using /-m/ as the regular object marker, with /-t/ occurring in only two forms. (See discussion in section 5.3.1.2.) Another unique characteristic of SP$_{V}$ is the series of first-person plural pronouns with a stem like /č°u(·)y-/. This stem is not attested in any other dialect or in any other South Patwin source. (See discussion in section 5.3.2.3.) The idiosyncrasies of SP$_{V}$ may be due to Suisun South Patwin (the dialect that Vallejo learned as a child) being a particularly divergent dialect of South Patwin. Or it could be because Vallejo learned the language only imperfectly and wrote it down only after a protracted period of not using the language. Merriam's attested forms are closer to the expected forms, but are still best considered tentative. (The page of pronoun forms in Merriam is inscribed with the warning "These are very shaky!")

One clear characteristic of South Patwin is that it lacks the first-person singular root form /na·-/, which is the regular form in all other dialects. South Patwin uses /ču·-/ instead for all of the 1SG pronouns. This is (relatively) well attested across all of the South Patwin material.

On the other hand an especially tentative form is /ʔewma/, which appears in isolation in a Vallejo word list, glossed simply 'those' (P. Vallejo, c:19.3.4). Based on Vallejo's gloss and the fact that /-ma/ is an attested allomorph of the plural suffix, I assume that this is a plural demonstrative in the subjective (unmarked) case. It may also be that /ʔewma/ is a singular demonstrative in the objective case, since /-ma/ is more likely to be an objective case marker than a plural, generally speaking. However, this latter interpretation would make Vallejo's gloss incorrect.

The series of inclusive pronouns attested in South Patwin is also tentative. They are attested only in Merriam's vocabulary (Merriam:V76.56–57), and none of them are glossed as one would expect. ⟨Ā´-pel-lā⟩, which appears to be the dual inclusive kinship-possessive pronoun *ʔepele(·)y*, is glossed 'Their (plural)' (emphasis added). ⟨Pel-lā´-num-min⟩, apparently the plural inclusive animate possessive pronoun *p'elé(·)nomin*, is glossed 'Ours (dual)'. ⟨Pā-lā-⟩, apparently the plural inclusive kinship-possessive *p'ele(·)y*, is glossed 'Our (dual)'. The form ⟨pele⟩ is also attested in Curtin (b:228), and is plausibly the inclusive plural subject pronoun, but there is no gloss in the source document.

Unlike in Hill Patwin and River Patwin, there is no evidence for the existence of a third-person personal pronoun series in South Patwin distinct from the demonstratives. This is reflected in the structures of tables A.15 and A.16, and I tentatively consider the lack of third-person personal pronouns to be a feature of South Patwin.

NOTES

1. Background

1. The low population estimate is due to Kroeber, who in his Patwin ethnography estimates "a total Patwin population of at least 6000 to 8000" (Kroeber1932:420). Kroeber's wording is careful, but his numbers are still likely to be misleadingly low, as he does not take into account drastic population loss due to epidemics of the first half of the nineteenth century (Cook 1943, 1955, 1976). The high number is based on the numbers and methodology reported in Cook (1976), as described below. It is likely that European diseases were already affecting California's population even before the nineteenth century, which would mean that the original, pre-Columbian population of Patwin-speaking peoples may have been significantly higher still (see, for example, Preston 2002).
2. Prior to 2013 the Wintuan languages were grouped into one language in the ISO 639-3 ontology as "Wintu" (wit). This overly general group was broken into three languages at the author's request.
3. Latham's term is derived from the name of a Patwin village in the Capay Valley (Merriam 1929).
4. This map was created by Jacquelyn Bjorkman, based on a map created by Bjorkman for Golla's 2011 book.
5. See Merriam (1967:271–72) for a discussion of his conversation with Mr. O'Brian, in which Merriam describes having difficulty understanding some of O'Brian's comments about Hill Patwin territory. The passage ends with Merriam speculating that, after all, the Hill Patwin groups O'Brian told him about may have been moved there during the Spanish period.
6. The Gibbs word list is published in Schoolcraft (Gibbs 1853) and in Powers (Powers 1877).
7. In this case Cook's methodology is to tally the number of distinct River Patwin villages mentioned in either Kroeber (1932) or Heizer and Hester (1970), and to assume an average of 500 people in each village (based on the average settlement size observed by early explorers in this area of the Sacramento River). We find forty distinct River Patwin villages mentioned in the two primary sources, making an estimated River Patwin population of twenty thousand (40 × 500).
8. Vallejo's description should be taken with a grain of salt, as the territory he identifies as Patwin or Suisun is certainly too large. Vallejo writes that the Patwin, under one chief, "occupied that region west from the Sierras to the ocean; and between the Rio Sacramento and the Rio Ruso [Russian River] on the

north" (P. Vallejo, c:10.1), but this area encompasses territory that is uncontroversially associated with the Miwok, Maiduan, Pomo, and Yukian languages and peoples, in addition to Patwin.

9. The call numbers for documents in this collection are "MIMSY 2001.43.*X*," where the *X* is a number or series of numbers identifying the individual document. When data from this collection is cited in this work, it is cited in the form "Vallejo (c:*X*.*p*)," where *X* is the document's individual call number and *p* is the page number within that document. A few documents in the collection have not been assigned individual call numbers (for reasons unknown); these must be cited individually: P. Vallejo (b, d, h).
10. Many thanks to Martha Vallejo McGettigan for calling attention to this important collection. Her own work in organizing and analyzing this material is ongoing.
11. The Bancroft has made their version of this collection available for viewing online via archive.org; this is the version consulted for this work. References to Merriam's Patwin materials in this work are given with list index numbers (i.e., V71–V76 and NH67–NH73), as indicated in the Bancroft's finding aid.
12. As Whistler puts it: "unreliably translated" and "phonetically abominable" (Whistler 1986:61).
13. In citations of Bright's notebooks and grammar I first give the book number (as in the SCOIL catalog) and then the page number within this book, as it appears on the page. Bright's page numbers begin with alphabetic characters indicating the identity of the speaker. A sample citation is Bright (c:1.G164), which reads: Bright's notebook 1, page G164.
14. In citations of Ultan's notebooks I first give the book number (as in the SCOIL catalog) and then the page number within this book, as it appears on the page.
15. Many thanks to Dr. Dorothea Theodoratus for helping to find Dr. Snyder's materials and making them available.
16. Whistler's seven notebooks are labeled A–G, which are used in citations thus: Whistler (d:B25) = Whistler's notebook B, page 25.
17. Barrett's 1919 paper on a Patwin religious ceremony is also of interest linguistically, though I have been asked not to consider this data for the present work.
18. Bright's recordings archived at SCOIL (catalog numbers BrightE.t001, BrightE.t002) are partial copies of this larger recording.
19. Thanks to Dr. Neil Alexander Walker for making me aware of this recording.
20. I generally refrain from taking the next logical step of positing Proto-Patwin forms based on the variety of forms in Patwin dialects. To make historical claims about Patwin before thorough comparative lexicography has been done on multiple Patwin dialects would be premature.
21. Note that this is the opposite order from generative rule-ordering approaches

for explaining allomorphy, which list the more restricted allomorphs first and the regular form last in an "elsewhere condition."

2. Phonemics and Phonetics

1. Much of the material in this chapter has been previously published as Lawyer (2015). Though the description remains almost entirely the same, some updated information can be found in sections 2.3.2, 2.3.9, and 2.3.10.1; section 2.4 is new. Any significant change to the description is noted in the text. This material is reused here in accordance with the terms of publication for the *International Journal of American Linguistics*.
2. These symbols are used in this work in keeping with previous publications on Wintuan languages (e.g., Whistler 1981; Pitkin 1984; Shepherd 2005), and should not be taken to suggest that the actual quality of Patwin vowels corresponds to the cardinal values of these symbols as defined by the International Phonetic Association (International Phonetic Association 1999). The phonetic quality of Patwin vowels is described in section 2.3.10.
3. The minimal pair *pʰo·* 'fire' / *po·* 'who' shown in table 2.5 was offered as a near-minimal pair in Lawyer (2015), where the vowel in *po·* was given as short. Although *po·* is often realized with a short vowel as [po] (see section 3.5.1) the vowel is now known to be underlyingly long.
4. Of the 451-language sample of the UCLA Phonological Segment Inventory Database (UPSID), only fourteen languages (≈3.1%) have these four series of plosives (Maddieson and Precoda). This calculation excludes /ʔ/, thus excluding any language in which /ʔ/ is the only plain plosive.
5. See Ohala (1983) for a more detailed phonetic discussion of this phenomenon.
6. See Maddieson (2011) for discussion of the areal distribution of this phenomenon in the languages of the world.
7. The following forms were used for Hill Patwin VOT measurements. All are expressions uttered in isolation in an elicitation session by Lodoga Hill Patwin speaker Oscar McDaniel (Ultan, b). In every case the VOT is measured for the initial consonant: *bá·lbalik* 'butterfly', *bak* 'wild cucumber', *pá·pa* 'Indian potato', *pá·tpat* 'flat tules', *pak* 'bone', *pʰákpʰak* 'egg', *pʰo·* 'fire', *p'ak* 'nailing', *p'áki* 'nailing', *dak* 'acorn flour', *dákʰa* 'belly', *táłčuro* 'bald', *tómo* 'worm', *tʰar* 'gray willow', *tʰátʰi* 'to pour out', *t'ákči* 'to slap', *t'ákči* 'to slap', *t'áłt'ałta* 'to try on', *t'ok* 'wood', *ká·ma* 'bed', *ko·l* 'mouth', *kʰap* 'wild grape', *kʰay* 'goose', *k'átibus* 'full', *k'ay* 'gopher', *k'ot* 'kangaroo rat'.
8. The following forms were used for River Patwin VOT measurements. All are expressions uttered in isolation in an elicitation session by River Patwin speaker Ida Mitchum (Swadesh and Melton). In every case the VOT is measured for the initial consonant: *bá·ro* 'eating', *bálusa* 'told', *béhna* 'morn-

ing', *bénta* 'big', *bo·* 'be', *pa·* 'now', *pá· beh* 'fresh', *pá·nti be* 'top', *pak* 'bone', *pókokwatu* 'yellow', *pó·mła* 'low', *pot* 'guts', *pʰákpʰak* 'egg', *pʰo·* 'fire', *pʰórohosa* 'broke', *pʰóspʰos* 'lungs', *dortʰusa* 'pushed', *to·kboʔita* 'limped', *tepuro* 'growing', *tʰá·say* 'gray-haired', *tʰa·w* 'left', *tʰáktʰusa* 'poured', *tʰáwła be* 'left side', *tʰo·ɬ* 'hill', *t'áɬmuʔuru bo* 'naked', *t'álta* 'lay down', *t'é·li* 'chest', *t'ok* 'stick', *t'óyusa* 'closed', *ká·lkal* 'slime', *ko·l* 'mouth', *kó·sta* 'steam', *kʰáluʔaro* 'different', *kʰáyłeyesa* 'threw away', *kʰódokʔohtu* 'skinny', *kʰonta* 'dry', *k'a·n* 'wing', *k'ánła be* 'armpit', *k'átusa* 'opened', *k'aw* 'the same', *k'om* 'big', *k'ó·tʔahtu* 'dirty'.

9. These are standard boxplots where the dark line in the middle indicates the median of the distribution, the enclosed box indicates the range from the first quartile to the third quartile, and the outer arms indicate the range from the minimum to the maximum recorded values. Statistically outlying values are not included in the boxplots, being represented in the figure by circles outside of the range of the boxplots. These boxplots, and all other plots in this paper, were generated using R (R Development Core Team 2011).
10. A multifactorial ANOVA model testing the influences of place and laryngeal category, and the interactions between these two factors, would be preferable to running multiple pairwise *t*-tests to statistically verify differences in means, as has been done in this section. Unfortunately the variance is not homogeneous in this data set (see below), thus an ANOVA model would produce invalid results. For completeness I can report here that a multifactorial ANOVA model shows significant effects of laryngeal series ($P < 0.001$) and place ($P < 0.001$), but not speaker ($P > 0.5$); it also shows a significant interaction effect between speaker and laryngeal series ($P < 0.05$). But, again, this model cannot be trusted because the data violates ANOVA's assumption of homogeneity of variance.
11. This section is not present in Lawyer (2015).
12. Lisker and Abramson use the range information only to gauge whether VOT values overlap for different laryngeal categories in each language. Cho and Ladefoged (1999) present mean VOTs for phonemes from a large number of languages, but do not give any information about VOT range or variance.
13. Flemming, Ladefoged, and Thomason (1994) use the term *glottal lag* when referring to the VOT of glottalized plosives in Montana Salish, defining this as "the interval between the release of the oral closure and the release of the glottal closure." In Patwin, at least, glottal lag and VOT amount to the same thing for the glottalized series, since periodic laryngeal vibration coincides with the glottalic release in these sounds. I have elected to present the VOTs of glottalized and nonglottalized speech sounds together here, for ease of comparison.
14. For a good discussion of speech sound initiation see Catford (1977:ch.5).
15. The chaotic nature of the wave shape for the final vowel in the /Cʔ/ example is incidental. It is due to the fact that this vowel is the final segment in an utter-

ance, thus having a heavily breathy quality in accordance with this speaker's usual mannerisms.

16. Ultan's observations about the dental /t/ were discovered only recently, so this information was not published in Lawyer (2015).
17. Ultan's observations about /w/ were discovered only recently, so this information was not published in Lawyer (2015).
18. The following forms were used for measurements of vocoid qualities. All are expressions uttered in isolation in an elicitation session by Lodoga Hill Patwin speaker Oscar McDaniel (Ultan, b). To measure vowels the primary-stressed vowels of the following expressions were used: *bak* 'wild cucumber', *kʰap* 'wild grape', *p'ak* 'nailing', *pak* 'bone', *pa·* 'now', *saká·kay* 'quail', *ʔew* 'this, here', *késči* 'hole', *péspes* 'property', *sékʔa* 'green', *séktu* 'chief', *tep* 'groin', *pʰe·ł* 'wild hemp', *sé·k'oro* 'to float', *t'e·t* 'big rope', *te·p* 'forked', *k'ir* 'ground', *łílaheta bos* 'shot', *t'ik* 'sore', *čí·di* 'stretch', *čí·li* 'star thistle', *k'i·l* 'gums', *k'i·r* 'cloud', *bok* 'milkweed', *t'ok* 'wood', *ko·l* 'mouth', *pʰo·* 'fire', *tʰo·k* 'tree', *buk* 'pus', *bus* 'stomach', *dul* 'head', *pu·s* 'nettle', *tʰú·bumabes* 'smell', *tu·s* 'face'. To measure semivowels the following expressions were used: *ʔew* 'this, here', *wiči·soro* 'stretch (tr.)', *ya·mel* 'yellow flower', *yeme* 'road'.
19. Finding the values of formants from a spectrogram is not entirely straightforward, especially given recording artifacts from old tapes. Vowels whose formants were too obscured to reliably measure were excluded from the sample. The values of each formant tend to change somewhat over the course of the pronunciation of a vowel, presenting another problem for finding a representative value for each formant. However, it is generally possible to find a portion of the middle of the vowel where the formants are relatively stable, and to take the mean formant values from this portion. This is the method used for the present description.
20. The values given for standard deviation in table 2.7 are not directly reflected in the ellipses in figure 2.6. The values in table 2.7 are standard deviation values for each formant individually, whereas the ellipses in figure 2.6 show standard deviation contours for models of the distribution of each vocoid in the Cartesian vowel space.
21. The information in this paragraph and the following paragraph is not present in Lawyer (2015).
22. The symbol ⟨ʌ⟩ is traditionally used to represent the English mid central vowel in words like *cup* and *hut*, in spite of its official designation as a back vowel in the International Phonetic Alphabet. (See Pullum and Ladusaw 1986:18.)
23. This confusion is of course exacerbated by the noncardinality of /i(·)/.
24. The following forms were used for measurements of unstressed vowel quality. All are expressions uttered in isolation in an elicitation session by Lodoga Hill Patwin speaker Oscar McDaniel (Ultan, b). Vowels used in the sample are indi-

cated with an underline: *łílaːhèta̱ bòs* ‘shot and wounded’, *sa̱ká·kày* ‘valley quail’, *ke̱lé·lày* ‘small perch’, *púyle̱* ‘measles’, *čí·di̱* ‘stretch’, *čí·li̱* ‘star thistle’, *késči̱* ‘hole’, *čóro̱* ‘head net’, *sé·k’oro̱* ‘floating’, *bu̱sú·li* ‘stomach’, *séktu̱* ‘captain’.

25. The following forms were used in the measurements of vowel duration. For the forms spoken by Lodoga Hill Patwin speaker Oscar McDaniel, all are expressions uttered in isolation in an elicitation session (Ultan, b). Vowels used in the sample are the primary-stressed vowels. For long vowels the following forms were used: *pa·* ‘now’, *saká·kay* ‘valley quail’, *pʰe·ł* ‘wild hemp’, *sé·k’oro* ‘floating’, *t’e·t* ‘big rope’, *te·p* ‘forked’, *čí·di* ‘stretch’, *čí·li* ‘star thistle’, *k’i·l* ‘gums’, *k’i·r* ‘cloud’, *tʰo·k* ‘tree’, *pu·s* ‘nettle’. For short vowels, the following forms were used: *pak* ‘bone’, *ʔew* ‘here’, *késči* ‘hole’, *péspes* ‘property’, *sékʔa* ‘green’, *séktu* ‘captain’, *tep* ‘groin’, *k’ir* ‘ground’, *łílaheta bos* ‘shot and wounded’, *t’ik* ‘pus’, *bok* ‘milkweed’, *t’ok* ‘wood’, *buk* ‘pus’, *bus* ‘stomach’, *duł* ‘head’.

    For the forms spoken by River Patwin speaker Ida Mitchum, all are expressions uttered in isolation in an elicitation session (Swadesh and Melton). Vowels used in the sample are the primary-stressed vowels. For long vowels the following forms were used: *si·* ‘teeth’, *dodó·k* ‘mucus’, *tahá·l* ‘tongue’, *ko·l* ‘mouth’, *łó·ho-botok* ‘black oak tree’, *no·p* ‘meat’, *só·robo·* ‘he listens’, *čú·sak-t’ok* ‘pitchwood’, *kú·saʔaro* ‘blind’, *lé·ni* ‘yesterday’, *me·m* ‘water’, *kotú·* ‘mushroom’, *letí·* ‘lips’, *tú·sma* ‘face’. For short vowels the following forms were used: *sála* ‘arm’, *čopól* ‘lake’, *t’ok* ‘stick’, *k’ánła be* ‘armpit’, *čočé* ‘back of neck’, *łéle-pita* ‘it changed’, *perimén* ‘throat’, *sem* ‘hand’, *ʔučús* ‘find’, *t’ekél* ‘palm of hand’, *ƛ’ebékmaro* ‘noise’, *kʰokʰí* ‘bark’.

26. This section was not present in Lawyer (2015).

3. Phonology

1. Some of the material in this chapter was previously published as a paper in Lawyer (2015), especially in sections 3.1 and 3.2. Analysis of Patwin phonology and morphology has advanced since the publication of the paper. This material is reused here in accordance with the terms of publication for the *International Journal of American Linguistics*.
2. In Lawyer (2015) this was described as a case of “static neutralization,” where neither surface nor underlying forms had aspirated or glottalized stops in syllable-final position. However, underlying aspirated consonants are in fact attested in syllable-final position, in CVC reduplication. See section 3.5.5.
3. The relative frequency of syllable-final /h/ in River Patwin was not reported in Lawyer (2015).
4. Theoretically minimal pairs of voicing are possible in syllable codas, though I have not yet found such a pair directly elicited. One such theoretical minimal pair would be *tʰebtʰi* ‘confluence’ / *tʰeptʰi* ‘hit-2.NSG.HORT’.
5. See section 8.2.2.2 for a discussion of the subjunctive suffix.

6. Syllable boundaries in the surface forms are indicated with periods, here and throughout this chapter.
7. See section 8.2.1.5 for a discussion of the remote past tense suffix.
8. See section 8.2.1.1 for a discussion of the finite suffix, and section 9.1 for a discussion of auxiliaries.
9. The forms [boh, beh, čeh] may then optionally undergo /h/ vocalization, creating the surface forms [bo(·), be(·), če(·)]. See section 3.5.3.
10. South Patwin probably also has the auxiliaries of the form /boh-, beh-/, but the finite suffix /-s/ is not present in South Patwin (see section 9.1.2). The finite suffix in South Patwin is a CV suffix /-t°i/, which need not be deleted to preserve syllable structure (see section 8.2.1.1).
11. In Lawyer (2015) I incorrectly attribute this transcription to Elizabeth Bright. In fact some of the pages in the second of Bright's notebooks (Bright, c:2) are in William Bright's handwriting, including this page. Elizabeth Bright's transcription of the same word, apparently taken down during the same elicitation session, is ⟨č̓ai·č̓ai·⟩ (Bright, c:3.IM5).
12. This generalization is derived from a rule stated by Whistler in his draft phonological description of Hill Patwin (Whistler, c:G11). Whistler's rule refers to word-final syllables, whereas my generalization applies to stem-final syllables. This correctly predicts that vowels may be deleted even from suffixed forms, for example /layuk-ʔa/ → [laykʔa]; /ma·yin-tu/ → [ma·yntu]. Whistler also does not specify that the coda must be stem-internal, though this is the case. Words where the coda is a suffix never exhibit this pattern of vowel deletion. For example /doyi-s/ 'give' inflected with the finite suffix /-s/ is never attested as *[doys].

    In Lawyer (2015:251), the River Patwin and South Patwin word for 'meadowlark' was offered as evidence that these vowel deletions should not be explained with a phonological rule. It was argued that since the rule never applied to the word for 'meadowlark', the anomalous stems /layk/ and /č'ayt/ were better explained as exceptional lexemes, rather than instances of a phonological rule. However, further lexicographical research has revealed that the River Patwin and South Patwin word for 'meadowlark' is in fact /hayu·k/, not /hayuk/ as reported in Lawyer (2015). Though a stress-initial form ⟨Hi-́yook⟩ /háyuk/ is attested in Merriam (1979:127,129), the underlying form is /hayu·k/, as shown in Whistler's attestation from River Patwin speaker Jennie Regalado ⟨hajú·k⟩ (Whistler, d:C86). Since the stem-final vowel is underlyingly long, and since it may attract stress, the vowel-deleting generalization is not expected to apply.
13. Patwin utterance-final /ʔ/ is similar to the junctural glottal that Callaghan describes for Lake Miwok and Bodega Miwok, which "marks final juncture after words ending in a vowel" (Callaghan 2003:53).

14. This distinction between Hill Patwin and River Patwin was not reported in Lawyer (2015).
15. Though syllable weight is traditionally a binary distinction between heavy and light, languages with three classes of syllable weight are attested, such as Klamath, Yupik, and Creek (Blevins 1995:214).
16. Note that not all of the hortative suffixes obligatorily condition rhotic assimilation.
17. The quality of the first vowel in the conditional suffix /-nini/ is uncertain. See section 8.2.7.
18. Due to the quality of the transcription, it is not known whether the [t] in (13h) is a geminate.
19. The phonetic rendering of (15a) is based on the re-elicitation by Whistler, published in the text of Whistler (1977a). Bright's original transcription is used in the example to show that the /r/ is present in the surface form of the word. In Whistler's published version only the morphological parse is shown: ⟨suduy-suduy-ṗir-bu⟩, from which the presence of [r] in the surface form could not be definitely concluded. I assume however that Whistler's rendition of the stem and suffixes are more phonetically accurate than Bright's.
20. See section 8.1 for a discussion of conjugational classes and stem forms.
21. The stems are /ʔuč-/ 'to catch', /ʔe·č-/ 'to steal', and /deč-/ 'to climb'. The suffixes are the exclusive hortative suffix /-le/, the negative suffix /-muʔu/, and the participle suffix /-ta/.
22. Orthographic equivalences are as follows. In Merriam (1979): ⟨ah⟩ = [a], ⟨ch⟩ = ⟨tch⟩ = ⟨ts⟩ = [č°], and ⟨]$_σ$´⟩ = stressed syllable. In Shafer (1961): ⟨tc⟩ = [č], ⟨¯,ˆ,ˋ⟩ are indications of putative tones, and ⟨'⟩ is a glottal stop. In Ultan: ⟨c⟩ = [č], and ⟨ċ⟩ = [č'] (Ultan, d). In Whistler: ⟨ċ⟩ = [č'], and ⟨ch⟩ = [čʰ] (Whistler, d). In Bright (Bright, c) and Morgan (1971): ⟨č̇⟩ = [č'].
23. The only attested counterexample is ⟨ʔɛ·č⟩ [ʔe·č] 'steal!' from Tebti Hill Patwin speaker Daisy Lorenzo (Ultan, d:6.88). The example is accompanied by a question mark and the note "slow speech" in parentheses. It is immediately followed by an instance of the same form with /č/ realized as [t]: ⟨ʔɛ·t⟩.
24. See section 4.6.2.1 for a discussion of nominals with multiple case suffixes.
25. See section 7.2 for more information about the morphology of cardinals.
26. Loanwords discussed in this section are shown in table 3.4, unless otherwise specified. Information about their derivation and example citations may be found in the table.
27. In Spanish orthography the graphemes ⟨b⟩ and ⟨v⟩ both signify the phoneme /b/.
28. The variant forms *kayi·nu* and *le·či* are not mentioned in Bright and Bright (1959).

4. Nominals and Nominal Morphology

1. For a description of the kinship-relational suffix, see section 5.3.1.3.4.
2. Whistler (1980:256) describes /-ma/ as a marker of "naturally or conventionally paired objects," but the plural usage in (34d) shows that /-ma/ is not restricted to paired objects.
3. The distinction between grammatical and semantic cases is widely accepted, though not unproblematic. A good overview of the distinction can be found in Kibort (2008).
4. The only arguable exception to the unmarked status of the subjective case is the first-person singular subjective pronoun *ču·*. See section 5.3.1.1.
5. The noun *sema·no* 'week' is inanimate, so it is unmarked for the objective case. That the noun phrase *ʔete·ma sema·no* is in the objective case can be seen in the morphological marking on the numeral *ʔete·ma* 'one (OBJ)'. See section 6.3 for discussion of case marking on numerals.
6. The object arguments of the verb *k'obo·li* 'pay' also appear in the objective case. Note the recipient in (37b) is the objective case pronoun *nat* 'me'. The patient of *k'obo·li* (i.e., what was paid) is also indicated in the objective case, as in *ʔa·na k'odoyma* 'lots of money (OBJ)' in (A).

(A) ⟨ʔa·na k̓odoyma ču k̓obo·lusa píma⟩

ʔa·na	k'odoy-ma	ču	k'obo·lu-sa	pima
lots	money-OBJ	1SG.SBJ	pay-PAST	DIST.OBJ

I paid a lot of money for it.

(Whistler, d:G71, HL) [HP_R]

7. *Genitive* is generally a preferable term to *possessive* for a case with a possessive function in comparative and typological literature (Haspelmath 2009:513). I use *possessive* here following the tradition of published work on Wintuan languages (Whistler 1980; Pitkin 1984; Shepherd 2005; etc.).
8. Rarely the /-no/ allomorph is contracted to /-n/, as in ⟨tc'i·´li sawa·´tun⟩ /č'i·li sawa·tu-n/ 'elk's horn' (Radin, c:7/144, AL).
9. The stem /ne·-/ 'mother' changes to /ni·-/ when preceded by the second-person possessive pronominal /ma-/ (Whistler 1980:208). The /-n/ on the stem in (44a) is the absolutive suffix /-·n/—see section 4.7.
10. "Aspect" in Wintuan nominals refers to the productive system of inflecting nouns for particular versus generic reference in Northern Wintuan languages. See Pitkin (1984).
11. One irregular nominal whose stem changes in semantic cases is the inanimate noun *dihi* 'home'. This word is the bare-stem *dihi* in the subjective and objec-

tive cases, but the stem changes to /di·/ in semantic cases, thus *di·ła* 'at home', *di·tuka* 'toward home', and so on.

12. See section 4.7 for a discussion of the absolutive suffix.
13. There is also productive double case marking on kinship terms in the possessive case. See section 4.6.1.3.
14. For example Marathi dative and instrumental case suffixes attach not to the bare stem of the noun, but to an already suffixed form of the stem called the "oblique stem." The resulting nouns have two case suffixes: the "oblique" suffix, followed by the instrumental or dative suffix (Masica 1991:233).
15. The co-occurrence of Sierra Miwok semantic case suffixes with accusative suffixes is not described outside of Broadbent's book. In the descriptions in Freeland (1951) and Callaghan (1987, 2003, 2014) Sierra Miwok semantic case suffixes co-occur only with the nominative suffix /-ʔ/.
16. Comitative marking on the noun implies a more or less equal relationship with the comitative nominal: "together with." Comitative marking on the verb implies a subordinate role for the object: "along with," "taking along." See section 8.2.4.4.
17. In the pronoun paradigm, one counterexample is attested: the proximal instrumental pronoun *ʔe·wsin* 'with this' (e.g., Radin, c:53/181, AL: ⟨'ɛ·´ucın⟩). This stem ends with a sonorant /w/, so would be expected to take the /-in/ allomorph of the instrumental case, but takes /-sin/ instead.
18. Note that the noun root in (55b) ends with /h/, but the intervening objective case suffix /-ma/ eradicates the environment that would condition the /-in/ allomorph of the locative case suffix.
19. Note that the prolative case is also attested marking a similar meaning, as in (61d).
20. Note the similarity to Proto-Costanoan (Ohlone) allative case suffix /-ta(k)/ ~ /-tka/ (Callaghan 2003:61).
21. The /-na·k/ allomorph is often attested with a short vowel, being subject to the general pattern of vowel shortening (see section 3.5.1).
22. Compare (53e, 53f), where the instrumental case marks the part of the agent's body used to carry out an event. Compare also (62b, 62c), where the prolative case is used to mark the part of the patient's body that is being acted upon.
23. The ablative is only used to express the cause when that cause is expressed as a nominal. When the cause is expressed with a subordinate clause, other constructions are used—usually clause chaining (see example 294).
24. Note that the vocative suffix has a short vowel here. This is an example of the pattern of vowel shortening described in section 3.5.1.
25. When *p'okse* 'brother's wife' takes the vocative suffix /-se·/, the stem changes to /p'ok/, avoiding the repetitive syllable sequence /sese·/. Thus the vocative of *p'okse* is *p'okse·* (Whistler 1980:217).

26. The occurrence of the verbalizer /-ho/ on the stem *ha·če* shows the productivity of the suffix at the time of European contact. Patwin *ha·če* is derived from Spanish *hacha* 'axe'.
27. For compound constructions involving verbs and directionals, see sections 7.1 and 8.5.

5. Pronouns

1. In these tables, and in this chapter generally, the pronouns are presented with morpheme boundaries indicated. Elsewhere in this work pronoun-internal morpheme boundaries are not indicated.
2. There are two attested exceptions where the root is /ma·-/ in the objective case: Lodoga Hill Patwin speaker Oscar McDaniel gives Ultan *mápelet* '2DU.OBJ' once, and Merriam attests one instance of *mat* '2SG.OBJ' in South Patwin.
3. Nonsingular forms are often used when addressing an in-law. See section 5.5.
4. Personal pronouns (of all three grammatical persons) are not attested in the instrumental case. This is likely to be an effect of semantics: it is unexpected for an expression referring to a person to appear in an instrumental function in a clause. Even outside of the pronouns, the instrumental case is attested only with nouns referring to nonpersons in Patwin. It is not known whether personal pronouns in the instrumental case are ungrammatical, or simply so rare as to be unattested.

   Another semantically driven formal distinction between personal pronouns and demonstratives is in the locative case, where the third-person personal pronouns appear only in the animate locative form (LOC$_{AN}$), whereas the demonstratives are attested in both the animate locative and the inanimate locative. This is expected, since personal pronouns are used only in reference to people (and people are always grammatically animate in Patwin), while demonstratives may refer either to grammatically animate or grammatically inanimate referents.
5. The impersonal root /pe·-/ takes the form /pe·y-/ in the word *pe·yła* 'when'. Although Whistler consistently transcribes this word as /pe·ła/, other written sources show evidence of the semivowel /y/. The semivowel is also clearly audible in the audio recording of River Patwin speaker Ida Mitchum (Swadesh and Melton). On the other hand the semivowel is distinctly absent in the subject, object, and verbalized forms of /pe·-/ in Hill Patwin and River Patwin sources. Other forms with the root /pe·-/ (inanimate possessive and instrumental) are too infrequently attested to detect the presence or absence of /y/; South Patwin sources are not reliable. The formally similar locational indefinite root /he·-/ shows no evidence of having a semivowel—even in the locative form. As clearly as Ida Mitchum says /pe·yła/, she says /he·ła/ just as clearly in the same recording session. In this work I adopt the most likely analysis: the

impersonal root is generally /pe·-/, and the locative form *pe·yla* 'when' is a lexically specified exception.

6. See Pitkin's dictionary for various Wintu interrogative words with the root /hE/ or /hek(e)/ (Pitkin 1985:149 ff.). Pitkin lists the latter root as {hek}, though almost all of its forms have a bisyllabic stem /heke-/. In his grammar Pitkin identifies the stem as /heke/, which he notes may be /hE/ 'interrogative demonstrative' + /kE/ 'optative' (Pitkin 1984:226).
7. The only subjective case pronoun that is (arguably) overtly marked is *ču·* '1SG.SBJ' in Hill Patwin and River Patwin—a single morpheme expressing its person, number, and case synthetically. Although *ču·* has no subjective case suffix, the root /ču·-/ does not occur outside of this pronoun in Hill Patwin and River Patwin, so the root itself could be said to explicitly indicate the subjective case. (In South Patwin this same pronoun *ču·* also occurs, but is analyzable as the regular first-person singular stem with a null subjective case marking.)
8. When /-t/ occurs on consonant-final stems such as the proximal stem *ʔew*, a harmonic vowel appears between the stem and the suffix, preventing word-final consonant clusters. See section 3.5.6.
9. He interviewed speakers at Sonoma, but long after South Patwin territory had been overrun by Euro-Americans and the population displaced in all directions.
10. Anecdotal evidence for a lack of meaning distinction comes from Daisy Lorenzo (HP_T), who tells Ultan that *p'ele·min* is the "short way" to say *p'ele·nomin* '1PL.INCL.$POSS_{AN}$' (Ultan, d:6.116).
11. Whistler uses the term *genitive* in a stronger sense: not just as a label for two series of possessive pronouns but as a separate case from the possessive case. For Whistler, the series I call inanimate possessive ($POSS_{IN}$) and animate possessive ($POSS_{AN}$) are in the possessive case, whereas the agentive pronouns ($POSS_V$) and kinship-possessive pronominals ($POSS_K$) are in the genitive case. There is no particular reason to consider these series to be distinct cases, in the sense that they would fill different functional roles in syntactic constructions. In fact there is some evidence that suggests they play the same functional role: they are interchangeable in kinship expressions. Kinship terms may appear either with a bound kinship-possessive pronominal or with an animate possessive pronoun, in free variation. See section 4.3.1.
12. When objective /-t/ occurs on dual pronouns, the resulting form is [-pelet]. The analysis of this form is ambiguous: it might be the two-syllable /-pele·/ followed by /-t/ or it might be the one-syllable /-pel/ followed by /-t/, where a morphophonological process intervenes to break up the aberrant word-final cluster /lt/ by inserting /e/ (see section 3.5.6). I analyze the dual suffix as /-pel/ here, since the second vowel in [-pelet] is always short, unlike the second vowel in the /-pele·/ allomorph.

13. Presumably the locative case codes animacy as well (as it does in nouns), but there are no attested animate locative demonstratives. On the other hand personal pronouns in the locative case always take the animate locative suffix /-tin/, as expected.
14. The animacy of the head nouns in these examples can be observed by the presence and absence of the objective case suffix. Animate nouns are marked with /-ma/ in the objective case, but inanimate nouns are not marked. Thus one can tell that *wilak* 'world' in (89a) is inanimate since it is the object but is not marked with /-ma/, whereas *pe·so* 'money' in (89b) and *mi·* 'tree' in (90b) are grammatically animate, taking the object marker. See section 4.6.1.2.
15. The form ⟨it⟩ is attested once in Merriam's South Patwin vocabulary (Merriam:V76), superficially appearing to be formally distinct from the more commonly attested *ʔu*t*. Merriam's ⟨it⟩ bears a tempting resemblance to the inanimate singular objective demonstratives just discussed, especially River Patwin *ʔe·s*: a root comprising a glottal stop followed by a front vowel, inflected with an object case suffix (objective case /-t/ would be the South Patwin analog of River Patwin /-s/). However, the one attestation of this form has an animate referent ('him'):

    (B) ⟨Choo-it win´-te⟩
    ču ? win-t°i
    1SG.SBJ ? see-FIN
    I see him.
    (Merriam:V76.59) [SP]

    It is therefore likely that Merriam's ⟨it⟩ is a misleadingly transcribed instance of the personal pronoun *ʔu*t* '3SG.OBJ'.
16. The syntax of (94b) is otherwise somewhat unclear. The final suffix may be a shortened allomorph of the suffix of certainty /-bot°i/. The ablative expression *wi·tinak* 'from a man, from being a man (?)' in this equative context is also unexplained.
17. Whistler (1977a, 1981) analyzes this verbalizing suffix and the verb *ʔu* 'to do, to say' as the same element—a kind of "auxiliary suffix," in the terminology of Whistler (1981). While there is a plausible historical relationship between these forms, here I analyze the suffix /-ʔu/ 'VBLZ' and the verb *ʔu* 'to do, to say' as two separate elements.
18. Two additional clause-linking demonstratives—*pi·ma* 'DIST.SG.OBJ.IN' and *pi·t* 'DIST.SG.OBJ.AN'—are probably best analyzed as nominal demonstratives rather than verbal demonstratives. Verbs do not generally take an objective case suffix unless they are functioning as relative clauses or complement

clauses. An object-marked pronoun functioning as a sentential adjunct may seem like a peculiar analysis as well, but nouns used as temporal adjuncts do appear in the objective case (see section 4.6.1.2).

19. Nonsingular nouns may also be used—see section 4.5.

6. Nominal Modifiers and the Noun Phrase

1. The exception to this rule is the multiplicative numeral *panom* 'twice', which is distinct from the stem /pampa-/ of the cardinal numeral *pampata* 'two'.
2. Many thanks to Ken Whistler for sending me a copy of his notes from this talk.
3. Note that the derivations given for 'six', 'seven', and 'nine' are historical derivations, not synchronic ones. For example the stem /serpo·ɬ-/ 'six' is historically related to /pono·ɬ/ 'three', but of the latter stem only /po·ɬ/ remains in /serpo·ɬ-/. Similarly in /serpote·-/ 'seven' and /panem(e)te·/ 'nine', only /te·/ remains of the component numeral /ʔete·/ 'one'.
4. Vowel length is only indicated in table 6.2 where it is found in Mason's word list, this being the only vocabulary that reliably indicates vowel length. Otherwise, only stressed syllables are shown (stress being relatively well attested in South Patwin sources).
5. The only River Patwin or Hill Patwin form in table 6.3 that does not come from Whistler (1979) is River Patwin *łeymat(in) pampak'ayi*, which is Thomas Odock's word for 'thirty', found in Waterman's notebook.
6. *Posepano* may instead mean 'seventeen' and is glossed as such in Dixon (1909). However, it is more likely that it means 'eighteen'. It is likely derived from /po(no)se(m)/ 'fifteen' + /panoł/ 'three' (the /a/ is archaic, from Proto-Wintuan). Whistler (1979) notes that the second element may be /panom/ 'twice', but this element is otherwise unattested finally in complex numerals. Instead /panom/ is always the first element in numerals, typically reduced to /pan/, and used to indicate a doubling of value. It is unlikely that it would indicate an increment of two when occurring as the last element in a complex numeral.
7. Colusa River Patwin speaker Thomas Odock gives a base-ten form for 'sixteen': ⟨pampasemtaLa sar̠poLta⟩ /pampasemta-ła/ 'ten-LOC' + /serpołta/ 'six' (Waterman:6). This is the only numeral that Odock gives between fourteen and twenty, so no definite comment can be made on this part of his numeral system.
8. This construction may be a reference to a system of counting, whereby a counter is set aside for each group of six. River Patwin speaker Jennie Regalado gives a similar form ⟨pán łome⟩ for 'ten', explaining that it refers to a system of counting beads, where a stick is set aside for each group (Whistler, d:E22). Where Regalado uses the phrase for two groups of five, other River Patwin speakers use *pan łomi* for two groups of six (Waterman:6, TO; Merriam:V75.1).

9. The presence of the auxiliary may mean that these expressions are best understood as clausal, whether as independent clauses (e.g., 'it is fourteen') or headless relative constructions ('that which is fourteen').
10. The underlying form of this auxiliary in South Patwin may be /beh/, but there is no evidence in these particular attested forms that the /h/ is present in the surface forms. It may have undergone /h/ vocalization (see section 3.5.3) or it may simply be untranscribed.
11. Whistler describes an additional relativizing suffix: /-bo, -be/ (Whistler 1977a, 1978, 1981). In my analysis this is not a relativizing suffix but an auxiliary verb. The auxiliary verb *bo·/be·* is common in Patwin clauses, including relative clauses.
12. Whistler analyzes /-sok/ as an instrumental and locative nominalizer, deriving deverbal nominals with meanings like "the thing with which one . . ." and "the place where one . . ." (Whistler 1977a: 174, 1981). This analysis is most suited to examples where /-sok/ derives single-word, headless relative constructions. However, since /-sok/ is also attested marking multiword relative clauses and relative constructions with head nominals, it is best analyzed as a relativizer.
13. In (136a) Radin's gloss suggests that the structure is a coordination, where only one of the coordinands is marked. However, Radin's glosses are not always accurate. (Note his incorrect reading of the number of women in this example.) It may be that the comitative suffix in (137a) is in fact best analyzed as having a true comitative meaning rather than a coordinating function, such that a more accurate gloss would be, 'The next morning, the two old women arrived with the old man.' Similarly ambiguous examples are found throughout the archival record. Note that (137b) has no such ambiguity.
14. This is not uncommon in the world's languages. See Dryer (2004) for a crosslinguistic discussion.
15. A better understanding of the long texts collected by Radin, Bright, Ultan, and Whistler may shed light on whether this is indeed a focus construction. Interestingly, though, the construction is not limited to situations of marked focus. Examples (141a), (141c), and (141d) are all sentences elicited in isolation, outside of narrative contexts.
16. Patwin fits all of Hale's criteria for a nonconfigurational language: free word order, the existence of linearly discontinuous expressions, and optional argument deletion ("null anaphora").
17. In (144) I depict the configurational structure of the clause as in classical standard theory: the root node is S dominates an NP node (the subject noun phrase) and a VP node (the verb phrase). The VP dominates the V node (the verb) and an NP node (the object noun phrase). I show no layers of structure in between these nodes and the terminal nodes (words), as this is only a rough sketch and not intended as a full syntactic analysis.

7. Directionals and Cardinals

1. For explanations of the morphology and syntax mentioned in this paragraph, see sections 7.1 and 7.2.
2. Both directionals and cardinals are attested in demonymic compound constructions with the noun *sel* 'person', however—see section 4.11.
3. Whistler includes *ʔetek* 'side' in his list of directionals (1977a:175), but this is morphologically an inanimate noun. It takes the locative case suffix /-ła/ when used as a locative adjunct in the clause, and is not attested with the directional suffixes discussed below.
4. The words *čenti* 'below' and *yelti* 'behind' have counterparts in Wintu that include the suffix /-ti/: *kenti* 'below, under' and *yelti* 'back of'. The suffix is also found on other Wintu directionals, as described in Pitkin (1984:263). Shepherd (2005:176) reconstructs a Proto-Wintuan directional locative */-ti/, though without clearly distinguishing Patwin stative /-ti/ 'at' from Patwin ablative /-ti/ 'from'. The Proto-Wintuan */-ti/ is likely to have been a stative suffix, since its reflexes on directionals in both Patwin and Wintu refer to static locations.
5. The directional *panti* seems to have the suffix /-ti/, and is analyzed as such in Whistler (1977a) and Lawyer (2015), but /panti/ is in fact a morphologically simplex stem. The stem */pan/ is never attested by itself in synchronic Patwin grammar, even as a bound form in compounds. Therefore I analyze *panti* as a morphologically simplex form, although it is likely to be etymologically related to the suffix /-ti/.
6. The words *kʰale·l* 'far' and *ʔole·l* 'up' have counterparts in Wintu that include the suffix /-e·l/: *kele·l* 'far' and *ʔole·l* 'up above' (Pitkin 1984:263). Pitkin glosses the Wintu suffix /-e·l/ as 'toward, in'. Shepherd reconstructs Proto-Wintuan */-e(·)l/ 'locative, toward, in (horizontally?)' (2005:37).
7. Kilak is a supernatural being, present in the indigenous religions of several ethnic groups of northern California. See Du Bois (2007:267) and Kroeber (1932:341).
8. This is distinct from the distribution of the stative and remote suffixes on directionals. On directionals they are mutually exclusive, never found together in the same word.

8. The Verb and Verbal Morphology

1. My first conjugation corresponds to Whistler (1981)'s base type I; my second conjugation corresponds to Whistler's base types IIA1, IIA3, IIB1, and IIB3; and my third conjugation class corresponds to Whistler's base types IIA2 and IIB2.
2. Long and short classes are not directly discernible in the South Patwin data, since the archival record does not consistently indicate vowel length. Indica-

tions of stress are generally the best evidence available for South Patwin vowel length. See discussion in section 8.1.3.

3. Tokens of these forms can all be found in Vallejo's word lists (e.g., P. Vallejo, c:23.8, 24.12, 26.6, 27.12).
4. Future research should address the South Patwin data as part of a comparative project including not only the other Patwin dialects but also Wintu and Nomlaki. This is beyond the scope of the present study. Curious readers should consult Shepherd's Proto-Wintuan lexical reconstructions (2005), but the amount of newly available South Patwin material may allow firmer conclusions about South Patwin lexicography than are found in that work.
5. Elsewhere in this work uncertain vowel length is indicated with a centered asterisk: V*.
6. Shepherd identifies a Wintu cognate /-s/ for Patwin /-s/ 'FIN' (2005:164). The Wintu /-s/ marks nouns for generic aspect (i.e. non-specific reference), and can also function as a nominalizer. Shepherd reconstructs Proto-Wintuan */-s/ 'nominalizer' from these, noting the presence of formally similar nominalizers in a number of other Penutian languages. Thus /-s/ may have a long history of semantic neutrality. The Patwin finite suffix may also function as a nominalizer—see section 8.4.2.
7. One major exception is the use of /-s/ for the voice of the narrator in traditional texts by some speakers (e.g., Nora Lowell and Harry Lorenzo in Whistler 1977a, 1978). The suffix /-s/ may be used here to avoid the temporal displacement associated with the past tense. Another attested marking for the narrative voice in texts is subjunctive /-mu/ (notably by Anderson Lowell in Radin, c). Sarah Gonzales (RP) uses only participles for the narrative voice in her rendition of the creation story (Bright, c:8.G43 ff.).
8. In (159b) the auxiliary stem /beh-/ is apparently realized as [bes], with the /h/ assimilating to the following /s/. This assimilation is not generally attested. It may be optional and rare or it may be a simple transcription error. Ultan's transcriptions are typically of high quality, so I leave the stem form as [bes] in the example.
9. Following the convention in section 6.5, the head of the relative construction in (164a) is shown in bold and the relative clause is delimited by square brackets.
10. Probably because /-ni/ 'RPAST' is never found without /-sa/ or /-ta·, -te·/ in Hill Patwin, Whistler (1981) in his study of Rumsey Hill Patwin verb morphology analyzes /-ni/ as fused with these two to make /-nisa/ 'remote past' and /-nita·/ 'remote past interrogative'. In the present study, since the /-ni/ element is clearly dissociated from following inflectional suffixes in River Patwin, I analyze /-ni/ as a separate suffix.

11. Because the only difference between the South Patwin finite suffix /-t°i/ and the future suffix /-t'i/ is one of laryngeal series, and because South Patwin sources do not show laryngeal distinctions other than voicing, it is generally ambiguous which of these suffixes is attested in any given South Patwin example. The future tense suffix seems to be sparsely attested in South Patwin, if at all.
12. The use of an additional inflectional suffix with /-t'i/ is thus optional. However, in the absence of an inflectional suffix, a particle is used to indicate whether the sentence is declarative (using the declarative particle *pi*) or interrogative (using the interrogative particle *pa*). See section 9.2.
13. Note that the subordinate clause in (184a) is a nominalization, with the subject appearing in the agentive form of the possessive case (POSS$_V$). The subordinate clause in (184b) is not a nominalization, the subject appearing in the subjective case.
14. For more on the nominalizing function of /-s/, see section 8.4.2.
15. Other speakers render traditional texts in other ways. Nora Lowell (HP$_C$) and Harry Lorenzo (HP$_R$) use an indicative declarative—the unmarked tense with /-s/—for the narrative voice (Bright, c:6.NL77 ff., 7.NL184 ff.; Whistler 1977a, 1978). Sarah Gonzales (RP) uses only participles for the narrative voice in her rendition of the creation story (Bright, c:8.G43 ff.).
16. Radin's gloss, 'The old man got up, built the fire, and then went to sleep', is not correct. *Č'iyake·* 'old man' is marked vocative, and the verb *di·hu* 'get up' is a hortative form. This is not a declarative statement, but an imperative one directed at the old man.
17. Other speakers use different markers for the narrative voice. Tebti Hill Patwin speakers Anderson Lowell and Daisy Lorenzo use the subjunctive /-mu/ (Radin, c), while Nora Lowell (HP$_C$) and Harry Lorenzo (HP$_R$) use the finite suffix /-s/ (Bright, c:6.NL77 ff., 7.NL184 ff.; Whistler 1977a, 1978).
18. There is one questionable attestation of /-taro/ by Lodoga Hill Patwin speaker Oscar McDaniel: ⟨wíntaro⟩ '(he) seen it' (Whistler, d:A89). Whistler annotates this line "unclear," however. This one questionable attestation stands against hundreds of attestations of the /-ta/ form by Mr. McDaniel.

    There is also one questionable attestation of /-taro/ in River Patwin: ⟨hařtařo ču⟩ 'I'm going' (Morgan 1971:25), but it is not clear who the speaker is that originated this utterance. Morgan's primary informant was River Patwin speaker Hazel (Gonzales) Erisey, but she used de Angulo's data from Cortina Hill Patwin speaker Fred Gonzales as well, and does not indicate the source for each example. In any case the /-taro/ form is attested only once in Morgan's grammar, while the /-ta/ form appears many times.
19. The applicative /-pa/ is always associated with an increase in valency and could therefore be properly described as a valence-changing suffix. Because /-pa/ is

part of the system of Patwin voice suffixes, I analyze it as primarily a voice suffix that also has a predictable effect on the predicate's valency.

20. The coexistence of a possessor and a subject argument for the verb in a passive sentence presents an interesting conundrum for theoretical syntax. Possessors are often characterized as the noun-phrase analog of the clausal subject (e.g., Jackendoff 1977:37 ff.); the status of a phrase with both a subject and a possessor is unclear. This interesting theoretical problem will not be addressed further here. Agents of passive clauses appearing in the possessive case is not unique to Patwin, and has in fact been identified as a frequent characteristic of Penutian languages (DeLancey and Golla 1997:189 ff.).
21. Increasing valency is generally seen as a definitional or prototypical property of a causative construction. For example Dixon's (2000) typology of causative constructions does not include causative constructions that can reduce transitivity (though he does mention their existence, calling them "quite rare").
22. The suffix /-pa/ is unlike the other Patwin voice suffixes in being consistently associated with a specific change in transitivity.
23. This final vowel could also be analyzed as a suffix /-i·/, which is unchanging and selects the hortative stem of the verb to which it attaches. However, almost every true suffix in Patwin begins with a consonant (with a few exceptions—see section 2.3.7). I therefore prefer to analyze this /i·/ as part of the verb stem proper, in the absence of evidence to the contrary.
24. The glosses are different in that the comitative participant in (227a) is translated as a count noun ("a gopher") while in (227b) it is translated as a mass noun ("some gopher"). Whether this difference is systematically related to the use of objective versus comitative case in this context cannot be determined from these two examples alone.
25. The form that the suffix would take on verbs of the first conjugation to avoid a three-consonant cluster is not known.
26. In nouns reduplication applies to the entire stem. See section 3.6.
27. The CV reduplication shown in (242) is not conditioned by the stem /hupu·-/, since there is also an example of the same stem with CVC reduplication in a different morphological context:

    (C) ⟨huphupuhtu⟩ /hup-hupu-htu/ 'diver'
    (< /hupu·/ 'dive'; Ultan, d:7.66, SG) [RP]

    The CVC reduplication of /hupu·-/ shown in (C) is from the same speaker as the CV reduplication of that stem in (242), and in the same elicitation session.
28. Note that /p^{h}u·ɬ-k^{h}o-/ 'lots of short blows' is a marked iterative, stressing an especially iterative event. The stem /p^{h}ułu-/ 'blow on' is itself iterative, as described above.

29. The suffix /-oho/ is formally anomalous, being the only verbal suffix to begin with a vowel. An alternative explanation is possible here—that the suffix is /-ho/ and is consistently associated with a change of inflectional class to /o/-final verbs of the second conjugation. The analysis of the suffix as /-oho/ is adopted here to simplify the explanation, such that change of inflectional class is not required. No other suffix is associated with a change of inflectional class.
30. River Patwin and Rumsey Hill Patwin use an overt nominalizing suffix /-s/ for 'food': *ba·s*.
31. The Lodoga Hill Patwin finite suffix /-bus/ is not attested in a nominalizing function.
32. Because words and phrases derived with /=men/ are lexicalized, I do not gloss the morpheme /=men/ outside of this section, but represent the derived expressions simply as stems with their own gloss.
33. Note also the Ohlone (Costanoan) nominalizers reconstructed for Proto-Costanoan as */-min/ and */-ṣ-min/ (Callaghan 2014:313–314). These are notable for their functional and formal similarity to Patwin /=men/ and /-s=men/. The Ohlone languages are geographically adjacent to the southwestern extent of Patwin territory, and may be deeply related to Wintuan languages (both are in the hypothesized Penutian superfamily).

9. The Clause

1. The contraction of /lu·mu-bus/ to [lu·bus] is irregular. The speaker (Oscar McDaniel) was evidently speaking quickly at the time of this elicitation, which is part of a series of barely glossed sentences that seem to form a connected narrative. Whistler and Ultan also record Mr. McDaniel uttering a different contraction of /lu·mu-bus/: [lumbus] (Whistler, d:B49; Ultan, d:2.76). This verb may be generally irregular for Mr. McDaniel.
2. For a discussion of these modal suffixes, see section 8.2.2.
3. The terms *clause chaining*, *final clause*, and *medial clause* are from the Oceanic and Papuan linguistics tradition. See Dooley (2010) for an overview of clause chaining. Clause chains are distinct from serial verb constructions (SVCs). In SVCs multiple verbs combine into a single predicate that is conceptualized as a single event (Aikhenvald and Dixon 2006). A clause chain is not restricted to such an interpretation. SVCs are similar to clause chains in that both concepts describe multiverb sentences with a single tensed verb and a series of non-finite verbs which are syntactically dependent.
4. In the examples in this section, medial clauses are represented in square brackets.
5. Because glottal stops are not transcribed in South Patwin sources, the suffix /-mele·/ cannot be readily distinguished from the subjunctive suffix allomorph /-m/ followed by the negative auxiliary *ʔele·*. Therefore it may be that the con-

struction /-mu/ 'SBJV' + *ʔele·* 'NEG' is also a way of expressing negation in South Patwin. However, convincing examples of this construction are not forthcoming. In particular, no instance of the /-mu/ allomorph of the subjunctive is attested in a negative construction; the /m/ and /ele·/ sequences are always adjacent in the South Patwin data. Therefore it is safest to assume that the negative marking attested in the South Patwin archive is the negative suffix /-mele·/.

6. I have presented the gloss in (303b) as it appears in the source. It appears in a list of eight interrogative sentences of the form "Can't he X?" where X is a common verb. However, (303b) has no overt interrogative marking. It is the only one of this series with the /-mur/ + *ʔele·* construction.
7. In River Patwin the expression *ʔur bo·* is attested as a way of saying "no." This is similar to the sentence in (304) but without a verb. A subject may also be added to this kind of expression: ⟨ʔʊrcu bɒ·⟩ *ʔur ču bo·* 'no, I don't want to' (Ultan, d:7.100, SG).
8. Some of the terminology in this section (*parameter, comparee, standard*) is drawn from Dixon's typology of comparative constructions (Dixon 2008).

Appendix

1. The only other instance of /-pele(·)-no-min/ recorded for any dialect is Cortina Hill Patwin /p'epélenomin/, which is also the only recorded instance of a dual animate possessive for the Cortina dialect.
2. These stories are derived from stories narrated to Elizabeth Bright by Cortina Hill Patwin speaker Nora Lowell, but Whistler checked the texts with Rumsey Hill Patwin speaker Harry Lorenzo. Chairman Lorenzo supplied Whistler with Rumsey forms where the Cortina forms were unfamiliar to him, so the texts can be considered to be "basically Cache Creek Hill Patwin"—that is, Rumsey Hill Patwin (Whistler 1977a:158).

REFERENCES

Archival Sources

Arroyo de la Cuesta, Felipe. [word list]. Terminos, y expressiones al Suisun de N.P. que me explico Samuel Capita =Page en 17 Enero de 1821. 1821. In "Lecciones de Yndios," BANC MSS C-C 63a, pp.23–24. The Bancroft Library, University of California, Berkeley. http://digitalassets.lib.berkeley.edu/bancbooks/ucb/text/bancms_63a_v1.pdf.

Barrett, S. A. (a). [audio recording]. Wintun songs and speeches, by Salvador (Wintun of Cortina Valley). 1909. Cylinder series 46: cylinders 24-1924–24-1959 (14-1491–14-1518) (Barrett #1–28). Hearst Museum of Anthropology, Berkeley.

——— (b). [slip file] [Vocabulary from Northern California languages]. File cards with Patwin vocabulary and some Wintun cultural information. 1909. Separate section of a comparative "vocabulary other than Pomo" (Miwok, Wintuan, Yuki, and Wappo). Survey of California and Other Indian Languages, University of California, Berkeley: Barrett.004. http://cla.berkeley.edu/item/63.

Bartlett, John R. [word list]. Miscellaneous vocabularies of thirty-two different tribes. Undated. MS 1627, National Anthropological Archives, Smithsonian Institution (183 pages). Partial photocopy at Survey of California and Other Indian Languages, University of California, Berkeley: Bartlett.001.

Bright, Elizabeth (a). [audio recording]. The Elizabeth Bright collection of Hill Patwin sound recordings. Hill Patwin. 1952. Spoken by Mrs. Nora Lowell. Berkeley Language Center: LA 20. http://cla.berkeley.edu/collection/10094.

——— (b). [grammar]. Patwin grammar. Two notebooks. Handwritten draft of a grammar. Circa 1952. Survey of California and Other Indian Languages, Berkeley: BrightE.002.004–005. http://dx.doi.org/doi:10.7297/X2000010.

——— (c). [notebook]. Patwin field notes. Eight notebooks. Collected 1952. Includes texts, vocabulary, and notes on grammar. Speakers Minnie Bill, Sarah Gonzales, Daisy Lorenzo, Nora Lowell, and Ida Mitchum. Survey of California and Other Indian Languages, Berkeley: BrightE.002.001–003,006–010. http://dx.doi.org/doi:10.7297/X2000010.

Curtin, Jeremiah (a). [word list]. Numerals from 1–10. 1889. In languages "Napa" (Coast Miwok), "San Jose" (Chochenyo Ohlone), "Stockton" (Plains Miwok), and "Suisun" (South Patwin); vocabulary of seventeen words in Stockton; and transmittal note. NAA MS 3701, National Anthropological Archives, Smithsonian Institution. Mistakenly cataloged as Wappo.

——— (b). [word list]. Yukian. 1884. Vocabularies of "Napa" (Coast Miwok), "Niles" (Chochenyo Ohlone), "Stockton" (Plains Miwok), and "Suisun" (South Patwin).

NAA MS 1456, National Anthropological Archives, Smithsonian Institution. Identification as Yukian is an error.

De Angulo, Jaime. [grammar]. The Patwin language. 1929. Data from speaker Fred Gonzales. Manuscripts at APS, in the American Council of Learned Societies Committee on Native American Languages collection: Mss.497.3.B63c P4b.1–4.

Haas, Mary. [notebook]. Patwin, Zuni, and Central Pomo word lists. Notebook with short vocabularies. Collected 1949–1950. Patwin from an interview with Ida and William Mitchum, Aug. 1950 in Williams, California. Survey of California and Other Indian Languages, Berkeley: Haas.067. http://cla.berkeley.edu/item/2593.

Halpern, A. M. (a). [Hill Patwin ethnographic notes]. Undated. Typed ethnographic notes on Hill Patwin. With speaker Daisy Lorenzo. Survey of California and Other Indian Languages, Berkeley: Halpern.031. http://dx.doi.org/doi:10.7297/X21J97N6.

——— (b). [archival documents]. Pomo Patwin Lower Lake field notes. Undated. Nine [orig. eleven] ruled notebooks, 602 pages in longhand pencil. Ethnological Documents of the Department and Museum of Anthropology, University of California, Berkeley, BANC FILM 2216 (reel 148). The Bancroft Library, University of California, Berkeley.

——— (c). [notebook]. Wintu, Patwin, and North Eastern Pomo notebooks. 1936. Part of Pitkin Papers, APS. Nine notebooks. Mss.Ms.Coll.78 Series I-D, Box Series I-1.

Hill, Dorothy. [collection]. The Dorothy Morehead Hill Collection. Audio recordings, transcriptions, manuscripts, and maps. Speakers Oscar McDaniel, Jennie Regalado, and others. Sometimes called the Dorothy J. Hill Collection. At the Special Collections of the Meriam Library, California State University, Chico. MSS 160.

Kelsey, C. E. [word list]. Some numerals from the California Indian languages. Circa 1903–1906. Includes numerals from the following tribal groups: Athapaskan (Tolowa, Kato, Hupa, Chilula); Chumash; Costanoan (San Lorenzo); Karok; Maidu (Tutudi [band] of Glenn Co.); Miwok; Pomo; Salinan (Milpitas); Shasta (Fort Jones, Yreka); Achomawi; Apwaraki (Susanville); Paiute; Mono; Panamint; Shoshonean (Tejon-Bakersfield, Morongo, Walker Basin, Tehachapi, Saboba, Temecula, Pala, Rincon, Cupa-Warner's Ranch, San Ysidro, Coahuila); Washo; Wiyot (Wishosk); Wintu(n); Patwin; Yana (Central); Yokuts; Yuki; Yuman (San Felipe, Pala, Mesa Grande, Santa Ysabel, Capitan Grande, Los Conejos, Sequam, Manzanita, Campo); Jacumba (Mexican); Yurok. Ethnological Documents of the Department and Museum of Anthropology, University of California, Berkeley, BANC FILM 2216 (reel 60, 114 typed carbon pages). The Bancroft Library, University of California, Berkeley.

Kroeber, A. L. (a). [notebook]. Wintun notes. Circa 1910. Notes with T. T. Waterman and River Patwin speaker Thomas Odock. A. L. Kroeber papers, BANC FILM 2049 (reel 118). The Bancroft Library, University of California, Berkeley.

——— (b). [notebooks]. Notebooks related to the Patwin language. Notebooks 201, 202, 206, 209, 210, and unnumbered. Collected 1909–1924. Speakers William Benjamin, William Bush, James Cooper, John Hudson, Hudson's mother Maggie, Carlos Lewis/Luis, Stephen Luluk, Tony Bill Mitchell, Thomas Odock, Julia Richards, Jim Tomaso Smith, Peter Wilson, and Bill Wylie. Part of the Pitkin Papers, APS: Mss.Ms.Coll.78 Series I-A, Box Series I-1.

——— (c). [slip file]. Patwin slipfile. Undated. Part of Pitkin Papers, APS. Ca. 1,800 slips. Mss.Ms.Coll.78 Series I-B, othertype Series, I Patwin Slipfile 1.

Kroeber, A. L., and T. T. Waterman (a). [audio recording]. Phonetic tracings: English and Wintun. 1909. Speaker Thomas Odock. A. L. Kroeber papers, BANC MSS C-B 925 (volume 6). The Bancroft Library, University of California, Berkeley. Photocopies in the Pitkin Papers, APS: Mss.Ms.Coll.78 Series I-D, Box Series I-1. Marked figs. 1–3, 5, 7.

Mason, John Alden. [word list]. Suisun vocabulary. 1916. About seventy words elicited from Dr. Platon M. G. Vallejo. Part of Pitkin Papers, APS: Mss.Ms.Coll.78 Series I-B, Box Series I-2.

McLendon, Sally. [audio recording]. The Sally McLendon collection of Northeastern Pomo sound recordings. 1958. Linguistic data; songs; conversation, untitled texts. Contains some Lodoga Hill Patwin. Five hours, twenty-eight minutes. Berkeley Language Center: LA 45.1. http://cla.berkeley.edu/item/15113.

Merriam, C. Hart. [notebooks]. Patwin vocabularies and natural history vocabularies. 1903–1936. From numerous dialects, with speakers Lewis James, George Bill, Jesse Berryessa, and Old Man McGill (Choo-hel′-mem-shel); Ant¯on Taylor (Chen′-po-sel); Tony Bill Mitchell, Bill Mitchell, Joe Mitchell, Bill Wiley, Ruth Wiley, and Helen Wiley Baker (Ko′-roo); and other unnamed speakers. C. Hart Merriam Papers, BANC FILM 1022 (reels 40–41 [V70–V76] and reel 56 [NH67–NH73]). The Bancroft Library, University of California, Berkeley.

Radin, Paul (a). [dictionary]. Patwin-English dictionary. Circa 1932. Manuscript at APS: Mss.497.3 B63c P4b.5. Photocopy of this is part of the Pitkin Papers, also at APS: Mss.Ms.Coll.78 Series I-B, Box Series I-2.

——— (b). [grammar]. A sketch of Patwin grammar. Handwritten manuscript. Circa 1932–1959. At APS in the Collection of the American Council of Learned Societies Committee of Native American Languages: Mss.497.3 B63c P4b.8.

——— (c). [manuscript]. Patwin texts. Ethnographic and folkloristic texts with English translations, from speaker Anderson Lowell and his mother. Collected 1932. Manuscript at APS: 497.3 B63c P4b.6–7.

——— (d). [notebook]. Wintun, Patwin notebook. 1931. Speakers Anderson Lowell and his mother. Part of Pitkin Papers, APS: Mss.Ms.Coll.78 Series I-A, Box Series I-1.

Rathburn, Robert. [notebook]. Patwin notebook. Elicited from River Patwin speaker Sarah Gonzales. 1969. Part of the Warren A. Snyder linguistic notes on Maidu and Patwin languages, BANC MSS 2012/120. The Bancroft Library, University of California, Berkeley.

Reeve, Richard H. [audio recording]. Interview with Harry Lorenzo, Rumsey Wintun. 1952. Interview about Mr. Lorenzo's life, Patwin culture and the Patwin language. Audio archived at the Sacramento State Department of Anthropology.

Snyder, Warren A. (a). [manuscript]. River Patwin: Preliminary phonemic analysis. Patwin phonemes and syllable structure. Typed manuscript with a few pencil notes. Not dated, but probably from the late 1960s or 1970 (pencil notes reflect a suggestion from Shipley in a letter dated March 1970). Part of the Warren A. Snyder linguistic notes on Maidu and Patwin languages, BANC MSS 2012/120. The Bancroft Library, University of California, Berkeley.

——— (b). [slip file]. River Patwin linguistic notes. 1969–1970. Part of the Warren A. Snyder linguistic notes on Maidu and Patwin languages, BANC MSS 2012/120. The Bancroft Library, University of California, Berkeley.

Swadesh, Morris, and Robert Melton [audio recording]. California, Colusa Katsil-dihi Ranch, Patwin. 1-hour audio recording of a River Patwin elicitation session with speaker Ida Benjamin Mitchum. 1953. Archived at Indiana University Archives of Traditional Music: 85-555-F, OT 7423.

Ultan, Donald (a). [audio recording]. River Patwin: Collected by Donald Ultan, spoken by Sarah Gonzales. River Patwin. 1962. Berkeley Language Center: LA 151. http://cla.berkeley.edu/collection/10044.

——— (b). [audio recording]. The Donald Ultan collection of Hill Patwin sound recordings. 1961. Spoken by Oscar McDaniel. Berkeley Language Center: LA 106. http://cla.berkeley.edu/collection/10023.

——— (c). Patwin [dictionary]. Part of Pitkin Papers, APS: Mss.Ms.Coll.78 Series I-B, Oversize 1: Folder Series IB-1–IB-6.

——— (d). [Hill Patwin field notes]. Seven field notebooks. Collected 1961–1962. Speakers Oscar McDaniel, Amelia Nunes, Nelson Lowell, Daisy Lorenzo, Sarah Gonzales, and Hazel Hanes. Original documents at APS (Mss.Ms.Coll.78). Microfilm copies (filmed 1964) at the Survey of California and Other Indian Languages, Berkeley: UltanD.m001. http://dx.doi.org/doi:10.7297/X23X84MJ.

Vallejo, Napoleon P. (a). [archival document]. Suysun numbers. Undated. Handwritten list of numerals in the South Patwin language. Napoleon cites his brother Platon Vallejo as the informant for these numbers. Two sheets. Original in collection of the Vacaville Heritage Council.

——— (b). [archival document]. The Lord's Prayer. Undated. Handwritten translation of the Lord's Prayer into South Patwin. Glossed in English. Three sheets. Manuscript in collection of the Vacaville Heritage Council.

Vallejo, Platon M. G. (a). [archival document]. Lord's Prayer in Suisun. Undated verifax copy of the Lord's Prayer and vocabulary in Suisun. Original dated 1890s and donated to the California Department of Natural Resources in 1953. Includes undated note from Francis A. Riddell to Mary Haas. Survey of California and Other Indian Languages, Berkeley: Vallejo.001.

——— (b). [archival document]. South Patwin numerals and word list. Undated. Two handwritten pages. Second page begins <Olelbo Tan oliáti –>. Manuscript in the Autry National Center. Vallejo Family Papers, Box 2, Folio 8 (no call number: MIMSY 2001.43.[x]).

——— (c). [archival document]. Suisun documents. Undated. Collection in the Autry National Center. Vallejo Family Papers, Box 2 (MIMSY 2001.43.X).

——— (d). [archival document]. Suisun-English Vocabulary. Undated. Two handwritten pages. Manuscript in the Autry National Center. Vallejo Family Papers, Box 2, Folio 8 (no call number: MIMSY 2001.43.[x]).

——— (e). [archival document]. The Angelic Salutation or "The Ave Maria." Speaker: Tomó. Typed sheet of two versions of the Angelic Salutation translated into South Patwin. One version is in paragraph form with no glosses or translation. The other version is glossed in English. Originally from the collection of Francisca V. McGettigan, copy in the collection of Martha McGettigan. Handwritten note at top of sheet: "TOMO, Indian from Suysun to PLATON VALLEJO, 1855 circa."

——— (f). [archival document]. The Apostles Creed. Undated. Typed sheet of two versions of the Apostles' Creed translated into South Patwin. One version is in paragraph form with no glosses or translation. The other version is glossed in English. Originally from the collection of Francisca V. McGettigan, copy in the collection of Martha McGettigan.

——— (g). [archival document]. The Lord's Prayer. Undated. Typed sheet of two versions of the Lord's Prayer translated into South Patwin. Undated. One version is in paragraph form with no glosses or translation. The other version is glossed in English, and is a partial version of Vallejo (AR[b]), with the second page missing. Originally from the collection of Francisca V. McGettigan, copy in the collection of Martha McGettigan.

——— (h). [archival document]. The Lord's Prayer, Angelic Salutation, and the Apostles' Creed in South Patwin. Undated. Two handwritten pages, pen with pencil additions. Manuscript in the Autry National Center. Vallejo Family Papers, Box 2, Folio 8 (no call number: MIMSY 2001.43.[x]).

——— (i). [archival document]. The Lord's Prayer in the Suysun dialect. Undated. Handwritten translation of the Lord's Prayer into South Patwin. No glosses or translation. Single sheet. Original manuscript in the collection of Martha McGettigan.

Waterman, T. T. [notebook]. S. E. Wintun notebook. Collected 1910. Speaker Thomas Odock. Part of Pitkin Papers, APS: Mss.Ms.Coll.78 Series I-A, Box Series I-1.

Whistler, Kenneth W. (a). [archival object]. Ethnobiological specimens with Patwin labels. Folder containing pressed flowers and a box with flora, a preserved goldfinch, and beetles. Survey of California and Other Indian Languages, Berkeley: Whistler.001. http://cla.berkeley.edu/item/1991.

——— (b). [audio recording]. The Kenneth W. Whistler collection of Hill Patwin sound recordings. Hill Patwin. 1975. Spoken by Oscar McDaniel. Berkeley Language Center: LA 105. http://cla.berkeley.edu/collection/10024.

——— (c). [manuscript]. Patwin phonology. A draft of a chapter from Whistler's never-completed *Handbook of California Indian Language Phonology*, with notes interspersed. 1984. Most text concerns the Cache Creek Hill dialect, with brief commentary on differences in the Grimes River dialect. Thirty-three pages.

——— (d). [notebook]. Patwin and Nomlaki Notebooks. Seven notebooks, labeled A–G. Collected 1975–1979. Scan housed at SCOIL, originals in researcher's possession. Speakers Oscar McDaniel, Harry Lorenzo, and Jennie Regalado. Survey of California and Other Indian Languages, Berkeley: Whistler.005. http://dx.doi.org/doi:10.7297/X2CV4FPF.

Wilson, H. B. [notebook]. Linguistic notes on Grimes Patwin. One field notebook. 1903. Speakers George Howell, Bob Wilson, George Byers, and Mary Byers. In Pitkin Papers at APS: Mss.Ms.Coll.78 Series I-A, Box Series IA-2.

Published Sources

Aikhenvald, Alexandra Y., and R. M. W. Dixon. 2006. *Serial Verb Constructions*. Oxford: Oxford University Press.

Aronoff, Mark. 1994. *Morphology by Itself: Stems and Inflectional Classes*. Linguistic Inquiry Monographs 22. Cambridge MA: MIT Press.

Barrett, S. A. 1908. "The Ethno-Geography of the Pomo and Neighboring Indians." *University of California Publications in Archaeology and Ethnology* 6, no. 1 (February): 1–332.

———. 1919. "The Wintun Hesi Ceremony." *University of California Publications in Archaeology and Ethnology* 14, no. 4 (March): 437–88.

Beeler, Madison S. 1954. "Sonoma, Carquinez, Umunhum, Coloma: Some Disputed Place Names." *Western Folklore* 13, no. 4 (October): 268–77.

Bennyhoff, James A. 1968. *The Ethnogeography of the Plains Miwok*. Center for Archaeological Research at Davis 5.

Bermúdez-Otero, Ricardo, and Ana R. Luís. 2016. "A View of the Morphome Debate." *The Morphome Debate*. Edited by Ana R. Luís and Ricardo Bermúdez-Otero. Oxford: Oxford University Press.

Blevins, Juliette. 1995. "The Syllable in Phonological Theory." *The Handbook of Phonological Theory*, edited by John A. Goldsmith, 206–44. Oxford: Blackwell.

Boas, Franz. 1911. "Introduction." *Handbook of American Indian Languages*, edited by Franz Boas, 5–83. Smithsonian Institution Bureau of American Ethnology Bulletin 40. Washington DC: Government Printing Office.

Boersma, Paul, and David Weenink. 2011. *Praat: Doing Phonetics by Computer*. Computer program. Version 5.2.25. http://www.praat.org/.

Bright, William. 1984. "Sibilants and Naturalness in Aboriginal California." In *American Indian Linguistics and Literature*, edited by William Bright, 31–54. Berlin: Mouton Publishers..

Bright, William, and Elizabeth Bright. 1959. "Spanish Words in Patwin." *Romance Philology* 13, no. 2 (November): 161–64.

Broadbent, Sylvia M. 1964. *The Southern Sierra Miwok Language*. Berkeley: University of California Press.

Callaghan, Catherine A. 1958. "California Penutian: History and Bibliography." *International Journal of American Linguistics* 24, no. 3 (July): 189–94.

———. 1987. *Northern Sierra Miwok Dictionary*. Berkeley: University of California Press.

———. 2003. "Proto-Utian (Miwok-Costanoan) Case System." *International Journal of American Linguistics* 69, no. 1 (January): 49–75.

———. 2014. *Proto Utian Grammar and Dictionary: With Notes on Yokuts*. Berlin: De Gruyter Mouton.

Campbell, Lyle. 1997. *American Indian Languages: The Historical Linguistics of Native America*. Oxford: Oxford University Press.

Catford, John C. 1977. *Fundamental Problems in Phonetics*. Bloomington: Indiana University Press.

Cho, Taehong, and Peter Ladefoged. 1999. "Variation and Universals in VOT: Evidence from 18 Languages." *Journal of Phonetics* 27, no. 2 (April): 207–29.

Cook, Sherburne F. 1943. *The Conflict between the California Indian and White Civilization II: The Physical and Demographic Reaction of the Nonmission Indians in Colonial and Provincial California*. Ibero-Americana 22. Republished in 1976 by the University of California Press.

———. 1955. "The Epidemic of 1830–1833 in California and Oregon." *University of California Publications in American Archaeology and Ethnology* 43, no. 3 (May): 303–26.

———. 1976. *The Population of the California Indians 1769–1970*. Berkeley: University of California Press.

Corbett, Greville G. 1991. *Gender*. Cambridge: Cambridge University Press.

Croft, William. 1994. "Voice: Beyond Control and Affectedness." In *Voice: Form and Function*, edited by Barbara Fox and Paul J. Hopper, 89–117. Typological Studies in Language 27. Amsterdam: John Benjamins.

Davies, William D., and Stanley Dubinsky. 2004. *The Grammar of Raising and Control: A Course in Syntactic Argumentation*. Oxford: Blackwell.

DeLancey, Scott, and Victor Golla. 1997. "The Penutian Hypothesis: Retrospect and Prospect." *International Journal of American Linguistics* 63, no. 1 (January): 171–202.

Dench, Alan, and Nicholas Evans. 1988. "Multiple Case-Marking in Australian Languages." *Australian Journal of Linguistics* 8(1): 1–47.
Diessel, Holger. 1999. *Demonstratives: Form, Function, and Grammaticalization.* Typological Studies in Language 42. Amsterdam: John Benjamins.
Dixon, R. M. W. 2000. "A Typology of Causatives: Form, Syntax and Meaning." In *Changing Valency: Case Studies in Transitivity*, edited by R. M. W. Dixon and Alexandra Y. Aikhenvald, 30–83. Cambridge: Cambridge University Press.
———. 2003. "Demonstratives: A Cross-Linguistic Typology." *Studies in Language* 27, no. 1 (January): 61–112.
———. 2008. "Comparative Constructions: A Cross-Linguistic Typology." *Studies in Language* 32, no. 4 (January): 787–817.
Dixon, R. M. W., and Alexandra Y. Aikhenvald, eds. 2000. *Changing Valency: Case Studies in Transitivity*. Cambridge: Cambridge University Press.
Dixon, Roland B. 1909. "Outlines of Wintun Grammar." In *Putnam Anniversary Volume: Anthropological Essays Presented to Frederic Ward Putnam in Honor of His Seventieth Birthday*, edited by Franz Boas, 461–76. New York: G. E. Stechert & Co.
Dixon, Roland B., and A. L. Kroeber. 1913a. "New Linguistic Families in California." *American Anthropologist* 15, no. 4 (October): 647–55.
———. 1913b. "Relationship of the Indian Languages of California." *Science* 37, no. 945 (February): 225.
———. 1919. "Linguistic Families of California." *University of California Publications in American Archaeology and Ethnology* 16, no. 3 (September): 47–118.
Dooley, Robert A. 2010. "Exploring Clause Chaining." SIL Electronic Working Papers 2010-001. http://www.sil.org/resources/publications/entry/7858.
Dryer, Matthew S. 2004. "Noun Phrases without Nouns." *Functions of Language* 11 (January): 43–76.
Du Bois, Cora. 2007. *The 1870 Ghost Dance.* Lincoln: University of Nebraska Press. Originally published 1939 by University of California Press: *Anthropological Records* 3:1.]
Dubin, Margaret. 2010. "'Pass Me That Squirrel, Toss Me My iPod': Language Learning at the Yocha Dehe Wintun Nation." *News from Native California* 23, no. 3 (Spring).
Eatough, Andrew. 1999. *Central Hill Nisenan Texts with Grammatical Sketch.* Berkeley: University of California Press.
Elliott, Evan. 2011. "Bringing the Hill Patwin into the North Coast Ranges Cultural Region." *Proceedings of the Society for California Archaeology* 25.
Falk, Yehuda N. 2001. *Lexical-Functional Grammar: An Introduction to Parallel Constraint-Based Syntax.* Stanford: CSLI.
Flemming, Edward, Peter Ladefoged, and Sarah Thomason. 1994. "Phonetic Structures of Montana Salish." UCLA Working Papers in Phonetics 87: Fieldwork Studies of Targeted Languages II. Los Angeles: UCLA Department of Linguistics.
Foster, Michael K. 1996. "Language and the Culture History of North America." In

Handbook of North American Indians. Vol. 17, *Languages*, edited by Ives Goddard, 64–110. Washington DC: Smithsonian Institution.

Freeland, L. S. 1951. *Language of the Sierra Miwok. Indiana University Publications in Anthropology and Linguistics* 6. Baltimore: Waverly Press.

Gibbs, George. 1853. "Vocabularies of Indian Languages in Northwest California." In *Information Respecting the History, Condition and Prospects of the Indian Tribes of the United States: Collected and prepared under the direction of the Bureau of Indian Affairs, per Act of Congress of March 3rd, 1847*, edited by Henry R. Schoolcraft, 428–34. Philadelphia: Lippencott, Grambo & Company. Reprint of volume published by the Nobu Press in 2011.

Goddard, Ives, ed. 1996. *Languages*. Vol. 17 of *Handbook of North American Indians*. Washington DC: Smithsonian Institution.

Golla, Victor. 2011. *California Indian Languages*. Berkeley: University of California Press.

Hale, Kenneth. 1983. "Warlpiri and the Grammar of Non-Configurational Languages." *Natural Language and Linguistic Theory* 1, no. 1 (March): 5–47.

Haspelmath, Martin. 2009. "Terminology of Case." In *The Oxford Handbook of Case*, edited by Andrej L. Malchukov and Andrew Spencer, 505–17. Oxford: Oxford University Press.

———. 2010. "Framework-Free Grammatical Theory." In *The Oxford Handbook of Grammatical Analysis*, edited by Bernd Heine and Heiko Narrog, 341–65. Oxford: Oxford University Press.

Heizer, Robert F. 1966. *Languages, Territories and Names of California Indian Tribes*. Berkeley: University of California Press.

Heizer, Robert F., and Thomas Roy Hester. 1970. "Names and Locations of Some Ethnographic Patwin and Maidu Villages." *Contributions of the University of California Archaeological Research Facility: Papers on California Ethnography* 9: 79–118.

Himmelmann, Nikolaus P. 2006. "Language Documentation: What Is It and What Is It Good For?" In *Essentials of Language Documentation*, edited by Jost Gippert, Nikolaus P. Himmelmann, and Ulrike Mosel, 1–30. Berlin: Mouton de Gruyter.

Hockett, Charles F. 1958. *A Course in Modern Linguistics*. New York: Macmillan.

Hodge, Frederick Webb, ed. 1907. *Handbook of American Indians North of Mexico*. Washington DC: Government Printing Office.

International Phonetic Association. 1999. *Handbook of the International Phonetic Association: A Guide to the Use of the International Phonetic Alphabet*. Cambridge: Cambridge University Press.

Jackendoff, Ray. 1977. *Syntax: A Study of Phrase Structure*. Linguistic Inquiry Monographs 2. Cambridge MA: MIT Press.

Johnson, Patti J. 1978. "Patwin." In *Handbook of North American Indians*. Vol. 8, *California*, edited by Robert F. Heizer and William C. Sturtevant, 350–60. Washington DC: Smithsonian Institution.

Karlsson, Fred. 1999. *Finnish: An Essential Grammar*. 2nd ed. New York: Routledge.

Keenan, Edward L., and Bernard Comrie. 1977. "Noun Phrase Accessibility and Universal Grammar." *Linguistic Inquiry* 8, no. 1 (Winter): 63–99.

Kibort, Anna. 2008. "Grammatical Features Inventory: Case." University of Surrey. http://dx.doi.org/10.15126/SMG.18/1.04.

Kroeber, A. L. 1925. *Handbook of the Indians of California*. Bureau of American Ethnology Bulletin 78. Washington DC: Government Printing Office.

———. 1932. "The Patwin and Their Neighbors." *University of California Publications in Archaeology and Ethnology* 29, no. 4 (February): 253–423.

———. 1957. "Ethnographic Interpretations 1–6." *University of California Publications in American Archaeology and Ethnology* 47, no. 2 (February): 191–234.

Ladefoged, Peter. 2001. *A Course in Phonetics*. 4th ed. Boston: Heinle and Heinle.

Ladefoged, Peter, and Ian Maddieson. 1996. *The Sounds of the World's Languages*. Oxford: Blackwell.

Latham, Robert. 1856. "On the Languages of Northern, Western, and Central America." *Proceedings of the Philological Society of London for 1856*, 57–115.

Lawyer, Lewis C. 2015. "Patwin Phonemics, Phonetics, and Phonotactics." *International Journal of American Linguistics* 81, no. 2 (April): 221–60.

Levy, Richard S. 1978. "Eastern Miwok." In *Handbook of North American Indians*. Vol. 8, *California*, edited by Robert F. Heizer and William C. Sturtevant, 398–413. Washington DC: Smithsonian Institution.

Lindau, Mona. 1984. "Phonetic Differences in Glottalic Consonants." *Journal of Phonetics* 12, no. 2 (April): 147–55.

Lindblom, Björn. 1990. "Explaining Phonetic Variation: A Sketch of the H & H Theory." In *Speech Production and Speech Modelling*, edited by William J. Hardcastle and Alain Marchal, 403–40. Dordrecht: Kluwer Academic Publishers.

Lisker, Leigh, and Arthur S. Abramson. 1964. "A Cross-Language Study of Voicing in Initial Stops: Acoustical Measurements." *Word* 20, no. 3 (December): 384–421.

Maddieson, Ian. 2011. "Voicing and Gaps in Plosive Systems." *The World Atlas of Language Structures Online*. Edited by Matthew S. Dryer and Martin Haspelmath. Munich: Max Planck Digital Library. http://wals.info/chapter/5.

Maddieson, Ian, and Kristin Precoda. UCLA Phonological Segment Inventory Database. Data accessed June 2011 through the web interface created by Henning Reetz. http://web.phonetik.uni-frankfurt.de/upsid.html.

Malchukov, Andrej L., Maria Koptjevskaja Tamm, Peter Cole, Gabriella Hermon, Jaklin Kornfilt, and Bernard Comrie. 2008. Leipzig Questionnaire on Nominalization and Mixed Categories. Draft version, July 2008. https://www.eva.mpg.de/lingua/tools-at-lingboard/pdf/Malchukov_MixedCategories_Questionnaire.pdf.

Martin, Jack B. 2000. "Creek Voice: Beyond Valency." In *Changing Valency: Case Studies in Transitivity*, edited by R. M. W. Dixon and Alexandra Y. Aikhenvald, 375–403. Cambridge: Cambridge University Press.

Masica, Colin P. 1991. *The Indo-Aryan Languages*. Cambridge: Cambridge University Press.

McKern, W. C. 1922. "Functional Families of the Patwin." *University of California Publications in Archaeology and Ethnology* 13, no. 7 (April): 235–58.

———. 1923. "Patwin Houses." *Phoebe Apperson Hearst Memorial Volume*, edited by A. L. Kroeber, 159–71. Berkeley: University of California Press.

Merriam, C. Hart. 1929. "The Cop-éh of Gibbs." *American Anthropologist* 31, no.1 (January–March): 136–37.

———. 1962. "Tribes of Wintoon Stock." In *Studies of California Indians*, edited by the staff of the Department of Anthropology of the University of California, 3–25. Berkeley: University of California Press.

———. 1966. "Ethnographic Notes on California Indian Tribes, Part I: Ethnographic Notes on California Indians." *Reports of the University of California Archaeological Survey* 68. Edited by Robert F. Heizer. Berkeley: University of California Archaeological Research Facility.

———. 1967. "Ethnographic Notes on California Indian Tribes, Part III: Ethnological Notes on Central California Indian Tribes." *Reports of the University of California Archaeological Survey* 68. Edited by Robert F. Heizer. Berkeley: University of California Archaeological Research Facility.

———. 1977. *Ethnogeographic and Ethnosynonymic Data from Central California Tribes*. Edited by Robert F. Heizer. Contributions to Native California Ethnology from the C. Hart Merriam Collection 2. Berkeley: University of California Archaeological Research Facility.

———. 1979. *Indian Names for Plants and Animals among California and Other Western North American Tribes*. Edited by Robert F. Heizer. Ballena Press Publications in Archaeology, Ethnology and History 14. Socorro NM: Ballena Press.

Mithun, Marianne. 1999. *The Languages of Native North America*. Cambridge: Cambridge University Press.

Moravcsik, Edith A. 1995. "Summing up Suffixaufnahme." In *Double Case: Agreement by Suffixaufnahme*, edited by Frans Plank, 451–84. Oxford: Oxford University Press.

Morgan, Bernadine Claire. 1971. "Phonemic and Preliminary Morphemic Analysis of River-Patwin." MA thesis, University of California, Davis.

Myers, William E. 1924. "Vocabularies: Wintun." In vol. 14 of *The North American Indian: Being a Series of Volumes Picturing and Describing the Indians of the United States, the Dominion of Canada, and Alaska*, edited by Edward S. Curtis and Frederick Webb Hodge, 220–29. Norwood: The Plimpton Press.

Ohala, John J. 1983. "The Origin of Sound Patterns in Vocal Tract Constraints." In *The Production of Speech*, edited by Peter F. MacNeilage, 189–216. New York: Springer.

Ojeda, Almerindo E. 2006. "Discontinuous Dependencies." In *Encyclopedia of*

Language and Linguistics, edited by Keith Brown, 624–30. 2nd ed. Amsterdam: Elsevier.

Perlmutter, David M., and Paul M. Postal. 1983. "Toward a Universal Characterization of Passivization." In *Studies in Relational Grammar 1*, edited by David M. Perlmutter, 3–29. Chicago: University of Chicago Press.

Pitkin, Harvey. 1984. *Wintu Grammar*. Berkeley: University of California Press.

———. 1985. *Wintu Dictionary*. Berkeley: University of California Press.

Plank, Frans. 1995. "(Re-)Introducing Suffixaufnahme." In *Double Case: Agreement by Suffixaufnahme*, edited by Frans Plank, 3–110. Oxford: Oxford University Press.

Powell, J. W. 1891. "Indian Linguistic Families of America, North of Mexico." In *Seventh Annual Report of the Bureau of Ethnology to the Secretary of the Smithsonian Institution, 1885–86*, edited by J. W. Powell, 1–142. Washington DC: Government Printing Office.

Powers, Stephen. 1877. *Tribes of California*. Washington DC: Government Printing Office.

Preston, William L. 2002. "Portents of Plague from California's Protohistoric Period." *Ethnohistory* 49, no. 1 (January): 69–121.

Pullum, Geoffrey K., and William A. Ladusaw. 1986. *Phonetic Symbol Guide*. Chicago: University of Chicago Press.

R Development Core Team. 2011. R: A Language and Environment for Statistical Computing. Open source software. Version 12.14.1. https://www.R-project.org/.

Rehg, Kenneth L. 2014. "On the Role and Utility of Grammars in Language Documentation and Conservation." In *The Art and Practice of Grammar Writing*, edited by Toshihide Nakayama and Keren Rice, 53–67. Language Documentation & Conservation Special Publication 8. Honolulu: University of Hawai'i Press.

Sag, Ivan A., Thomas Wasow, and Emily M. Bender. 2003. *Syntactic Theory: A Formal Introduction*. Stanford: CSLI.

Sapir, Edward. 1929. "Central and North American Languages." In *Encyclopaedia Britannica*, 5: 138–41. 14th ed. London: Encyclopaedia Britannica Company.

Sawyer, Jesse O. 1965. *English-Wappo Vocabulary*. Berkeley: University of California Press.

Schlichter, Alice. 1981. *Wintu Dictionary*. Survey Reports 2. Berkeley: Survey of California and Other Indian Languages.

Shafer, Robert. 1961. "Tones in Wintun." *Anthropological Linguistics* 3, no. 6 (June): 17–30. [Speakers Charlie Wright (Hill Patwin) and Jim Perdue (River Patwin).]

Shepherd, Alice. 2005. *Proto-Wintun*. Berkeley: University of California Press.

Silverstein, Michael. 1979. "Penutian: An Assessment." In *The Languages of Native America: Historical and Comparative Assessment, edited by Lyle Campbell and Marianne Mithun*, 650–91. Austin: University of Texas Press.

Spence, Justin. 2015. "Managing Uncertainty in Archival Linguistic Research." Paper presented at the 89th Annual Meeting of the Linguistic Society of America, Portland, Oregon. January.

Steele, Susan. 1987. "Constituency and Luiseño Argument Structure." In *Discontinuous Constituency*, edited by Geoffrey J. Huck and Almerindo E. Ojeda, 341–75. Syntax and Semantics 20. Orlando: Academic Press.

Swadesh, Morris. 1954. "On the Penutian Vocabulary Survey." *International Journal of American Linguistics* 20, no. 2 (April): 123–33.

Tarpent, Marie-Lucie. 1997. "Tsimshianic and Penutian: Problems, Methods, Results, and Implications." *International Journal of American Linguistics* 63, no. 1 (January): 65–112.

Tatsch, Sheri Jean. 2006. "The Nisenan: Dialects & Districts of a Speech Community." PhD thesis, University of California, Davis.

Whalen, D. H., and Gary F. Simons. 2012. "Endangered Language Families." *Language* 88, no. 1 (March): 155–73.

Whistler, Kenneth W. 1976. "Patwin Folk-Taxonomic Structures." MA thesis, University of California Berkeley.

———. 1977a. "Deer and Bear Children." In *Northern California Texts*, edited by Victor Golla and Shirley Silver, 158–78. International Journal of American Linguistics Native American Texts Series 2. Chicago: University of Chicago Press.

———. 1977b. "Wintun Prehistory: An Interpretation Based on Linguistic Reconstruction of Plant and Animal Nomenclature." In *Proceedings of the Third Berkeley Linguistic Society Meeting*, edited by Kenneth W. Whistler et al., 157–74. Berkeley: Berkeley Linguistics Society.

———. 1978. "Mink, Bullethawk, and Coyote." In *Coyote Stories*, edited by William Bright, 51–61. International Journal of American Linguistics Native American Texts Series 1. Chicago: University of Chicago Press.

———. 1979. "Patwin Numerals: A Reconstruction and Its Cultural Implications." Paper delivered at University of California, Santa Barbara, March.

———. 1980. "Proto-Wintun Kin Classification: A Case Study in Reconstruction of a Complex Semantic System." PhD diss., University of California, Berkeley.

———. 1981. "Ablaut in Hill Patwin." *Survey Report* No.1. Berkeley: Survey of California and Other Indian Languages, 42–94.

———. 1986. "Evidentials in Patwin." In *Evidentiality: The Linguistic Coding of Epistemology*, edited by Wallace Chafe and Johanna Nichols, 60–74. Norwood NJ: Ablex.

Wilson, Norman L., and Arlean H. Towne. 1978. "Nisenan." In *Handbook of North American Indians*. Vol. 8, *California*, edited by Robert F. Heizer and William C. Sturtevant, 387–97. Washington DC: Smithsonian Institution.

In Studies in the Native Languages of the Americas

The Miami-Illinois Language
By David J. Costa

Caddo Verb Morphology
By Lynette R. Melnar

A Grammar of Crow (Apsáalooke Aliláau)
By Randolph Graczyk

Topic and Discourse Structure in West Greenlandic Agreement Constructions
By Anna Berge

A Reference Grammar of Kotiria (Wanano)
By Kristine Stenzel

A Grammar of Patwin
Lewis C. Lawyer

CPSIA information can be obtained
at www.ICGtesting.com
Printed in the USA
LVHW091233041221
705033LV00007B/2

9 781496 230423